The Life Of Trust : Being A Narrative Of The Lord's Dealings With George Müller

Müller, George, 1805-1898,
Lincoln, Heman, 1821-1887

Nabu Public Domain Reprints:

You are holding a reproduction of an original work published before 1923 that is in the public domain in the United States of America, and possibly other countries. You may freely copy and distribute this work as no entity (individual or corporate) has a copyright on the body of the work. This book may contain prior copyright references, and library stamps (as most of these works were scanned from library copies). These have been scanned and retained as part of the historical artifact.

This book may have occasional imperfections such as missing or blurred pages, poor pictures, errant marks, etc. that were either part of the original artifact, or were introduced by the scanning process. We believe this work is culturally important, and despite the imperfections, have elected to bring it back into print as part of our continuing commitment to the preservation of printed works worldwide. We appreciate your understanding of the imperfections in the preservation process, and hope you enjoy this valuable book.

ASHLEY DOWN ORPHAN HOUSES, BRISTOL, ENG.

THE LIFE OF TRUST:

BEING A

NARRATIVE OF THE LORD'S DEALINGS

WITH

GEORGE MÜLLER,

WRITTEN BY HIMSELF.

With an Introduction

BY FRANCIS WAYLAND.

A NEW EDITION, BROUGHT DOWN TO THE PRESENT TIME, INCLUDING HIS VISIT TO AMERICA.

NEW YORK:
SHELDON AND COMPANY,
1878.

Entered according to Act of Congress, in the year 1873, by
GOULD AND LINCOLN,
In the office of the Librarian of Congress, at Washington.

Copyright, 1877, by SHELDON & CO.

EDITOR'S PREFACE

TO THE NEW REVISED EDITION.

THE first American edition of the LIFE OF TRUST was published in 1860, under the editorial supervision of Rev. H. L. Wayland, D.D. His work was performed with rare judgment and skill. From the "Narrative" of Mr. Müller, in four parts, the last published in 1856, and from the four "Annual Reports" issued in 1857, 1858, 1859, and 1860, he condensed into less than one-fourth of the space, a comprehensive view of the life and work of Mr. Müller, omitting nothing of essential value. The repetition from year to year, of similar events, incidents and illustrations, made the reduction an imperative necessity. He divided, also, the Narrative into chapters, and prefixed to each chapter a brief statement of the leading subjects introduced. By such judicious editorial labor, the American edition was made more attractive than the English works from which it was condensed. It was more compact for use, involved fewer repetitions, and supplied a Table of Contents, by which the reader could be guided. The work has had a large and steady sale, and many Christian hearts have been led by it to a stronger faith in the LIVING GOD.

The stereotype plates were destroyed in the great fire of November 9th and 10th, 1872, and the Publishers requested me to prepare a new edition of the work. Thirteen years having passed since the first edition was published, years rich in labors and in fruits to Mr. Müller, it seemed important that some record should be made of this important period. Since 1860, three new Orphan Houses have been opened, accommodating more than thirteen hundred orphans; and the expenses of the establishment have been increased threefold. But God has proportioned the grace to the trial. The barrel of meal has not wasted, nor the cruse of oil failed. The supply has been equal to the demand. Several chapters have been added, giving a brief sketch of the growth and prosperity of the institution from 1860 to the present time. It exhibits the same daily providential care which marked the earlier history of Mr. Muller's labors. To give place to the new matter, without swelling the volume to an inconvenient size, paragraphs have been dropped here and there from the former edition, where it seemed possible to omit them, without interrupting the narrative, or weakening the force of its lessons.

With the changes indicated, and the insertion of fine full-page wood engravings of each of the five Orphan Houses, the work is sent forth anew to encourage Christians to daily faith in a present and LIVING GOD. Mr. Muller's life is an eloquent sermon on the POWER OF FAITH. If science denies that God can interpose to overrule or guide his laws, an appeal may be made to this testimony of personal experience during nearly forty years. If Mr. Galton and Prof. Tyndall ask for proofs of the value of prayer in common life, they may be directed to the BRISTOL ORPHAN HOUSES, for the facts of which they are in search. The facts are numerous, direct, and attested by witnesses whose veracity cannot be impeached. Mr. Muller claims that these facts prove the POWER AND WILLINGNESS OF GOD TO ANSWER PRAYER. He invites candid men to examine them, and pass judgment on his theory.

HEMAN LINCOLN.

NEWTON CENTRE, *May* 26, 1873.

AUTHOR'S PREFACE.

IT was only after the consideration of many months, and after much self-examination as to my motives, and after much earnest prayer, that I came to the conclusion to write this work. I have not taken one single step in the Lord's service concerning which I have prayed so much. My great dislike to increasing the number of religious books would, in itself, have been sufficient to have kept me forever from it, had I not cherished the hope of being instrumental in this way to lead some of my brethren to value the Holy Scriptures more, and to judge by the standard of the Word of God the principles on which they act. But that which weighed more with me than anything, was, that I have reason to believe, from what I have seen among the children of God, that many of their trials arise either from want of confidence in the Lord as it regards temporal things, or from carrying on their business in an unscriptural way. On account, therefore, of the remarkable way in which the Lord has dealt with me as to temporal things, I feel that I am a debtor to the church of Christ, and that I ought, for the benefit of my poorer brethren especially, to make known the way in which I have been led. In addition to this, I know that to many souls the Lord has blessed what I have told them about the way in which he has led me, and therefore it seemed a duty to use such means, whereby others also, with whom I could not possibly converse, might be benefited. That which induced me finally to determine to write this

Narrative was, that if the Lord should permit the book to sell, I might, by the profits arising from the sale, be enabled in a greater degree to help the poor brethren and sisters among whom I labor, —a matter which, just at that time, weighed much on my mind. I therefore began to write. But after three days I was obliged to lay the work aside on account of my other pressing engagements. Subsequently, I was laid aside on account of an abscess; and being unable, for many weeks, to walk about as usual, though able to work at home, I had time for writing. When the manuscript was nearly completed I gave it to a brother to look over, that I might have his judgment; and the Lord so refreshed his spirit through it, that he offered to advance the means for having it printed, with the understanding that if the book should not sell he would never consider me his debtor. By this offer not a small obstacle was removed, as I have no means of my own to defray the expense of printing. These last two circumstances, connected with many other points, confirmed me that I had not been mistaken when I had come to the conclusion that it was the will of God that I should serve his church in this way.

The fact of my being a foreigner, and therefore but very imperfectly acquainted with the English language, I judged to be no sufficient reason for keeping me from writing. The Christian reader, being acquainted with this fact, will candidly excuse any inaccuracy of expression.

For the poor among the brethren this Narrative is especially intended, and to their prayers I commend it in particular.

GEORGE MÜLLER.

CONTENTS.

INTRODUCTION XVII

CHAPTER I.

BOYHOOD AND YOUTH.

1805 — 1825.

BIRTH — EARLY DISHONESTY — INSENSIBILITY — CONFIRMATION IN THE STATE CHURCH — DISSOLUTENESS OF LIFE — THE HARD WAY OF TRANSGRESSORS — THE GYMNASIUM AT NORDHAUSEN — THE UNIVERSITY AT HALLE — ROVINGS 47

CHAPTER II.

THE PRODIGAL'S RETURN.

1825 — 1826.

A TREASURE FOUND — DAWNING OF THE NEW LIFE — THE PEACE OF GOD — "I AM COME TO SET A MAN AT VARIANCE AGAINST HIS FATHER" — "LET HIM THAT HEARETH SAY COME" — THE FIRST SERMON — DELIGHT IN THE LORD — A COMMON ERROR — THE FOUNTAIN NEGLECTED 54

CHAPTER III.

SELF-DEDICATION.

1826 — 1829.

DESIRE FOR MISSIONARY LABOR — PROVIDENTIAL RELEASE FROM MILITARY SERVICE — VISIT AT HOME — LED TO THE LAND OF HIS FUTURE LABORS — PROGRESS IN RELIGIOUS KNOWLEDGE — DESIRE FOR IMMEDIATE USEFULNESS 63

CHAPTER IV.

LEANING ON JESUS.

1830 — 1832.

A DOOR OPENED — TOKENS FOR GOOD — TRUST EXERCISED IN THE STUDY AND MINISTRY OF THE WORD — THE SWORD OF THE SPIRIT — TRUSTING IN GOD FOR DAILY BREAD — BLESSEDNESS OF WAITING UPON THE LORD — "OWE NO MAN" — "ACCORDING TO YOUR FAITH BE IT UNTO YOU" — THE GIFT OF FAITH, AND THE GRACE OF FAITH 74

CHAPTER V.

MINISTRY AT BRISTOL BEGUN.

1832 — 1835.

"HERE HAVE WE NO CONTINUING CITY" — CAUTION TO THE CHRISTIAN TRAVELLER — NEW TOKENS FOR GOOD — THE WAY MADE CLEAR — MEETINGS FOR INQUIRY — NO RESPECT OF PERSONS WITH GOD — FRANKE, "BEING DEAD, YET SPEAKETH" — DAILY BREAD SUPPLIED — A PECULIAR PEOPLE 95

CHAPTER VI.

THE SCRIPTURAL KNOWLEDGE INSTITUTION.

1834 — 1835.

UNSCRIPTURAL CHARACTER OF THE EXISTING RELIGIOUS AND BENEVOLENT SOCIETIES — A NEW INSTITUTION PROPOSED — GOD'S WORD THE ONLY RULE, AND GOD'S PROMISE THE ONLY DEPENDENCE — "IN EVERYTHING LET YOUR REQUEST BE MADE KNOWN UNTO GOD" — EARNEST OF THE DIVINE BLESSING ON THE INSTITUTION — BEREAVEMENT — HELPER SEASONABLY SENT — REWARD OF SEEKING GOD'S FACE 109

CHAPTER VII.

HOME FOR DESTITUTE ORPHANS.

1835 — 1836.

FRANKE'S WORKS FOLLOW HIM — A GREAT UNDERTAKING CONCEIVED — REASONS FOR ESTABLISHING AN ORPHAN HOUSE — PRAYER FOR GUIDANCE — TREASURE LAID UP IN HEAVEN — IN PRAYER AND IN FAITH THE WORK IS BEGUN . .124

CHAPTER VIII.

THE FIELD WIDENING.

1836—1837.

AN UNEXPECTED OBSTACLE — IMPLICIT SUBMISSION — A SECOND ORPHAN HOUSE PROPOSED — AN ENCOURAGING TEXT — THE NEW ORPHAN HOUSE OPENED — COMPLETED ANSWER TO PRAYER — PROGRESS OF THE LORD'S WORK — THE OVERSIGHT OF THE FLOCK 136

CHAPTER IX.

TRIAL.

1838.

THE MINISTRY OF SICKNESS — PEACE OF MIND — JESUS A PRESENT HELP — DEEP POVERTY — PLEADING WITH GOD — UNITED PRAYER 148

CHAPTER X.

DELIVERANCE.

1838.

"PERPLEXED BUT NOT IN DESPAIR" — FAITH JUSTIFIED — A LESSON OF OBEDIENCE — BOUNTIFUL SUPPLIES — SPIRITUAL INGATHERING — A DAY OF MERCIES — TIMELY AID — A SEASON OF PLENTY — OBEDIENCE REWARDED 158

CHAPTER XI.

ASKING AND RECEIVING.

1839.

HELP FOR THE POOR SAINTS — THE UNFAILING BANK — MEANS EXHAUSTED — LIBERALITY OF A LABORING SISTER — "HE KNOWETH OUR FRAME" — REDEEMING THE TIME — GODLINESS PROFITABLE UNTO ALL THINGS . 172

CHAPTER XII.

PLENTY AND WANT.

1840.

A PURE OFFERING REQUIRED — A JOURNEY PROPOSED — SEASONABLE PROVISION — LOOKING ONLY TO THE LORD — THE WRATH OF MAN PRAISING GOD — A PROMISE FULFILLED — BENEFIT OF TRIAL — NEW SPRINGS OPENED — BEFORE THEY CALL I WILL ANSWER — TRUST IN GOD COMMENDED — SPIRITUAL BLESSINGS 184

CHAPTER XIII.

FAITH STRENGTHENED BY EXERCISE.

1841.

A WANT SUPPLIED — RESOURCES EXCEEDING THE DEMAND — EVIL OF SURETYSHIP — POWER OF CHRISTIAN LOVE — GOD'S WORD THE FOOD OF THE SOUL — PREPARATION FOR THE HOUR OF TRIAL — POVERTY — DEPENDING ONLY ON THE LIVING GOD 199

CHAPTER XIV.

WALKING IN DARKNESS.

1841—1842.

"GOD'S WAY LEADS INTO TRIAL" — GROUNDS OF THANKFULNESS — PROTRACTED DARKNESS — CAST DOWN, BUT NOT DESTROYED — TRUST IN GOD COMMENDED — THE MEANS OF ITS ATTAINMENT — REVIEW OF THE WORK 212

CHAPTER XV.

PROSPERITY.

1842—1843.

ABUNDANT SUPPLIES — RESTING ON THE WRITTEN WORD — "SEEKING AND FINDING" — ERRONEOUS IMPRESSIONS REMOVED — PERSEVERING AND PREVAILING PRAYER ANSWERED — "LENGTHENING THE CORDS AND STRENGTHENING THE STAKES" — A FOURTH ORPHAN HOUSE 235

CHAPTER XVI.

STEWARDSHIP.

1844.

EARTHLY AND HEAVENLY TREASURES — SEEKING THE KINGDOM OF GOD — FELLOWSHIP WITH THE FATHER — THE CHRISTIAN MERCHANT — EXAMPLES — MISTAKES 252

CHAPTER XVII.

REAPING BOUNTIFULLY.

1845 — 1846.

AN UNEXPECTED REQUEST — DELIBERATION — A GREAT UNDERTAKING — RELIANCE ON THE RESOURCES OF THE LIVING GOD — AN ANSWER EXPECTED AND RECEIVED — PRAYER FOR FAITH AND PATIENCE — FURTHER PROOFS OF DIVINE FAVOR — THE BLESSEDNESS OF DEVISING LIBERAL THINGS . 286

CHAPTER XVIII.

FAITH CONFIRMED BY PROSPERITY.

1846 — 1848.

THE SPIRIT OF SUPPLICATION BESTOWED AND PRAYER ANSWERED — THE TIME OF MAN'S NEED AND OF GOD'S BOUNTY — FAITH NOT SHAKEN — DEALING ONLY WITH GOD — THE NEEDED AMOUNT FURNISHED — PERPETUAL "NEED" — NOT WEARY IN GOD'S WORK — JOY IN ANSWERED PRAYER — FOUR REQUESTS GRANTED — "CONTINUING INSTANT IN PRAYER" — THE BUILDING COMMENCED — PERSONAL HISTORY — A MARKED DELIVERANCE 309

CHAPTER XIX.

CONTINUED MERCIES.

1848 — 1850.

HUMBLE BEGINNINGS — DEVISING LIBERAL THINGS — THE ORPHANS PROVIDED FOR — A MEMORABLE DAY — MONEY "AT INTEREST" — MEANS FROM AN UNEXPECTED SOURCE — THE PROGRESS OF THE NEW ORPHAN HOUSE — MEANS PROVIDED FOR ITS COMPLETION — INEXPRESSIBLE DELIGHT IN GOD — REVIEW OF THE TWO YEARS PAST 327

CHAPTER XX.

A NEW VICTORY OF FAITH.

1850 — 1851.

PAST MERCIES A ENCOURAGEMENT TO NEW UNDERTAKINGS — A HOUSE FOR SEVEN HUNDRED ORPHANS PROPOSED — WALKING BY FAITH — COUNSEL SOUGHT FROM GOD — THE PURPOSE FORMED — DELIGHT IN THE MAGNITUDE AND DIFFICULTY OF THE DESIGN 348

CHAPTER XXI.

UNVARYING PROSPERITY.

1851 — 1852.

DESIRES FOR MORE ENLARGED USEFULNESS GRATIFIED — A LARGE DONATION ANTICIPATED AND RECEIVED — REVIEW OF 1851 — PERSONAL EXPERIENCE — BUILDING FUND FOR THE SECOND NEW ORPHAN HOUSE — DOUBT RESISTED — WAITING ON GOD NOT IN VAIN — REVIEW OF 1852 368

CHAPTER XXII.

REAPING IN JOY.

1852 — 1854.

EXPECTING GREAT THINGS FROM GOD — MUNIFICENT DONATION — INCREASING USEFULNESS OF THE SCRIPTURAL KNOWLEDGE INSTITUTION — ACCESS TO GOD THROUGH FAITH IN CHRIST — A VOICE FROM MOUNT LEBANON — BENEFIT OF WAITING GOD'S TIME — CAREFUL STEWARDSHIP — FAITH, THE ONLY RELIANCE — "THIS POOR WIDOW HATH CAST IN MORE THAN THEY ALL" — GREATER ACHIEVEMENTS OF FAITH ANTICIPATED — COUNSEL TO TRACT DISTRIBUTORS — A NEW AND SEVERE TRIAL OF FAITH 377

CHAPTER XXIII.

THREE YEARS OF PROSPERITY.

1854 — 1857.

THE SITE SELECTED — SIX THOUSAND ORPHANS IN PRISON — HOW TO ASK FOR DAILY BREAD — REVIEW OF TWENTY-FOUR YEARS — "TAKE NO THOUGHT FOR THE MORROW" — INSURANCE AGAINST BAD DEBTS . . 399

CHAPTER XXIV.

SUMMARY.

1857 — 1860.

THE HOUSE FOR FOUR HUNDRED OPENED — PRAYER MORE THAN ANSWERED — THE RESORT IN TROUBLE — AN OUTPOURING OF THE SPIRIT ON THE ORPHANS — LAND FOR A NEW BUILDING PURCHASED — " BUT ONE LIFE TO SPEND FOR GOD " — " SCATTERING, YET INCREASING " — A MEMORABLE YEAR — THE GERM OF THE IRISH REVIVAL — LETTER FROM AN ORPHAN — THE FRUIT OF SIX MONTHS' PRAYER — THE RESULTS OF THE WORK — REVIVAL AMONG THE ORPHANS................................218

CHAPTER XXV.

1860 — 1868

GREAT PROSPERITY — FEWER TRIALS — INFLUENCE — THIRD ORPHAN HOUSE — PRAYING FOR HELPERS, AND FOR OTHER NEEDS — REGULAR CONTRIBUTORS — REVIVALS — FOURTH ORPHAN HOUSE..............442

CHAPTER XXVI.

1868 — 1872.

DONATIONS — FIFTH ORPHAN HOUSE — HABITS OF BENEVOLENCE — DEATH OF MRS. MÜLLER — MR. WRIGHT AN ASSOCIATE — PLACES FOR THE ORPHANS — OBJECTS OF THE INSTITUTION — ORPHANS LEAVING THE INSTITUTION — SPECIMEN OF ARTICLES DONATED — NOTE FROM MR. MULLER RESPECTING BOOKS AND ACCOUNTS — ANNUAL REPORT FOR 1872..........463

CHAPTER XXVII.

A VISIT TO THE ORPHAN HOUSES — ATTENDING CHURCH — INTERNAL ARRANGEMENTS — FOOD — EDUCATION — HEALTH...............480

CHAPTER XXVIII.

A REVIEW OF FIVE YEARS' WORK — CONTINENTAL TRAVELS, AND VISIT IN AMERICA...................................492

INTRODUCTION.

WHAT is meant by the prayer of faith? is a question which is beginning to arrest, in an unusual degree, the attention of Christians. What is the significance of the passages both in the New Testament and the Old which refer to it? What is the limit within which they may be safely received as a ground of practical reliance? Were these promises limited to prophetical or apostolical times; or have they been left as a legacy to all believers until the end shall come?

Somehow or other, these questions are seldom discussed either from the pulpit or the press. I do not remember to have heard any of them distinctly treated of in a sermon. I do not know of any work in which this subject is either theoretically explained or practically enforced. It really seems as if this portion of Revelation was, by common consent, ignored in all our public teachings. Do not men believe that God means what he appears plainly to have asserted? or, if we believe that he means it, do we fear the charge of fanaticism if we openly avow that we take him at his word?

The public silence on this subject does not, however, prevent a very frequent private inquiry in respect to it. The thoughtful Christian, when in his daily reading of the Scriptures he meets with any of those wonderful promises made to believing prayer, often pauses to ask himself, What can these words mean? Can it be that God has made such promises as these to me, and to such men as I am? Have I really permission to commit all my little affairs to a God of infinite wisdom, believing that he will take charge of them and direct them according to the promptings of boundless love and absolute omniscience? Is prayer really a power with God, or is it merely an expedient by which our own piety may be cultivated? Is it not merely a power (that is, a stated antecedent accompanied by the idea of causation), but is it a transcendent power, accomplishing what no other power can, overruling all other agencies, and rendering them subservient to its own wonderful efficiency? I think there are few devout readers of the Bible to whom these questions are not frequently suggested. We ask them, but we do not often wait for an answer. These promises seem to us to be addressed either to a past or to a coming age, but not to us, at the present day. Yet with such views as these the devout soul is not at all satisfied If an invaluable treasure is here reserved for the believer, he asks, why should I not receive my portion of it? He cannot doubt that God has, in a remarkable manner, at various times, answered his prayers; why should he not always answer them? and why should not the believer always draw near to God in full confidence that he will do as he has said? He may remember that the prayer which has been manifestly answered was the offspring of deep humility, of conscious unworthiness, of utter self-negation, and of simple and earnest reliance on the promises of God through the mediation of Christ. Why should not his prayers be always of the same character? With the apostles of old he pours out his soul in the petition, "Lord, increase our faith."

And yet it can scarcely be denied that the will of God has been distinctly revealed on this subject. The promises made to believing prayer are explicit, numerous, and diversified. If we take them in their simple and literal meaning, or if in fact we give to them any reasonable interpretation whatever, they seem to be easily understood. Our difficulty seems to be this the promise is so "exceeding great" that we cannot conceive God really to mean what he clearly appears to have revealed. The blessing seems too vast for our comprehension; we "stagger at the promises, through unbelief," and thus fail to secure the treasure which was purchased for us by Christ Jesus.

It may be appropriate for us to review some of the passages which refer most directly to this subject: —

"Ask, and it shall be given you; seek, and ye shall find; knock, and it shall be opened unto you; for *every one* that asketh receiveth, and he that seeketh findeth, and to him that knocketh *it shall* be opened." "If ye then, being evil, know how to give good gifts unto your children, *how much more* shall your Father which is in heaven give good things to them that *ask* him?"[1]

In the Gospel of Luke the same words are repeated, with a single variation at the close. "If ye, being evil, know how to give good gifts unto your children, how much more shall your heavenly Father give the *Holy Spirit to them that ask him?*"[2]

"I say unto you that if two of you shall agree on earth as touching anything that they shall ask, it shall be done for them of my Father which is in heaven. For where two or three are gathered together in my name, there am I in the midst of them."[3]

"Jesus answered and said unto them, Verily I say unto you, if ye have faith, and doubt not, ye shall not only do that which is done to the fig-tree, but also ye shall say to this mountain, Be thou removed, and be thou cast into the sea, and it shall be done. And *all things whatsoever* ye shall ask in prayer, believing, ye shall receive."[4]

The same promise, slightly varied in form, is found in the Gospel of Mark. "*Have faith in God.* For verily I say unto you that whosoever shall say to this mountain, Be thou removed, and be thou cast into the sea, and shall not doubt in his heart, but shall believe that those things which he hath said shall come to pass, he shall have whatever he saith. Therefore I say unto you,

---

[1] Matthew vii. 7-11.
[2] Luke xi. 13.
[3] Matthew xviii. 19, 20.
[4] Matthew xxi. 21, 22.

Whatsoever things ye desire, when ye pray, believe that ye receive them, and ye shall have them."[1]

Now I do not pretend that we are obliged to receive these words literally. Unless, however, we believe the Saviour to have spoken repeatedly on the same subject, at random, and with no definite meaning, we must understand him to have asserted that things impossible by the ordinary laws of material causation are possible by faith in God. I do not perceive, if we allow these words to have any meaning whatever, that we can ascribe to them any other significance.

"Verily I say unto you, He that believeth in me, the works that I do shall he do also; and greater works than these shall he do, because I go unto my Father. And whatsoever ye shall ask in my name, that I will do, that the Father may be glorified in the Son. If ye shall ask anything in my name I will do it."[2]

"Verily I say unto you, Whatsoever ye shall ask the Father in my name, he will give it you. Hitherto ye have asked nothing in my name. Ask, and ye shall receive, that your joy may be full."[3]

"The effectual, fervent prayer of a righteous man *availeth much;*"[4] that is, it is a real power, a positive energy. The apostle illustrates what he means by availing prayer by the example of Elias, a man subject to like passions as we are: "He prayed earnestly that it might not rain, and it rained not on the earth by the space of three years and six months; and he prayed again, and the heavens gave rain, and the earth brought forth her fruit."[5]

The conditions on which prayer will be heard are in various places specified, but particularly in John xv. 7.: "If ye abide in me and my words abide in you, ye shall *ask what ye will,* and it shall be done unto you." That is, if I understand the passage, prevalence in prayer is conditioned by the conformity of our

---

[1] Mark xi. 22-24. [2] John xiv. 12-14. [3] John xvi. 23, 24.
[4] James v. 16. [5] V. 17, 18.

souls to the will of God; "if ye abide in me and my words abide in you." On this condition, and on this only, may we ask what we will, with the assurance that it will be done unto us. Faith, in its most simple meaning, is that temper of the mind in the creature which responds to every revealed perfection of the Creator. Just according to the degree in which this correspondence exists, is the promise made that we shall have whatsoever we ask.

It is evident, from the eleventh of Hebrews, that the views of the Apostle Paul concerning faith were entirely in harmony with the passages recited above. He reviews the lives of the most eminent saints, for the express purpose of showing that the impressive events in their history, whether physical or moral, were controlled entirely by faith. He sums up the whole in this remarkable language: —

"And what shall I say more? For the time would fail me to tell of those who *through faith* subdued kingdoms, wrought righteousness, obtained promises, stopped the mouths of lions, quenched the violence of fire, escaped the edge of the sword, out of weakness were made strong, waxed valiant in fight, turned to flight the armies of the aliens; women received their dead raised to life again; and others were tortured, not accepting deliverance, that they might obtain a better resurrection." We are, I think, taught by this passage that the apostle believed faith to be a power capable of transcending and modifying every other agency, by which changes became possible which to every other known power were impossible. We see that in this catalogue of the victories of faith he includes the subjection of almost every form of what we call natural laws. The whole passage seems an illustration of the meaning of our Lord, when he says, "If ye have faith as a grain of mustard seed, ye shall say to this sycamine tree, Be thou removed and planted in the midst of the sea, and it shall obey you."

It seems then apparent that the doctrine of the peculiar and wonderful power of the prayer of faith is as clearly revealed in the Scriptures as any other doctrine. It would seem evident, at any rate, from the passages just quoted, that the Apostle Paul understood the teachings of our Saviour to mean what they say. From the general tenor of the Scriptures I think we may learn two important truths: First, that there is a certain state of mind in a devout soul to which God has promised all that it asks, subject, however, as to the manner of the answer, to the dictates of his infinite wisdom and goodness; and, second, that in granting such petitions he does not always limit his action within the ordinary or acknowledged laws of matter or of mind. I do not perceive how we can interpret the passages above cited, as well as many others, without giving them a meaning at least as extensive as this.

Why is it, then, that this whole range of revealed truth has so generally been looked upon as an unknown and unexplored region? Why should we limit either the goodness or the power of God by our own knowledge of what we call the laws of nature? Why should we not admit that "there are more things in heaven and earth than are dreamed of in our philosophy"? In a universe governed by moral law, why should not moral laws take precedence of all others? Why should we deny that there is a power in prayer to which we have not commonly attained? We are straitened in ourselves, and suppose that we are straitened in God. We interpret the gracious promises of our most loving Father in heaven by the rule of our own imperfect and unbelieving piety. We ask for light from without, while the light can only come from a more elevated piety within. We ask for examples of the effects of faith at the present day, corresponding to those spoken of in the sacred Scriptures. Thoughtful men acknowledge that there must be a meaning in these promises, which they have not yet understood, and they see plainly that the kingdom of God can never come with power until this prevalence in prayer shall have become a matter of universal attainment; and yet they dare hardly believe that God is as good as he has revealed himself to be.

There have, nevertheless, from time to time, occurred, what plainly appear to be, remarkable instances of answers to prayer. Many of them have faded from recollection, with the generation in which they occurred; those which are remembered, however, seem to teach us that God is a living God now as truly as in times past. The history of persecutions is always filled with remarkable answers to prayer. The rescue of Peter from the power of the Sanhedrim in one case, and from the power of Herod in another, has been a thousand times repeated in the history of the church of Christ. The answer to prayer for divine direction as to the time and manner of performing some Christian service, to which an individual has felt himself specially called, has frequently been very remarkable. The biographies of the early and of many of the later Friends are replete with such instances. Any one who will read the edifying memoirs of George Fox, John Woolman, William Allen, and Stephen Grellet, will find what I have alluded to, abundantly exemplified. The well-authenticated accounts of the late revivals in this country and in Ireland teach us that most remarkable instances of answers to prayer were of almost daily occurrence. In the last century a single instance deserves particular remembrance; it was the founding of Franke's Orphan House at Halle. It seemed to him to be a Christian duty to attempt something for the relief of orphans, and he commenced the undertaking. From time to time, as the number of applicants increased, the means for their support was provided, in answer, as he firmly believed, to fervent and unceasing prayer. Thus an extensive establishment was reared, which has continued to the present day, providing education and support for thousands of the poor and destitute, and it has been for a century and a half one of the most honored of the charitable institutions of the continent of Europe.

The most remarkable instance of the efficacy of prayer with

which I am acquainted, is that recorded in the following pages. It seems, in fact, to be a practical illustration of the meaning of those passages of Scripture which I have already recited. A young German Christian, friendless and unknown, is conscious of what he believes to be a call from the Lord to attempt something for the benefit of the poor vagabond children of Bristol. He is at this time preaching the gospel to a small company of believers, from whom, at his own suggestion, he receives no salary, being supported day by day by the voluntary offerings of his brethren. Without the promise of aid from any being but God, he commences his work. In answer to prayer, funds are received as they are needed, and the attempt succeeds beyond his expectation. After a few years he is led to believe that God has called him to establish a house for the maintenance and education of orphans. He was impelled to this effort, not only from motives of benevolence, but from a desire to convince men that God was a LIVING GOD, as ready now as ever to answer prayer; and that, in the discharge of any duty to which he calls us, we may implicitly rely upon his all-sufficient aid in every emergency.

Mr. Müller was led to undertake this work in such a manner that aid could not be expected from any being but God. He did not of course expect God to create gold and silver and put them into his hands. He knew, however, that God could incline the hearts of men to aid him, and he believed, if the thing that he attempted was of Him, that he would so incline them, in answer to prayer, as his necessities should require. Most men in making such an attempt would have spread the case before the public, employed agents to solicit in its behalf, and undertaken nothing until funds adequate to the success of the enterprise had been already secured. But Mr. Müller, true to his principles, would do no such thing. From the first day to the present moment he has neither directly nor indirectly solicited either of the public or of an individual a single penny. As necessities arose he simply laid his case before God and asked of him all that he needed, and the supply has always been seasonable and unfailing.

The conductors of benevolent enterprises generally consider it important to publish the names of donors, appealing thus to what is considered an innocent desire in man to let our good deeds be known, and thus also to stimulate others to do likewise. Ignoring every motive of this kind, Mr. Muller made it his rule to publish the name of no contributor. When the name was known to him, which, however, was not often the case, he made a private acknowledgment; while in his printed account he only made known the sum received, and the date of its reception. In this manner, forsaking every other reliance but God, and in childlike simplicity looking to him alone for the supply of every want, all that he needed was furnished as punctually as if, in possession of millions, he had drawn from time to time on his banker.

Thus has he continued from, I think, the year 1834. By degrees the establishment increased, and it was necessary to leave the hired houses in which the children had thus far been accommodated. Land was purchased, and a building was erected in the vicinity of Bristol. This was soon filled to overflowing, and another building was demanded. This was erected, and it also was very soon filled. These buildings were sufficient to accommodate seven hundred orphans. At the present moment, a third building, larger than either, is in the process of erection, and is to be finished in the course of the ensuing summer. When this shall be completed, accommodations will have been provided for eleven hundred and fifty orphans. These expensive buildings have been erected; the land has been purchased on which they stand; this multitude of children has been clothed and fed and educated; support and remuneration have been provided for all the necessary teachers and assistants, and all this has been done by a man who is not worth a dollar. He has never asked any one but God for whatever they needed, and from the beginning they have never wanted a meal, nor have they ever allowed them selves to be in debt. There seems in this to be something as remarkable as if Mr. Muller had commanded a sycamine tree to be removed and planted in the sea, and it had obeyed him

But this is not all. Mr. Muller saw that there was a great demand for copies of the Holy Scriptures, both in Great Britain and on the Continent, and he commenced the work of Bible distribution. This so rapidly extended itself that he was soon obliged to open in Bristol a large Bible House. He believed that great good might be done by the circulation of religious tracts, and he has carried out his work extensively. He was moved to make an attempt to aid and even to support missionaries among the heathen, as well as other good men, of various denominations, who, with very inadequate means of living, were preaching the gospel to the poor and destitute at home. He began to aid them as their necessities came to his knowledge, and now one hundred such men are depending on him, wholly or in part, for support.

Here, then, we certainly behold a remarkable phenomenon. A single man, wholly destitute of funds, is supporting and educating seven hundred orphans, providing everything needful for their education, is in himself an extensive Bible and Tract and Missionary Society, the work is daily increasing in magnitude, and the means for carrying it on are abundantly supplied, while he is connected with no particular denomination, is aided by no voluntary association, and he has asked the assistance of not a single individual. He has asked no one but God, and all his wants have been regularly supplied. In these labors of love he has, up to the present time, expended nearly a million of dollars. It is thus that he has endeavored to show to an unbelieving world that God is a living God, and that he means what he has said in every one of his promises.[1]

---

[1] The following brief statistics will show the magnitude of the work already accomplished —

The number of pupils hitherto instructed in all the day, evening, and Sunday schools, is 13,124 The whole number of *orphans* educated within the establishment is 1,153 Of the 700 now in the Institution, 260 are hopefully pious. Missionaries aided at the

INTRODUCTION.   XXVII

I have referred to Mr. Muller as if he were the sole agent in this work. This, however, is by no means true. His co-workers in the Institution are all of the same spirit as himself. Mr. Craik, a gentleman from Scotland, has been with him from the beginning, has shared in all the labors and responsibilities of these vast undertakings, and has been specially blessed as a preacher of the gospel. The remuneration of all the assistants is contingent on the means received in answer to prayer. When sacrifices are to be made, they are all prompt to make them, and they do not expect an answer to prayer until they have contributed, from their own scanty wages, whatever can be spared after providing for their actual necessities.

The last report of Mr. Müller's labors has just been received. From this we learn another interesting fact. It seems that the late revival in Ireland is indirectly connected with these labors in

---

present time, 100. Since 1834 there have been circulated, — Bibles, 24,768, Testaments, 15,100, Psalms, 719, other portions of Scripture, 1,876, or, total, 42,463 Bibles or portions of Scripture Tracts and books (not pages, but separate publications), 11,493,174.

Two large buildings have been erected, a third is in the process of erection , the land on which they stand has been purchased. The expense of the orphan work alone has amounted to £133,528 sterling, and the expenses are daily increasing

The contributions by which these expenditures have been met have been sent from every quarter of the globe The largest amounts have been, as might be expected, from England, Scotland, Ireland, and Wales, but to these may be added the Cape of Good Hope, Mt Lebanon, Demerara, Newport, R I , New York, Philadelphia, California, France, Holland, Sardinia, Australia, etc , etc

[1] *Since the above statement by Dr. Wayland, Dec , 1860, Mr Muller says, in his last report, 1872.* "The work goes steadily on — we want nothing Faith is above circumstances No war, no fire, no water, no mercantile panic, no loss of friends, no death, can touch it It goes on its own steady course. It triumphs over all difficulties"

Since the commencement more than £500,000 ($2,500,000) have been received 23,000 children or grown-up persons have been taught in the various schools, *entirely* supported by the funds of the Institution, besides the tens of thousands who have been benefited in the schools, which were *assisted* by its funds; more than 64,000 Bibles, 85,000 Testaments, and 100,000 smaller portions of the Holy Scriptures, in various languages, also thirty-nine millions of tracts and books, in several different languages, have been circulated There have been, from the first, missionaries assisted by its funds, and of late years more than 150 in number On this object alone £104,000 ($520,000) have been expended. 3,575 orphans have been under our care and five large houses, at the expense of £115,000 ($575 000), have been erected and fitted up for the accommodation of 2,050 orphans. As to the spiritual results, I will here say nothing, indeed, eternity alone can unfold them —*Ed. revised edition.*

Bristol. A pious young Irishman read "The Dealings of the Lord with George Muller," and received from it new views of the power of believing prayer. He felt the need of prayer for the perishing around him, and determined by prayer and conversation to labor for their salvation. First, however, he asked that God would give him an associate. This prayer was granted. These two then united in earnest prayer for some additions to their number. This prayer was granted. In this manner a small company was united in asking for an outpouring of the Holy Spirit on their neighborhood. They devoted themselves to prayer and to labor among the people by whom they were surrounded. Their prayers were answered. The Spirit was poured out, twenty-five souls were converted. Multitudes united with them in supplication. They went from place to place, praying and laboring for the conversion of men; and thus the work extended, until the whole district of Ulster was visited with that remarkable outpouring of the Holy Spirit.

All these we suppose to be indisputable facts. If in any respect there has been a misstatement, or even an exaggeration, the means are abundant for detecting it. The whole work has been carried on in the presence and under the inspection of the whole city of Bristol. There stand those large and expensive buildings. There are seen the seven hundred orphans, who are in every respect admirably cared for. Everything has been paid for, for Mr. Muller is never in debt. His poverty is well known, and he will not accept of any money as a provision for his future necessities. His accounts have been annually audited by a competent committee. There is not the man living who can contradict his assertion, " I never asked aid from a single individual." Hundreds weekly visit the Institution, and no one has ever found in it anything at variance with Mr. Muller's published statements. Last of all, the Rev. Dr Sawtell, a gentleman known to thousands in this country, has added his independent testimony to the truth of all that is here related. More conclusive evidence to the truth of facts cannot be desired.

To account for a fact is to refer it to some general law whose existence is already established. When it is therefore asked, How shall these facts be accounted for? we inquire, to what known law can they be referred? They cannot certainly be referred to any known law of human action. How would we decide if a similar case should occur in physics? Suppose a series of experiments should be made daily for twenty-five years in chemistry or mechanics, with the same invariable result, and this result could be referred to no previously established law,— to what conclusion should we arrive? There could be but one conclusion in which all men of science would unite. They would all declare that a new law had been discovered, and would modify their systems accordingly. It seems to me that on all sound philosophical principles we are bound to come to the same conclusion in the present case. We can refer these facts to no other law than to that announced by the Saviour in his promise to answer the prayer of faith. There is no reason to suppose that in the case of Mr. Müller and his associates there is anything exceptional or peculiar. What God has done for them we cannot doubt that, under the same conditions, he will do for every other believing disciple of Christ.

What, then, are the conditions of this remarkable experiment, if such we may call it? They are something like the following. A poor, unknown man is convinced that it is his duty, as a servant of Christ, to labor in several ways for the relief of the temporal and spiritual wants of the ignorant and destitute. He consecrates himself to the work by dedicating to it his time and labor, and whatever pecuniary means should come into his possession. He resolved that he would neither appeal to any of the ordinary motives which dispose men to humanity, nor even solicit aid from any human being, but simply make his wants known to God, believing that, if he was doing the work of God, the divine promise was pledged in his behalf. Not only did he trust in God that all the pecuniary aid which he needed would be furnished, but that, in answer to prayer, all needed wisdom would be given him in the conduct of his complicated and arduous undertakings. The result has met his most sanguine expectations. The institution has increased to a most magnificent charity, aside from its missionary, Bible, and tract operations; all its wants have been from time to time supplied; and it is at the present moment carried on upon precisely the same principles on which it commenced. We cannot resist the conclusion that if any one will undertake any other Christian work in a similar spirit, and on the same principles, his labor will be attended with a similar result.

While we believe this, however, we do not pretend to affirm that just such immediate results will always be seen. This would be to limit the omniscience of God by the short-sighted ignorance of man. It may best suit the purposes of infinite goodness to answer the prayer of faith by crosses and disappointments; but these in the end shall be found in the most signal manner to promote the object to be accomplished. While the disciples were praying and laboring for the extension of the kingdom of Christ in Jerusalem, it seemed a strange answer to prayer that they should be driven out of the city; but the meaning of it was evident when churches arose in Phenice and Cyprus and Antioch, and it became manifest that the gospel was designed not for Jews alone, but for the whole family of man. Paul devoted himself with unquenchable zeal to the salvation of men, and, with a fervid eloquence which has given him a place among the noblest orators of antiquity, delighted to spend his life in persuading men to be reconciled to God. He was a man whose confidence in God was as unshaken as any whose history has been recorded by the pen of inspiration. It doubtless was to the disciples of that age, as well as to himself, a most unaccountable dispensation that he should have been impeded in his great work by the necessity of composing dissensions and rectifying errors which were constantly arising in the churches which he had planted, and, most of all, that so many years of his life should have been spent in prison. Yet it is to these, at the time untoward circumstances, that we owe the writing of those epistles which occupy so large a portion of the volume of inspiration, and without which the message of God to man would not have been completed. In no other way could his prayer to be useful to the cause of Christ have been so fully answered.

With this understanding of the promise granted to the prayer of faith, I do not see why we should not take the case of Mr. Müller as an example for our imitation. Whoever attains to this same simple desire in all things to do the will of God, and to the same childlike trust in his promises, may, I think, hope for a similar blessing. God is no respecter of persons. "If *any* man *do his will*, him he heareth." And all the teaching of the Scriptures confirms us in this belief. The passages which we have quoted at the commencement of this paper, with hundreds of others, all lead to the same conclusion. In the Scriptures every form of illustration is used to impress upon us the conviction that God is indeed our Father, and that he delights to grant our requests for anything that is for our benefit, and specially that he pledges himself to direct by his counsel, and aid by his providence, every one who honestly labors to promote the cause of true benevolence and real religion.

If this be so, how important is this subject in its bearing on individual effort. No Christian, though the poorest and humblest, ever need despair of doing a noble work for God. He need never wait until he can obtain the co-operation of the multitude or the wealthy. Let him undertake what he believes to be his duty, on ever so small a scale, and look directly to God for aid and direction. If it be a seed which God has planted, it will take root, grow, and bear fruit, "*having seed within itself.*" "It is better to trust in God than to put confidence in man; it is better to trust in God than to put confidence in princes." A multitude of cases can be adduced to prove that this course is in harmony with the designs of God. It is abundantly shown in the case of Mr. Muller. Take the case of Robert Raikes. Suppose that he had established no school until a powerful association, formed from ecclesiastical dignitaries, millionaires, and the multitude, had united in his support, his effort could hardly have escaped ridiculous failure. On the contrary, he simply established a school by himself. It was a seed which God had planted, and its fruit now shakes like Lebanon.

On the contrast which is seen between the plan of Mr. Muller and the plans by which our missionary and other benevolent operations are conducted, it is unnecessary to enlarge. If Mr Müller is right, I think it is evident that we are all wrong. We cannot go into this subject in detail. We may, however, be permitted to remark, that the means which are frequently employed to secure the approbation and pecuniary aid of worldly men, in carrying forward the cause of Christ, are intensely humiliating. It would seem as though God was the last being to be relied on in carrying forward the work which he has given us to do.

But it is time to bring these remarks to a close. We commend this most unpretending of narratives to the thoughtful consideration of Christians of all denominations. We have greatly overrated the teaching of these facts, if they do not furnish strong incentives to A LIFE OF HOLY EXERTION, AND IMPART AN UNWONTED AND POWERFUL MOTIVE TO EARNEST AND BELIEVING PRAYER. F. W.

PROVIDENCE, December 17, 1850.

DR. SAWTELL'S PREFATORY LETTER.

THE following Letter from Rev. Dr. Sawtell, chaplain to British and American seamen at Havre, France, a gentleman well known in this country, coming directly from the scenes to which it refers, and abundantly confirming the statements given by Mr. Muller himself, while it bears the impress of a warm and hearty appreciation of his work of faith and labor of love, — this *outside view* is a fitting opening to the volume.

To Rev. Francis Wayland, D.D.

My dear Sir: Your repeated request that I should furnish a brief statement of what I know personally of that extraordinary work of faith connected with the Orphan Houses at Ashley Down, near Bristol, England, is so in accordance with the expressed wish of thousands throughout the land, that, however sorely pressed with other duties, I do not feel at liberty to disregard it; and more especially as it is to introduce to American Christians "The Lord's Dealings with George Muller," — a book the intrinsic merits of which, in so far as it exemplifies the power of a living, active faith, and its peculiar adaptation to meet the wants of God's people in the present age, has, to my mind, no parallel out of the Bible. I rejoice in my heart that a new edition is so soon to be issued from the American press in a condensed form.

I shall confine myself to a few simple facts, connected with my own personal knowledge, which serve only to confirm all that is stated in the Narrative. The facts themselves need no coloring;

the more simply they are stated, the more eloquently do they speak to the head and the heart; the less they are varnished, the brighter they shine. And, as to Mr. Muller himself, anything in the shape of eulogy would be as foreign to good taste as it would be offensive and painful to one whom the Lord delighteth to honor. Indeed, so sensitive is he on this point, that, if he hears any one speaking of the Orphan Houses as "Mr. Muller's Asylum," he repudiates the thought, and exclaims, "No, they are God's Orphan Houses."

THE FACTS.

For the last five years my duties have called me frequently to England, Scotland, and Ireland, but I do not remember making one of these preaching tours without hearing more or less of what many called "A standing miracle at Bristol;" — *A man sheltering, feeding, clothing, educating, and making comfortable and happy, hundreds of poor orphan children, with no funds of his own, and no possible means of sustenance, save that which God sent him in answer to prayer.* Of course, such facts, coming from undoubted authority, and oft-repeated, could not fail to arrest my attention, and cause me to ponder deeply these things in my own heart; and every new fact that came to my ears served only to increase an irrepressible desire to "turn aside and see this great sight."

I confess, on my first visit, in March, 1860, I had reserved to myself a wide margin for deductions and disappointment; but, after a few days of careful investigation, I left Bristol exclaiming, with the Queen of Sheba, "The half had not been told me." Here I saw, indeed, seven hundred orphan children fed and provided for, by the hand of God, in answer to prayer, as literally and truly as Elijah was fed by ravens with meat which the Lord provided. And now, after an absence of nine months, I am here again, moving about among these seven hundred children, examining their writing, and the progress they have made in the various branches of study, and their different kinds of work, — listening to their sweet voices in songs of praise to the God of the orphan, — passing through all parts of these vast buildings, that have been erected for their accommodation, — conducting their family worship, and addressing four hundred of them at one time, and three hundred at another, assembled in their respective dining-halls, the most silent, attentive, and earnest listeners I ever addressed; then enjoying hours of sweet converse and prayer with Mr Muller himself, — a privilege for which I shall ever thank God. Oh, it is good to be here!

But to the Orphan Houses themselves. These are all built of stone, in the most complete and thorough manner. No pains have been spared in rendering them convenient, comfortable, and safe for children, and with special reference to warmth, light, ventilation, and cleanliness; and while all is in good taste, and exceedingly chaste and neat, it is all plain — nothing for show or ornament. House No. 1 is fitted up for the accommodation of three hundred orphans, No. 2 for four hundred; both completely furnished and completely filled. No. 3, now in the course of erection, with its walls up, and partly under roof, is planned for the accommodation of four hundred and fifty orphans; and so rapidly are applications coming in that nearly four hundred are already registered on their books; so that no sooner will it be completed than, with God's blessing, it will be filled with helpless orphans. The entire cost of these buildings, and the manner of obtaining the funds, I will state in Mr. Muller's own words· "Without any one having been personally applied to for anything by me, the sum of £133,528, 14s. has been given to me for the orphans, as the result of prayer to God, since the commencement of the work, which sum includes the amount received for the building fund, for the houses already built, and the one now in progress"

But if we would have correct views of the entire work, and understand what God is willing to do in answer to the prayer of faith, we must not confine our eyes or thoughts to the seven hundred orphans. There are here in Bristol four day schools for poor children, with three hundred and thirty-nine pupils, instructed by believers upon scriptural principles, and one Sunday school, such as we call, in the United States, "a Mission School," with one hundred and sixty children, besides an adult school in which Christian teachers are employed, two evenings in the week, to teach reading and writing; all these schools have been entirely supported out of the funds sent in answer to prayer. In reference to this adult school, Mr. Muller says: "Those who teach them take the opportunity of speaking to the scholars about the way of salvation, and make remarks on portions of the word of God which may be read; and thus many have been led to care about their souls, and to go regularly to hear the gospel preached." In summing up the results in connection with all these various schools, Mr. Muller thus remarks: "Since March, 1834, there have been 6,945 children in the day schools, 2,952 in the adult schools, and 3,227 in the Sunday schools, making a total of 13,124 souls that have been brought under habitual instruction in the things of God, besides the many thousands in the schools in the various parts of England, Ireland, Scotland, British Guiana, the West Indies, and East Indies, which have been, to a greater or less degree, assisted," and all, too, let the reader remember, from funds sent to Mr. Muller in answer to prayer.

Nor is this all. During the past year, and out of the same funds sent in answer to prayer, there have been expended for the circulation of the Holy Scriptures the sum of £5,681, 13s. 3½d; also, more than five thousand pounds, or *twenty-five thousand dollars*, to aid missionary efforts in various parts of the world; and the total amount received since 1834, to aid the blessed work of missions in home and foreign fields, is £34,495, 3s. 4d. Added to all this is the sum of £8,064, 12s. 6½d. expended since 1840 for the circulation of religious books and tracts, by which sum 11,493,174 books and tracts have been circulated. Thus we see that for these various objects, disconnected with the orphans, there has been sent in to Mr. Muller, since March, 1834, the sum of £51,777, 14s. 11d, which, added to the sum for the orphans, makes a total of £185,306, 8s. 11d., — *nearly one million of dollars*, sent to Mr. Muller from various parts of the Christian world, and from thousands who never saw him, all in answer to prayer, to aid him in carrying forward his benevolent work in saving souls and to honor and glorify God.

Is it any wonder that men of little faith, and slow of heart to believe what God says, should look upon all this as a 'standing miracle"? But quite otherwise does Mr. Muller regard it. "Think not,' says he, in his Narrative, "that I have the *gift of faith*, that gift of which we read in 1 Cor. xii. 9, mentioned in connection with the 'gifts of healing, the working of miracles,' etc." "It is true," he adds, "that the faith I am enabled to exercise is altogether God's own gift, but it is the self-same faith found in every believer, the growth of which I am most sensible of; for by little and little it has been increasing for the last thirty years."

Now, if it be true that Mr. Muller has received from God no extraordinary gift, beyond that which is common to every believer, it becomes a solemn and momentous question, and one to be pondered deeply and prayerfully, *By what means has this ordinary faith in him attained to such marvellous strength?* Whence came he in possession of that mysterious key by which he is able to unlock the store-houses of God's treasures, and, as it were, help himself to whatever he needs? Day by day, year after year, does this man of God receive the most extraordinary answers to prayer, and by which he is able to carry forward the most stupendous and complicated works of benevolence, while the like precious faith in others is so small and feeble as to be utterly powerless in moving God's loving heart in the bestowment of blessings. "Is there not a cause?" And ought not such facts and such questions to startle every believer into the most thorough searchings of heart to discover the cause of his *little* faith? Let us not attempt, as the manner of some is, to evade the issue, by resolving it all into the sovereignty of God. True it is, God's sovereignty is all-pervading, and as manifest in the Chinese as it is in the British empire; but were an inquisitive child to inquire into the cause of the difference between the well-developed, elastic foot of an Englishman, and the little, dwarfish stump of a Chinese, no Christian parent would consider it a logical or scriptural answer to charge it all upon God's sovereignty. God acts as sovereign in giving to the infant a foot, and certain laws of physical development, in common with its other members; but when the mother, in the pride of her heart, bandages that foot so tight that the laws of development become nugatory and powerless, in that case the sovereignty of God ceased where the bandaging commenced. Just so it is with faith. Being seated with Mr. Muller at his own table, a few evenings since, the subject of faith naturally became the topic of conversation, when he beautifully remarked, "The first germ of faith in the soul is very much like a new-born infant in the cradle, very small and very weak, and its future growth and increase of strength as much depend on its daily, constant exercise as do the physical developments of the child; yes," continued he, "I can now as easily trust God for thirty-five thousand pounds as I could at first for *five thousand*."

Now, may not Mr. Muller's experience on this vital and fundamental principle of our holy religion reveal to us the secret cause of our own weak faith? We fold it up, as it were, in a napkin, lay it carefully away, and treat it as a tender but foolish mother does her offspring: afraid of the open air, it will take cold, it must not walk out, it will fall and break its limbs; it must not take nutritious food, it is so delicate. Thus the poor, unfortunate child never rises to the full strength and vigor of manhood. So is it with that class of believers who do little else than to nurse and sing a kind of lullaby over their puny faith; it must never venture out of sight, or upon a stormy sea in a dark night, or, in other words, *never trust God*. O, what a misnomer to call this faith! and what is it worth, even if it can be called faith? So far as the wants of this perishing world are concerned, it is as worthless as the one talent buried in the earth, and if sufficient to save the soul, it can be saved "only as by fire." Let us not fail here to mark well the difference between these two grains of faith, both small and weak at the beginning, but one, by daily vigorous exercise, increases and grows into such mighty strength "that as a prince it hath power with God," while the other for want of exercise, sinks into imbecility, and becomes powerles for good.

Let us notice, also, the circumstances into which Mr Muller voluntarily threw himself and family, for the very purpose of affording opportunity for the exercise of his faith, — giving away all he possessed, laying by nothing for the future, — thus placing himself and family upon a level with the poorest child, and forcing his faith, as it were, into the severest exercise, by looking to God for daily bread, no less for himself and family than for the seven hundred orphans dependent upon his bounty. Nor can he be persuaded to accept any money, or gifts of any kind, unless with the privilege of laying it at once upon God's altar, to advance the cause and kingdom of his blessed Redeemer. The following facts and correspondence exhibit Mr. Muller's views and real character on this subject.

In October, 1856, a gentleman, in admiration of the services which Mr. Muller had rendered to poor orphans, and to mankind in general, sent him *one hundred pounds*, as the commencement of a fund for the future maintenance of himself and family. Mr. Muller's reply is so characteristic, and so beautifully exemplifies the simplicity of his childlike faith, that I give it in full : —

"MY DEAR SIR: I hasten to thank you for your kind communication, and to inform you that your check for one hundred pounds has safely come to hand.

"I have no property whatever, nor has my dear wife; nor have I had one single shilling regular salary as minister of the Gospel for the last twenty-six years, nor as the Director of the Orphan House and the other objects of the Scriptural Knowledge Institution for Home and Abroad. When I am in need of anything, I fall on my knees and ask God that he would be pleased to give me what I need, and he puts it into the heart of some one or other to help me. Thus all my wants have been amply supplied during the last twenty-six years, and I can say, to the praise of God, I have lacked nothing. My dear wife and my only child — a daughter twenty-four years old — are of the same mind with me. Of this blessed way of living none of us are tired, but become, day by day, more convinced of its blessedness.

"I have never thought it right to make provision for myself or my dear wife and daughter, except in this way, that when I saw a case of need, such as an aged widow, or a sick person, or a helpless infant, I would use my means freely which God had given me, fully believing that if either myself, or my dear wife or daughter, at some time or other should be in need of anything, God would richly repay what was given to the poor, considering it as lent to himself.

"Under these circumstances, I am unable to accept your kindness of the gift of one hundred pounds, *towards making a provision for myself and family;* for so I understand your letter. Any gift given to me, unasked for, by those who have it in their heart to help me to supply my personal and family expenses, I thankfully accept; or any donation given to me for the work of God in which I am engaged, I also thankfully accept, as a steward for the orphans, etc.; but your kind gift seems to me especially given to *make a provision for myself*, which I think would be displeasing to my heavenly Father, who has so bountifully given me my daily bread hitherto. But should I have misunderstood the meaning of your letter, be pleased to let me know it. I hold the check till I hear again from you.

"In the mean time, my dear sir, however you meant your letter, I am deeply sensible of your kindness, and daily pray that God would be pleased richly to recompense you for it, both temporally and spiritually.

"I am, dear sir,
"Yours very gratefully,
"GEORGE MÜLLER."

Two days after the above letter was written, Mr. Muller received a reply, desiring him to use the one hundred pounds for the orphans, and within five days more he received an additional *two hundred pounds* for the benefit of the orphans, from the same individual, who up to that time was unknown to Mr. Muller, nor has he ever seen him since.

Here, then, we discover the secret of Mr. Muller's strong faith. He will not suffer himself to be placed in a condition where he cannot exercise it at all times and in all places. This is the soil, dear readers, into which Mr. Muller cast his faith, which at the beginning was like a grain of mustard-seed, very small, but now, behold, a great tree, where I see with my own eyes seven hundred little birds lodging in the branches thereof; and so rapidly and vigorously does it shoot out new branches, that in a few months four hundred and fifty more will be warbling their sweet notes of praise beneath its wide-spreading foliage. But this is not all, Mr. Müller not only casts the seed into good soil, but he is careful to keep it well watered with the dews of heaven; and this he does " by prayer and supplication, with thanksgiving, making known his requests unto God," and by reading and studying the Holy Scriptures; or, as he modestly expressed himself in conversation, "I am habitually given to the reading of the word of God, coupled with meditation on the same; and everything connected with myself or my service I turn into prayer."

Now, most men would consider such a stupendous work as his a reasonable excuse for cutting short their closet duties. Not so with Mr. Muller. It is in the closet, shut up with God and the Bible, that he girds up the loins of his mind, and burnishes his armor for the battles of the day. It is very beautiful, also, to notice the confidence and childlike simplicity with which he receives everything, and believes every word that God has spoken, and the increased relish and zest with which he daily and hourly returns to God's holy word is very peculiar; as though he was in constant communication with heaven, and receiving fresh letters of instruction and precious promises daily and hourly from his heavenly Father. Hence, he never studies the Bible for others, but for himself, to find out what his Father requires of him; and, studying thus, he seems so impregnated with God's truth, that when he speaks of God, of Christ, of the Holy Spirit, and the great salvation, you are reminded of the words of our Saviour, John vii. 38, for from him seem to flow "rivers of living waters." And the more strikingly does this appear from his primitive style of preaching. Never taking a text, but reading a whole chapter, more or less, he literally teaches his hearers out of the Scriptures, pouring forth such floods of light upon that given passage that his people very soon become mighty in the Scriptures.

His prayers, also, are as peculiar as his preaching, — great simplicity in language; while humbleness, meekness, gentleness, and fervency of spirit are so manifest, that he recalls to your mind a very dear child, who, having had much forgiven, loves much, and whose tender father, before whom it stands, is so rich, so benevolent, so forgiving, that it asks and obtains great blessings, while the deep sense of its own unworthiness keeps the child's heart very tender and very humble. But the most remarkable feature noticeable in his prayers is the asking of everything in the name, through the merits, and for the sake of the Lord Jesus Christ. I do not mean that the fact itself is peculiar, but the great stress he lays upon the honor and glory due to Christ, — Christ's precious blood; Christ our Teacher, our great atoning High Priest; Christ the Resurrection and the Life; Christ the Exalted, Glorified One; Christ our Mediator, Intercessor, and Advocate. To honor and glorify Christ, and magnify his name above every name, seems to be the all-pervading theme which fills his heart and moves his tongue.

But it is not meet that I keep the reader longer from this remarkable narrative of the "Lord's Dealings" with the man himself. In this he tells his own story, and it is marvellous in our eyes. Would that it were translated into every language in Christendom, and might find its way into every family; for, to my mind, it contains the most important, the most instructive and impressive lesson to the child of God that can be found in any uninspired book, the like of which has never appeared since the days of the Apostles. This is no hasty opinion, but a solemn conviction, after days and weeks of diligent search, and the most thorough investigation, in the very city and on the very grounds where these wonderful things have transpired. And if God raised up a Luther in the sixteenth century, to scatter the clouds and disperse the darkness of that age, and to restore to his people that glorious doctrine of "JUSTIFICATION BY FAITH," so long buried beneath the rubbish of Papal superstition, why should it be thought a thing incredible that the same glorious God should, in our day, raise up a Muller to rear this "Monument" on Ashley Down, in the face of all Christendom, to prove that the God of the Bible, whom we serve, is still the "Living God," the hearer and answerer of prayer; and that the faith taught by Luther, and by which alone we can be justified before God, is not a *dead*, but a living, active, practical faith, which has in it the power of an endless life, and a power that can move the heart and the hand of Him who moves the world?

MR. MULLER'S PERSONAL APPEARANCE.

He is tall, rather slender, standing six feet in his boots, and of a remarkably fine figure, with a grave, German face, and dark-brownish eyes that kindle into a pleasing, benevolent expression in conversation. His dress is the very same in cut and color that he wore in the German university (his coat a long-tail frock), all in black, except the snow-white neck-tie, fastened with a common plain pin in front, the ends hid beneath a waistcoat buttoned up so high as to hide everything but the cravat; making his whole general appearance, whether in the pulpit or in the street, a perfect model of neatness and order. Hi hair is rather coarse, and black as jet.

HIS SCHOLARSHIP.

He is master of six languages, — Latin, Greek, Hebrew, German, French and English, — and reads and understands the Dutch, and two or three Oriental languages, but does not profess to be master of them. His attainments in Biblical literature are the most thorough, and I may say the most extraordinary.

HIS LIBRARY.

It consists of a Hebrew Bible, three Greek Testaments, a Greek Concordance and Lexicon, with some half-dozen different versions of the Holy Scriptures, and copies of the best translations into those several languages of which he is master. *These* constitute his *entire library!*

HIS HABITS AND MANNER OF STUDY AND PREACHING.

He rises early, enters his closet, shuts the door, opens his Bible, offers a short prayer especially to invoke the guidance of God's Spirit upon the reading and meditation of his holy word, then reads and meditates verse by verse, chapter by chapter, till his whole soul becomes impressed with God's presence and impregnated with God's teachings; then he bows himself, and, like Samson hold of the middle pillars, he wrestles with God, till, like Israel, he prevails. His habit of reading the Scriptures is to go straight and regularly through them, both the Old and New Testaments at the same time: that is, to read in the Old one part of the day, and in the New the other. He has strong objections to that *hop, skip and jump* method that some practise in reading the Bible, or the habit of opening it at random. When asked how often he had gone through the Bible in this way, his answer was, "I cannot tell, but probably more than a hundred times." His preaching is altogether *expository*, reading a whole chapter, or part of one, or parts of two chapters, according to the connection, and then drawing out of the passage such rich treasures, so many things new and old, that I felt it to be worth crossing the Atlantic to hear them. For three Sabbaths I sat under his teachings, and heard him twice each day. Though he invited me to preach for him, I declined, for the very reason that I could not afford to lose the precious opportunity of hearing him. The happy results of his method of preaching are seen in the numbers of men and women connected with his churches who have become mighty in the Scriptures, and are better qualified to expound them, and to guide inquiring souls to Christ, than many a young minister who has spent his three years in a theological seminary. Let no one imagine that this kind of preaching becomes dry and heavy. Never have I listened to more burning words and touching eloquence than occasionally burst from the lips of this man of God, and especially when he turns to the young, and, with all the tenderness and pathos of a loving father, pleads with them "to seek now the Lord while he may be found, and call upon him whilst he is near."

SELLING JEWELRY SENT IN FOR THE BENEFIT OF THE ORPHANS — IS IT SINFUL?

His answer to me was in substance the following: "If I believed it to be sinful, I would smash it all up, though it took *ten thousand pounds* per annum from the orphans' support. I have searched the Scriptures and made it a subject of prayer. I do not find a command in the Bible against it. I find enough to guide myself in its use; so with my dear wife and daughter. We think a meek, quiet, and humble spirit the best of all ornaments, and the only ornament a Christian needs. But if we lay down a rule and adopt it as a principle to regulate others, consistency would require us not to stop at mere jewelry; other rich and costly articles of dress, etc., must be discarded, and who is wise enough to draw the right line, unless God has spoken explicitly on the subject? No; these things must be regulated from within. The conscience must be kept quickened, and the love of Christ must constrain one in the regulation of these things." Mr. Muller's consistent, prayerful, and godly life, connected with his wonderful study and knowledge of the Bible, gives weight to his opinions on all questions of this kind.

GENERAL READING, ETC.

"I have no time," said he, "for that." From his assistants (to whom I am indebted for many facts of a personal nature which Mr. Muller himself would never have disclosed) I learned that the way he kept himself at all posted up with regard to the stirring events of the day was by conversation at table with his associates, teachers, matrons, etc., who were expected to have a little more time for general reading. His morning hours, after his closet duties are over, are spent in his family, opening his letters, packages, etc., marking with his pencil and separating them into such divisions or classes that his three clerks or assistants can understand their respective duties. He reaches the Orphan Houses between ten and eleven o'clock; there he remains till six or seven in the evening, attending to and overseeing a great variety of things. The amount of labor he performs is amazing, and the almost endless variety would render insane, one would think, most other men. Yet he is never ruffled, never looks anxious or out of temper, — always calm and placid, and in a prayerful frame of mind, casting all his cares upon the Lord, who careth for him. I doubt whether I shall ever see his like again this side heaven. If I am not a better man in future, possessing more of the spirit of Christ, more faith, more of the spirit of prayer and of holy living, for having spent three weeks at his feet, surely my case is a very sad one indeed. I have not time to say more on this fertile subject at present.

Let the dear people of God in America gaze upon this "Monument" brought to their view in this narrative, till by prayer and supplication they shall obtain for themselves more of the "like precious faith," — that faith without which it is impossible to please God, —

that faith that worketh by love and purifieth the heart, — that faith that removes mountains of obstacles out of our path, — that faith that takes hold on God's strength, and is the substance of things hoped for, and the evidence of things not seen. O Lord, bless the reading of this book to the increase of our faith, and the faith of all thy dear children, is the prayer of

E. N. SAWTELL.

PUBLISHERS' NOTICE.

THIS valuable book has now been brought down five years later than the last edition, or from 1872 to 1877. The work has been done by Rev. E. P Thwing, under the personal supervision of Mr Muller, who is now in this country. It gives a full account of Mr. Muller's labors for the past five years

THE LIFE OF TRUST.

CHAPTER I.

BOYHOOD AND YOUTH.

1805 — 1825.

BIRTH — EARLY DISHONESTY — INSENSIBILITY — CONFIRMATION IN THE STATE CHURCH — DISSOLUTENESS OF LIFE — THE HARD WAY OF TRANSGRESSORS — THE GYMNASIUM AT NORDHAUSEN — THE UNIVERSITY AT HALLE — ROVINGS.

I WAS born at Kroppenstaedt, near Halberstadt, in the kingdom of Prussia, September 27, 1805. In January, 1810, my parents removed to Heimersleben, about four miles from Kroppenstaedt, where my father was appointed collector in the excise.

My father, who educated his children on worldly principles,[1] gave us much money, considering our age. The result was, that it led me and my brother into many sins. Before I was ten years old, I repeatedly took of the government money which was intrusted to my father, and which he had to make up; till one day, as he had repeatedly missed money, he detected my theft, by depositing a counted sum in the room where I was, and leaving me to myself for a while. Being thus left alone, I took some of

---

[1] The opinion is often entertained that persons who become eminent for power in prayer and nearness of communion with God, owe their attainments to natural excellence of character, or to peculiarly favoring circumstances of early education. The narrative of the youth of Müller exhibits the fallaciousness of this view, and shows that the attainments which he made are within the reach of any one who will "ask of God, tnat giveth to *all men liberally* and upbraideth not." — ED.

the money, and hid it under my foot in my shoe. When my father, after his return, had counted and missed the money, I was searched and my theft detected.

When I was between ten and eleven years of age I was sent to Halberstadt, there to be prepared for the university; for my father's desire was that I should become a clergyman; not, indeed, that thus I might serve God, but that I might have a comfortable living. My time was now spent in studying, reading novels, and indulging, though so young, in sinful practices. Thus it continued till I was fourteen years old, when my mother was suddenly removed. The night she was dying, I, not knowing of her illness, was playing at cards till two in the morning, and on the next day, being the Lord's day, I went with some of my companions in sin to a tavern, and then we went about the streets half intoxicated.

This bereavement made no lasting impression on my mind. I grew worse and worse. Three or four days before I was confirmed, and thus admitted to partake of the Lord's Supper, I was guilty of gross immorality; and the very day before my confirmation, when I was in the vestry with the clergyman to confess my sins, after a formal manner, I defrauded him; for I handed over to him only the twelfth part of the fee which my father had given me for him. In this state of heart, without prayer, without true repentance, without faith, without knowledge of the plan of salvation, I was confirmed, and took the Lord's Supper, on the Sunday after Easter, 1820. Yet I was not without some feeling about the solemnity of the thing, and stayed at home in the afternoon and evening, whilst the other boys and girls, who had been confirmed with me, walked about in the fields.

My time till midsummer, 1821, was spent partly in study, but in a great degree in playing the piano-forte and guitar, reading novels, frequenting taverns, forming resolutions to become different, yet breaking them almost as fast as they were made. My money was often spent on my sinful pleasures, through which I was now and then brought into trouble, so that once, to satisfy my hunger, I stole a piece of coarse bread, the allowance of a soldier who was quartered in the house where I lodged.

At midsummer, 1821, my father obtained an appointment at Schoenebeck, near Magdeburg, and I embraced the opportunity of entreating him to remove me to the cathedral classical school of Magdeburg; for I thought that if I could but leave my companions in sin, and get out of certain snares, and be placed under other tutors, I should then live a different life. My father consented, and I was allowed to leave Halberstadt, and to stay at Heimersleben till Michaelmas. Being thus quite my own master, I grew still more idle, and lived as much as before in all sorts of sin. When Michaelmas came, I persuaded my father to leave me at Heimersleben till Easter, and to let me read the classics with a clergyman living in the same place. I was now living on the premises belonging to my father, under little real control, and intrusted with a considerable sum of money, which I had to collect for my father, from persons who owed it to him. My habits soon led me to spend a considerable part of this money, giving receipts for different sums, yet leaving my father to suppose I had not received them.

In November, I went on a pleasure excursion to Magdeburg, where I spent six days in much sin, and though my absence from home had been found out by my father before I returned from thence, yet I took all the money I could obtain, and went to Brunswick, after I had, through a number of lies, obtained permission from my tutor. I spent a week at Brunswick in an expensive hotel. At the end of the week my money was expended. I then went, without money, to another hotel, in a village near Brunswick, where I spent another week in an expensive way of living. At last, the owner of the hotel, suspecting that I had no money, asked for payment, and I was obliged to leave my best clothes as security. I then walked about six miles, to Wolfenbuttel, went to an inn, and began again to live as if I had plenty of money. On the second or third morning I went quietly out of the yard and then ran off; but being suspected and observed, and therefore seen to go off, I was immediately called after, and so had to return. I was arrested, and being suspected to be a thief, was examined for about three hours, and then sent to jail. I now found myself, at the age of sixteen, an inmate of the same dwelling with thieves and murderers. I was locked up in this place day and night, without permission to leave my cell.

I was in prison from Dec. 18, 1821, to January 12, 1822, when the keeper told me to go with him to the police office. Here I found that the commissioner before whom I had been tried, had acquainted my father with my conduct; and thus I was kept in prison till my father sent the money which was needed for my travelling expenses, to pay my debt in the inn, and for my maintenance in the prison. So ungrateful was I now for certain little kindnesses shown to me by a fellow-prisoner, that, although I had promised to call on his sister, to deliver a message from him, I omitted to do so; and so little had I been benefited by this, my chastisement, that, though I was going home to meet an angry father, only two hours after I had left the town where I had been imprisoned, I chose an avowedly wicked person as my travelling companion for a great part of my journey.

My father, who arrived two days after I had reached Heimersleben, after having severely beaten me, took me home to Schoenebeck, intending, at Easter, to send me to a classical school at Halle, that I might be under strict discipline and the continual inspection of a tutor. Easter came, and I easily persuaded him to let me stay at home till Michaelmas. But after that period he would not con sent to my remaining any longer with him, and I left home, pretending to go to Halle to be examined. But having a hearty dislike to the strict discipline of which I had heard, I went to Nordhausen, and had myself examined to be received into that school. I then went home, but never told my father a word of all this deception till the day before my departure, which obliged me to invent a whole chain of lies. He was then very angry; but at last, through my entreaties and persuasion, he gave way and allowed me to go. This was in October, 1822.

I continued at Nordhausen two years and six months. During this time I studied with considerable diligence the Latin classics, French, history, my own language, etc.; but did little in Hebrew, Greek, and the mathematics. I lived in the house of the director, and got, through my conduct, highly into his favor, so much so that I was held up by him in the first class as an example to the rest. I used now to rise regularly at four, winter and summer, and generally studied all the day, with little exception, till ten at night.

But whilst I was thus outwardly gaining the esteem of my fellow-creatures, I did not care in the least about God, but lived secretly in much sin, in consequence of which I was taken ill, and for thirteen weeks confined to my room. During my illness I had no real sorrow of heart, yet, being under certain natural impressions of religion, I read through Klopstock's works without weariness. I cared nothing about the word of God. I had about three hundred books of my own, but no Bible. Now and then I felt that I ought to become a different person, and I tried to amend my conduct, particularly when I went to the Lord's Supper, as I used to do twice every year, with the other young men. The day previous to attending that ordinance, I used to refrain from certain things; and on the day itself I was serious, and also swore once or twice to God, with the emblem of the broken body in my mouth, to become better, thinking that for the oath's sake I should be induced to reform. But after one or two days were over, all was forgotten, and I was as bad as before.

At Easter, 1825, I became a member of the University of Halle, and that with very honorable testimonials. I thus obtained permission to preach in the Lutheran Establishment; but I was as truly unhappy and as far from God as ever. I had made strong resolutions now at last to change my course of life, for two reasons: first, because, without it, I thought no parish would choose me as their pastor; and, secondly, that without a considerable knowledge of divinity, I should never get a good living. But the moment I entered Halle, the university town, all my resolutions came to nothing. Being now more than ever my own master, I renewed my profligate life afresh, though now a student of *divinity*. Yet in the midst of it all I had a desire to renounce this wretched life, for I had no enjoyment in it, and had sense enough left to see the end, one day or other, would be miserable. But I had no sorrow of heart on account of offending God.

One day, when I was in a tavern with some of my wild fellow-students, I saw among them one of my former school-fellows, named Beta, whom I had known four years before at Halberstadt, but whom at that time I had despised, because he was so quiet and serious. It now appeared well to me to choose him as my friend, thinking that, if I could but have better companions, I should by that means improve my own conduct. "*Cursed be the man that trusteth in man, and maketh flesh his arm.*"

This Beta was a backslider. When formerly he was so quiet at school, I have reason to believe it was because the Spirit of God was working on his heart; but now, having departed from the Lord, he tried to put off the ways of God more and more, and to enjoy the world of which he had known but little before. *I* sought his friendship, because I thought it would lead me to a steady life; and *he* gladly formed an acquaintance with me, as he told me afterwards, because he thought it would bring him into gay society.

At the commencement of August, Beta and I, with two other students, drove about the country for four days. When we returned, instead of being truly sorry on account of this sin, we thought of fresh pleasures; and as my love for travelling was stronger than ever, through what I had seen on this last journey, I proposed to my friends to set off for Switzerland. The obstacles in the way, the want of money, and the want of the passports, were removed by *me*. For, through forged letters from our parents, we procured passports, and through pledging all we could, particularly our books, we obtained as much money as we thought would be enough. Forty-three days we were day after day travelling, almost always on foot.

I had now obtained the desire of my heart. I had seen Switzerland. But still I was far from being happy. I was on this journey like Judas; for, having the common purse, I was a thief. I managed so that the journey cost me but two thirds of what it cost my friends. I had, by many lies, to satisfy my father concerning the travelling expenses. During the three weeks I stayed at home, I determined to live differently for the future. I was different for a few days; but when the vacation was over, and fresh students came, and, with them, fresh money, all was soon forgotten.

CHAPTER II.

THE PRODIGAL'S RETURN.

1825 — 1826.

A TREASURE FOUND — DAWNING OF THE NEW LIFE — THE PEACE OF GOD — "I AM COME TO SET A MAN AT VARIANCE AGAINST HIS FATHER" — "LET HIM THAT HEARETH SAY COME" — THE FIRST SERMON — DELIGHT IN THE LORD — A COMMON ERROR — THE FOUNTAIN NEGLECTED.

THE time was now come when God would have mercy upon me. At a time when I was as careless about him as ever, he sent his Spirit into my heart.

I had no Bible, and had not read it for years. I went to church but seldom; but, from custom, I took the Lord's Supper twice a year. I had never heard the gospel preached. I had never met with a person who told me that he meant, by the help of God, to live according to the Holy Scriptures. In short, I had not the least idea that there were any persons really different from myself except in degree.

On Saturday afternoon, about the middle of November, 1825, I had taken a walk with my friend Beta. On our return he said to me that he was in the habit of going on Saturday evenings to the house of a Christian, where there was a meeting. On further inquiry, he told me that they read the Bible, sang, prayed, and read a printed sermon. No sooner had I heard this than it was to me as if I had found something after which I had been seeking all my life long. We went together in the evening. As I did not know the manners of believers, and the joy they have in seeing poor sinners, even in any measure, caring about the things of God, I made an apology for coming. The kind answer of the dear brother I shall never forget. He said: "Come as often as you please; house and heart are open to you." We sat down and sang a hymn. Then brother Kayser, now a missionary in Africa, fell on his knees and asked a blessing on our meeting. This kneeling down made a deep impression upon me; for I had never either seen any one on his knees, nor had I ever myself prayed on my knees. He then read a chapter and a printed sermon; for no regular meetings for expounding the Scriptures were allowed in Prussia, except an ordained clergyman was present. At the close we sang another hymn, and then the master of the house prayed. Whilst he prayed, my feeling was something like this: "I could not pray as well, though I am much more learned than this illiterate man." The whole made a deep impression on me. I was happy; though, if I had been asked why I was happy, I could not have clearly explained it.

When we walked home, I said to Beta: "All we have seen on our journey to Switzerland, and all our former pleasures, are as nothing in comparison with this evening." Whether I fell on my knees when I returned home, I do not remember; but this I know, that I lay peaceful and happy in my bed. This shows that the Lord may begin his work in different ways. For I have not the least doubt that on that evening he began a work of grace in me, though I obtained joy without any deep sorrow of heart, and with scarcely any knowledge. But that evening was the turning-point in my life. The next day and Monday, and once or twice besides, I went again to the house of this brother, where I read the Scriptures with him and another brother; for it was too long for me to wait till Saturday came again.

Now my life became very different, though not so that all sins were given up at once. My wicked companions were given up; the going to taverns was entirely discontinued; the habitual practice of telling falsehoods was no longer indulged in; but still a few times after this I spoke an untruth. I read the Scriptures, prayed often, loved the brethren, went to church from right motives, and stood on the side of Christ, though laughed at by my fellow-students.

In January, 1826, I began to read missionary papers, and was greatly stirred up to become a missionary myself. I prayed frequently concerning this matter, and thus made more decided progress for a few weeks. About Easter, 1826, I saw a devoted young brother, named Hermann Ball, a learned man, and of wealthy parents, who, constrained by the love of Christ, preferred laboring in Poland among the Jews as a missionary to having a comfortable living near his relations. His example made a deep impression on me. The Lord smiled on me, and I was, for the first time in my life, able fully and unreservedly to give up myself to him.

At this time I began truly to enjoy the peace of God which passeth all understanding. In my joy I wrote to my father and brother, entreating them to seek the Lord, and telling them how happy I was; thinking that, if the way to happiness were but set before them, they would gladly embrace it. To my great surprise, an angry answer was returned About this period the Lord sent a believer, Dr. Tholuck, as professor of divinity to Halle, in consequence of which a few believing students came from other universities. Thus also, through becoming acquainted with other brethren, the Lord led me on.

My former desire to give myself to missionary service returned, and I went at last to my father to obtain his permission, without which I could not be received into any of the German missionary institutions. My father was greatly displeased, and particularly reproached me, saying that he had expended so much money on my education, in hope that he might comfortably spend his last days with me in a parsonage, and that he now saw all these prospects come to nothing. He was angry, and told me he would no longer consider me as his son. But the Lord gave me grace to remain steadfast. He then entreated me, and wept before me; yet even this by far harder trial the Lord enabled me to bear. After I had left my father, though I wanted more money than at any previous period of my life, as I had to remain two years longer in the university, I determined never to take any more from him; for it seemed to me wrong, so far as I remember, to suffer myself to be supported by him, when he had no prospect that I should become what he would wish me to be, namely, a clergyman with a good living. This resolution I was enabled to keep.

Shortly after this had occurred, several American gentlemen, three of whom were professors in American colleges, came to Halle for literary purposes, and, as they did not understand German, I was recommended by Dr. Tholuck to teach them. These gentlemen, some of whom were believers, paid so handsomely for the instruction which I gave them, and for the lectures of certain professors which I wrote out for them, that I had enough and to spare. Thus did the Lord richly make up to me the little which I had relinquished for his sake. "*O fear the Lord, ye his saints: for there is no want to them that fear him.*"

Whitsuntide, and the two days following, I spent in the house of a pious clergyman in the country; for all the ministers at Halle, a town of more than twenty thousand inhabitants, were unenlightened men. God greatly refreshed me through this visit. Dear Beta was with me. On our return we related to two of our former friends, whose society we had not quite given up, though we did not any longer live with them in sin, how happy we had been on our visit. I then told them how I wished they were as happy as ourselves. They answered, We do not feel that we are sinners. After this I fell on my knees, and asked God to show them that they were sinners. Having done so, I went into my bedroom, where I continued to pray for them. After a little while, I returned to my sitting room and found them both in tears, and both told me that they now felt themselves to be sinners. From that time a work of grace commenced in their hearts.

Though very weak and ignorant, yet I had now, by the grace of God, some desire to benefit others, and he who so faithfully had once served Satan, sought now to win souls for Christ. I circulated every month about three hundred missionary papers. I also distributed a considerable number of tracts, and often took my pockets full in my walks, and distributed them, and spoke to poor people whom I met. I also wrote letters to some of my former companions in sin. I visited, for thirteen weeks, a sick man, who, when I first began to speak to him about the things of God, was completely ignorant of his state as a sinner, trusting for salvation in his upright and moral life. After some weeks, however, the Lord allowed me to see a decided change in him, and he afterwards repeatedly expressed his gratitude that I had been sent to him by God to be the means of opening his blind eyes.

Having heard that there was a schoolmaster living in a village about six miles from Halle, who was in the habit of holding a prayer meeting at four o'clock every morning, with the miners, before they went into the pit, giving them also an address, I thought he was a believer; and as I knew so very few brethren, I went to see him, in order, if it might be, to strengthen his hands. About two years afterwards, he told me that when I came to him first he knew not the Lord, but that he had held these prayer meetings merely out of kindness to a relative, whose office it was, but who had gone on a journey; and that those addresses which he had read were not his own, but copied out of a book. He also told me that he was much impressed with my kindness, and what he considered condescension on my part in coming to see him, and this, together with my conversation, had been instrumental in leading him to care about the things of God, and I knew him ever afterwards as a true brother.

This schoolmaster asked me whether I would not preach in his parish, as the aged clergyman would be very glad of my assistance. Up to this time I had never preached; yet I thought that by taking a sermon, or the greater part of one, written by a spiritual man, and committing it to memory, I might benefit the people. I set about putting a printed sermon into a suitable form, and committing it to memory. There is no joy in man's own doings and choosings. I got through it, but had no enjoyment in the work. It was on August 27, 1826, at eight in the morning, in a chapel of ease. There was one service more, in the afternoon, at which I needed not to have done anything; but having a desire to serve the Lord, though I often knew not how to do it scripturally, and knowing that this aged and unenlightened clergyman had had this living for forty-eight years, and having, therefore, reason to believe that the gospel scarcely ever had been preached in that place, I had it in my heart to preach again in the afternoon. It came to my mind to read the fifth chapter of Matthew, and to make such remarks as I was able. I did so. Immediately upon beginning to expound "Blessed are the poor in spirit," etc., I felt myself greatly assisted; and whereas in the morning my sermon had not been simple enough for the people to understand it, I now was listened to with the greatest attention, and I think was also understood. My own peace and joy were great. I felt this a blessed work.

On my way to Halle I thought, this is the way I should like always to preach. But then it came immediately to my mind that such sort of preaching might do for illiterate country people, but that it never would do before a well-educated assembly in town. I thought the truth ought to be preached at all hazards, but it ought to be given in a different form, suited to the hearers. Thus I remained unsettled in my mind as it regards the mode of preaching;

and it is not surprising that I did not then see the truth concerning this matter, for I did not understand the work of the Spirit, and therefore saw not the powerlessness of human eloquence. Further, I did not keep in mind that if the most illiterate persons in the congregation can comprehend the discourse, the most educated will understand it too; but that the reverse does not hold true.

It was not till three years afterwards that I was led, through grace, to see what I now consider the right mode of preparation for the public preaching of the word. But about this, if God permit, I will say more when I come to that period of my life.

It was about this time that I formed the plan of exchanging the University of Halle for that of Berlin, on account of there being a greater number of believing professors and students in the latter place. But the whole plan was formed without prayer, or at least without earnest prayer. When, however, the morning came on which I had to apply for the university testimonials, the Lord graciously stirred me up prayerfully to consider the matter; and finding that I had no sufficient reason for leaving Halle, I gave up the plan, and have never had reason to regret having done so.

The public means of grace by which I could be benefited were very few. Though I went regularly to church when I did not preach myself, yet I scarcely ever heard the truth; for there was no enlightened clergyman in the town. And when it so happened that I could hear Dr. Tholuck, or any other godly minister, the prospect of it beforehand, and the looking back upon it afterwards, served to fill me with joy. *Now and then I walked ten or fifteen miles to enjoy this privilege.*

Another means of grace which I attended, besides the Saturday-evening meetings in brother Wagner's house, was a meeting every Lord's-day evening with the believing students, six or more in number, increased, before I left

Halle, to about twenty. In these meetings, one or two, or more, of the brethren prayed, and we read the Scriptures, sang hymns, and sometimes also one or another of the brethren spoke a little in the way of exhortation, and we read also such writings of godly men as were calculated for edification. I was often greatly stirred up and refreshed in these meetings; and twice, being in a backsliding state, and therefore cold and miserable, I opened my heart to the brethren, and was brought out of that state through the means of their exhortations and prayers.

As to the other means of grace, I would say, I fell into the snare into which so many young believers fall, the reading of religious books in preference to the Scriptures. I read tracts, missionary papers, sermons, and biographies of godly persons. I never had been at any time of my life in the habit of reading the Holy Scriptures. When under fifteen years of age, I occasionally read a little of them at school; afterwards God's precious book was entirely laid aside, so that I never read one single chapter of it till it pleased God to begin a work of grace in my heart. Now the scriptural way of reasoning would have been: God himself has consented to be an author, and I am ignorant about that precious book, which his Holy Spirit has caused to be written through the instrumentality of his servants, and it contains that which I ought to know, the knowledge of which will lead me to true happiness; therefore I ought to read again and again this most precious book of books, most earnestly, most prayerfully, and with much meditation; and in this practice I ought to continue all the days of my life. But instead of acting thus, my difficulty in understanding it, and the little enjoyment I had in it, made me careless of reading it; and thus, like many believers, I practically preferred, for the first four years of my divine life, the works of uninspired men to the oracles of the living God. The consequence was, that I remained a babe, both in knowledge and grace.

The last and most important means of grace, prayer, was comparatively but little used by me. I prayed, and prayed often, and in general, by the grace of God, with sincerity; but had I prayed as earnestly as I have of late years, I should have made much more rapid progress.

CHAPTER III.

SELF-DEDICATION.

1826 — 1829.

DESIRE FOR MISSIONARY LABOR — PROVIDENTIAL RELEASE FROM MILITARY SERVICE — VISIT AT HOME — LED TO THE LAND OF HIS FUTURE LABORS — PROGRESS IN RELIGIOUS KNOWLEDGE — DESIRE FOR IMMEDIATE USEFULNESS.

IN August, 1827, I heard that the Continental Society in England intended to send a minister to Bucharest, the residence of many nominal German Christians, to help an aged brother in the work of the Lord. After consideration and prayer, I offered myself for this work to Professor Tholuck, who was requested to look out for a suitable individual; for with all my weakness I had a great desire to live wholly for God. Most unexpectedly my father gave his consent, though Bucharest was above a thousand miles from my home, and as completely a missionary station as any other. I now prepared with earnestness for the work of the Lord. I set before me the sufferings which might await me. And he who once so fully served Satan was now willing, constrained by the love of Christ, rather to suffer affliction for the sake of Jesus than to enjoy the pleasures of sin for a season. I also prayed with a degree of earnestness concerning my future work.

One day, at the end of October, the above-mentioned brother, Hermann Ball, missionary to the Jews, stated that he feared, on account of his health, he should be obliged to give up laboring among the Jews. When I heard this, I felt a peculiar desire to fill up his place. About this very time, also, I became exceedingly fond of the Hebrew language, which I had cared about very little up to that time, and which I had merely studied now and then, from a sense of duty. But now I studied it, for many weeks, with the greatest eagerness and delight. Whilst I thus from time to time felt a desire to fill up Brother Ball's place, and whilst I thus greatly delighted in the study of Hebrew, I called, in the evening of November 17, on Dr. Tholuck. In the course of conversation he asked me whether I had ever had a desire to be a missionary to the Jews, as I might be connected with the London Missionary Society for promoting Christianity among them, for which he was an agent. I was struck with the question, and told him what had passed in my mind, but added that it was not proper to think anything about that, as I was going to Bucharest; to which he agreed.

When I came home, however, these few words were like fire within me. The next morning I felt all desire for going to Bucharest gone, which appeared to me very wrong and fleshly, and I therefore entreated the Lord to restore to me the former desire for laboring on that missionary station. He graciously did so almost immediately. My earnestness in studying Hebrew, and my peculiar love for it, however, continued.

About ten days after, Dr. Tholuck received a letter from the Continental Society, stating that, on account of the war between the Turks and Russians, it appeared well to the committee for the time being to give up the thought of sending a minister to Bucharest, as it was the seat of war between the two armies. Dr. Tholuck then asked me again what I now thought about being a missionary to the Jews. My reply was that I could not then give an answer, but that I would let him know, after I had prayerfully considered the matter. After prayer and consideration, and consulting with experienced brethren, in order that they might probe my heart as to my motives, I came to this conclusion, that I ought to offer myself to the committee, leaving it with the Lord to do with me afterwards as it might seem good in his sight. Accordingly, Dr. Tholuck wrote, about the beginning of December, 1827, to the committee in London.

It was not before March, 1828, that he received an answer from London respecting me, in which the committee put a number of questions to me, on the satisfactory answers to which my being received by them would depend. After replying to this first communication, I waited daily for an answer, and was so much the more desirous of having it, as my course in the university was completed. At last, on June 13, I received a letter from London, stating that the committee had determined to take me as a missionary student for six months on probation, provided that I would come to London.

I had now had the matter before me about seven months, having supposed not only that it would have been settled in a few weeks, but also, that, if I were accepted, I should be sent out immediately, as I had passed the university. Instead of this, not only seven months passed over before the decision came, but I was also expected to come to London; and not only so, but though I had from my infancy been more or less studying, and now at last wished actively to be engaged, it was required that I should again become a student. For a few moments, therefore, I was greatly disappointed and tried. But on calmly considering the matter, it appeared to me but right that the committee should know me personally, and that it was also well for me to know them more intimately than merely by correspondence, as this afterwards would make our connection much more comfortable. I determined, therefore, after I had seen my father, and found no difficulty on his part, to go to London.

There was, however, an obstacle in the way of my leaving the country. Every Prussian male subject is under the necessity of being for three years a soldier, provided his state of body allows it; but those who have had a classical education up to a certain degree, and especially those who have passed the university, need to be only one year in the army, but have to equip and maintain themselves during that year. I could not obtain a passport out of the country till I had either served my time or had been exempted by the king himself. The latter I hoped would be the case; for it was a well-known fact that those who had given themselves to missionary service had always been exempted. Certain brethren of influence, living in the capital, to whom I wrote on the subject, wrote to the king; but he replied that the matter must be referred to the ministry and to the law, and no exception was made in my favor.

My chief concern now was how I might obtain a passport for England, through exemption from military duty. But the more certain brethren tried, though they knew how to set about the matter, and were also persons of rank, the greater difficulty there appeared to be in obtaining my object; so that in the middle of January, 1829, it seemed as if I must immediately become a soldier. There was now but one more way untried, and it was at last resorted to. A believing major, who was on good terms with one of the chief generals, proposed that I should actually offer myself for entering the army, and that then I should be examined as to my bodily qualifications, in the hope that, as I was still in a very weak state of body, I should be found unfit for military service. In that case it would belong to the chief general finally to settle the matter; who, being a godly man himself, on the major's recommendation, would, no doubt, hasten the decision, on account of my desire to be a missionary to the Jews.

Thus far the Lord had allowed things to go, to show me, it appears, that all my friends could not procure me a passport till his time was come. But now it was come. The King of kings had intended that I should go to England, because he would bless me there and make me a blessing, though I was at that time, and am still, most unworthy of it; and, therefore, though the king of Prussia had not been pleased to make an exemption in my favor, yet now all was made plain, and that at a time when hope had almost been given up, and when the last means had been resorted to. I was examined, and was declared to be unfit for military service. With a medical certificate to this effect, and a letter of recommendation from the major, I went to this chief general, who received me very kindly, and who himself wrote instantaneously to a second military physician, likewise to examine me *at once*. This was done, and it was by him confirmed that I was unfit. Now, the chief general himself, as his adjutants happened to be absent, in order to hasten the matter, wrote, with his own hands, the papers which were needed, and I got a complete dismissal, and that for life, from all military engagements.

On February 5 I arrived at my father's house; it was the place where I had lived as a boy, and the scene of many of my sins, my father having now returned to it after his retirement from office. There were but three persons in the whole town with whom my soul had any fellowship. One of them was earning his daily bread by thrashing corn. As a boy I had in my heart laughed at him. Now I sought him out, having been informed that he was a brother, to acknowledge him as such, by having fellowship with him, and attending a meeting in his house on the Lord's-day evening. My soul was refreshed, and his also. Such a spiritual feast as meeting with a brother was a rare thing to him.

I left my father's house on February 10, and about February 22 arrived at Rotterdam. My going to England by the way of Rotterdam was not the usual way; but, consulting with a brother in Berlin, who had been twice in England, I was told that this was the cheapest route. My asking this brother, to be profited by his experience, would have been quite right, had I, besides this, like Ezra, sought of the Lord the right way.[1] But I sought unto men only, and not at all unto the Lord, in this matter. When I came to Rotterdam, I found that no vessels went at that time from that port to London, on account of the ice having just broken up in the river. Thus I had to wait nearly a month at Rotterdam, and needed much more time than I should have required to go by way of Hamburg, and also much more money.

On March 19, 1829, I landed in London. Soon after my arrival, I heard one of the brethren speak of Mr. Groves, a dentist, who, for the Lord's sake, had given up his profession, which brought him at least £1,500[2] a year, and who intended to go as a missionary to Persia, with his wife and children, simply trusting in the Lord for temporal supplies. This made such an impression on me, and delighted me so, that I not only marked it down in my journal, but also wrote about it to my German friends.

I came to England weak in body, and, in consequence of much study, as I suppose, I was taken ill on May 15, and was soon, at least in my own estimation, apparently beyond recovery. The weaker I became in body, the happier I was in spirit. Never in my whole life had I seen myself so vile, so guilty, so altogether what I ought not to have been, as at this time. It was as if every sin of which I had been guilty was brought to my remembrance; but at the same time I could realize that all my sins were completely forgiven, — that I was washed and made clean, completely clean, in the blood of Jesus. The result of this was great peace. I longed exceedingly to depart and be with Christ.

---

[1] Then I proclaimed a fast, to seek of God a right way for us, and for our little ones, and for all our substance. — Ezra viii. 21.

[2] To avoid the necessity of reducing the sums named to federal money, it may be stated that a pound (£) is equal to about $4.83, a sovereign to the same, a shilling (s.) to about 28 cts. and a penny (d.) to 2 cts. For convenience of computation, when exactness is not required, we may call the pound $5.00, and the shilling 25 cts. — ED.

When my medical attendant came to see me, my prayer was something like this: "Lord, thou knowest that he does not know what is for my real welfare, therefore do thou direct him." When I took my medicine, my hearty prayer each time was something like this: "Lord, thou knowest that this medicine is in itself nothing, no more than as if I were to take a little water. Now please, O Lord, to let it produce the effect which is for my real welfare, and for thy glory. Let me either be taken soon to thyself, or let me be soon restored; let me be ill for a longer time, and then taken to thyself, or let me be ill for a longer time, and then restored. O Lord, do with me as seemeth thee best!"

After I had been ill about a fortnight, my medical attendant unexpectedly pronounced me better. As I recovered but slowly, my friends entreated me to go into the country for change of air. I thought that it might be the will of God that I should do so, and I prayed therefore thus to the Lord: "Lord, I will gladly submit myself to thy will, and go, if thou wilt have me to go. And now let me know thy will by the answer of my medical attendant. If, in reply to my question, he says it would be very good for me, I will go; but if he says it is of no great importance, then I will stay." When I asked him, he said that it was the best thing I could do. I was then enabled willingly to submit, and accordingly went to Teignmouth.

A few days after my arrival at Teignmouth, the chapel, called Ebenezer, was reopened, and I attended the opening. I was much impressed by one of those who preached on the occasion. For though I did not like all he said, yet I saw a gravity and solemnity in him different from the rest. After he had preached, I had a great desire to know more of him; and, being invited by two brethren of Exmouth, in whose house he was staying, to spend some time with them, I had an opportunity of living ten days with him under the same roof. It was at this time that God began to show me that his word alone is our standard of judgment in spiritual things; that it can be explained only by the Holy Spirit; and that in our day, as well as in former times, he is the teacher of his people. The office of the Holy Spirit I had not experimentally understood before that time. Indeed, of the office of each of the blessed persons, in what is commonly called the Trinity, I had no experimental apprehension. I had not before seen from the Scriptures that the Father chose us before the foundation of the world; that in him that wonderful plan of our redemption originated, and that he also appointed all the means by which it was to be brought about. Further, that the Son, to save us, had fulfilled the law, to satisfy its demands, and with it also the holiness of God; that he had borne the punishment due to our sins, and had thus satisfied the justice of God. And, further, that the Holy Spirit alone can teach us about our state by nature, show us the need of a Saviour, enable us to believe in Christ, explain to us the Scriptures, help us in preaching, etc. It was my beginning to understand this latter point in particular, which had a great effect on me; for the Lord enabled me to put it to the test of experience, by laying aside commentaries, and almost every other book, and simply reading the word of God and studying it. The result of this was, that the first evening that I shut myself into my room, to give myself to prayer and meditation over the Scriptures, I learned more in a few hours than I had done during a period of several months previously. *But the particular difference was, that I received real strength for my soul in doing so.* I now began to try by the test of the Scriptures the things which I had learned and seen, and found that only those principles which stood the test were really of value.

My stay in Devonshire was most profitable to my soul. My prayer had been, before I left London, that the Lord would be pleased to bless my journey to the benefit of my body and soul. In the beginning of September I returned to London, much better in body; and as to my soul, the change was so great that it was like a second conversion. After my return to London, I sought to benefit my brethren in the seminary, and the means which I used were these: I proposed to them to meet together every morning from six to eight for prayer and reading the Scriptures; and that then each of us should give out what he might consider the Lord had shown him to be the meaning of the portion read. One brother in particular was brought into the same state as myself; and others, I trust, were more or less benefited. Several times, when I went to my room after family prayer in the evening, I found communion with God so sweet that I continued in prayer till after twelve, and then, being full of joy, went into the room of the brother just referred to; and finding him also in a similar frame of heart, we continued praying until one or two; and even then I was a few times so full of joy that I could scarcely sleep, and at six in the morning again called the brethren together for prayer.

After I had been for about ten days in London, and had been confined to the house on account of my studies, my health began again to decline; and I saw that it would not be well, my poor body being only like a wreck or brand brought out of the devil's service, to spend my little remaining strength in study, but that I now ought to set about actual engagement in the Lord's work. I wrote to the committee of the Society, requesting them to send me out at once; and, that they might do so more comfortably, to send me as a fellow-laborer with an experienced brother. However, I received no answer.

After having waited about five or six weeks, in the mean time seeking, in one way or other, to labor for the Lord, it struck me that, considering myself called by the Lord to preach the gospel, I ought to begin at once to labor among the Jews in London, whether I had the title of missionary or not. In consequence of this, I distributed tracts among the Jews, with my name and residence written on them, thus inviting them to conversation about the things of God; preached to them in those places where they most numerously collect together; read the Scriptures regularly with about fifty Jewish boys; and became a teacher in a Sunday school. In this work I had much enjoyment, and the honor of being reproached and ill-treated for the name of Jesus. But the Lord gave me grace, never to be kept from the work by any danger, or the prospect of any suffering.

Mr. Müller was led, toward the close of 1829, to doubt the propriety of continuing under the patronage of the London Society. It seemed to him unscriptural for a servant of Christ to put himself under the control and direction of any one but the Lord. A correspondence with the Society, evincing on his part, and on their part, entire kindness and love, resulted in a dissolution of his relation to them. He was left free to preach the gospel wherever Providence might open the way.

On December 30, I went to Exmouth, where I intended to spend a fortnight in the house of some Christian friends. I arrived at Exmouth on December 31, at six in the evening, an hour before the commencement of a prayer-meeting at Ebenezer Chapel. My heart was burning with a desire to tell of the Lord's goodness to my soul. Being, however, not called on, either to speak or pray, I was silent. The next morning, I spoke on the difference between being a *Christian* and *a happy Christian*, and showed whence it generally comes that we rejoice so little in the Lord. This, my first testimony, was blessed to many believers, that God, as it appears, might show me that he was with me. At the request of several believers,

I spoke again in the afternoon, and also proposed a meeting in the chapel every morning at ten, to expound the Epistle to the Romans. The second day after my arrival, a brother said to me, "I have been praying for this month past that the Lord would do something for Lympstone, a large parish where there is little spiritual light. There is a Wesleyan chapel, and I doubt not you would be allowed to preach there." Being ready to speak of Jesus whenever the Lord might open a door, yet so that I could be faithful to the truths which he had been pleased to teach me, I went, and easily obtained liberty to preach twice on the next day, being the Lord's day.

CHAPTER IV.

LEANING ON JESUS.

1830 — 1832.

A DOOR OPENED — TOKENS FOR GOOD — TRUST EXERCISED IN THE STUDY AND MINISTRY OF THE WORD — THE SWORD OF THE SPIRIT — TRUSTING IN GOD FOR DAILY BREAD — BLESSEDNESS OF WAITING UPON THE LORD — "OWE NO MAN" — "ACCORDING TO YOUR FAITH BE IT UNTO YOU" — THE GIFT OF FAITH, AND THE GRACE OF FAITH.

AFTER I had preached about three weeks at Exmouth and its neighborhood, I went to Teignmouth, with the intention of staying there ten days, to preach the word among the brethren with whom I had become acquainted during the previous summer, and to tell them of the Lord's goodness to me. In the evening, Monday, I preached for Brother Craik, at Shaldon, in the presence of three ministers, none of whom liked the sermon; yet it pleased God, through it, to bring to the knowledge of his dear Son a young woman. How differently does the Lord judge from man! Here was a particular opportunity for the Lord to get glory to himself. A foreigner was the preacher, with great natural obstacles in the way, for he was not able to speak English with fluency; but he had a desire to serve God, and was by this time also brought into such a state of heart as to desire that God alone should have the glory, if any good were done through his instrumentality.

On Tuesday evening, I preached at Ebenezer Chapel, Teignmouth, the same chapel at the opening of which I became acquainted with the brother whom the Lord had afterwards used as an instrument of benefiting me so much.

During the week ensuing, Mr. M. preached almost daily at the same place, a blessing attending his labors.

By this time, the request that I might stay at Teignmouth, and be the minister of the above chapel, had been repeatedly expressed by an increasing number of the brethren; but others were decidedly against my remaining there. This opposition was instrumental in settling it in my mind that I should stay for a while, at least until I was formally rejected.

I preached again three times on the Lord's day, none saying we wish you not to preach, though many of the hearers did not hear with enjoyment. Some of them left, and never returned; some left, but returned after a while. Others came to the chapel who had not been in the habit of attending there previous to my coming. There was a great stir, a spirit of inquiry, and a searching of the Scriptures, whether these things were so. And, what is more than all, God set his seal upon the work, in converting sinners. Twelve weeks I stood in this same position, whilst the Lord graciously supplied my temporal wants, through two brethren, unasked for. After this time, the whole little church, eighteen in number, unanimously gave me an invitation to become their pastor. They offered to supply my temporal wants by giving me fifty-five pounds a year, which sum was afterwards somewhat increased, on account of the increase of the church.

That which I now considered the best mode of preparation for the public ministry of the word, no longer adopted from necessity, on account of want of time, but from deep conviction, and from the experience of God's blessing upon it, both as it regards my own enjoyment, the benefit of the saints, and the conversion of sinners, is as follows: First, I do not presume to know myself what is best for the hearers, and I therefore ask the Lord, in the first place, that he would graciously be pleased to teach me on what subject I shall speak, or what portion of his word I shall expound. Now, sometimes it happens that, previous to my asking him, a subject or passage has been in my mind, on which it has appeared well for me to speak. In that case, I ask the Lord whether I should speak on this subject or passage. If, after prayer, I feel persuaded that I should, I fix upon it, yet so that I would desire to leave myself open to the Lord to change it if he please. Frequently, however, it occurs that I have no text or subject in my mind, before I give myself to prayer for the sake of ascertaining the Lord's will concerning it. In this case, I wait some time on my knees for an answer, trying to listen to the voice of the Spirit to direct me. If, then, a passage or subject, whilst I am on my knees, or after I have finished praying for a text, is brought to my mind, I again ask the Lord, and that sometimes repeatedly, especially if, humanly speaking, the subject or text should be a peculiar one, whether it be his will that I should speak on such a subject or passage. If, after prayer, my mind is peaceful about it, I take this to be the text, but still desire to leave myself open to the Lord for direction, should he please to alter it, or should I have been mistaken. Frequently, also, in the third place, it happens that I not only have no text nor subject on my mind previous to my praying for guidance in this matter, but also I do not obtain one after once, or twice, or more times praying about it. I used formerly at times to be much perplexed when this was the case, but, for more than twenty years, it has pleased the Lord, in general at least, to keep me in peace about it. What I do is, to go on with my regular reading of the Scriptures, where I left off the last time, praying (whilst I read) for a text, now and then also laying aside my Bible for prayer, till I get one. Thus it has happened that I have had to read five, ten, yea, twenty chapters, before it has pleased the Lord to give me a text; yea, many times I have even had to go to the place of meeting without one, and obtained it, perhaps, only a few minutes before I was going to speak; but I have never lacked the Lord's assistance at the time of preaching, provided I had earnestly sought it in private. The preacher cannot know the particular state of the various individuals who compose the congregation, nor what they require, but the Lord knows it; and if the preacher renounces his own wisdom, he will be assisted by the Lord; but if he will choose in his own wisdom, then let him not be surprised if he should see little benefit result from his labors.

Before I leave this part of the subject, I would just observe one temptation concerning the choice of a text. We may see a subject to be so very full that it may strike us it would do for some other occasion. For instance, sometimes a text brought to one's mind for a week-evening meeting may appear more suitable for the Lord's day, because then there would be a greater number of hearers present. Now, in the first place, we do not know whether the Lord ever will allow us to preach on another Lord's day; and, in the second place, we know not whether that very subject may not be especially suitable for some or many individuals present just that week-evening. Thus I was once tempted, after I had been a short time at Teignmouth, to reserve a subject which had been just opened to me for the next Lord's day. But being able, by the grace of God, to overcome the temptation by the above reasons, and preaching about it at once, it pleased the Lord to bless it to the conversion of a sinner, and that too an individual who meant to come but that once more to the chapel, and to whose case the subject was most remarkably suited.

2. Now, when the text has been obtained in the above way, whether it be one, or two, or more verses, or a whole chapter or more, I ask the Lord that he would graciously be pleased to teach me by his Holy Spirit whilst meditating over it. Within the last twenty-five years, I have found it the most profitable plan to meditate with my pen

in my hand, writing down the outlines as the word is opened to me. This I do, not for the sake of committing them to memory, nor as if I meant to say nothing else, but for the sake of clearness, as being a help to see how far I understand the passage. I also find it useful afterwards to refer to what I have thus written. I very seldom use any other help besides the little I understand of the original of the Scriptures, and some good translations in other languages. My chief help is prayer. I have NEVER in my life begun to study one single part of divine truth without gaining some light about it when I have been able really to give myself to prayer and meditation over it. But *that* I have often found a difficult matter, partly on account of the weakness of the flesh, and partly, also, on account of bodily infirmities and multiplicity of engagements. This I most firmly believe, that no one ought to expect to see much good resulting from his labors in word and doctrine, if he is not much given to prayer and meditation.

3. Having prayed and meditated on the subject or text, I desire to leave myself entirely in the hands of the Lord. I ask him to bring to my mind what I have seen in my closet concerning the subject I am going to speak on, which he generally most kindly does, and often teaches me much additionally whilst I am preaching.

In connection with the above, I must, however, state that it appears to me there is a preparation for the public ministry of the word which is even more excellent than the one spoken of. It is this; to live in such *constant* and *real* communion with the Lord, and to be so *habitually* and *frequently* in meditation over the truth, that without the above *effort*, so to speak, we have obtained food for others, and know the mind of the Lord as to the subject or the portion of the word on which we should speak.

That which I have found most beneficial in my experience for the last twenty-six years in the public ministry of the word, is *expounding* the Scriptures, and especially the going now and then through a whole gospel or epistle. This may be done in a twofold way, either by entering minutely into the bearing of every point occurring in the portion, or by giving the general outlines, and thus leading the hearers to see the meaning and connection of the whole. The benefits which I have seen resulting from *expounding* the Scriptures, are these: 1. The hearers are thus, with God's blessing, led to the Scriptures. They find, as it were, a *practical* use of them in the public meetings. This induces them to bring their Bibles, and I have observed that those who at first did not bring them, have afterwards been induced to do so; so that, in a short time, few (of the believers at least) were in the habit of coming without them. This is no small matter; for everything which in our day will lead believers to value the Scriptures is of importance. 2. The expounding of the Scriptures is in general more beneficial to the hearers than if, on a single verse, or half a verse, or two or three words of a verse, some remarks are made, so that the portion of Scripture is scarcely anything but a motto for the subject; for few have grace to meditate much over the word, and thus exposition may not merely be the means of opening to them the Scriptures, but may also create in them a desire to meditate for themselves. 3. The expounding of the Scriptures leaves to the hearers a connecting link, so that the reading over again the portion of the word which has been expounded brings to their remembrance what has been said, and thus, with God's blessing, leaves a more lasting impression on their minds. This is particularly of importance as it regards the illiterate, who sometimes have neither much strength of memory nor capacity of comprehension. 4. The *expounding* of large portions of the word, as the whole of a gospel or an epistle, besides leading the *hearer* to see the connection of the whole, has also this particular benefit for the *teacher*, that it leads him, with God's blessing, to the consideration of portions of the word which otherwise he might not have considered, and keeps him from speaking too much on favorite subjects, and leaning too much to particular parts of truth, which tendency must surely sooner or later injure both himself and his hearers. Expounding the word of God brings little honor to the preacher from the *unenlightened* or *careless* hearer, but it tends much to the benefit of the hearers in general.

Simplicity in expression, whilst the truth is set forth, is, in connection with what has been said, of the utmost importance. It should be the aim of the teacher to speak so that children, servants, and people who cannot read may be able to understand him, so far as the natural mind can comprehend the things of God. It ought also to be remembered that there is, perhaps, not a single congregation in which there are not persons of the above classes present, and that if *they* can understand, the well-educated or literary persons will understand likewise; but the reverse does not hold good. It ought further to be remembered that the expounder of the truth of God speaks for God, for eternity, and that it is not in the least likely that he will benefit the hearers, except he use plainness of speech, which nevertheless needs not to be vulgar or rude. It should also be considered that if the preacher strive to speak according to the rules of this world, he may please many, particularly those who have a literary taste; but, in the same proportion, he is less likely to become an instrument in the hands of God for the conversion of sinners, or for the building-up of the saints. For neither eloquence nor depth of thought makes the truly great preacher, but such a life of prayer and meditation and spirituality as may render him a vessel meet for the Master's use, and fit to be employed both in the conversion of sinners and in the edification of the saints.

Becoming convinced, after a prayerful examination of the Scriptures, that baptism should be administered only by immersion, Mr. Müller was then baptized in the spring of 1830.

It was so usual for me to preach with particular assistance, especially during the first months of this year, that once, when it was otherwise, it was much noticed by myself and others. The circumstance was this. One day, before preaching at Teignmouth, I had more time than usual, and therefore prayed and meditated about six hours in preparation for the evening meeting, and I thought I saw many precious truths in the passage on which I had meditated. It was the first part of the first chapter of the epistle to the Ephesians. After I had spoken a little time, I felt that I spoke in my own strength, and I, being a foreigner, felt particularly the want of words, which had not been the case before. I told the brethren that I felt I was left to myself, and asked their prayers. But after having continued a little longer, and feeling the same as before, I closed, and proposed that we should have a meeting for prayer, that the Lord still might be pleased to help me. We did so, and I was particularly assisted the next time.

On October 7, 1830, I was united by marriage to Miss Mary Groves, sister of the brother whose name has already been mentioned. This step was taken after prayer and deliberation, from a full conviction that it was better for me to be married; and I have never regretted since either the step itself or the choice, but desire to be truly grateful to God for having given me such a wife.

About this time, I began to have conscientious objections against any longer receiving a stated salary. My reasons against it were these: —

1. The salary was made up by pew-rents; but pew-rents are, according to James ii. 1–6, against the mind of the Lord, as, in general, the poor brother cannot have so good a seat as the rich. 2. A brother may *gladly* do something towards my support if left to his own time; but, when the

quarter is up, he has perhaps other expenses, and I do not know whether he pays his money grudgingly, and of necessity, or cheerfully; but God loveth a cheerful giver. Nay, *I knew it to be a fact* that sometimes it had not been convenient to individuals to pay the money when it had been asked for by the brethren who collected it. 3. Though the Lord had been pleased to give me grace to be faithful, so that I had been enabled not to keep back the truth when he had shown it to me; still, I felt that the pew-rents were a snare to the servant of Christ. It was a temptation to me, at least for a few minutes, at the time when the Lord had stirred me up to pray and search the word respecting the ordinance of baptism, because thirty pounds of my salary was at stake if I should be baptized.

For these reasons, I stated to the brethren, at the end of October, 1830, that I should for the future give up having any regular salary. After I had given my reasons for doing so, I read Philippians iv., and told the saints that if they still had a desire to do something towards my support, by voluntary gifts, I had no objection to receive them, though ever so small, either in money or provisions. A few days after, it appeared to me that there was a better way still; for, if I received personally every single gift offered in money, both my own time and that of the donors would be much taken up; and in this way, also, the poor might, through temptation, be kept from offering their pence, a privilege of which they ought not to be deprived; and some also might in this way give more than if it were not known who was the giver, so that it would still be doubtful whether the gift were given grudgingly or cheerfully. For these reasons especially, there was a box put up in the chapel, over which was written that whoever had a desire to do something towards my support might put his offering into the box.

At the same time, it appeared to me right that henceforth I should ask no man, not even my beloved brethren and sisters, to help me, as I had done a few times, according to their own request, as my expenses, on account of travelling much in the Lord's service, were too great to be met by my usual income. For, unconsciously, I had thus again been led, in some measure, to trust in an arm of flesh, going to man instead of going to the Lord at once. *To come to this conclusion before God required more grace than to give up my salary.*

About the same time, also, my wife and I had grace given to us to take the Lord's commandment, "Sell that ye have, and give alms," Luke xii. 33, literally, and to carry it out. Our staff and support in this matter were Matthew vi. 19-34, John xiv. 13, 14. We leaned on the arm of the Lord Jesus. It is now twenty-five years since we set out in this way, and *we do not in the least regret the step we then took.* As I have written down how the Lord has been pleased to deal with us since, I shall be able to relate some facts concerning this matter, as far as they may tend to edification.

Nov. 18, 1830. Our money was reduced to about eight shillings. When I was praying with my wife in the morning, the Lord brought to my mind the state of our purse, and I was led to ask him for some money. About four hours after, a sister said to me, "Do you want any money?" "I told the brethren," said I, "dear sister, when I gave up my salary, that I would for the future tell the Lord *only* about my wants." She replied, "But he has told me to give you some money. About a fortnight ago, I asked him what I should do for him, and he told me to give you some money; and last Saturday it came again powerfully to my mind, and has not left me since, and I felt it so forcibly last night that I could not help speaking of it to brother P." My heart rejoiced, seeing the Lord's faithfulness, but I thought it better not to tell her about our circumstances, lest she should be influenced to give accordingly; and I also was assured that, if it were of the Lord, she could not but give. I therefore turned the conversation to other subjects, but when I left she gave me two guineas. We were full of joy on account of the goodness of the Lord. I would call upon the reader to admire the gentleness of the Lord, that he did not try our faith much at the commencement, but allowed us to see his willingness to help us, before he was pleased to try it more fully.

The next Wednesday I went to Exmouth, our money having then again been reduced to about nine shillings. I asked the Lord on Thursday, when at Exmouth, to be pleased to give me some money. On Friday morning, about eight o'clock, whilst in prayer, I was particularly led to ask again for money; and before I rose from my knees I had the fullest assurance that we should have the answer that very day. About nine o'clock I left the brother with whom I was staying, and he gave me half a sovereign, saying, "Take this for the expenses connected with your coming to us." I did not expect to have my expenses paid, but I saw the Lord's fatherly hand in sending me this money within one hour after my asking him for some. But even then I was so fully assured that the Lord would send more that very day, or had done so already, that, when I came home about twelve o'clock, I asked my wife whether she had received any letters. She told me she had received one the day before from a brother in Exeter, with three sovereigns. Thus even my prayer on the preceding day had been answered. The next day one of the brethren came and brought me four pounds, which was due to me of my former salary, but which I could never have expected, as I did not even know that this sum was due to me. Thus I received, within thirty hours, in answer to prayer, seven pounds ten shillings.

About Christmas, when our money was reduced to a few shillings, I asked the Lord for more; when, a few hours after, there was given to us a sovereign by a brother from Axminster. This brother had heard much against me, and was at last determined to hear for himself, and thus came to Teignmouth, a distance of forty miles; and having heard about our manner of living, gave us this money.

With this closes the year 1830. Throughout it the Lord richly supplied all my temporal wants, though at the commencement of it I had no certain human prospect for one single shilling: so that, even as it regards temporal things, I had not been in the smallest degree a loser in acting according to the dictates of my conscience; and as it regards spiritual things, the Lord had dealt bountifully with me, and had condescended to use me as an instrument in doing his work.

On the 6th, 7th, and 8th of Jan. 1831, I had repeatedly asked the Lord for money, but received none. On the evening of January 8, I left my room for a few minutes, and was then tempted to distrust the Lord, though he had been so gracious to us in that he not only up to that day had supplied all our wants, but had given us also those answers of prayer which have been in part just mentioned. I was so sinful, for about five minutes, as to think it would be of no use to trust in the Lord in this way. I also began to say to myself, that I had perhaps gone too far in living in this way. But, thanks to the Lord! this trial lasted but a few minutes. He enabled me again to trust in him, and Satan was immediately confounded; for when I returned to my room the Lord had sent deliverance. A sister in the Lord had brought us two pounds four shillings: so the Lord triumphed, and our faith was strengthened.

Jan. 10. To-day, when we had again but a few shillings, five pounds were given to us, which had been taken out of the box. I had, once for all, told the brethren who had the care of these temporal things, to have the kindness to let me have the money every week; but as these beloved brethren either forgot to take it out weekly, or were ashamed to bring it in such small sums, it was generally taken out every three, four, or five weeks. As I had stated to them, however, from the commencement, that I desired to look neither to man nor the box, but to the living God, I thought it not right on my part to remind them of my request to have the money weekly, lest it should hinder the testimony which I wished to give, of trusting in the living God alone It was on this account that on January 28, when we had again but little money, though I had seen the brethren, on January 24, open the box and take out the money, I would not ask the brother, in whose hands it was, to let me have it; but standing in need of it, as our coals were almost gone, I asked the Lord to incline his heart to bring it; and but a little time afterwards it was given to us, even one pound eight shillings and sixpence.

I would here mention, that, since the time I began living in this way, I have been kept from speaking, either directly or indirectly, about my wants, at the time I was in need. The only exception is, that in a few instances, twenty years or more since, I have, at such times, spoken to *very poor* brethren in the way of encouraging them to trust in the Lord, telling them that I had to do the same, being myself in similar straits; or, in a few instances, where it was needful to speak about my own want, lest I should appear unfeeling, in that I did not help at all, in cases of distress or not as much as might have been expected.

On February 14, we had again very little money, and, whilst praying, I was led to ask the Lord graciously to supply our wants; and *the instant that I got up from my knees* a brother gave me one pound, which had been taken out of the box.

On March 7, I was again tempted to disbelieve the faithfulness of the Lord, and though I was not miserable, still, I was not so fully resting upon the Lord that I could triumph with joy. It was *but one hour after*, when the Lord gave me another proof of his faithful love. A Christian lady brought five sovereigns for us, with these words written in the paper: "I was an hungered, and ye gave *me* meat; I was thirsty, and ye gave *me* drink," etc.

April 16. This morning I found that our money was reduced to three shillings; and I said to myself, I must now go and ask the Lord earnestly for fresh supplies. But before I had prayed, there was sent from Exeter, two pounds, as a proof that the Lord hears before we call.

I would observe here, by the way, that if any of the children of God should think that such a mode of living leads away from the Lord, and from caring about spiritual things, and has the effect of causing the mind to be taken up with the question, What shall I eat?—What shall I drink?—and Wherewithal shall I be clothed?—I would request him prayerfully to consider the following remarks: 1. I have had experience of both ways, and know that my present mode of living, as to temporal things, is connected with less care. 2. Confidence in the Lord, to whom alone I look for the supply of my temporal wants, keeps me, when a case of distress comes before me, or when the Lord's work calls for my pecuniary aid, from anxious reckoning like this: Will my salary last out? Shall I have enough myself the next month? etc. In this my freedom, I am, by the grace of God, generally, at least, able to say to myself something like this: My Lord is not limited; he can again supply; he knows that this present case has been sent to me: and thus, this way of living, so far from *leading to anxiety*, is rather the means of *keeping from it*. And truly it was once said to me by an individual,—You can do such and such things and need not to lay by, for the church in the whole of Devonshire cares about your wants. My reply was: The Lord can use not merely any of the saints throughout Devonshire, but those throughout the world, as instruments to supply my temporal wants. 3. This way of living has often been the means of reviving the work of grace in my heart, when I have been getting cold; and it also has been the means of bringing me back again to the Lord, after I have been backsliding. For it will not do, — it is not possible to live in sin, and at the same time, by communion with God, to draw down from heaven everything one needs for the life that now is. 4. Frequently, too, a fresh answer to prayer, obtained in this way, has been the means of quickening my soul, and filling me with much joy.

May 12. A sister has been staying for some time at Teignmouth on account of her health; and when she was about to return home to-day, we saw it the Lord's will to invite her to stay with us for some time, as we knew that she would stay longer if her means allowed it. We were persuaded that, as we saw it to be the Lord's will to invite her, he himself would pay the expenses connected with her stay. About the time when she came to our house, a parcel with money was sent from Chumleigh. A few weeks before, I had preached at Chumleigh and in the neighborhood. The brethren, knowing about my manner of living, after my departure collected some money for me, and thus, in small offerings (one hundred and seven altogether, as I have been told), two pounds and one penny halfpenny were given. Thus the Lord paid for the expenses connected with our sister's staying with us.

June 12. Lord's day. On Thursday last I went with brother Craik to Torquay, to preach there. I had only about three shillings with me, and left my wife with about six shillings at home. I asked the Lord repeatedly for money; but when I came home my wife had only about three shillings left, having received nothing. We waited still upon the Lord. Yesterday passed away, and no money came. We had ninepence left. This morning we were still waiting upon the Lord, and looking for deliverance. We had only a little butter left for breakfast, sufficient for brother E. and a relative living with us, to whom we did not mention our circumstances, that they might not be made uncomfortable. After the morning meeting, brother Y.

most unexpectedly opened the box, and, in giving me quite as unexpectedly the money at such a time, he told me that *he and his wife could not sleep last night, on account of thinking that we might want money.* The most striking point is, that after I had repeatedly asked the Lord, but received nothing, *I then prayed yesterday that the Lord would be pleased to impress it on brother Y. that we wanted money, so that he might open the box.* There was in it one pound eight shillings and tenpence halfpenny.

Nov. 16. This morning I proposed united prayer respecting our temporal wants. Just as we were about to pray, a parcel came from Exmouth. In prayer we asked the Lord for meat for dinner, having no money to buy any. After prayer, on opening the parcel, we found, among other things, a ham, sent by a brother at Exmouth, which served us for dinner.

Nov. 19. We had not enough to pay our weekly rent; but the Lord graciously sent us again to-day fourteen shillings and sixpence. I would just observe, that we never contract debts, which we believe to be unscriptural (according to Romans xiii. 8); and therefore we have no bills with our tailor, shoemaker, grocer, butcher, baker, etc.; but all we buy we pay for in ready money. The Lord helping us, we would rather suffer privation than contract debts. Thus we always know how much we have, and how much we have a right to give away. I am well aware that many trials come upon the children of God, on account of not acting according to Rom. xiii. 8.

Nov. 27. Lord's day. Our money had been reduced to two pence halfpenny; our bread was hardly enough for this day. I had several times brought our need before the Lord. After dinner, when I returned thanks, I asked him to give us our daily bread, meaning literally that he would send us bread for the evening. Whilst I was praying, there was a knock at the door of the room. After I had concluded, a poor sister came in, and brought us some of her dinner, and from another poor sister five shillings. In the afternoon she also brought us a large loaf. Thus the Lord not only literally gave us bread but also money.

After we had, on December 31, 1831, looked over the Lord's gracious dealings with us during the past year, in providing for all our temporal wants, we had about ten shillings left. A little while after, the providence of God called for that, so that not a single farthing remained Thus we closed the old year, in which the Lord had been so gracious in giving to us, without our asking any one, — 1. Through the instrumentality of the box, thirty-one pounds fourteen shillings. 2. From brethren of the church at Teignmouth, in presents of money, six pounds eighteen shillings and sixpence. 3. From brethren living at Teignmouth and elsewhere, not connected with the church at Teignmouth, ninety-three pounds six shillings and twopence. Altogether, one hundred and thirty-one pounds eighteen shillings and eightpence. There had been likewise many articles of provision and some articles of clothing given to us, worth at least twenty pounds. I am so particular in mentioning these things, to show that we are never losers from acting according to the mind of the Lord. For had I had my regular salary, humanly speaking, I should not have had nearly as much : but whether this would have been the case or not, this is plain, that I have not served a hard master, and that is what I delight to show.

Jan. 7, 1832. We had been again repeatedly asking the Lord to-day and yesterday to supply our temporal wants, having no means to pay our weekly rent, and this evening, as late as eleven o'clock, a brother gave us nineteen shillings and sixpence, — a proof that the Lord is not limited to time.

Jan. 14. This morning we had nothing but dry bread with our tea; only the second time since we have been living by simple faith upon Jesus for temporal supplies. We have more than forty pounds of ready money in the house for two bills,[1] which will not be payable for several weeks; but we do not consider this money to be our own, and would rather suffer great privation, God helping us, than take of it. We were looking to our Father, and he has not suffered us to be disappointed. For when now we had but threepence left, and only a small piece of bread, we received two shillings and five shillings.

Feb. 18. This afternoon I broke a bloodvessel in my stomach, and lost a considerable quantity of blood. I was very happy immediately afterwards. February 19. This morning, Lord's day, two brethren called on me, to ask me what arrangement there should be made to-day, as it regarded the four villages, where some of the brethren were in the habit of preaching, as, on account of my not being able to preach, one of the brethren would need to stay at home to take my place. I asked them, kindly, to come again in about an hour, when I would give them an answer. After they were gone the Lord gave me faith to rise. I dressed myself, and determined to go to the chapel. I was enabled to do so, though so weak when I went, that walking the short distance to the chapel was an exertion to me. I was enabled to preach this morning with as loud and strong a voice as usual, and for the usual length of time. After the morning meeting, a medical friend called on me, and entreated me not to preach again in the afternoon, as it might greatly injure me. I told him that I should indeed consider it great presumption to do so had the Lord not given me faith. I preached again in the afternoon, and this medical friend called again, and said the same concerning the evening meeting. Nevertheless, having faith, I preached again in the evening. After each

---

[1] One bill I had to meet for a brother, the other was for money which, in the form of a bill, I had sent to the Continent; but in both cases the money was in my hands before the bills were given.

meeting I became stronger, which was a plain proof that the hand of God was in the matter.

Feb. 20. The Lord enabled me to rise early in the morning, and to go to our usual prayer meeting, where I read, spoke, and prayed. Afterwards I wrote four letters, expounded the Scriptures at home, and attended the meeting again in the evening. February 21. I attended the two meetings as usual, preached in the evening, and did my other work besides. February 22. To-day I attended the meeting in the morning, walked afterwards six miles with two brethren, and rode to Plymouth. February 23. I am now as well as I was before I broke the bloodvessel. In relating the particulars of this circumstance, I would earnestly warn every one who may read this not to imitate me in such a thing if he has no faith; but if he has, it will, as good coin, most assuredly be honored by God. I could not say that if such a thing should happen again I would act in the same way; for when I have been not nearly so weak as when I had broken the bloodvessel, having no faith, I did not preach; yet, if it were to please the Lord to give me faith, I might be able to do the same, though even still weaker than at the time just spoken of.

About this time I repeatedly prayed with sick believers till they were restored. *Unconditionally* I asked the Lord for the blessing of bodily health (a thing which I could not do now), and almost always had the petition granted. In some instances, however, the prayer was not answered. In the same way, whilst in London, November, 1829, in answer to my prayers, I was immediately restored from a bodily infirmity, under which I had been laboring for a long time, and which has never returned since. The way in which I now account for these facts is as follows. It pleased the Lord, I think, to give me in such cases something like the gift (not grace) of faith, so that unconditionally I could ask and look for an answer. The difference between the *gift* and the *grace* of faith seems to me this. According to *the gift of faith*, I am able to do a thing, or believe that a thing will come to pass, the not doing of which, or the not believing of which, *would not be sin;* according to *the grace of faith*, I am able to do a thing, or believe that a thing will come to pass, respecting which I have the word of God as the ground to rest upon, and, therefore, the not doing it, or the not believing it, *would be sin.* For instance, *the gift of faith* would be needed to believe that a sick person should be restored again, though there is no human probability, for *there is no promise to that effect; the grace of faith* is needed to believe that the Lord will give me the necessaries of life, if I first seek the kingdom of God and his righteousness, for *there is a promise to that effect.*[1]

March 18. These two days we have not been able to purchase meat. The sister in whose house we lodge gave us to-day part of her dinner. We are still looking to Jesus for deliverance. We want money to pay the weekly rent and to buy provisions. March 19. Our landlady sent again of her meat for our dinner. We have but a halfpenny left. I feel myself very cold in asking for money; still, I hope for deliverance, though I do not see whence money is to come. We were not able to buy bread to-day as usual. March 20. This has been again a day of very great mercies. In the morning we met round our breakfast which the Lord had provided for us, though we had not a single penny left. The last halfpenny was spent for milk. We were then still looking to Jesus for fresh supplies. We both had no doubt that the Lord would interfere. I felt it a trial that I had but little earnestness in asking the Lord; and had this not been the case, perhaps we might have had our wants sooner supplied. We have about seven pounds in the house; but considering it no longer our own, the Lord kept us from taking of it, with

[1] Matt. vi

the view of replacing what we had taken, as formerly I might have done. The meat which was sent yesterday for our dinner was enough also for to-day. Thus the Lord had provided another meal. Two sisters called upon us about noon, who gave us two pounds of sugar, one pound of coffee, and two cakes of chocolate. Whilst they were with us, a poor sister came and brought us one shilling from herself and two shillings and sixpence from another poor sister. Our landlady also sent us again of her dinner, and also a loaf. Our bread would scarcely have been enough for tea, had the Lord not thus graciously provided. In the afternoon, the same sister who brought the money brought us also, from another sister, one pound of butter and two shillings, and from another sister five shillings.

CHAPTER V.

MINISTRY AT BRISTOL BEGUN.

1832—1835.

"HERE HAVE WE NO CONTINUING CITY"—CAUTION TO THE CHRISTIAN TRAVELLER—NEW TOKENS FOR GOOD—THE WAY MADE CLEAR—MEETINGS FOR INQUIRY—NO RESPECT OF PERSONS WITH GOD—FRANKE, "BEING DEAD, YET SPEAKETH"—DAILY BREAD SUPPLIED—A PECULIAR PEOPLE.

APRIL 8. I have felt much this day that Teignmouth is no longer my place, and that I shall leave it. I would observe that in August of 1831 I began greatly to feel as if my work at Teignmouth were done, and that I should go somewhere else. I was led to consider the matter more maturely, and at last had it settled in this way,—that it was not likely to be of God, because, for certain reasons, I should *naturally* have liked to leave Teignmouth. Afterwards, I felt quite comfortable in remaining there. In the commencement of the year 1832, I began again much to doubt whether Teignmouth was my place, or whether my gift was not much more that of going about from place to place, seeking to bring believers back to the Scriptures, than to stay in one place and to labor as a pastor. I resolved to try whether it were not the will of God that I should still give myself to pastoral work among the brethren at Teignmouth; and with more earnestness and faithfulness than ever I was enabled to give myself to this work, and was certainly much refreshed and blessed in it; and I saw immediately blessings result from it. This my experience seemed more than ever to settle me at Teignmouth. But notwithstanding this, the impression that my work was done there came back after some time, as the remark in my journal of April 8 shows, and it became stronger and stronger. There was one point remarkable in connection with this. Wherever I went I preached with much more enjoyment and power than at Teignmouth, the very reverse of which had been the case on my first going there. Moreover, almost everywhere I had many more hearers than at Teignmouth, and found the people hungering after food, which, generally speaking, was no longer the case at Teignmouth.

April 11. Felt again much that Teignmouth will not much longer be my residence. April 12. Still feel the impression that Teignmouth is no longer my place. April 13. Found a letter from brother Craik, from Bristol, on my return from Torquay, where I had been to preach. He invites me to come and help him. It appears to me, from what he writes, that such places as Bristol more suit my gifts. O Lord, teach me! I have felt this day more than ever that I shall soon leave Teignmouth. I fear, however, there is much connected with it which savors of the flesh, and that makes me fearful. It seems to me as if I should shortly go to Bristol, if the Lord permit. April 14. Wrote a letter to brother Craik, in which I said I should come, if I clearly saw it to be the Lord's will. Have felt again very much to-day, yea, far more than ever, that I shall soon leave Teignmouth.

April 15. Lord's day. This evening I preached, as fully as time would permit, on the Lord's second coming. After having done so, I told the brethren what effect this doctrine had had upon me, on first receiving it, even to determine me to leave London, and to preach throughout the kingdom; but that the Lord had kept me chiefly at Teignmouth for these two years and three months, and that it seemed to me now that the time was near when I should leave them. I reminded them of what I told them when they requested me to take the oversight of them, that I could make no certain engagement, but stay only so long with them as I should see it to be the Lord's will to do so There was much weeping afterwards. But I am now again in peace.

April 16. This morning I am still in peace. I am glad I have spoken to the brethren, that they may be prepared, in case the Lord should take me away I left to-day for Dartmouth, where I preached in the evening. I had five answers to prayer to-day. 1. I awoke at five, for which I had asked the Lord last evening. 2. The Lord removed from my dear wife an indisposition under which she had been suffering. It would have been trying to me to have had to leave her in that state. 3. The Lord sent us money. 4. There was a place vacant on the Dartmouth coach, which only passes through Teignmouth. 5. This evening I was assisted in preaching, and my own soul refreshed.

April 21. I would offer here a word of warning to believers. Often the work of the Lord itself may be a temptation to keep us from that communion with him which is so essential to the benefit of our own souls. On the 19th I had left Dartmouth, conversed a good deal that day, preached in the evening, walked afterwards eight miles, had only about five hours' sleep, travelled again the next day twenty-five miles, preached twice, and conversed very much besides, went to bed at eleven, and arose before five. All this shows that my body and spirit required rest, and, therefore, however careless about the Lord's work I might have appeared to my brethren, I ought to have had a great deal of quiet time for prayer and reading the word, especially as I had a long journey before me that day, and as I was going to Bristol, which in itself required much prayer. Instead of this, I hurried to the prayer-meeting, after a few minutes' private prayer. But let none think that public prayer will make up for closet communion. Then again, afterwards, when I ought to have withdrawn myself, as it were, by force, from the company of beloved brethren and sisters, and given my testimony for the Lord, (and, indeed, it would have been the best testimony I could have given them,) by telling them that I needed secret communion with the Lord, I did not do so, but spent the time, till the coach came, in conversation with them. Now, however profitable in some respects it may have been made to those with whom I was on that morning, yet my own soul needed food; and not having had it, I was lean, and felt the effects of it the whole day; and hence I believe it came that I was dumb on the coach, and did not speak a word for Christ, nor give away a single tract, though I had my pockets full on purpose.

April 22. This morning I preached at Gideon Chapel, Bristol. In the afternoon I preached at the Pithay Chapel. This sermon was a blessing to many, many souls; and many were brought through it to come afterwards to hear brother Craik and me. Among others it was the means of converting a young man who was a notorious drunkard, and who was just again on his way to a public house, when an acquaintance of his met him, and asked him to go with him to hear a foreigner preach. He did so; and from that moment he was so completely altered, that he never again went to a public house, and was so happy in the Lord afterwards that he often neglected his supper, from eagerness to read the Scriptures, as his wife told me. He died about five months afterwards. This evening I was much instructed in hearing brother Craik preach. I am now fully persuaded that Bristol is the place where the Lord will have me to labor.

April 27. It seems to brother Craik and myself the Lord's will that we should go home next week, in order that in quietness, without being influenced by what we see here, we may more inquire into the Lord's will concerning us. It especially appears to us much more likely that we should come to a right conclusion among the brethren and sisters in Devonshire, whose tears we shall have to witness, and whose entreaties to stay with them we shall have to hear, than here in Bristol, where we see only those who wish us to stay.

April 28. It still seems to us the Lord's will that we should both leave soon, to have quiet time for prayer concerning Bristol. April 29. I preached this morning on Rev. iii. 14–22. As it afterwards appeared, that testimony was blessed to many, though I lacked enjoyment in my own soul. This afternoon brother Craik preached in a vessel called the Clifton Ark, fitted up for a chapel. In the evening I preached in the same vessel. These testimonies also God greatly honored, and made them the means of afterward bringing several, who then heard us, to our meeting-places. How was God with us, and how did he help us, thereby evidently showing that he himself had sent us to this city!

April 30. It was most affecting to take leave of the dear children of God, dozens pressing us to return soon, many with tears in their eyes. The blessing which the Lord has given to our ministry seems to be very great. We both see it fully the Lord's will to come here, though we do not see under what circumstances. A brother has promised to take Bethesda Chapel for us, and to be answerable for the payment of the rent; so that thus we should have two large chapels. I saw, again, two instances to-day in which my preaching has been blessed.

May 1. Brother Craik and I left this morning for Devonshire.

May 3. I saw several of the brethren to-day, and felt so fully assured that it is the Lord's will that I should go to Bristol, that I told them so. This evening I had a meeting with the three deacons, when I told them plainly about it; asking them, if they see anything wrong in me concerning this matter, to tell me of it. They had nothing to say against it; yea, though much wishing me to stay, they were convinced themselves that my going is of God.

May 5. One other striking proof to my mind that my leaving Teignmouth is of God, is, that some truly spiritual believers, though they much wish me to stay, themselves see that I ought to go to Bristol.

May 7. Having received a letter from Bristol on May 5, it was answered to-day in such a way that the Lord may have another opportunity to prevent our going thither if it be not of him.

May 15. Just when I was in prayer concerning Bristol, I was sent for to come to brother Craik. Two letters had arrived from Bristol. The brethren assembling at Gideon accept our offer to come under the conditions we have made, *i. e.*, for the present, to consider us only as ministering among them, but not in any fixed pastoral relationship, so that we may preach as we consider it to be according to the mind of God, *without reference to any rules among them; that the pew-rents should be done away with; and that we should go on, respecting the supply of our temporal wants, as in Devonshire.* We intend, the Lord willing, to leave in about a week, though there is nothing settled respecting Bethesda Chapel.

May 21. I began to-day to take leave of the brethren at Teignmouth, calling on each of them. It has been a trying day. Much weeping on the part of the saints. Were I not so fully persuaded that it is the will of God we should go to Bristol, I should have been hardly able to bear it.

May 22. The brethren at Teignmouth say that they expect us soon back again. *As far as I understand the way in which God deals with his children, this seems very unlikely.* Towards the evening, the Lord, after repeated prayer, gave me Col. i. 21–23 as a text for the last word of exhortation. It seemed to me best to speak as little as possible about myself, and as much as possible about Christ. I scarcely alluded to our separation, and only commended myself and the brethren, in the concluding prayer, to the Lord. The parting scenes are very trying.

but my full persuasion is that the separation is of the Lord. May 23. My wife, Mr. Groves, my father-in-law, and I left this morning for Exeter. Dear brother Craik intends to follow us to-morrow.

We had unexpectedly received, just before we left Teignmouth, about fifteen pounds, else we should not have been able to defray all the expenses connected with leaving, travelling, etc. By this, also, the Lord showed his mind concerning our going to Bristol.

The following record will now show to the believing reader how far what I have said concerning my persuasion that it was the will of God that we should go to Bristol has been proved by facts.

May 25, 1832. This evening we arrived at Bristol. May 27. This morning we received a sovereign, sent to us by a sister residing in *Devonshire*, which we take as an earnest that the Lord will provide for us here also. May 28. When we were going to speak to the brethren, who manage the temporal affairs of Gideon Chapel, about giving up the pew-rents, having all the seats free, and receiving the free-will offerings through a box, — a matter which was not quite settled on their part, as brother Craik and I had thought, — we found that the Lord had so graciously ordered this matter for us that there was not the least objection on the part of these brethren.

June 4. For several days we have been looking about for lodgings, but finding none plain and cheap enough, we were led to make this also a subject of earnest prayer; and now, immediately afterwards, the Lord has given us such as are suitable. We pay only eighteen shillings a week for two sitting-rooms and three bedrooms, coals, and attendance. It was particularly difficult to find *cheap* furnished lodgings, having five rooms in the same house, which we need, as brother Craik and we live together. How good is the Lord to have thus appeared for us, in answer to prayer, and what an encouragement to commit everything to him in prayer!

June 25. To-day it was finally settled to take Bethesda Chapel for a twelvemonth, on condition that a brother at once paid the rent, with the understanding that, if the Lord shall bless our labors in that place, so that believers are gathered together in fellowship, he expects them to help him; but if not, that he will pay all. This was the only way in which we could take the chapel; for we could not think it to be of God to have had this chapel, though there should be every prospect of usefulness, if it had made us in any way debtors.

July 6. To-day we commenced preaching at Bethesda Chapel. It was a good day. July 13. To-day we heard of the first cases of cholera in Bristol. July 16. This evening, from six to nine o'clock, we had appointed for conversing at the vestry, one by one, with individuals who wished to speak to us about their souls. There were so many that we were engaged from six till twenty minutes past ten.

These meetings we have continued ever since, twice a week, or once a week, or once a fortnight, or once a month, as our strength and time allowed it, or as they seemed needed. We have found them beneficial in the following respects: —

1. Many persons, on account of timidity, would prefer coming at an appointed time to the vestry to converse with us, to calling on us in our own house. 2. The very fact of appointing a time for seeing people, to converse with them in private concerning the things of eternity, has brought some, who, humanly speaking, never would have called upon us under other circumstances; yea, it has brought even those who, though they thought they were concerned about the things of God, yet were completely ignorant; and thus we have had an opportunity of speaking to them. 3. These meetings have also been a great

encouragement to ourselves in the work, for often, when we thought that such and such expositions of the word had done no good at all, it was through these meetings found to be the reverse; and likewise, when our hands were hanging down, we have been afresh encouraged to go forward in the work of the Lord, and to continue sowing the seed in hope, by seeing at these meetings fresh cases in which the Lord has condescended to use us as instruments, particularly as in this way instances have sometimes occurred in which individuals have spoken to us about the benefit which they derived from our ministry, not only a few months before, but even as long as two, three, and four years before.

For the above reasons I would particularly recommend to other servants of Christ, especially to those who live in large towns, if they have not already introduced a similar p'an, to consider whether it may not be well for them also to set apart such times for seeing inquirers. Those meetings, however, require much prayer, to be enabled to speak aright to all those who come, according to their different need; and one is led continually to feel that one is not sufficient of one's self for these things, but that our sufficiency can be alone of God. These meetings also have been by far the most wearing-out part of all our work, though at the same time the most refreshing.

July 18. To-day I spent the whole morning in the vestry, to procure a quiet season. This has now for some time been the only way, on account of the multiplicity of engagements, to make sure of time for prayer, reading the word, and meditation. July 19. I spent from half-past nine till one in the vestry, and had real communion with the Lord. The Lord be praised, who has put it into my mind to use the vestry for a place of retirement!

Aug. 5. *When all our money was gone to-day, the Lord again graciously supplied our wants.* Aug. 6. This afternoon, from two till after six, brother Craik and I spent in the vestry, to see the inquirers. We have had again, in seeing several instances of blessing upon our labors, abundant reason brought before us to praise the Lord for having sent us to Bristol.

Aug. 13. This evening one brother and four sisters united with brother Craik and me in church-fellowship at Bethesda, *without any rules, desiring only to act as the Lord shall be pleased to give us light through his word.*

Sept. 17. This morning the Lord, in addition to all his other mercies, has given us a little girl, who, with her mother, is doing well.

Oct. 1. A meeting for inquirers this afternoon from two to five. Many more are convinced of sin through brother Craik's preaching than my own. This circumstance led me to inquire into the reasons, which are probably these: 1. That brother Craik is more spiritually minded than I am. 2. That he prays more earnestly for the conversion of sinners than I do. 3. That he more frequently addresses sinners, as such, in his public ministrations, than I do. This led me to more frequent and earnest prayer for the conversion of sinners, and to address them more frequently as such. The latter had never been intentionally left undone, but it had not been so frequently brought to my mind as to that of brother Craik. Since then, the cases in which it has pleased the Lord to use me as an instrument of conversion have been quite as many as those in which brother Craik has been used.

Feb. 9, 1833. I read a part of Franke's life. The Lord graciously help me to follow him, as far as he followed Christ. Most of the Lord's people whom we know in Bristol are poor, and if the Lord were to give us grace to live more as this dear man of God did, we might draw much more than we have as yet done out of our heavenly Father's bank for our poor brethren and sisters. March 2. A man in the street ran up to brother Craik and put a paper containing ten shillings into his hand, saying, "That is for you and Mr. Müller," and went hastily away. May 28. This morning, whilst sitting in my room, the distress of several brethren and sisters was brought to my mind, and I said to myself, "O that it might please the Lord to give me means to help them!" About an hour afterwards I received sixty pounds from a brother whom up to this day I never saw, and who then lived, as he does still, a distance of several thousand miles.

May 29. Review of the last twelve months, as it regards the fruits of our labors in Bristol: 1. The total number of those added to us within the year has been one hundred and nine. 2. There have been converted through our instrumentality, *so far as we have heard and can judge respecting the individuals,* sixty-five. 3. Many backsliders have been reclaimed, and many of the children of God have been encouraged and strengthened in the way of truth.

June 12. I felt, this morning, that we might do something for the souls of those poor boys and girls, and grown-up or aged people, to whom we have daily given bread for some time past, in establishing a school for them, reading the Scriptures to them, and speaking to them about the Lord. This desire was not carried out. The chief obstacle in the way was a pressure of work coming upon brother Craik and me just about that time. Shortly after, the number of the poor who came for bread increased to between sixty and eighty a day, whereby our neighbors were molested, as the beggars were lying about in troops in the street, on account of which we were obliged to tell them no longer to come for bread. This thought ultimately issued in the formation of the Scriptural Knowledge Institution, and in the establishment of the Orphan Houses.

Dec. 17. This evening brother Craik and I took tea with a family, of whom five had been brought to the knowledge of the Lord through our instrumentality. As an encouragement to brethren who may desire to preach the gospel in a language not their own, I would mention that the first member of this family who was converted came merely out of curiosity to hear my foreign accent, some words having been mentioned to her which I did not pronounce properly.

Dec. 31. In looking over my journal, I find, —
1. That at least two hundred and sixty persons (according to the number of names we have marked down, but there have been many more) have come to converse with us about the concerns of their souls. Out of these, one hundred and fifty-three have been added to us in fellowship these last eighteen months, sixty of whom have been brought to the knowledge of the Lord through our instrumentality.

2. In looking over the Lord's dealings with me as to temporal things, I find that he has sent me, during the past year, —

1. In freewill offerings through the boxes, *as my part*	£152	14	5¼
2. Presents in money given to me	25	1	3
3. Presents in clothes and provisions, worth, at least .	20	0	0
4. A brother sent me, from a distance	60	0	0
5. We live free of rent, which is worth *for our part* .	10	0	0
	£267	15	8¼

It is just now four years since I first began to trust in the Lord alone for the supply of my temporal wants. My little all I then had, at most worth one hundred pounds a year, I gave up for the Lord, having then nothing left but about five pounds. The Lord greatly honored this little sacrifice, and he gave me, in return, not only as much as I had given up, but considerably more. For during the first year, he sent me already, in one way or other, including what came to me through family connection, about one hundred and thirty pounds. During the second year, one hundred and fifty-one pounds eighteen shillings and eight pence. During the third year, one hundred and ninety-five pounds three shillings. During this year, two hundred and sixty-seven pounds fifteen shillings and eight and one fourth pence. The following points require particular notice: 1. During the last three years and three months I never have asked any one for anything; but, by the help of the Lord, I have been enabled at all times to bring my wants to him, and he graciously has supplied them all. 2. At the close of each of these four years, though my income has been comparatively great, I have had only a few shillings or nothing at all left; and thus it is also to-day, by the help of God. 3. During the last year a considerable part of my income has come from a distance of several thousand miles from a brother whom I never saw. 4. Since we have been obliged to discontinue the giving away of bread to about fifty poor people every day, on account of our neighbors, our income has not been during the second part of this year nearly so great, scarcely one half as much, as during the first part of it.

January 9, 1834. Brother Craik and I have preached during these eighteen months, once a month, at Brislington, a village near Bristol, but have not seen any fruit of our labors there. This led me to-day very earnestly to pray to the Lord for the conversion of sinners in that place. I was also, in the chapel, especially led to pray again about this, and asked the Lord in particular that he would be pleased to convert, at least, one soul this evening that we might have a little encouragement. I preached with much help, and I hope there has been good done this evening. The Lord did according to my request. There was a young man brought to the knowledge of the truth.

Jan 14. I was greatly tried by the difficulty of fixing upon a text from which to preach on the morning of October 20, and at last preached without enjoyment. To-day I heard of a NINTH instance in which this very sermon has been blessed.

Jan. 31. This evening a Dorcas Society was formed among the sisters in communion with us, but not according to the manner in which we found one when we came to Bristol; for, as we have dismissed all teachers from the Sunday School who were not real believers, so now believing females only will meet together to make clothes for the poor. The being mixed up with unbelievers had not only proved a barrier to spiritual conversation among the sisters, but must have been also injurious to both parties in several respects. One sister, now united to us in fellowship, acknowledged that the being connected with the Dorcas Society, previous to her conversion, had been, in a measure, the means of keeping her in security; as she thought that, by helping on such like things, she might gain heaven at last. O that the saints, in *faithful* love, according to the word of God (2 Cor. vi. 14–18), might be more separated in all spiritual matters from unbelievers, and not be unequally yoked together with them!

CHAPTER VI.

THE SCRIPTURAL KNOWLEDGE INSTITUTION.

1834 — 1835.

UNSCRIPTURAL CHARACTER OF THE EXISTING RELIGIOUS AND BENEVOLENT SOCIETIES — A NEW INSTITUTION PROPOSED — GOD'S WORD THE ONLY RULE, AND GOD'S PROMISE THE ONLY DEPENDENCE — "IN EVERYTHING LET YOUR REQUEST BE MADE KNOWN UNTO GOD" — EARNEST OF THE DIVINE BLESSING ON THE INSTITUTION — BEREAVEMENT — HELPER SEASONABLY SENT — REWARD OF SEEKING GOD'S FACE.

FEB. 21. I was led this morning to form a plan for establishing, upon scriptural principles, an institution for the spread of the gospel at home and abroad. I trust this matter is of God. Feb. 25. I was led again this day to pray about the forming of a new Missionary Institution, and felt still more confirmed that we should do so.

[Some readers may ask why we formed a *new* Institution for the spread of the gospel, and why we did not unite with some of the religious societies, already in existence, seeing that there are several missionary, Bible, tract, and school societies. I give, therefore, our reasons, in order to show that nothing but the desire to maintain a good conscience led us to act as we have done. For as, by the grace of God, we acknowledge the word of God as the only rule of action for the disciples of the Lord Jesus, we found, in comparing the then existing religious societies with the word of God, that they departed so far from it, that we could not be united with them, and yet maintain a good conscience. I only mention here the following points.

1. The *end* which these religious societies propose to themselves, and which is constantly put before their mem-

bers, is, that the world will gradually become better and better, and that at last the whole world will be converted To this end, there is constantly reference made to the passage in Habakkuk ii. 14 : "For the earth shall be filled with the knowledge of the glory of the Lord, as the waters cover the sea ; " or the one in Isaiah xi. 9 : "For the earth shall be full of the knowledge of the Lord, as the waters cover the sea." But that these passages can have no reference to the present dispensation, but to the one which will commence with the return of the Lord, — that in the present dispensation things will not become spiritually better, but rather worse, — and that in the present dispensation it is not the whole world that will be converted, but only a people gathered out from among the Gentiles for the Lord, — is clear from many passages of the divine testimony, of which I only refer to the following : Matt. xiii. 24–30, and verses 36–43, 2 Tim. iii. 1–13, Acts xv. 14.

A hearty desire for the conversion of sinners, and earnest prayer for it to the Lord, is quite *scriptural;* but it is *unscriptural* to expect the conversion of the whole world. *Such an end* we could not propose to ourselves in the service of the Lord.

2. But that which is worse, is, the connection of those religious societies with the world, which is completely contrary to the word of God (2 Cor. vi. 14–18). In temporal things the children of God need, whilst they remain here on earth, to make use of the world; but when the work to be done requires that those who attend to it should be possessed of spiritual life (of which unbelievers are utterly destitute), the children of God are bound, by their loyalty to their Lord, entirely to refrain from association with the unregenerate. But, alas ! the connection with the world is but too marked in these religious societies; for every one who pays a guinea, or, in some societies, half a guinea, is considered as a member. Although such an individual may live in sin; although he may manifest to every one

that he does not know the Lord Jesus; if only the guinea or the half-guinea be paid, he is considered a member and has a right as such to vote. Moreover, whoever pays a larger sum, for instance, ten pounds or twenty pounds, can be, in many societies, a member for life, however openly sinful his life should be for the time, or should become afterwards. Surely such things ought not to be.

3. The means which are made use of in these religious societies to obtain money for the work of the Lord are also in other respects unscriptural; for it is a most common case to *ask* the *unconverted* for money, which even Abraham would not have done (Genesis xiv. 21–24); and how much less should *we* do it, who are not only forbidden to have fellowship with unbelievers in all such matters (2 Cor. vi. 14–18), but who are also in fellowship with the Father and the Son, and can therefore obtain everything from the Lord which we possibly can need in his service, without being obliged to go to the unconverted world! How altogether differently the first disciples acted, in this respect, we learn from 3 John 7.

4. Not merely, however, in these particulars is there a connection with the world in these religious societies; but it is not a rare thing for even committee members (the individuals who manage the affairs of the societies) to be manifestly unconverted persons, if not open enemies to the truth; and this is suffered because they are rich, or of influence, as it is called.

5. It is a most common thing to endeavor to obtain for patrons and presidents of these societies and for chairmen at the public meetings, persons of rank or wealth, to attract the public. Never once have I known a case of a POOR, but very devoted, wise, and experienced servant of Christ being invited to fill the chair at such public meetings. Surely, the Galilean fishermen, who were apostles, or our Lord himself, who was called the carpenter, would not have been called to this office, according to these prin-

ciples. These things ought not so to be among the disciples of the Lord Jesus, who should not judge with reference to a person's fitness for service in the church of Christ by the position he fills in the world, or by the wealth he possesses.

6. Almost all these societies contract debts, so that it is a comparatively rare case to read a report of any of them without finding that they have expended more than they have received, which, however, is contrary both to the spirit and to the letter of the New Testament. (Rom. xiii. 8.)

Now, although brother Craik and I were ready, by the grace of God, heartily to acknowledge that there are not only many true children of God connected with these religious societies, but that the Lord has also blessed their efforts in many respects, notwithstanding the existence of these and other principles and practices which we judged to be unscriptural; yet it appeared to us to be his will that we should be entirely separate from these societies (though we should be considered as singular persons, or though it should even appear that we despised other persons, or would elevate ourselves above them), in order that, by the blessing of God, we might direct the attention of the children of God in those societies to their unscriptural practices; and we would rather be entirely unconnected with these societies than act contrary to the Holy Scriptures. We therefore separated entirely from them, although we remained united in brotherly love with individual believers belonging to them, and would by no means judge them for remaining in connection with them, if they do not see that such things are contrary to Scripture. But seeing them to be so ourselves, we could not with a clear conscience remain. After we had thus gone on for some time, we considered that it would have an injurious tendency upon the brethren among whom we labored, and also be at variance with the spirit of the gospel of Christ, if we did nothing at all for missionary objects, the circulation of the Holy Scriptures, tracts, etc., and we were therefore led, for these and other reasons, to do something for the spread of the gospel at home and abroad, however small the beginning might be.]

March 5. This evening, at a public meeting, brother Craik and I stated the principles on which we intend to carry on the institution which we propose to establish for the spread of the gospel at home and abroad. There was nothing outwardly influential either in the number of people present or in our speeches. May the Lord graciously be pleased to grant his blessing upon the institution, which will be called " The **Scriptural** Knowledge Institution, for Home and Abroad."

I. THE PRINCIPLES OF THE INSTITUTION.

1. We consider every believer bound, in one way or other, to help the cause of Christ, and we have scriptural warrant for expecting the Lord's blessing upon our work of faith and labor of love; and although, according to Matt. xiii. 24-43, 2 Tim. iii. 1-13, and many other passages, the world will not be converted before the coming of our Lord Jesus, still, while he tarries, all scriptural means ought to be employed for the ingathering of the elect of God.

2. The Lord helping us, we do not mean to seek the patronage of the world; *i. e.*, we never intend to ask *unconverted* persons of rank or wealth to countenance this Institution, because this, we consider, would be dishonorable to the Lord. In the name of our God we set up our banners, (Ps. xx. 5); he alone shall be our patron, and if he helps us we shall prosper, and if he is not on our side we shall not succeed.

3. We do not mean to *ask* unbelievers for money (2 Cor. vi. 12-18); though we do not feel ourselves warranted to

refuse their contributions, if they of their own accord should offer them. Acts xxviii. 2–10.

4. We reject altogether the help of unbelievers in managing or carrying on the affairs of the Institution. 2 Cor. vi. 14–18.

5. We intend never to enlarge the field of labor by contracting debts (Rom. xiii. 8), and afterwards appealing to the Church of Christ for help, because this we consider to be opposed both to the letter and the spirit of the New Testament; but in secret prayer, God helping us, we shall carry the wants of the Institution to the Lord, and act according to the means that God shall give.

6. We do not mean to reckon the success of the Institution by the amount of money given, or the number of Bibles distributed, etc., but by the Lord's blessing upon the work (Zech. iv. 6); and we expect this in the proportion in which he shall help us to wait upon him in prayer.

7. While we would avoid aiming after needless singularity, we desire to go on simply according to Scripture, without compromising the truth; at the same time thankfully receiving any instruction which experienced believers, after prayer, upon scriptural ground, may have to give us concerning the Institution.

II. THE OBJECTS OF THE INSTITUTION.

1. To *assist* day schools, Sunday schools, and adult schools, in which instruction is given upon *scriptural principles*, and as far as the Lord may give the means, and supply us with suitable teachers, and in other respects make our path plain, to establish schools of this kind. With this we also combine *the putting of poor children to such day schools*.

a. By day schools upon scriptural principles, we understand day schools in which the teachers are godly persons, — in which the way of salvation is scripturally pointed out, — and in which no instruction is given opposed to the principles of the gospel.

b. Sunday schools, in which all the teachers are believers, and in which the Holy Scriptures are alone the foundation of instruction, are such only as the Institution assists with the supply of Bibles, Testaments, etc.; for we consider it unscriptural that any persons who do not profess to know the Lord themselves should be allowed to give religious instruction.

c. The Institution does not assist any adult school with the supply of Bibles, Testaments, spelling-books, etc., except the teachers are believers.

2. To circulate the Holy Scriptures.

3. The third object of this Institution is to aid missionary efforts.

We desire to assist those missionaries whose proceedings appear to be most according to the Scriptures.

March 7. To-day we have only one shilling left. This evening, when we came home from our work, we found a brother, our tailor, waiting for us, who brought a new suit of clothes both for brother Craik and me, which a brother, whose name was not to be mentioned, had ordered for us.

April 23. Yesterday and to-day I asked the Lord to send us twenty pounds, that we might be able to procure a larger stock of Bibles and Testaments than our small funds of the Scriptural Knowledge Institution would allow us to purchase; and this evening a sister, unasked, promised to give us that sum, adding that she felt a particular pleasure in circulating the Holy Scriptures, as the simple reading of them had been the means of bringing her to the knowledge of the Lord.

June 8. Lord's day. I obtained no text yesterday, notwithstanding repeated prayer and reading of the word.

This morning I awoke with these words: "My grace is sufficient for thee." As soon as I had dressed myself, I turned to 2 Cor. xii. to consider this passage; but in doing so, after prayer, I was led to think that I had not been directed to this portion for the sake of speaking on it, as I at first thought, and I therefore followed my usual practice in such cases, *i. e.*, to read on in the Scriptures where I left off last evening. In doing so, when I came to Heb. xi. 13-16, I felt that this was the text. Having prayed, I was confirmed in it, and the Lord was pleased to open this passage to me. I preached on it with great enjoyment. It pleased God greatly to bless what I said on that passage, and at least one soul was brought through it to the Lord.

June 25. These last three days I have had very little real communion with God, and have therefore been very weak spiritually, and have several times felt irritability of temper.

June 26. I was enabled, by the grace of God, to rise early, and I had nearly two hours in prayer before breakfast. I feel now this morning more comfortable.

July 11. I have prayed much about a master for boys' school, to be established in connection with our little Institution. Eight have applied for the situation, but none seemed to be suitable. Now, at last, the Lord has given us a brother who will commence the work.

Oct. 9. Our little Institution, established in dependence upon the Lord, and supplied by him with means, has now been seven months in operation, and through it have been benefited with instruction, — 1. In the Sunday school, about 120 children. 2. In the adult school, about 40 adults. 3. In the two day schools for boys and the two day schools for girls, 209 children, of whom 54 have been entirely free; the others pay about one third of the expense. There have been also circulated 482 Bibles, and 520 New Testaments. Lastly, fifty-seven pounds have been spent to aid missionary exertion. The means which the Lord has sent us, as the fruit of many prayers, during these seven months, amount to one hundred and sixty-seven pounds ten shillings and halfpenny.

Oct. 28. We heard a most affecting account of a poor little orphan boy, who for some time attended one of our schools, and who seems there, as far as we can judge, to have been brought to a real concern about his soul, through what I said concerning the torments of hell, and who some time ago was taken to the poorhouse, some miles out of Bristol. He has expressed great sorrow that he can no longer attend our school and ministry. May this, if it be the Lord's will, lead me to do something also for the supply of the *temporal* wants of poor children, the pressure of which has caused this poor boy to be taken away from our school!

Nov. 4. I spent the greater part of the morning in reading the word and in prayer, and asked also for our daily bread, for we have scarcely any money left. Nov. 5. I spent almost the whole of the day in prayer and reading the word. I prayed also again for the supply of our temporal wants; but the Lord has not as yet appeared. Nov. 8. Saturday. The Lord has graciously again supplied our temporal wants during this week, though at the commencement of it we had but little left. I have prayed much this week, for money, more than any other week, as far as I remember, since we have been in Bristol. The Lord has supplied us through our selling what we did not need, or by our being paid what was owed to us.

Dec. 10. To-day we found that a departed brother had left both to brother Craik and me twelve pounds.

Dec. 31, 1834. 1. Since brother Craik and I have been laboring in Bristol, 227 brethren and sisters have been added to us in fellowship. Out of the 227 who have been added to us, 103 have been converted through our instrumentality, and many have been brought into the liberty of the gospel, or reclaimed from backsliding. Forty-seven young converts are at Gideon, and fifty-six at Bethesda. 2. The income which the Lord has given me during this year is: —

1. My part of the freewill offerings through the boxes	£135 13 2¼
2. Money given to me by saints in and out of Bristol	92 7 6
Altogether	£228 0 8¼
3. Besides this, many articles in provisions, clothing, and furniture, worth to us about	60 0 0

Jan. 1, 1835. We had last evening an especial prayer meeting, for the sake of praising the Lord for all his many mercies, which we have received during the past year, and to ask him to continue to us his favor. Jan. 13. I visited from house to house the people living in Orange street, and saw in this way the families living in nine houses, to ascertain whether any individuals wanted Bibles, whether they could read, whether they wished their children put to our day schools or Sunday school, with the view of helping them accordingly. This afforded opportunities to converse with them about their souls.

Jan. 15. This morning I went again from house to house in Orange street. I should greatly delight in being frequently engaged in such work, for it is a most important one; but our hands are so full with other work that we can do but little in this way. Jan. 21. Received, in answer to prayer, from an unexpected quarter, five pounds, for the Scriptural Knowledge Institution. The Lord pours in, whilst we seek to pour out. For during the past week, merely among the poor, in going from house to house, fifty-eight copies of the Scriptures were sold at reduced prices, the going on with which is most important, but will require much means.

Jan. 28. I have, for these several days, prayed much

to ascertain whether the Lord will have me to go as a missionary to the East Indies, and I am most willing to go, if he will condescend to use me in this way. Jan. 29. I have been greatly stirred up to pray about going to Calcutta as a missionary. May the Lord guide me in this matter! (After all my repeated and earnest prayer in the commencement of 1835, and willingness on my part to go, if it were the Lord's will, still, he did not send me.)

Feb. 25. In the name of the Lord, and in dependence upon him alone for support, we have established a fifth day school for poor children, which to-day has been opened. We have now two boys' schools and three girls' schools.

Mr. Muller having determined to visit Germany, chiefly on missionary business, reached London February 27, and writes: —

This morning I went to the Alien Office for my passport. On entering the office, I saw a printed paper, in which it is stated that every alien neglecting to renew every six months his certificate of residence, which he receives on depositing his passport, subjects himself to a penalty of fifty pounds, or imprisonment. This law I have ignorantly broken ever since I left London, in 1829. It appeared to me much better to confess at once that I had ignorantly done so than now wilfully break it; *trusting in the Lord as it regarded the consequences of the step.* I did so, and *the Lord inclined the heart of the officer with whom I had to do to pass over my non-compliance with the law, on account of my having broken it ignorantly.* Having obtained my passport, I found an unexpected difficulty in the Prussian ambassador refusing to sign it, as it did not contain a description of my person, and therefore I needed to prove that I was the individual spoken of in the passport. This difficulty was not removed for three days, when, *after earnest prayer,* through a paper signed by some citizens of

London, to whom I am known, the ambassador was satisfied. This very difficulty, when once the Lord had removed it, afforded me cause for thanksgiving: for I now obtained a *new* passport, worded in a way that, should I ever need it again, will prevent similar difficulties.

Mr. Müller was absent for five weeks, during which time he experienced many answers to prayer and encouragements to faith.

April 15. Bristol. Yesterday, at one, we landed in London. In answer to prayer, I soon obtained my things from the custom-house, and reached my friends in Chancery Lane a little before two.

June 3. To-day we had a public meeting on account of the Scriptural Knowledge Institution for Home and Abroad. It is now fifteen months since, in dependence upon the Lord for the supply of means, we have been enabled to provide poor children with schooling, circulate the Holy Scriptures, and aid missionary labors. During this time, though the field of labor has been continually enlarging, and though we have now and then been brought low in funds, the Lord has never allowed us to be obliged to stop the work. We have been enabled during this time to establish three day schools, and to connect with the Institution two other charity day schools, which, humanly speaking, otherwise would have been closed for want of means. The number of the children that have been thus provided with schooling, in the day schools only, amounts to 439. The number of copies of the Holy Scriptures which have been circulated is 795 Bibles and 753 New Testaments. We have also sent, in aid of missionary labors in Canada, in the East Indies, and on the Continent of Europe, one hundred and seventeen pounds, eleven shillings. The whole amount of the free-will offerings put into our hands for carrying on this work from March 5, 1834, to May 19, 1835, is £363 12s. 0¾d.

June 22. This morning at two my father-in-law died. June 25. Our little boy is so ill that I have no hope of his recovery. The Lord's holy will be done concerning the dear little one. June 26. My prayer, last evening, was that God would be pleased to support my dear wife under the trial, should he remove the little one; and to take him soon to himself, thus sparing him from suffering. I did not pray for the child's recovery. It was but two hours after that the dear little one went home. I am so fully enabled to realize that the dear infant is so much better off with the Lord Jesus than with us, that I scarcely feel the loss at all, and when I weep I weep for joy.

July 31. To-day brother C———r, formerly a minister in the establishment, who came to us a few days since, began, in connection with the Scriptural Knowledge Institution, to go from house to house to spread the truth as a city missionary. [This was a remarkable interposition of God. Brother Craik had before this, for some months, been unable, on account of bodily infirmity, to labor in the work of the schools, the circulation of the Scriptures, etc., and my own weakness, shortly after brother C———r's arrival, increased so that I was obliged to give up the work entirely. How gracious, therefore, of the Lord to send brother C———r, that thus the work might go on! Up to July, 1837 this beloved brother was enabled to continue in his work, and thus this little Institution was in a most important way enlarged as it regards the field of labor.]

Aug. 24. I feel very weak, and suffer more than before from the disease. I am in doubt whether to leave Bristol entirely for a time. I have no money to go away for a change of air. I have had an invitation to stay for a week with a sister in the country, and I think of accepting the invitation, and going to-morrow. August 26. To-day I had five pounds given to me *for the express purpose of using change of air.* August 29. To-day I received another five pounds *for the same purpose.*

Aug. 30. To-day, for the first Lord's day since our arrival in Bristol, I have been kept from preaching through illness. How mercifully has the Lord dealt in giving me so much strength for these years! I had another five pounds sent *to aid me in procuring change of air.* How kind is the Lord in thus providing me with the means for leaving Bristol! Sept. 2. Went with my family to Portishead.

Sept. 15. As I clearly understood that the person who lets me his horse has no license, I saw that, being bound as a believer to act according to the laws of the country, I could use it no longer; and as horse exercise seems most important, humanly speaking, for my restoration, and as this is the only horse which is to be had in the place, we came to the conclusion to leave Portishead to-morrow. *Immediately after,* I received a kind letter from a brother and two sisters in the Lord, who live in the Isle of Wight, which contained a fourth invitation, more pressing than ever, to come and stay with them for some time. In addition to this, they wrote that they had repeatedly prayed about the matter, and were persuaded that I ought to come. This matter has been to-day a subject for prayer.

Sept. 16. We came this morning to the conclusion that *I* should go to the Isle of Wight; but we saw not how my wife and child and our servant could accompany me, as we had not sufficient money for travelling expenses; and yet this seemed of importance. The Lord graciously removed the difficulty this evening; for we received *most unexpectedly and unasked for,* five pounds and thirteen shillings, which was owed to us, and also, when we had already retired to rest, a letter was brought, containing a present of two pounds. How very, very kind and tender is the Lord!

Sept. 19. This evening we arrived at our friends' in the Isle of Wight, by whom we were most kindly received.

Oct. 9. I have many times had thoughts of giving in print some account of the Lord's goodness to me, for the instruction, comfort, and encouragement of the children of God. I have considered to-day all the reasons for and against, and find that there are scarcely any against, and many for it.

Nov. 15. Bristol. Brother C——r and I have been praying together, the five last days, that the Lord would be pleased to send us means for carrying on the work of the Scriptural Knowledge Institution. This evening, a brother gave me six shillings and one penny, being money which he formerly used to pay towards the support of a trade club, which he has lately given up for the Lord's sake. Nov. 18. This evening thirty pounds were given to me; twenty-five pounds for the Scriptural Knowledge Institution, and five pounds for myself. This is a most remarkable answer to prayer. Brother C——r and I have prayed repeatedly together during the last week concerning the work, and especially that the Lord would be pleased to give us the means to continue, and even enlarge the field. In addition to this, I have several times asked for a supply for myself, and he has kindly granted both these requests. O that I may have grace to trust him more and more!

CHAPTER VII.

HOME FOR DESTITUTE ORPHANS.

1835 — 1836.

FRANKE'S WORKS FOLLOW HIM — A GREAT UNDERTAKING CONCEIVED — REASONS FOR ESTABLISHING AN ORPHAN HOUSE — PRAYER FOR GUIDANCE — TREASURE LAID UP IN HEAVEN — IN PRAYER AND IN FAITH, THE WORK IS BEGUN.

NOVEMBER 20. This evening I took tea at a sister's house, where I found Franke's life. I have frequently, for a long time, thought of laboring in a similar way, on a much smaller scale; not to imitate Franke, but in reliance upon the Lord. May God make it plain! Nov. 21. To-day I have had it very much impressed on my heart, no longer merely to *think* about the establishment of an orphan house, but actually to set about it, and I have been very much in prayer respecting it, in order to ascertain the Lord's mind. Nov. 23. To-day I had ten pounds, sent from Ireland, for our Institution. The Lord, in answer to prayer, has given me, in a few days, about fifty pounds. I had asked only for forty pounds. This has been a great encouragement to me, and has still more stirred me up to think and pray about the establishment of an orphan house. Nov. 25. I have been again much in prayer yesterday and to-day about the orphan house, and am more and more convinced that it is of God. May he in mercy guide me!

It may be well to enter somewhat minutely upon the reasons which led me to establish an orphan house. Through my pastoral labors, through my correspondence, and through brethren who visited Bristol, I had constantly cases brought before me, which proved that one of the especial things which the children of God needed in our day, was, *to have their faith strengthened.* I might visit a brother who worked fourteen or even sixteen hours a day at his trade, the necessary result of which was, that not only his body suffered, but his soul was lean, and he had no enjoyment in God. I might point out to him that he ought to work less, in order that his bodily health might not suffer, and that he might gather strength for his inner man, by reading the word of God, by meditation over it, and by prayer. The reply, however, I generally found to be something like this: " But if I work less, I do not earn enough for the support of my family. Even now, whilst I work so much, I have scarcely enough." There was no trust in God, no real belief in the truth of that word, " Seek ye first the kingdom of God, and his righteousness, and all these things shall be added unto you." I might reply something like this: " My dear brother, it is not your work which supports your family, but the Lord; and he who has fed you and your family when you could not work at all, on account of illness, would surely provide for you and yours, if, for the sake of obtaining food for your inner man, you were to work only for so many hours a day as would allow you proper time for retirement. And is it not the case now that you begin the work of the day after having had only a few hurried moments for prayer; and when you leave off your work in the evening, and mean then to read a little of the word of God, are you not too much worn out in body and mind to enjoy it, and do you not often fall asleep whilst reading the Scriptures, or whilst on your knees in prayer?" The brother would allow it was so; he would allow that my advice was good; but still I read in his countenance, even if he should not have actually said so, " How should I get on if I were to *carry out* your advice?" I longed therefore, to have something to point the brother to, as a visible proof that our God and Father is the same faithful God that he ever was, — as willing as ever to PROVE himself the LIVING GOD, in our day as formerly, *to all who put their trust in him.*

Again; sometimes I found children of God tried in mind by the prospect of old age, when they might be unable to work any longer, and therefore were harassed by the fear of having to go into the poorhouse. If in such a case I pointed out to them how their heavenly Father has always helped those who put their trust in him, they might not *say* that times have changed; but yet it was evident enough that God was not looked upon by them as the LIVING God. I longed to set something before the children of God whereby they might see that he does not forsake, even in our day, those who rely upon him.

Another class of persons were brethren in business, who suffered in their souls, and brought guilt on their consciences, by carrying on their business almost in the same way as unconverted persons do. The competition in trade, the bad times, the over-peopled country, were given as reasons why, if the business were carried on simply according to the word of God, it could not be expected to do well. Such a brother, perhaps, would express the wish that he might be differently situated, but very rarely did I see *that there was a stand made for God; that there was the holy determination to trust in the living God, and to depend on him, in order that a good conscience might be maintained.* To this class, likewise, I desired to show by a visible proof that God is unchangeably the same.

Then there was another class of persons, individuals who were in professions in which they could not continue with a good conscience, or persons who were in an unscriptural position with reference to spiritual things; but both classes feared, on account of the consequences, to give up the profession in which they could not abide with God, or to leave their position, lest they should be thrown out of employment. My spirit longed to be instrumental in strengthening their faith, by giving them not only instances from the word of God of his willingness and ability to help all those who rely upon him, but *to show them by proofs* that he is the same in our day. I well knew *that the word of God ought to be enough;* but I considered that I ought to lend a helping hand to my brethren, if by any means, by this visible proof to the unchangeable faithfulness of the Lord, I might strengthen their hands in God; for I remembered what a great blessing my own soul had received through the Lord's dealings with his servant A. H. Franke, who, in dependence upon the living God alone, established an immense orphan house, which I had seen many times with my own eyes. I therefore judged myself bound to be the servant of the church of Christ in the particular point on which I had obtained mercy; namely, *in being able to take God by his word, and to rely upon it.*

All these exercises of my soul, which resulted from the fact that so many believers with whom I became acquainted were harassed and distressed in mind, or brought guilt on their consciences on account of not trusting in the Lord, were used by God to awaken in my heart the desire of setting before the church at large, and before the world, a proof that he has not in the least changed; and this seemed to me best done by the establishing of an orphan house. It needed to be something which could be seen, even by the natural eye. Now, if I, a poor man, simply by prayer and faith, obtained, *without asking any individual*, the means for establishing and carrying on an orphan house, there would be something which, with the Lord's blessing, might be instrumental in strengthening the faith of the children of God, besides being a testimony to the consciences of the unconverted of the reality of the things of God.

This, then, was the primary reason for establishing the orphan house. I certainly did from my heart desire to be used by God to benefit the bodies of poor children, bereaved of both parents, and seek in other respects, with the help of God, to do them good for this life. I also particularly longed to be used by God in getting the dear orphans trained up in the fear of God; but still, the first and primary object of the work was, and still is, that God might be magnified by the fact that the orphans under my care are provided with all they need, only *by prayer and faith,* without any one being asked by me or my fellow-laborers, whereby it may be seen that God is FAITHFUL STILL, and HEARS PRAYER STILL. That I was not mistaken, has been abundantly proved since November, 1835, both by the conversion of many sinners who have read the accounts which have been published in connection with this work, and also by the abundance of fruit that has followed in the hearts of the saints, for which, from my inmost soul, I desire to be grateful to God, and the honor and glory of which not only is due to him alone, but which I, by his help, am enabled to ascribe to him.

Nov. 28. I have been, every day this week very much in prayer concerning the orphan house, chiefly entreating the Lord to take away every thought concerning it out of my mind if the matter be not of him; and have also repeatedly examined my heart concerning my motives in the matter. But I have been more and more confirmed that it is of God.

Dec. 2. I have again these last days prayed much about the orphan house, and have frequently examined my heart, that if it were at all my desire to establish it for the sake of gratifying myself I might find it out. To that end I have also conversed with brother Craik about it, that he might be instrumental in showing me any hidden corruption of my heart concerning the matter, or any other scriptural reason against my engaging in it. The one only reason which ever made me at all doubt as to its being of God that *I* should engage in this work, is the multiplicity of engagements which I have already. But if the matter be of God, he will in due time send suitable individuals, so that comparatively little of my time will be taken up in this service.

This morning I asked the Lord especially that he would be pleased to teach me through the instrumentality of brother C.; and I went to him, that he might have an opportunity of probing my heart. For as I desire only the Lord's glory, I should be glad to be instructed through the instrumentality of any brother, if the matter be not of him. But brother C., on the contrary, greatly encouraged me in it. Therefore, I have this day taken the first actual step in the matter, in having ordered bills to be printed, announcing a public meeting on Dec. 9, at which I intend to lay before the brethren my thoughts concerning the orphan house, as a means of ascertaining more clearly the Lord's mind concerning the matter. Dec. 5. This evening I was struck, in reading the Scriptures, with these words: "Open thy mouth wide, and I will fill it." I was led to apply this scripture to the orphan house, and asked the Lord for premises, one thousand pounds, and suitable individuals to take care of the children. Dec. 7. To-day I received the first shilling for the orphan house.

Dec. 9. This afternoon the first piece of furniture was given, — a large wardrobe. This afternoon and evening I was low in spirit as it regards the orphan house, but as soon as I began to speak at the meeting I received peculiar assistance from God. After the meeting, ten shillings were given to me. *There was purposely no collection*, nor did any one speak besides myself; for it was not in the least intended to work upon the feelings, for I sought to be quite sure concerning the mind of God. After the meeting, a sister offered herself for the work. I went home, happy in the Lord, and full of confidence that the matter will come to pass, though but ten shillings have been given. Dec. 10. I have sent to the press a statement, which contains the substance of what I said at the meeting last evening

I have received a letter, in which a brother and sister wrote thus: "We propose ourselves for the service of the intended orphan house, if you think us qualified for it; also to give up all the furniture, etc., that the Lord has given us, for its use; and to do this without receiving any salary whatever, believing that if it be the will of the Lord to employ us, he will supply all our need," etc. In the evening a brother brought, from several invividuals, three dishes, twenty-eight plates, three basins, one jug, four mugs, three saltstands, one grater, four knives, and five forks.

Dec. 12. While I was praying this morning that the Lord would give us a fresh token of his favor concerning the orphan house, a brother brought three dishes, twelve plates, one basin, and one blanket. After this had been given, I thanked God, and asked him to give even this day another encouragement. Shortly after, fifty pounds were given, and that by an individual from whom, for several reasons, I could not have expected this sum. Thus the hand of God appeared so much the more clearly. Even then I was led to pray that this day the Lord would give still more. In the evening, accordingly, there were sent, by a sister, twenty-nine yards of print. Also a sister offered herself for the work. Dec. 13. A brother was influenced this day to give four shillings per week, as long as the Lord gives the means; eight shillings were given by him as two weeks' subscription. To-day a brother and sister offered themselves, with all their furniture, and all their provisions which they have in the house, if they can be usefully employed in the concerns of the orphan house.

Dec. 14. To-day a sister offered her services for the work. In the evening another sister offered herself for the institution. Dec. 15. A sister brought, from several friends, ten basins, eight mugs, one plate, five dessert spoons, six teaspoons, one skimmer, one toasting-fork, one flour-dredge, three knives and forks, one sheet, one pillow-case, one table-cloth; also one pound. In the afternoon were sent fifty-five yards of sheeting, and twelve yards of calico. Dec. 16. I took out of the box in my room one shilling. Dec. 17. I was rather cast down last evening and this morning about the matter, questioning whether I ought to be engaged in this way, and was led to ask the Lord to give me some further encouragement. This evening a brother brought a quantity of household articles, and told me that it had been put into the heart of an individual to send to-morrow one hundred pounds.

Dec. 18. This afternoon the same brother brought the hundred pounds above referred to. Since the publication of the second edition, it has pleased the Lord to take to himself the donor of this hundred pounds, and I therefore give, in this present edition, some further account of the donation and the donor.

A. L. was known to me almost from the beginning of my coming to Bristol, in 1832. She earned her bread by needle-work, by which she gained from two shillings to five shillings per week; the average, I suppose, was not more than three shillings sixpence, as she was weak in body. But I do not remember ever to have heard her utter a word of complaint on account of earning so little. Some time before I had been led to establish an orphan house, her father had died, through which event she had come in possession of four hundred and eighty pounds, which sum had been left to her (and the same amount to her brother and two sisters) by her grandmother, but of which her father had had the interest during his lifetime. The father, who had been much given to drinking, died in debt, which debts the children wished to pay; but the rest, besides A. L., did not like to pay in full, and offered to the creditors twenty-five per cent., which they gladly accepted, as they had not the least legal claim upon the children. After the debts had been paid according to this agreement, sister A. L. said to herself, "However sinful my father may have been, yet he was my father, and as I have the means of paying his debts to the full amount, I ought, as a believing child, to do so, seeing that my brother and sisters will not do it." She then went to all the creditors secretly, and paid the full amount of the debts, which took forty pounds more of her money, besides her share, which she had given before. Her brother and two sisters now gave fifty pounds each of their property to their mother; but A. L. said to herself, "I am a *child of God;* surely I ought to give my mother twice as much as my brothers and sisters." She therefore gave her mother one hundred pounds. Shortly after this she sent me the hundred pounds towards the orphan house. I was not a little surprised when I received this money from her, for I had always known her as a poor girl, and I had never heard anything about her having come into the possession of this money, and her dress had never given me the least indication of an alteration in her circumstances. Before, however, accepting this money from her, I had a long conversation with her, in which I sought to probe her as to her motives, and in which I sought to ascertain whether, as I had feared, she might have given this money in the feeling of the moment, without having counted the cost. But I had not conversed long with this beloved sister, before I found that she was, in this particular, a quiet, calm, considerate follower of the Lord Jesus, and one who desired, in spite of what human reason might say, to act according to the words of our Lord, "Lay not up for yourselves treasures upon earth." "Sell that ye have, and give alms." When I remonstrated with her, in order that I might see whether she counted the cost, she said to me, "The Lord Jesus has given his *last* drop of blood for me, and should I not give him this hundred pounds?" She would also have me take five pounds for the poor saints in communion with us. I mention here particularly that this dear sister kept all these things to herself, and did them as much as possible in secret; and during her lifetime, I suppose, not six brethren and sisters among us knew that she had ever possessed four hundred and eighty pounds, or that she had given one hundred pounds towards the orphan house.

I relate one instance more. August 4, 1836, seven months and a half after she had given the hundred pounds, she came one morning to me, and said: "Last evening I felt myself particularly stirred up to pray about the funds of the Scriptural Knowledge Institution; but whilst praying, I thought, *what good is it for me to pray for means, if I do not give when I have the means*, and I have therefore brought you these five pounds." As I had reason to believe that, by this time, by far the greater part of her money was gone, I again had a good deal of conversation with her, to see whether she really did count the cost, and whether this donation also was given unto the Lord, or from momentary excitement, in which case it was better not to give the money. However, she was at this time also steadfast, grounded upon the word of God, and evidently constrained by the love of Christ; and all the effect my conversation had upon her was, that she said, "You must take five shillings in addition to the five pounds, as a proof that I give the five pounds cheerfully." And thus she constrained me to take the five pounds and five shillings. —Four things are especially to be noticed about this beloved sister, with reference to all this period of her earthly pilgrimage: 1. She did all these things in secret, avoiding to the utmost all show about them, and thus proved that she did not desire the praise of man 2. She remained, as before, of an humble and lowly mind, and she proved thus that she had done what she did unto the Lord, and not unto man. 3. Her dress remained, during all the time that she had this comparative abundance, the same as before. It was clean, yet as simple and as inexpensive as it was at the time when all her income consisted of three shillings and sixpence, or at most five shillings per week. There was not the least difference as to her lodging, dress, manner of life, etc. She remained in every way the poor handmaid of the Lord, as to all outward appearance. 4. But that which is as lovely as the rest, she continued working at her needle all this time. She earned her two shillings-sixpence, or three shillings, or a little more, a week, by her work, as before; whilst she gave away the money in sovereigns or five-pound notes. At last all her money was gone, and that some years before she fell asleep; and as her bodily health never had been good as long as I had known her, and was now much worse, she found herself peculiarly dependent upon the Lord, who never forsook her, up to the last moments of her earthly course. Her body became weaker and weaker, in consequence of which she was able to work very little, for many months before she died; but the Lord supplied her with all she needed, though she never asked for anything. For instance, a sister in communion with us sent her, for many months, all the bread she used. Her mouth was full of thanksgiving, even in the midst of the greatest bodily sufferings.

Dec. 31. This evening we had a special meeting for prayer and praise. There have been received into the church, during the past year, 59. There are men in communion with us, 95. I have received for my temporal wants, in freewill offerings, presents, etc., £285 1s. 1¼d.

During January to May of 1836, numerous donations were made of furniture, provisions, half-worn clothing, and money (varying from one hundred pounds to a halfpenny). Encouraged by these *unsolicited* offerings, Mr. Müller determined to open the Orphan House.

April 21. This day was set apart for prayer and

thanksgiving concerning the Orphan House, as it is now opened. In the morning, several brethren prayed, and brother Craik spoke on the last verses of Psalm xx. In the afternoon, I addressed our day and Sunday school children, the orphans, and other children present. In the evening we had another prayer meeting. There are now seventeen children in the Orphan House.

May 6. I have now been for some years, and especially these last few months, more or less thinking and praying respecting publishing a short account of the Lord's dealings with me. To-day I have at last settled to do so, and have begun to write.

May 16. For these several weeks our income has been little; and though I had prayed many times that the Lord would enable us to put by the taxes, yet the prayer remained unanswered. In the midst of it all, my comfort was, that the Lord would send help by the time it would be needed. One thing particularly has been a trial to us of late, far more than our own temporal circumstances, which is, that we have scarcely, in any measure, been able to relieve the distress among the poor saints. To-day, the Lord, at last, after I had many times prayed to him for these weeks past, answered my prayers, there being seven pounds twelve shillings and one farthing given to me as my part of the freewill offerings through the boxes, — two five-pound notes having been put in yesterday, one for brother Craik and one for me. Thus the Lord has again delivered us, and answered our prayers, and that *not one single hour too late;* for the taxes have not as yet been called for. May he fill my heart with gratitude for this fresh deliverance, and may he be pleased to enable me more and more to trust in him, and to wait patiently for his help.

CHAPTER VIII.

THE FIELD WIDENING.

1836 — 1837.

AN UNEXPECTED OBSTACLE — IMPLICIT SUBMISSION — A SECOND ORPHAN HOUSE PROPOSED — AN ENCOURAGING TEXT — THE NEW ORPHAN HOUSE OPENED — COMPLETED ANSWER TO PRAYER — PROGRESS OF THE LORD'S WORK — THE OVERSIGHT OF THE FLOCK.

MAY 18, 1836. In the foregoing pages, a statement has been given of the success with which the Lord has been pleased to crown the prayers of his servant respecting the establishment of an Orphan House in this city. The subject of my prayer was that he would graciously provide a house, either as a loan or as a gift, or that some one might be led to pay the rent for one; further, that he would give me one thousand pounds for the object, and likewise suitable individuals to take care of the children. A day or two after, I was led to ask, in addition to the above, that he would put it into the hearts of his people to send me articles of furniture, and some clothes for the children. In answer to these petitions, many articles of furniture, clothing, and food were sent; a conditional offer of a house, as a gift, was made; individuals proposed themselves to take care of the children, and various sums of money were given, varying from one hundred pounds to a halfpenny.

It may be well to state that the above results have followed in answer to prayer, without any one having been asked by me for one single thing; from which I have refrained, not on account of want of confidence in the brethren, or because I doubted their love to the Lord, but that I might see the hand of God so much the more clearly.

So far as I remember, I brought even the most minute circumstances concerning the Orphan House before the Lord in my petitions, being conscious of my own weakness and ignorance. There was, however, one point I never had prayed about, namely, that the Lord would send children; for I naturally took it for granted that there would be plenty of applications. The appointed time came, and not even one application was made. This circumstance now led me to lie low before my God in prayer, and to examine my heart once more as to all the motives concerning it; and being able, as formerly, to say that his glory was my chief aim, *i. e.*, that it might be seen that it is not a vain thing to trust in the living God, and still continuing in prayer, I was at last brought to this state, that I could say *from my heart* that I should rejoice in God being glorified in this matter, though it were *by bringing the whole to nothing*. But as still, after all, it seemed to me more tending to the glory of God to establish and prosper the Orphan House, I could then ask him heartily to send applications. I enjoyed now a peaceful state of heart concerning the subject, and was also more assured than ever that God would establish it. *The very next day* the first application was made, and within a short time forty-three applied. I rented the house No. 6, Wilson street, as being, on account of its cheapness and largeness, very suitable.

I have mentioned that we intended to take in the children from the seventh to the twelfth year. But after six applications had been made for children between four and six years of age, it became a subject of solemn prayerful consideration, whether, as long as there were vacancies, such children should not be received, though so young. I came at last to the conclusion to take in the little girls under seven years of age, for whom application had been made. Further, it had been repeatedly brought before me, how desirable it would be to establish also, in this city, an Orphan House for *male* children, and there were even articles sent for *little orphan boys*. Partly, then, on account of these reasons; and partly because the Institution already opened was quite filled in a few days; and partly because the Lord has done hitherto far above what I could have expected; I have at last, after repeated prayer, come to the conclusion, in the name of the Lord, and in dependence upon him alone for support, to propose the establishment of an Infant Orphan House.

June 3. From May 16 up to this day I have been confined to the house, and a part of the time to my bed, on account of a local inflammation, which keeps me from walking. Almost every day during this time I have been able to continue writing a narrative of the Lord's dealings with me, which had been again laid aside after May 7, on account of a number of pressing engagements. It is very remarkable that the greatest objection against writing it for the press was want of time. Now, through this affliction, which leaves my mind free, and gives me time, on account of confinement to the house, I have been able to write about a hundred quarto pages.

June 14. This morning brother C——r and I prayed unitedly, chiefly about the schools and the circulation of the Scriptures. Besides asking for blessings upon the work, we have also asked the Lord for the means which are needed; for on July 1, seventeen pounds ten shillings will be due for the rent of school-rooms, and besides this, we want at least forty pounds more to go on with the circulation of the Scriptures, to pay the salaries of the masters, etc. Towards all this we have only about seven pounds. I also prayed for the remainder of the thousand pounds for the Orphan House.

June 21. This evening brother C——r and I found that the Lord had not only been pleased to send us, through the offerings which have come in during the last week, in answer to our prayers, the seventeen pounds ten shillings which will be due for the rent of two school-rooms on July 1, but that we have five pounds more than is needed. Thus the Lord once more has answered our prayers.

July 28. For some weeks past we have not been able to pay the salary of the masters and governesses *a month in advance*, but have been obliged to pay it *weekly*. Brother C——r and I have lately prayed repeatedly together respecting the funds, but we were now brought so low, that we should not have been able to pay even this *weekly* salary of the teachers, had not the Lord most remarkably helped us again to-day. For, besides one pound, which was given to us, this evening a brother gave eight pounds, which sum had been made up by a number of his workmen *paying weekly one penny each*, of their own accord, towards our funds. The money had been collecting for many months, and, in this our necessity, it had been put into the heart of this brother to bring it.

July 29. This evening, from six to half-past nine, we had a meeting for inquirers. There came twelve fresh cases before us.

Oct. 1. To-day, in dependence upon the Lord alone for means, we engaged a brother as a master for a sixth day school. On account of the many deliverances which we have had of late, we have not hesitated to enlarge the field, as another boys' school was greatly needed.

Oct. 5. This evening twenty-five pounds were given to me for the Scriptural Knowledge Institution. Thus the Lord has already given the means of defraying the expenses of the new boys' school for some months to come.

Oct. 19. To-day, after having many times prayed respecting the matter, I have at last engaged a sister as matron for the Infant Orphan House, never having been able, up to this day, to meet with an individual who seemed suitable, though there has been money enough in hand, for some time past, for commencing this work, and there have been applications made for several infant orphans.

Oct. 25. To-day we obtained, without any trouble, through the kind hand of God, very suitable premises for the Infant Orphan House.

Nov. 5. There were given by a brother one hundred pounds, fifty pounds of which were previously promised, to insure the rent for premises. It is a remarkable fact, concerning this donation, that I had, in December of last year, repeatedly asked the Lord to incline the heart of this brother to give these hundred pounds, and I made a memorandum of this prayer in my journal of December 12, 1835. On January 25, 1836, fifty pounds were promised by him, and on November 5, fifty pounds besides that sum were given; but it was not till some days after, that I remembered that the very sum for which I had asked the Lord had been given. When it came to my mind that this prayer had been noted down in my journal, and I showed it to the donor, we rejoiced together; *he*, to have been the instrument in giving, and *I* to have had the request granted.

Nov. 30. On account of many pressing engagements, I had not been led, for some time past, to pray respecting the funds. But *being in great need*, I was led, yesterday morning, earnestly to ask the Lord; and in answer to this petition a brother gave me, last evening, ten pounds. He had had it in his heart, for several months past, to give this sum, but had been hitherto kept from it, not having the means. Just now, in this our great necessity, the Lord furnished him with the means, and we were helped in this way. In addition to these ten pounds, I received last evening a letter with five pounds, from a sister whom I never saw, and who has been several times used by God as an instrument to supply our wants. She writes thus: "It has been so much on my mind lately to send you some money, that I feel as if there must be some need, which the Lord purposes to honor me by making me the instrument of supplying. I therefore enclose you five pounds, all I have in the house at this moment."

Dec. 9. One pound, with Mark ix. 36–7: "And taking a little child, he set him in the midst of them," etc., a most encouraging passage for this work, the force of which I had never felt before.

Dec. 15. This day was set apart for prayer and thanksgiving respecting the Infant Orphan House, which was opened on Nov. 28. In the morning we had a prayer meeting. In the afternoon, besides prayer and thanksgiving, I addressed the children of our day schools and the orphans, about 350, on Ecclesiastes xii. 1.

Dec. 31. We had this evening a prayer meeting to praise the Lord for his goodness during the past year, and to ask him for a continuance of his favors.

During the past year there have been received into the church, 52; and the Lord has been pleased to give me, as it regards my temporal supplies, £232 11s. 9d.

REVIEW OF THE YEAR 1836.

In addition to the items mentioned above, donations were received during the year, of money, food, clothes, books, boxes, coal-hods, ornaments (to be sold), etc.; also, the offer of gratuitous medical attendance, and medicine. Up to the close of 1836, seven hundred and seventy pounds and ninepence halfpenny had been given, and forty pounds promised.

Jan. 2, 1837. This evening the two churches had again an especial prayer meeting.

Jan. 5. To-day a sister called and told me about the conversion of her father, who, in his eightieth year, after having for many years lived openly in sin, is at last brought to the knowledge of the Lord. This sister had long prayed for the conversion of her father, and at last, though only after twenty years, the Lord gave her the desire of her heart.

May 18. There are now sixty-four children in the two Orphan Houses, and two more are expected, which will fill the two houses.

May 28. The narrative of some of the Lord's dealings with me is now near being published, which has led me again most earnestly this day week, and repeatedly since, to ask the Lord that he would be pleased to give me what is wanting of the one thousand pounds, for which sum I have asked him on behalf of the orphans; for though, in my own mind, the thing is as good as done, so much so that I have repeatedly been able to thank God that he will surely give me every shilling of that sum, yet to others this will not be enough. As the whole matter, then, about the Orphan House had been commenced for the glory of God, that in this way before the world and the church there might be another visible proof that the Lord delights in answering prayer; and as there was yet a part of the thousand pounds wanting; and *as I earnestly desired the book might not leave the press* before every shilling of that sum had been given in answer to prayer, *without one single individual having been asked by me for anything*, that thus I might have the sweet privilege of bearing my testimony for God in this book; — for these reasons, I say, I have given myself earnestly to prayer about this matter since May 21. On May 22 came in seven pounds and ten shillings, and on May 23, three pounds. On May 24, a lady, whom I never saw before, called on me, and gave me forty pounds. This circumstance has greatly encouraged me; for the Lord showed me thereby, afresh, his willingness to continue to send us *large sums*, and that they can even come from individuals whom we have never seen before.

June 15. To-day I gave myself once more earnestly to prayer respecting the remainder of the thousand pounds. This evening five pounds were given, so that now the whole sum is made up. During eighteen months and ten days this petition has been brought before God almost daily. From the moment I asked till the Lord granted it fully, I had never been allowed to doubt that he would give every shilling of that sum. Often have I praised him beforehand, in the assurance that he would grant my request. The thing after which we have especially to seek in prayer is, that we believe that we receive, according to Mark xi. 24: "*What things soever ye desire, when ye pray, believe that ye receive them, and ye shall have them.*"

As the Lord has so greatly condescended to listen to my prayers, and as I consider it one of the particular talents which he has entrusted to me to exercise faith upon his promises, as it regards my own temporal wants and those of others; and as an Orphan House for *boys* above seven years of age seems greatly needed in this city; and as also without it we know not how to provide for the little *boys* in the Infant Orphan House, when they are above seven years of age, I purpose to establish an Orphan House for about forty boys above seven years of age.

July 12. The same friend who gave me on May 24, 1837, forty pounds for the orphans, and whom, up to that time, 1 had never seen, gave four hundred and sixty pounds more being altogether five hundred pounds.

It is now three years and four months since brother Craik and I began, in dependence upon the Lord for funds, to seek to help the spread of the gospel through the instrumentality of schools, the circulation of the Holy Scriptures, and by aiding missionary exertions. Since then there have been circulated, through our instrumentality, 4,030 copies of the Scriptures; four day schools, for poor children, have been *established* by us; 1,119 children have been instructed in the six day schools, and 353 children are now in those six day schools. Besides this, a Sunday school and an adult school have been supplied with all they needed, and missionary exertions in the East Indies, in Upper Canada, and on the continent of Europe, have been aided. In addition to this, the word of God has been preached from house to house among the poor, in connection with the Scriptural Knowledge Institution, by brother C———r, within the last two years.

On the fifteenth of August, 1837, the preceding portion of this narrative was published.

Aug. 17. To-day two more children were received into the Infant Orphan House, which makes up our full number, sixty-six in the Girls' and Infant Orphan Houses.

Sept. 2. I have been looking about for a house for the orphan boys, these last three days. Everything else has been provided. The Lord has given suitable individuals to take care of the children, money, etc. In his own time he will give a house also.

Sept. 19. It was to-day particularly impressed upon my heart that I ought to seek for more retirement, though the work should *apparently* suffer ever so much; and that arrangements should be made whereby I may be able to visit the brethren more, as an *unvisited* church will sooner or later become an *unhealthy church*. Pastors, as fellow-laborers, are greatly needed among us.

Sept. 28. I have for a long time been too much outwardly engaged. Yesterday morning I spent about three hours in the vestry at Gideon, to be able to have more time for retirement. I meant to do the same in the afternoon, but before I could leave the house I was called on, and thus one person after the other came, till I had to go out. Thus it has been again to-day.

Oct. 16. For a long time past Brother Craik and I have felt the importance of more pastoral visiting, and it has been *one of our greatest trials* that we have been unable to give more time to it. This evening we had purposely a meeting of the two churches, at which brother Craik and I, and a brother from Devonshire, spoke on: I. The importance of pastoral visiting. II. The particular obstacles which hindered us in attending to it. III. The question whether there was any way of removing some of the obstacles.

I. As to the importance of pastoral visiting, the following points were mentioned: 1. Watching over the saints. by means of visiting them, to prevent coldness, or to recover them from backsliding. 2. To counsel and advise them in family affairs, in their business, and in spiritual matters. 3. To keep up that loving and familiar intercourse which is so desirable between saints and those who have the oversight of them. These visits should be, if possible, frequent; but in our case there have been several obstacles in the way.

II. The particular obstacles in our case are: 1. The largeness of the number who are in communion with us. One hundred would be quite as many as we have strength to visit regularly, and as often as would be desirable; but there are nearly four hundred in fellowship with us. 2. The distance of the houses of the saints from our own dwellings, as many live more than two miles off. 3. The Lord's blessing upon our labors. Not one year has passed away, since we have been in Bristol, without more than fifty having been added to our number, each of whom, in general, needed several times to be conversed with before being admitted into fellowship. 4. That brother Craik and I have each of us the care of two churches. At the first sight it appears as if the work is thus divided, but the double number of meetings, etc., nearly double the work. 5. The mere ruling, and taking care, in general, of a large body of believers, irrespective of the other work, takes much more time, and requires much more strength, than the taking care of a small body of believers, as we, by grace, desire not to allow known sin among us. 6. The position which we have in the church at large brings many brethren to us who travel through Bristol, who call on us, or lodge with us, and to whom, according to the Lord's will, we have to give some time. 7. In my own case, an extensive needful correspondence. 8. The weakness of body on the part of both of us. When the preaching is done, — when strangers who lodge with us are gone, — when the calls at our house are over, — when the needful letters, however briefly, are written, — when the necessary church business is settled, — our minds are often so worn out that we are glad to be quiet. 9. But suppose we have bodily strength remaining, after the above things have been attended to, yet the frame of mind is not always so as that one could visit. After having been particularly tried by church matters, which in so large a body does not rarely occur, or being cast down in one's own soul, one may be fit for the closet, but not for visiting the saints. 10. Lastly, in my own case, no small part of my time is taken up by attending to the affairs of the Orphan Houses, schools, the circulation of the Scriptures, the aiding missionary efforts, and other work connected with the Scriptural Knowledge Institution.

III. What is to be done under these circumstances? 1. In the days of the apostles there would have been more brethren to take the oversight of so large a body as we are. The Lord has not laid upon us a burden which is too heavy for us; he is not a hard Master. It is evident that he does not mean us *even to attempt to visit all the saints* as much as is evidently needful, and much less as frequently as it would be desirable. We mention this, to prevent uncomfortable feelings on the part of the dear saints under our pastoral care, who find themselves not as much visited as they used to be when we came to Bristol, when the number of them was not seventy, and now it is about four hundred, and when in many other respects the work in our hands was not half so much as it is now, and when we had much more bodily strength. 2. It is therefore evident that there are other pastors needed; not nominal pastors, but such as the Lord has called, to whom he has given a pastor's heart and pastoral gifts. 3. Such may be raised up by the Lord from our own number, or the Lord may send them from elsewhere. 4. But in the mean time we should at least see whether there are not helpers among us. 5. As to the work itself, in order that time may be saved, it appears desirable that the two churches, Bethesda and Gideon, should be united into one, that the breaking of bread should be alternately, and that the number of weekly meetings should be reduced.

Oct. 21. To-day the Lord has given me a house for the Orphan Boys, in the same street in which the other two Orphan Houses are.

Mr. Muller's health having suffered from his cares, money was sent him from unexpected sources, to be used in travelling and recreation.

REVIEW OF THE YEAR 1837.

1. There are now eighty-one children in the three Orphan Houses, and nine brethren and sisters, who have the care of them. Ninety, therefore, daily sit down to table. Lord, look on the necessities of thy servant!

2. The schools require as much help as before; nay, more, particularly the Sunday school, in which there are at present about 320 children, and in the day schools about 350. Lord, thy servant is a poor man; but he has trusted in thee, and made his boast in thee, before the sons of men; therefore let him not be confounded! Let it not be said all this was enthusiasm, and therefore it is come to naught!

3. My temporal supplies have been £307 2s. 6½d.

CHAPTER IX.

TRIAL.

1838.

THE MINISTRY OF SICKNESS — PEACE OF MIND — JESUS A PRESENT HELP — DEEP POVERTY — PLEADING WITH GOD — UNITED PRAYER.

JANUARY 6, 1838. I feel little better in my head, though my general health seems improved; but my kind physician says I am much better, and advises now change of air. This evening a sister, who resides about fifty miles from hence, and who is quite unacquainted with the medical advice given to me this morning, sent me fifteen pounds for the express purpose of change of air; and wrote that she felt assured, from having been similarly afflicted, that nothing would do me so much good, humanly speaking, as quiet and change of air.

Jan. 7. This is the ninth Lord's day that I have been kept from ministering in the word. My affliction is connected with a great tendency to irritability of temper; yea, with some satanic feeling, foreign to me even naturally.

Jan. 10. To-day I went with my family to Trowbridge.
Jan 14. Lord's day. I have spent several hours in prayer to-day, and read on my knees, and prayed for two hours over Psalm lxiii. God has blessed my soul much to-day. My soul is now brought into that state that I delight myself in the will of God, as it regards my health. Yea, I can now say, *from my heart*, I would not have this disease removed till God, by its means, has bestowed the blessing for which it was sent.

His health remaining feeble, Mr. M. left England on April 6, for Germany, and returned to Bristol, May 7. He continues his narrative: —

May 8. This evening I went to the prayer meeting at Gideon. I read Psalm ciii., and was able to thank the Lord publicly for my late affliction. This is the first time that I have taken any part in the public meetings of the brethren since November 6, 1837.

July 12. The funds, which were this day twelvemonth about seven hundred and eighty pounds, are now reduced to about twenty pounds; but, thanks be to the Lord, my faith is as strong or stronger, than it was when we had the larger sum in hand; nor has he at any time, from the commencement of the work, allowed me to distrust him. Nevertheless, as our Lord will be inquired of, and as real faith is manifested as such by leading to prayer, I gave myself to prayer with brother T——, of the Boys' Orphan House, who had called on me, and who, besides my wife and brother Craik, is the only individual to whom I speak about the state of the funds. While we were praying, an orphan child from Frome was brought, and some believers at Frome, having collected among them five pounds, sent this money with the child. Thus we received the first answer at a time of need. *We have given notice for seven children to come in, and purpose to give notice for five more, though our funds are so low, hoping that God will look on our necessities.*

July 17, 18. These two days we have had two especial prayer meetings, from six to nine in the evening, to commend publicly to the Lord the Boys' Orphan House. Our funds are now very low. There are about twenty pounds in hand, and in a few days thirty pounds, at least, will be needed; but I *purposely* avoided saying anything about our present necessities, and spoke only to the praise of God, about the abundance with which our gracious Father, " the

Father of the fatherless," has hitherto supplied us. This was done in order that the hand of God, in sending help, may be so much the more clearly seen.

July 22. This evening I was walking in our little garden, meditating on Heb. xiii. 8, "Jesus Christ, the same yesterday, and to-day, and forever." Whilst meditating on his unchangeable love, power, wisdom, etc., and turning all, as I went on, into prayer respecting myself; and whilst applying likewise his unchangeable love, and power, and wisdom, etc., both to my present spiritual and temporal circumstances, — all at once the present need of the Orphan Houses was brought to my mind. Immediately I was led to say to myself, Jesus in his love and power has hitherto supplied me with what I have needed for the orphans, and in the same unchangeable love and power he will provide me with what I may need for the future. A flow of joy came into my soul whilst realizing thus the unchangeableness of our adorable Lord. About one minute after, a letter was brought me, enclosing a bill for twenty pounds.

Aug. 18. I have not one penny in hand for the orphans. In a day or two again many pounds will be needed. My eyes are to the Lord. Evening. Before this day is over, I have received from a sister five pounds. She had some time since put away her trinkets, to be sold for the benefit of the orphans. This morning, whilst in prayer, it came to her mind, "I have this five pounds, and owe no man anything, therefore it would be better to give this money at once, as it may be some time before I can dispose of the trinkets." She therefore brought it, little knowing that there was not a penny in hand.

Aug. 29. To-day sixteen believers were baptized. Among those who were baptized was an aged brother of above eighty-four years, and one above seventy. For the latter, his believing wife had prayed thirty-eight years, and at last the Lord answered her prayers in his conversion.

Aug. 31. I have been waiting on the Lord for means,

as the matron's books from the Girls' Orphan House have been brought, and there is no money in hand to advance for housekeeping. But, as yet, the Lord has not been pleased to send help. As the matron called to-day for money, one of the laborers gave two pounds of his own, for the present necessities.

Sept. 1. The Lord in his wisdom and love has not yet sent help. Whence it is to come, need not be my care. But *I believe* God will, in due time, send help. His hour is not yet come. As there was money needed in the Boys' Orphan House also, the same brother just alluded to gave two pounds for that also. Thus we were delivered at this time likewise. But now his means are gone. This is the most trying hour that as yet I have had in the work, as it regards means; but I know that I shall yet praise the Lord for his help.

Sept. 5. Our hour of trial continues still. The Lord mercifully has given enough to supply our daily necessities; but he gives *by the day* now, and almost *by the hour*, as we need it. Nothing came in yesterday. I have besought the Lord again and again, both yesterday and to-day. It is as if the Lord said: "Mine hour has not yet come." But I have faith in God. I believe that he surely will send help, though I know not whence it is to come. Many pounds are needed within a few days, and there is not a penny in hand. This morning two pounds were given, for the present necessities, by one of the laborers in the work. Evening. This very day the Lord sent again some help to encourage me to continue to wait on him, and to trust in him. As I was praying this afternoon respecting the matter, I felt fully assured that the Lord would send help, and praised him beforehand for his help, and asked him to encourage our hearts through it. I have been also led, yesterday and to-day, to ask the Lord especially that he would not allow my faith to fail. A few minutes after I had prayed, brother T—— came and brought four pounds one shilling and fivepence, which had come in in several small donations. He told me, at the same time, that to-morrow the books would be brought from the Infant Orphan House, when money must be advanced for housekeeping. I thought for a moment it might be well to keep three pounds of this money for that purpose. But it occurred to me immediately, "*Sufficient unto the day is the evil thereof.*" The Lord can provide by to-morrow much more than I need; and I therefore sent three pounds to one of the sisters whose quarterly salary was due, and the remaining one pound one shilling and fivepence to the Boys' Orphan House for housekeeping. Thus I am still penniless. My hope is in God; he will provide.

Sept. 6. This morning the books were brought from the Infant Orphan House, and the matron sent to ask when she should fetch them, implying when they would have been looked over, and when money would be advanced for housekeeping. I said "to-morrow," though I had not a single penny in hand. About an hour after, brother T—— sent me a note, to say that he had received one pound this morning, and that last evening a brother had sent twenty-nine pounds of salt, forty-four dozen of onions, and twenty-six pounds of groats.[1]

Sept. 7. The time had come that I had to send money to the Infant Orphan House, but the Lord had not sent any more. I gave, therefore, the pound which had come in yesterday, and two shillings and twopence which had been put into the box in my house, trusting to the good Lord to send in more.

Sept 8. It has not pleased my gracious Lord to send me help as yet. Yesterday and to-day I have been pleading with God eleven arguments why he would be graciously pleased to send help. The arguments which I plead with God are: —

---

[1] Groats. Oats or other grain, with the hulls removed. — ED.

1. That I set about the work for the glory of God, *i. e.*, that there might be a visible proof, by God supplying, *in answer to prayer only*, the necessities of the orphans, that he is the *living* God, and most willing, even in *our* day, to answer prayer; and that, therefore, he would be pleased to send supplies.

2. That God is the "Father of the fatherless," and that he, therefore, as their father, would be pleased to provide. Psalm lxviii. 5.

3. That I have received the children in the name of Jesus, and that therefore he, in these children, has been received, and is fed, and is clothed; and that therefore he would be pleased to consider this. Mark ix. 36, 37.

4. That the faith of many of the children of God has been strengthened by this work hitherto, and that, if God were to withhold the means for the future, those who are weak in faith would be staggered; whilst, by a continuance of means, their faith might still farther be strengthened.

5. That many enemies would laugh, were the Lord to withhold supplies, and say, Did we not foretell that this enthusiasm would come to nothing?

6. That many of the children of God who are uninstructed, or in a carnal state, would feel themselves *justified* to continue their alliance with the world in the work of God, and to go on as heretofore in their unscriptural proceedings respecting similar institutions, so far as the obtaining of means is concerned, if he were not to help me.

7. That the Lord would remember that I am his child, and that he would graciously pity me, and remember that *I* cannot provide for these children, and that therefore he would not allow this burden to be upon me long without sending help.

8. That he would remember likewise my fellow-laborers in the work, who trust in him, but who would be tried were he to withhold supplies.

9. That he would remember that I should have to dismiss the children from under our scriptural instruction to their former companions.

10. That he would show that those were mistaken who said, that, *at the first*, supplies might be expected, while the thing was new, but not afterwards.

11. That I should not know, were he to withhold means, what construction I should put upon all the many most remarkable answers to prayer which he had given me heretofore in connection with this work, and which most fully have shown to me that it is of God.

In some small measure I now understand experimentally, the meaning of that word " *how long,*" which so frequently occurs in the prayers of the Psalms. But even now, by the grace of God, my eyes are unto him only, and I believe that he will send help.

Sept. 10. Monday morning. Neither Saturday nor yesterday had any money come in. It appeared to me now needful to take some steps on account of our need, *i. e.*, to go to the Orphan Houses, call the brethren and sisters together (who, except brother T——, had never been informed about the state of the funds), state the case to them, see how much money was needed for the present, tell them that amidst all this trial of faith I still believed that God would help, and to pray with them. Especially, also, I meant to go for the sake of telling them that no more articles must be purchased than we have the means to pay for, but to let there be nothing lacking in any way to the children, as it regards nourishing food and needful clothing; for I would rather at once send them away than that they should lack. I meant to go for the sake also of seeing whether there were still articles remaining which had been sent for the purpose of being sold, or whether there were any articles really needless, that we might turn them into money. I felt that the matter was now come to a solemn crisis. About half-past nine sixpence came in, which had been put anonymously into the box at Gideon Chapel. This money seemed to me like an earnest that God would have compassion and send more. About ten, after I had returned from brother Craik, to whom I had unbosomed my heart again, whilst once more in prayer for help, a sister called who gave two sovereigns to my wife for the orphans, stating that she had felt herself stirred up to come, and that she had delayed coming already too long. A few minutes after, when I went into the room where she was, she gave me two sovereigns more, and all this without knowing the least about our need. Thus the Lord most mercifully has sent us a little help, to the great encouragement of my faith. A few minutes after I was called on for money from the Infant Orphan House, to which I sent two pounds, and one pound sixpence to the Boys' Orphan House, and one pound to the Girls' Orphan House.

To-day I saw a young brother who, as well as one of his sisters, has been brought to the knowledge of the Lord through my Narrative.

Sept. 11. The good Lord, in his wisdom, still sees it needful to keep us very low. But this afternoon brother T—— called, and told me that one of our fellow-laborers had sold his metal watch, and two gold pins, for one pound one shilling, that nine shillings sixpence had come in, and that two of our fellow-laborers had sent two lots of books of their own, nineteen and twenty-one in number, to be sold for the orphans.

Sept. 12. Still the trial continues. Only nine shillings came in to-day, given by one of the laborers. In the midst of this great trial of faith the Lord still mercifully keeps me in great peace. He also allows me to see that our labor is not in vain; for yesterday died Leah Cullhford, one of the orphans, about nine years old, truly converted, and brought to the faith some months before her departure.

Sept. 13. No help has come yet. This morning I found it was absolutely needful to tell the brethren and sisters about the state of the funds, and to give necessary directions as to going into debt, etc. We prayed together, and had a very happy meeting. They all seemed comfortable. Twelve shillings sixpence was taken out of the boxes in the three houses, twelve shillings one of the laborers gave, and one pound one shilling had come in for needlework done by the children. One of the sisters, who is engaged in the work, sent a message after me, not to trouble myself about her salary, for she should not want any for a twelvemonth.

Sept. 14. I met again this morning with the brethren and sisters for prayer, as the Lord has not yet sent help. After prayer one of the laborers gave me all the money he had, sixteen shillings, saying that it would not be upright to pray, if he were not to give what he had. One of the sisters told me that in six days she would give me six pounds, which she had in the savings-bank for such a time of need. Up to this day, the matrons of the three houses had been in the habit of paying the bakers and the milkman weekly, *because they had preferred to receive the payments in this way*, and sometimes it had thus been also with the butcher and grocer. But now, as the Lord deals out to us *by the day*, we consider it would be wrong to go on any longer in this way, as the week's payment might become due, and we have no money to meet it; and thus those with whom we deal might be inconvenienced by us, and we be found acting against the commandment of the Lord, "Owe no man anything." (Rom. xiii. 8.) From this day, and henceforward, whilst the Lord gives to us our supplies by the day, we purpose, therefore to pay at once for every article as it is purchased, and never to buy anything except we can pay for it at once, however much it may seem to be needed, and however much those with whom we deal may wish to be paid only by the week. The little which was owed was paid off this day.

Sept. 15. *Saturday.* We met again this morning for prayer. God comforts our hearts. We are looking for help. I found that there were provisions enough for to-day and to-morrow, but there was no money in hand to take in bread as usual, in order that the children might not have newly baked bread. This afternoon one of the laborers, who had been absent for several days from Bristol, returned, and gave one pound. This evening we met again for prayer, when I found that ten shillings sixpence more had come in since the morning. With this one pound ten shillings sixpence we were able to buy, even this Saturday evening, the usual quantity of bread (as it might be difficult to get stale bread on Monday morning), and have some money left. God be praised, who gave us grace to come to the decision not to take any bread to-day, as usual, nor to buy anything for which we cannot pay at once. We were very comfortable, thankfully taking this money out of our Father's hands, as a proof that he still cares for us, and that, in his own time, he will send us larger sums.

CHAPTER X.

DELIVERANCE.

1838.

"PERPLEXED BUT NOT IN DESPAIR"—FAITH JUSTIFIED—A LESSON OF OBE-
DIENCE—BOUNTIFUL SUPPLIES—SPIRITUAL INGATHERING—A DAY OF
MERCIES—TIMELY AID—A SEASON OF PLENTY—OBEDIENCE REWARDED.

SEPTEMBER 17. The trial still continues. It is now more and more trying, even to faith, as each day comes. But I am sure God will send help, if we can but wait. One of the laborers had had a little money come in, of which he gave twelve shillings sixpence; another laborer gave eleven shillings eightpence, being all the money she had left; this, with seventeen shillings sixpence, which partly had come in, and partly was in hand, enabled us to pay what needed to be paid, and to purchase provisions, so that nothing yet, in any way, has been lacking. This evening I was rather tried respecting the long delay of larger sums coming; but being led to go to the Scriptures for comfort, my soul was greatly refreshed, and my faith again strengthened, by Psalm xxxiv., so that I went very cheerfully to meet with my dear fellow-laborers for prayer. I read to them the Psalm, and sought to cheer their hearts through the precious promises contained in it.

Sept. 18. Brother T. had twenty-five shillings in hand, and I had three shillings. This one pound eight shillings enabled us to buy the meat and bread which were needed, a little tea for one of the houses, and milk for all; no more than this is needed. Thus the Lord has provided not only for this day, but there is bread for two days in hand. Now, however, we are come to an extremity. The funds are exhausted. The laborers who had a little money have given as long as they had any left. Now observe how the Lord helped us! A lady from the neighborhood of London, who brought a parcel with money from her daughter, arrived four or five days since in Bristol, and took lodgings next door to the Boys' Orphan House. This afternoon she herself kindly brought me the money, amounting to three pounds two shillings and sixpence. We had been reduced so low as to be on the point of selling those things which could be spared; but this morning I had asked the Lord, if it might be, to prevent the necessity of our doing so. That the money had been so near the Orphan Houses for several days without being given, is a plain proof that it was from the beginning in the heart of God to help us; but, because he delights in the prayers of his children, he had allowed us to pray so long; also to try our faith, and to make the answer much the sweeter. It is indeed a precious deliverance. I burst out into loud praises and thanks the first moment I was alone after I had received the money. I met with my fellow-laborers again this evening for prayer and praise; their hearts were not a little cheered. This money was this evening divided, and will comfortably provide for all that will be needed to-morrow.[1]

Sept. 20. Morning. The Lord has again kindly sent in a little. Last evening was given to me one shilling and sixpence, and this morning one pound three shillings. Evening. This evening the Lord sent still further supplies; eight pounds eleven shillings and twopence halfpenny came in, as a further proof that the Lord is not unmindful of us. There was in the box of the Girls' Orphan House

---

[1] In July, 1845, he thus refers to this day:— "I have been only once tried in spirit, and that was on Sept 18th, 1838, when, for the first time, the Lord seemed not to regard our prayer But when he did send help at that time, and I saw that it was only for the trial of our faith, and not because he had forsaken the work that we were brought so low, my soul was so strengthened and encouraged, that I have not only not been allowed to distrust the Lord, but *I have not even been cast down when in the deepest poverty*, since that time."

one pound one shilling, and in that of the Boys' Orphan House one pound seven shillings and twopence halfpenny. One of the laborers, in accordance with her promise this day week, gave six pounds three shillings. About eighteen months ago she saw it right no longer to have money for herself in the savings-bank, and she therefore, in her heart, gave the money which she had there to the Orphan Houses, intending to draw it in a time of need. Some time since (she told me this evening) she drew a part of it to buy several useful articles for the Orphan Houses; now the sum was reduced to six pounds. When she found out the present need, she went this day week to the savings-bank, and gave notice that she wished to draw her money to-day.

Sept. 22. Both yesterday and to-day we have again assembled for prayer and praise. We are in no immediate want, but on the 29th, nineteen pounds ten shillings will be due for the rent of the three Orphan Houses. To-day there was only four shillings and sevenpence in hand for the other objects of the institution, though it was the pay day for some of the teachers. My comfort was the *living* God. During this week he had helped me so repeatedly and in such a remarkable way, as it regards the Orphan Houses, that it would have been doubly sinful not to have trusted in him for help under this fresh difficulty. No money came in this morning. About two, the usual time when the teachers are paid, a sovereign was given, with which I went immediately to brother T., who attends to this part of the work, to pay, at least in part, the weekly salaries. I found that he had received a sovereign in the morning. By means of this sovereign, together with the one which I had received *just at the moment when it was needed*, we were helped through this day.

Sept. 29. Saturday evening. Prayer has been made for several days past respecting the rent, which is due this day. I have been looking out for it, though I knew not whence a shilling was to come. This morning brother T. called on me, and, as no money had come in, we prayed together, and continued in supplication from ten till a quarter to twelve. Twelve o'clock struck, the time when the rent ought to have been paid, but no money had been sent. For some days past I have repeatedly had a misgiving, whether the Lord might not disappoint us, in order that we might be led *to provide by the week, or the day, for the rent.* This is the second, and only the second, complete failure as to answers of prayer in the work, during the past four years and six months. The first was about the half-yearly rent of Castle-Green school-rooms, due July 1, 1837, which had come in only in part by that time. I am now fully convinced that the rent ought to be put by daily or weekly, as God may prosper us, in order that the work, even as to this point, may be a testimony. May the Lord, then, help us to act accordingly, and may he now mercifully send in the means to pay the rent!

Oct. 2. Tuesday evening. The Lord's holy name be praised! He hath dealt most bountifully with us during the last three days! The day before yesterday five pounds came in for the orphans. O, how kind is the Lord! Always before there has been actual want he has sent help Yesterday came in one pound ten shillings more. Thus the expenses of yesterday for housekeeping were defrayed. The Lord helped me also to pay yesterday the nineteen pounds ten shillings for the rent. The means for it were thus obtained: One of the laborers had received through his family ten pounds, and five pounds besides from a sister in the Lord, also some other money. Of this he gave sixteen pounds, which, with the three pounds ten shillings that were left of the above-mentioned five pounds, made up nineteen pounds ten shillings, the sum which was needed. This day we were again greatly reduced. There was no money in hand to take in bread, as usual, for the Boys' and Infant Orphan Houses. But again the Lord helped. A sister who had arrived this afternoon from Swansea brought one pound seven shillings, and one of the laborers sold an article, by means of which he was able to give one pound thirteen shillings. Thus we had three pounds, — one pound for each house, — and could buy bread before the day was over. Hitherto we have lacked nothing!

Oct. 9. To-day we were brought lower than ever. The provisions would have lasted out only to-day, and the money for milk in one of the houses could only be made up by one of the laborers selling one of his books. The matron in the Boys' Orphan House had this morning two shillings left. When in doubt whether to buy bread with it, or more meat, to make up the dinner with the meat which she had in the house, the baker called, and left three quarterns of bread as a present. In this great need, some money having been given to one of the laborers, he gave two pounds of it, by which we were able to buy meat, bread, and other provisions.

Oct. 10. The coals in the Infant Orphan House are out, and nearly so in the other two houses. Also the treacle casks in all the three houses are nearly empty. On this account we ask the Lord for fresh supplies.

Oct. 11. The "Father of the fatherless" has again shown his care over us. An orphan from Devonshire arrived last evening. With her were sent two pounds five shillings and sixpence. The sister who brought her gave also a silver tea-pot, sugar-basin, and cream-jug, of the weight of forty-eight ounces, having found true riches in Christ. There were also in the boxes nine shillings. One of the laborers paid for a ton of coals. We obtained sixteen pounds sixteen shillings for the silver articles. Thus we were helped through the heavy expenses of the following days.

Oct. 12. To-day seven brethren and sisters were added to us in fellowship, and eight were proposed. May the Lord send helpers for the work!

Oct. 15. I knew that there **would** be money needed

this morning for many things in the Orphan Houses, and my heart was therefore lifted up to the Lord. Just when I was going to meet my fellow-laborers for prayer, I received from Trowbridge four pounds. There had come in also at the Orphan Houses seven shillings and threepence. To this one of the laborers added one pound. Thus I was enabled abundantly to supply all that was wanted, and to pay for a cask of treacle and a ton of coals. We are now, however, cast again on the love of our Lord for further supplies, as there is neither anything in hand, nor have the laborers any more of their own to give.

Oct. 16. I was looking up to the Lord for help early this morning, when, almost immediately afterwards, brother T. came, and brought two silver tablespoons and six teaspoons, which had been left anonymously, yesterday afternoon, at the Girls' Orphan House. This afternoon I received twelve pounds from Staffordshire.

Oct. 22. To-day our funds were again quite low. In the Infant Orphan House only twopence was left, and very little in the other two houses. But the Lord most manifestly again answered prayer, by sending four pounds three shillings and one penny.

Oct. 27. Thanks to our adorable Lord! this day also we have not been confounded; for there were six shillings in the box at the Infant Orphan House, and six shillings came in for things which had been given to be sold. To this one of the laborers added eighteen shillings. By means of this one pound ten shillings we have been able to meet all pressing demands, and to procure provisions for to-day and to-morrow.

Oct. 30. This has been again a day of peculiar mercies in reference to the funds. Whilst I was in prayer respecting them a brother brought two and a quarter yards of cloth. He had bought it for himself, but afterwards, considering that he had sufficient clothes, he gave it to be sold for the orphans. This evening a sister gave me twenty pounds, ten of which were for the orphans and ten for the other objects.

Nov. 7. The funds are now again completely exhausted.

Nov. 13. This morning our want was again great. I have twenty pounds in hand, which have been put by for rent, but, for the Lord's honor, I would not take of it. Nothing had come in, and the laborers had scarcely anything to give. I went, however, to the Orphan Houses to pray with my fellow-laborers, and, if it might be, to comfort them, and see what could be done. When I came there I found that nineteen shillings and sixpence had come in this morning. On inquiry I heard that only two shillings and sixpence more were needed to carry us through the day. This one of the laborers was able to add of his own. Thus the Lord has again helped us out of our difficulty. One of the laborers gave some things which he could do without, and another gave a workbox to be sold for the orphans. Before this day has come to an end, the Lord has sent in one pound two shillings and fourpence more, so that we have also a little for to-morrow.

Nov. 21. Never were we so reduced in funds as to-day. There was not a single halfpenny in hand between the matrons of the three houses. Nevertheless, there was a good dinner, and by managing so as to help one another with bread, etc., there was a prospect of getting over this day also; but for none of the houses had we the prospect of being able to take in bread. When I left the brethren and sisters at one o'clock, after prayer, I told them that we must wait for help, and see how the Lord would deliver us at this time. I was sure of help, but we were indeed straitened. When I came to Kingsdown, I felt that I needed more exercise, being very cold, wherefore I went not the nearest way home, but round by Clarence-place. About twenty yards from my house I met a brother who walked back with me, and after a little conversation gave me ten pounds to be handed over to the brethren, the deacons, towards providing the poor saints with coals, blankets, and warm clothing; also five pounds for the orphans, and five pounds for the other objects of the Scriptural Knowledge Institution. The brother had called twice while I was gone to the Orphan Houses, and had I now been *one half minute* later I should have missed him. But the Lord knew our need, and therefore allowed me to meet him.

Nov. 24. This again has been a very remarkable day. We had as little in hand this morning as at any time, and yet several pounds were needed. But God, who is rich in mercy, and whose word so positively declares that none who trust in him shall be confounded, has helped us through this day also. While I was in prayer about ten in the morning, respecting the funds, I was informed that a gentleman had called to see me. He came to inform me that a lady had ordered three sacks of potatoes to be sent to the Orphan Houses. Never could they have come more seasonably. This was an encouragement to me to continue to expect help. When I came to the prayer meeting, about twelve o'clock, I heard that two shillings had come in, also one pound for a guitar, which had been given for sale. The payment for this guitar had been expected for many weeks. It had been mentioned among us repeatedly that it might come just at a time when we most needed it; and oh, how true! But with all this we could not have put by the rents for this week, amounting to thirty shillings. One of the laborers therefore gave his watch to the orphan fund, under this condition, that should the Lord not enable us before Dec. 21 to make up this deficiency, it should be sold, but not otherwise, as he needs it in the Lord's service. [A few days after the Lord gave the means to put by the thirty shillings, and thirty shillings besides for the next week's rent.] Thus the Lord helped us through this day, and with it brought us to the close of one more week.

Nov. 28. This is perhaps of all days the most remarkable as yet, so far as it regards the funds. When I was in prayer this morning respecting them, I was enabled firmly to believe that the Lord would send help, though all seemed dark as to natural appearances. At twelve o'clock I met as usual with the brethren and sisters for prayer. There had come in only one shilling, which was left last evening anonymously at the Infant Orphan House, and which, except twopence, had already been spent, on account of the great need. I heard also that an individual had gratuitously cleaned the timepiece in the Infant Orphan House, and had offered to keep the timepieces in the three houses in repair. Thus the Lord gave even in this a little encouragement, and a proof that he is still mindful of us. On inquiry I found that there was everything needful for the dinner in all the three houses; but neither in the Infant nor Boys' Orphan Houses was there bread enough for tea, nor money to buy milk. Lower we had never been, and perhaps never so low. We gave ourselves now unitedly to prayer, laying the case in simplicity before the Lord. Whilst in prayer there was a knock at the door, and one of the sisters went out. After the two brethren who labor in the Orphan Houses and I had prayed aloud, we continued for a while silently in prayer. As to myself, I was lifting up my heart to the Lord to make a way for our escape, and in order to know if there were any other thing which I could do with a good conscience, besides waiting on him, so that we might have food for the children. At last we rose from our knees. I said, "God will surely send help." The words had not quite passed over my lips, when I perceived a letter lying on the table, which had been brought whilst we were in prayer. It was from my wife, containing another letter from a brother with ten pounds for the orphans. The evening before last I was asked by a brother whether the balance in hand for the orphans would be as great this time, when the accounts would be made up, as the last time. My answer was that it would be as great as the Lord pleased. The next morning this brother was moved to remember the orphans, and to send to-day ten pounds, which arrived after I had left my house, and which, on account of our need, was forwarded immediately to me. The brother who sent the ten pounds for the orphans sent likewise ten pounds to be divided between brother Craik and me, with the object of purchasing new clothes for ourselves.

Dec. 6. This afternoon I received one hundred pounds from a sister, — fifty for the orphans, and fifty for the school, Bible, and missionary fund. This same sister, who earns her bread with her own hands, had given, on October 5, 1837, fifty pounds towards the Boys' Orphan House, and gave for the necessities of the poor saints, in August, 1838, one hundred pounds more; for she had been made willing to act out those precious exhortations: "Having food and raiment, let us be therewith content." "Sell that ye have, and give alms; provide yourselves bags which wax not old, a treasure in the heavens that faileth not, where no thief approacheth, neither moth corrupteth." "Lay not up for yourselves treasures upon earth, where moth and rust doth corrupt, and where thieves break through and steal; but lay up for yourselves treasures in heaven, where neither moth nor rust doth corrupt, and where thieves do not break through nor steal." Respecting the fifty pounds which have been given of this sum for the school, Bible, and missionary fund, it is worthy of remark, that we would not order reference Bibles till we had the means. We had repeatedly prayed respecting this want of Bibles, and particularly again this morning. It had been also much laid on our hearts to-day to request that the Lord would enable us to have the Report printed, which we could not do unless he first sent the means. Lastly, we had also repeatedly asked him to supply us so largely, if it were his will, as that at the time of the public meetings we might be able to speak again of abundance. For though for some months past the time has been fixed for the public meetings, without any reference to the state of the funds, nevertheless, it might have had the appearance that we had convened the brethren for the sake of telling them about our poverty, and thus to induce them to give.

Dec. 11, 12, and 13. On the evenings of these three days there were public meetings, at which I gave an account of the Lord's dealing with us in reference to the Orphan Houses and the other objects of the Scriptural Knowledge Institution. As the work, and particularly that of the Orphan Houses, was begun for the benefit of the church at large, it appeared well to us that from time to time it should be publicly stated how the Lord had dealt with us in reference to it; and as, on Dec. 9, the third year had been completed since the commencement of the orphan work, this seemed to be a suitable time for having these meetings.

I notice briefly the following particulars respecting the first three objects of the Scriptural Knowledge Institution. 1. There is at present — December, 1838 — a Sunday school supported by it, which contains four hundred and sixty-three children. This part of the work calls for particular thanksgiving; for during these last eighteen months the number of the children has been nearly three times as great as it used to be. Five of the scholars have been converted within the last two years, and are now in fellowship with the church, and three of them are teachers in the school. 2. There is in connection with the Institution an adult school, in which, since the commencement of the work, above one hundred and twenty adults have been instructed, and in which at present twelve are taught to read. 3. The Institution has entirely supported, since its commencement, several day schools for poor children, and within the last two years six of such, — three for boys and three for girls. The number of all the children that have had schooling in the day schools through the medium of the Institution, since its formation, amounts to 1,534; the number of those at present in the six days schools is 342. 4. During the last two years there have been circulated 1,884 copies of the Scriptures in connection with the Institution, and since the beginning of the work, March 5, 1834, 5,078 copies. 5. For missionary purposes have been laid out £74, 18s. 4d. 6. The total of the income for the first three objects, during the last two years, was £1.129, 13s 1d.; the total of the expense, £1,111, 13s. 7½d.

There are, at present 86 orphans in the three houses, i. e., 31 in the Girls' Orphan House, 31 in the Infant Orphan House, and 24 in the Boys' Orphan House. The whole number of orphans who have been under our care from April 11, 1836, to Dec. 9, 1838, amounts to 110.

The total of the income for the orphans, from Dec. 9, 1836, to Dec. 9, 1838, has amounted to £1,341, 4s. 7d; the total of the expenses to £1,664, 4s. 0¾d There was two years ago a balance of £373, 4s. 8¼d. in hand, and now the balance is £50, 5s. 3d.

Dec. 16. There was a paper anonymously put into the box at Bethesda Chapel containing four pounds ten shillings. In the paper was written, "For the rent of the Orphan Houses, from Dec 10 to Dec. 31, 1838. 'Oh, taste and see that the *Lord is good: blessed* is the man that *trusteth in him!*'" In order that the reader may be able to enter into the value of this donation, I would request him to read over once more what I wrote under "Sept. 29" of this year. [The individual who gave these four pounds ten shillings for the rent of the Orphan Houses for the first three weeks after the public meetings, at which the matter about the rent, for the instruction of the brethren, was fully stated, continued for three years, up to Dec. 10, 1841, to give regularly, but anonymously, one pound ten shillings a week for the same purpose, which was exactly the sum required every week for the rent of those three houses. Thus the Lord rewarded our faithfulness in carrying out the light which he had given us. But the chief blessing resulting from this circumstance I consider to be this, — that several brethren, who earn their bread by the labor of their hands, have learned through this circumstance that it is the will of the Lord they should lay by their rent weekly. I beseech those brethren who are not pursuing this course to do so, and they will soon prove by experience the benefit of acting on scriptural principles even as it regards this life.]

Dec. 17. To-day eleven brethren and sisters were proposed for fellowship.

Dec. 20. As the expenses for the orphans have been above forty-seven pounds within the last six days, and as but little above thirteen pounds have come in, and as the money for printing the Report had to be kept back, in order that we might not be in debt, we were again to-day very low in funds, though it is but six days since the public meetings. As I knew that to-morrow several pounds would be needed to supply the matrons, I gave myself this morning to prayer. About a quarter of an hour afterwards I received three pounds, the payment of a legacy left by a sister, who fell asleep in Jesus several months since, in Ireland. Besides this I received from the brother through whom the legacy was paid, two pounds ten shillings for the orphan fund. With these five pounds ten shillings I hope to be able to meet the expenses of to-morrow.

Dec. 22. *A solemn day.* I received to-day the information that my brother died on October 7. "*Shall not the Judge of all the earth do right?*" must be the stay of the believer at such a time, and, by grace, it is my stay now. *I know* that the Lord is glorified in my brother, whatever his end has been. May the Lord make this event a lasting blessing to me, especially in leading me to earnestness in prayer for my father.

REVIEW OF THE YEAR 1838.

1. As to the church. There are 405 at present in fellowship with us; 61 having been added last year, of whom 36 have been brought among us to the knowledge of the truth

2 As to my temporal supplies. The Lord has been pleased to give me during the past year £350, 4s. 8d

During no period of my life had I such need of means, on account of my own long illness and that of my dear wife, and on account of the *many* and *particular* calls for means, as during the past year; but also during no period of my life has the Lord so richly supplied me. Truly, it must be manifest to all that I have served a most kind Master, during this year also, and that, even for this life, it is by far the best thing to seek to act according to the mind of the Lord as to temporal things!

CHAPTER XI.

ASKING AND RECEIVING.

1839.

HELP FOR THE POOR SAINTS — THE UNFAILING BANK — MEANS EXHAUSTED — LIBERALITY OF A LABORING SISTER — "HE KNOWETH OUR FRAME" — REDEEMING THE TIME — GODLINESS PROFITABLE UNTO ALL THINGS.

JANUARY 1, 2, and 3, 1839. We have had three especial church prayer meetings these three days. The year commenced with mercies. *In the first hour* of the year there came in for the orphans two pounds seven shillings, which were given after our usual prayer meeting on Dec. 31, which this time lasted from seven in the evening till after midnight.

Jan. 20. For some time past it has appeared to me that the words, " Ye have the poor with you always, and whensoever ye will ye may do them good," which the Lord spoke to his disciples, *who were themselves very poor*, imply that the children of God, as such, have power with God to bring temporal blessings upon poor saints or poor unbelievers through the instrumentality of prayer. Accordingly, I have been led to ask the Lord for means to assist poor saints; and at different times he has stirred up his children to intrust me with sums both large and small, *for that especial object;* or has, by some means or other, put money at my disposal, which I might so use. In like manner I had been asking again for means, a few days since, to be able more extensively to assist the poor saints in communion with us, as just now many of them are not merely tried by the *usual* temporal difficulties arising from its being winter, but especially from the high price of bread.

And now this evening the Lord has given me the answer to my prayer. When I came home from the meeting I found a brother at my house who offered to give me ten pounds a week, for twelve weeks, towards providing the poor saints with coals and needful articles of clothing, but chiefly with bread. [Accordingly, this brother sent me, two days afterwards, one hundred and twenty pounds, whereby very many, especially poor widows, were greatly assisted, chiefly with flour and bread. This money just lasted till the price of bread was reduced from ninepence halfpenny to sevenpence halfpenny.]

Feb. 7. This day has been one of the most remarkable days as it regards the funds. There was no money in hand. I was waiting upon God. I had asked him repeatedly, but no supplies came. Brother T. called, between eleven and twelve o'clock, to tell me that about one pound two shillings would be needed, to take in bread for the three houses and to meet the other expenses; but we had only two shillings ninepence, which yesterday had been taken out of the boxes in the Orphan Houses. He went to Clifton to make arrangements for the reception of the three orphans of our sister Loader, who fell asleep on the fourth; for, though we have no funds in hand, the work goes on, and our confidence is not diminished. I therefore requested him to call, on his way back from Clifton, to see whether the Lord might have sent any money in the mean time. When he came I had received nothing, but one of the laborers, having five shillings of his own, gave it. It was now four o'clock. I knew not how the sisters had got through the day. Toward the close of the day I went to the Girls' Orphan House, to meet with the brethren for prayer. When I arrived there I found that a box had come for me from Barnstable. The carriage was paid, else there would have been no money to pay for it. (See how the Lord's hand is in the smallest matters!) The box was opened, and it contained, in a letter from a sister, ten pounds, of which eight pounds was for the orphans, and two pounds for the Bible Fund; from brethren at Barnstable, two pounds eleven shillings twopence; and from another brother, five shillings. Besides this, there were in the box four yards of merino, three pairs of new shoes, two pairs of new socks; also six books for sale; likewise a gold pencil-case, two gold rings, two gold drops of earrings, a necklace and a silver pencil-case. On inquiry how the sisters had been carried through the day, I found it thus: everything was in the houses which was needed for dinner. After dinner a lady from Thornbury came and bought one of my Narratives and one of the Reports, and gave three shillings besides. About five minutes afterwards the baker came to the Boys' Orphan House. The matron of the Girls' Orphan House, seeing him, went immediately with the six shillings sixpence which she had just received (to prevent his being sent away, as there was no money in hand at the Boys' Orphan House), and bought bread to the amount of four shillings sixpence. The two remaining shillings, with the little which was in hand, served to buy bread for the Girls' Orphan House. By the donations sent in the box I was enabled to give a rich supply to the matrons before the close of the day.

Feb. 13. This evening five pounds were given me, which had come in under the following circumstances: A gentleman and lady visited the Orphan Houses, and met at the Boys' Orphan House two ladies who were likewise visiting. One of the ladies said to the matron of the Boys' Orphan House, "Of course you cannot carry on these Institutions without a good stock of funds." The gentleman, turning to the matron, said, "Have you a good stock?" She replied, "Our funds are deposited in a bank which cannot break." The tears came into the eyes of the inquiring lady. The gentleman, on leaving, gave to the master of the boys five pounds, which came in *when I had not a penny in hand.*

March 5. To-day, however, I knew that there would be

again several pounds required, as, besides the daily provisions, there were coals needed, the treacle casks in two houses were empty, and there were but five shillings in hand. I gave myself therefore to prayer this morning. WHILST I WAS IN PRAYER Q. Q. sent a check for seven pounds ten shillings.

April 13. I conversed with another of the orphans, who seems to have been truly converted, and who has walked consistently for many months. To-morrow she will be united with the saints in communion.

April 14. To-day five pounds eightpence came in for the orphans, one pound of which is one of the most remarkable gifts that we have ever had. A poor brother, with a large family and small wages, — there are eight in the family, and he had fifteen shillings wages till lately, when they were raised to eighteen shillings, — put by this money by little and little of what was given him by his master for beer. This brother, who was converted about five years ago, was before that time a notorious drunkard.

July 2. To-day were given to me, *when there was not one shilling in hand*, fifty pounds, for the school, Bible, and missionary fund.

July 15. Monday. To-day two pounds seven shillings threepence were needed for the orphans, but we had nothing. How to obtain the means for a dinner, and for what else was needed, I knew not. My heart was perfectly at peace, and unusually sure of help, though I knew not in the least whence it was to come. Before brother T. came, I received a letter from India, written in May, with an order for fifty pounds for the orphans. I had said last Saturday to brother T. that it would be desirable to have fifty pounds, as the salaries of all my fellow-laborers are due, the three treacle casks empty, all the provision stores exhausted, several articles of clothing needed, and worsted for the boys to go on with their knitting.

Aug. 22. In my morning walk, when I was reminding

the Lord of our need, I felt assured that he would send help this day. My assurance sprang from our need; for there seemed no way to get through the day without help being sent. After breakfast I considered whether there was anything which might be turned into money for the dear children. Among other things there came under my hands a number of religious pamphlets which had been given for the benefit of the orphans; but all seemed not nearly enough to meet the necessities of the day. In this our deep poverty, after I had gathered together the few things for sale, a sister, *who earns her bread by the labor of her hands,* brought eighty-two pounds. This sister had seen it to be binding upon believers in our Lord Jesus to act out his commandments: "Sell that ye have (sell your possessions) and give alms," Luke xii. 33; and "Lay not up for yourselves treasures upon earth," Matt. vi. 19. Accordingly, she had drawn her money out of the bank and stocks, being two hundred and fifty pounds, and had brought it to me at three different times, for the benefit of the orphans, the Bible, missionary, and school fund, and the poor saints. About two months ago she brought me one hundred pounds more, being the produce of some other possessions which she had sold, the half of which was to be used for the school, Bible, and missionary fund, and the other half for the poor saints. This eighty-two pounds which she has brought to-day is the produce of the sale of her last earthly possession. [At the time I am preparing this fifth edition for the press, more than sixteen years have passed away, and this sister has never expressed the least regret as to the step she took, but goes on quietly laboring with her hands to earn her bread.]

Sept. 4. I have been led to pray whether it is the Lord's will that I should leave Bristol for a season, as I have for the last fortnight been suffering from indigestion, by which my whole system is weakened, and thus the nerves of my head are more than usually affected. There are, however, two hindrances in the way, — want of means for the orphans, and want of means for my own personal expenses. To-day I have received a check from Q. Q. for seven pounds ten shillings for the orphans, which came, therefore, very seasonably. Also four pounds besides have come in since the day before yesterday.

Sept. 5. To-day a sister sent me five pounds for myself, to be used for the benefit of my health. She had heard that my health is again failing. I do not lay by money for such purposes; but whenever I really need means, whether for myself or others, the Lord sends them, in answer to prayer; for he had in this case again given me prayer respecting means for myself, and for the orphans, that my way might be made plain as to leaving Bristol for a season.

Sept. 7. Trowbridge. This has been a very good day. I have had much communion with the Lord. How kind to take me from the work in Bristol for a season, to give me more communion with himself! I remembered the Lord's especial goodness to me in this place at the commencement of last year. How kind has he also been since! I prayed much for myself, for the church at large, for the saints here and in Bristol, for my unconverted relatives, for my dear wife, and that the Lord would supply my own temporal necessities, and those of the orphans; and *I know that he has heard me.* I am surrounded with kind friends in the dear saints, under whose roof I am, and feel quite at home. My room is *far better* than I need; yet an easy chair *in this my weak state of body*, to kneel before in prayer, would have added to my comfort. In the afternoon, without having a hint about it, I found an easy chair put into my room. I was struck with the kindness, the especial kindness of my heavenly Father, in being mindful of the smallest wants and comforts of his child. Having had more prayer than usual, I found that my intercourse with the saints at tea was with unction, and more than usually profitable.

Sept. 9. I returned to Bristol, to go from hence to

morrow to Exeter, if the Lord permit, on account of my health. I had been earnestly asking the Lord, while I was staying at Trowbridge that he would be pleased to send in supplies for the orphans before I go into Devonshire, and I had the fullest assurance that means would come in before I left Bristol. I therefore asked my wife, on my return, how much had come in, and found that it was only eight pounds nine shillings seven and three-fourths pence. This was not nearly as much as I had expected, and would not answer the end for which I had particularly asked means, *i. e.,* that I might be able to leave enough for several days. My reply, therefore, was according to the faith given to me, and judging from the earnestness and confidence of my prayer *that the Lord would send more before I left.* About an hour after, brother Craik brought me ten pounds, and also a letter, in which the arrival of a large box full of articles, to be sold for the benefit of the orphans, is announced.

Upon his return from his journey, Mr. M. writes: —

During my stay at Plymouth, I was stirred up afresh to early rising, a blessing, the results of which I have not lost since. That which led me to it was the example of the brother in whose house I was staying, and a remark which he made in speaking on the sacrifices in Leviticus, "that as not the refuse of animals was to be offered up, *so the best part of our time* should be especially given to communion with the Lord." I had been, on the whole, rather an early riser during former years. But since the nerves of my head had been so weak, I thought that, as the day was long enough for my strength, it would be best for me not to rise early, in order that thus the nerves of my head might have the longer quiet. On this account I rose only between six and seven, and sometimes after seven. For the same reason also I brought myself *purposely* into the habit of sleeping a quarter of an hour, or half an hour, after dinner: as I thought I found benefit from it, in quieting the nerves of my head. In this way, however, my soul had suffered more or less every day, and sometimes considerably, as now and then unavoidable work came upon me before I had had sufficient time for prayer and reading the word. After I had heard the remark to which I have alluded, I determined that, whatever my body might suffer, I would no longer let the most precious part of the day pass away while I was in bed. By the grace of God I was enabled to begin the very next day to rise earlier, and have continued to rise early since that time. I allow myself now about seven hours' sleep, which, though I am far from being strong, and have much to tire me mentally, I find is quite sufficient to refresh me. In addition to this I gave up the sleeping after dinner. The result has been that I have thus been able to procure long and precious seasons for prayer and meditation before breakfast; and as to my body, and the state of the nervous system in particular, I have been *much better* since. Indeed, I believe that the very worst thing I could have done for my weak nerves was to have lain an hour or more longer in bed than I used to do before my illness; for it was the very way to keep them weak. As this may fall into the hands of some children of God who are not in the habit of rising early, I make a few more remarks on the subject.

I. It might be asked, how much time shall I allow myself for rest? The answer is, that no rule of universal application can be given, as all persons do not require the same measure of sleep, and also the same persons, at different times, according to the strength or weakness of their body, may require more or less. Females also, being generally weaker in body, require more sleep than males. Yet, from what I can learn, it is the opinion of medical persons that men in health do not require more than between six and seven hours' sleep, and females no more than between seven and eight hours; so that it would be rather *an exception* for a man to require more than seven and a woman more than eight hours. But my decided advice, at the same time, is, that children of God would be careful not to allow themselves *too little* sleep, as there are few men who can do with less than six hours' sleep, and yet be well in body and mind, and few females who can do with less than seven hours. Certain it is that for a long time, as a young man, before I went to the university, I went to bed regularly at ten and rose at four, studied hard, and was in good health; and certain also, that since I have allowed myself only about seven hours, from the time of my visit at Plymouth in Oct. 1839, I have been much better in body, and in my nerves in particular, than when I was eight or eight hours and a half in bed.

II. If it be asked, But why should I rise early? The reply is, "To remain too long in bed" is, 1. *Waste of time*, which is unbecoming a saint, who is bought by the precious blood of Jesus, with his *time* and all he has, to be used for the Lord. If we sleep more than is needful for the refreshment of the body, it is wasting the time with which the Lord has intrusted us as a talent, to be used for his glory, for our own benefit, and the benefit of the saints and the unbelievers around us. 2. To remain too long in bed *injures the body*. Just as when we take too much food, we are injured thereby, so as it regards sleep. Medical persons would readily allow that the lying longer in bed than is needful for the strengthening of the body does *weaken* it. 3. *It injures the soul.* The lying too long in bed not merely keeps us from giving the most precious part of the day to prayer and meditation, but this sloth leads also to *many other evils*. Any one need but make the experiment of spending one, two, or three hours in prayer and meditation before breakfast, either in his room, or with his Bible in his hand in the fields, and he will soon find out the beneficial effect which early rising has upon the outward and inward man. I beseech all my brethren and sisters into whose hands this may fall, and who are not in the habit of rising early, to make the trial, and they will praise the Lord for having done so.

III. It may lastly be said, But how shall I set about rising early? My advice is, 1. Commence at once, delay it not. To-morrow begin to rise. 2. But do not depend upon your own strength. This may be the reason why before this you may have begun to rise early, but have given it up. As surely as you depend upon your own strength in this matter, it will come to nothing. In every good work we depend upon the Lord, and in this thing we shall feel *especially* how weak we are. If any one rises, that he may give the time which he takes from sleep to prayer and meditation, let him be sure that Satan will try to put obstacles into the way. 3. Do trust in the Lord for help. You will honor him if you *expect* help from him in this matter. Give yourself to prayer for help, expect help, and you will have it. 4. Use, however, in addition to this, the following means: *a.* Go early to bed. If you stay up late, you cannot rise early. Let no society and no pressure of engagements keep you from going *habitually* early to bed. If you fail in this, you neither can nor ought to get up early, as your body requires rest. Keep also particularly in mind, that neither for the body nor soul is it the same thing whether you go to bed *late* and rise *late*, or whether you go to bed *early* and rise *early*. Even medical persons will tell you how injurious it is to sit up late, and to spend the morning hours in bed; but how much more important still is it to retire early and to rise early, in order to *make sure of time for prayer and meditation before the business of the day commences*, and to devote to those exercises that part of our time when the mind and the body are *most fresh*, in order thus to obtain spiritual strength for the conflict, the trials, and the work of the day. *b.* Let some one call you, if possible, at the time which you have determined before

God that you will rise; or procure, what is still better, an alarum, by which you may regulate almost to a minute the time when you wish to rise. For about twelve shillings a little German clock with an alarum may be bought almost in every town. Though I have very many times been awakened by the Lord, in answer to prayer, almost to the minute when I desired to rise; yet I thought it well to procure an alarum to assist me in my purpose of rising early; not indeed as if it could give the least help, without the Lord's blessing, for I should remain in bed notwithstanding the noise of the alarum, were he not to give me grace to rise; but simply looking upon it as a means. *c.* Rise at once when you are awake. Remain not a minute longer in bed, else you are likely to fall asleep. *d.* Be not discouraged by feeling drowsy and tired in consequence of your rising early. This will soon wear off. You will after a few days feel yourself stronger and fresher than when you used to lie an hour or two longer than you needed. *e.* Allow yourself always the same hours for sleep. Make no change except sickness oblige you.

On December 10, 11, and 12 we had public meetings, at which the account of the Lord's dealings with us in reference to the Orphan Houses and the other objects of the Scriptural Knowledge Institution was given. It is now — December 10, 1839 — five years and nine months since the Scriptural Knowledge Institution has been in operation.

During the last year also, 1. We have been enabled to continue to provide all the needful expenses connected with the six day schools, three for boys and three for girls. The number of the children who are at present in them amounts to 286. The number of all the children that have had schooling in the day schools, through the medium of the Institution, since its formation, amounts to 1,795. 2 There are at present 226 children in the Sunday school 3 There are 14 taught to read in the adult school, and there have been about 130 adults instructed in that school since the formation of the Institution. 4. There have been circulated, during the last year, 514 copies of the Scriptures, and 5,592 since March 5, 1834. 5. There have been laid out, during the last year, £91, 6s for missionary purposes. 6. There have been received into the three Orphan Houses, from December 9, 1838, to December 9, 1839, 16 orphans. There are at present 96 orphans in the three houses. The number of all the orphans who have been under our care from April 11, 1836, to December 9, 1839, amounts to 126.

For the Orphan Houses, *without any one having been asked for anything by us*, the sum of £3,067, 8s. 9¼d. has been given, *entirely as the result of prayer to God*, from the commencement of the work up to December 9, 1839.

The total of the expenses connected with the objects of the Institution, exclusive of the Orphan Houses, from November 19, 1838, to November 19, 1839, is £542, 13s. The balance in hand on November 19, 1839, was 18s. 5d.

The total of the expenses connected with the three Orphan Houses, from December 9, 1838, to December 9, 1839, is £960, 9s. 2¼d. The balance in hand on December 9, 1839, was £46, 8s 1d.

Dec. 31. My health is much better than for years. My mental powers also are as good as they have been at any time during the last three years. I ascribe this to God's blessing, through the instrumentality of early rising, and plunging my head into cold water when I rise.

1. As to the church: During the last year have been added 115; of whom 34 have been brought to the knowledge of the Lord among us.

2. As to my temporal supplies, the Lord has been pleased to give me, during the past year, £313, 2s. 5d.

CHAPTER XII.

PLENTY AND WANT.

1840.

A PURE OFFERING REQUIRED — A JOURNEY PROPOSED — SEASONABLE PROVISION — LOOKING ONLY TO THE LORD — THE WRATH OF MAN PRAISING GOD — A PROMISE FULFILLED — BENEFIT OF TRIAL — NEW SPRINGS OPENED — BEFORE THEY CALL I WILL ANSWER — TRUST IN GOD COMMENDED — SPIRITUAL BLESSINGS.

JANUARY 1, 1840. This morning, about one hour after midnight, I received a paper with some money sealed up in it for the orphans. A few minutes afterwards, I remembered that the individual who gave it was in debt, and I was aware that she had been repeatedly asked by her creditors for payment. I resolved, therefore, without opening the paper, to return it, as no one has a right to give whilst in debt. This was done *when I knew there was not enough in hand to meet the expenses of the day.* About eight this morning, a brother brought five pounds, which he had received just then from his mother, for the orphans. Observe, the brother is led to bring it *at once!*

Jan. 25. I have been much in prayer this week about going to Germany: 1. To see certain brethren who purpose to go as missionaries to the East Indies; and, 2. To see my father once more. I am led to go just now, instead of delaying it, because my health is again so failing that it seems desirable I should leave Bristol at all events; and thus I could continue to serve in the work of the Lord, and yet attend to the benefit of my health at the same time. Lord, keep me from making a mistake in this matter!

Mr. Muller's absence lasted from Feb. 3 to March 9. Under the latter date he writes: —

During the whole time of my absence the Lord not only supplied all the need of the orphans, but on my return I found more in hand than there was when I left. The donations, which came in during my absence, amount to between eighty and ninety pounds.

March 26. On the 17th of this month I received the following letter from a brother who several times had been used by the Lord as an instrument in supplying our need, and who also, two months since, sent thirty pounds.

"I have received a little money from ———. Have you any *present* need for the Institution under your care? I know you do not *ask*, except indeed of Him whose work you are doing: but to *answer when asked* seems another thing, and a right thing. I have a reason for desiring to know the present state of your means towards the objects you are laboring to serve, viz., should you *not have* need, other departments of the Lord's work, or other people of the Lord, *may have* need. Kindly then inform me, and to what amount, *i. e.*, what amount you at this present time need, or can profitably lay out."

At the time when this letter came we were indeed in need. Nevertheless, I considered that, as I have hitherto acted (*i. e.*, telling the Lord alone about our need), I ought to continue to do, as otherwise the principal object of the work, to be a help to the saints generally, by seeking to lead them to increased dependence upon God *alone*, through this Institution, would be frustrated. I answered therefore the letter in substance as follows: —

"Whilst I thank you for your love, and whilst I agree with you, that, in general, there is a difference between *asking for money* and *answering when asked*, nevertheless in our case I feel not at liberty to speak about the state of our funds, as the primary object of the work in my hands is to lead those who are weak in faith to see that there is *reality* in dealing with God *alone.*"

After having sent off the answer, I was again and again led to pray to the Lord in this way: "Lord, thou knowest that for thy sake I did not tell this brother about our need. Now, Lord, show afresh that there is *reality* in speaking to thee *only* about our need, and speak therefore to this brother, so that he may help us."

To-day, in answer to this my request, this brother sent one hundred pounds. Thus I have means for establishing the infant school, and for ordering more Bibles. Also the orphans are again supplied for a week; for when the money came in, there was *not one penny* in hand for them.

April 7. This evening I received information from my little half brother that my dear father died on March 30. During no period did I pray more frequently or more earnestly for the conversion of my dear aged parent than during the last year of his life; but, at all events, it did not please the Lord to let me *see* the answer to my prayers.

April 9. We are on the point of sending some money to the East Indies for missionary objects. *Whilst I was on my knees* respecting this object, five pounds was brought for it.

May 3. Last evening a brother was baptized, who on the first Lord's day of this year came with his intended wife to Bethesda Chapel. Both were in an unconverted state. Only since April 1, forty-one persons have come to us to speak about their souls.

May 8. There are four believers staying at my house, and to-day we had only a few shillings of our own money left. I gave myself, therefore, to prayer for means for our own personal expenses. In answer to my request, I received this morning five pounds.

May 10. To-day five of the orphans were baptized. There are now fourteen of them in fellowship.

May 26. Nothing had come in. My engagements kept

me from going to the Orphan House till seven in the evening, when the laborers met together for prayer. When we met I found that one of them had given seventeen shillings, which had been divided between the three houses. This, with the little which had been left yesterday, had procured all necessary articles. We are now very poor.

May 27. We met for prayer at eleven this morning. No money had come in, but there was enough for dinner in all the houses. This morning the last coals were used in the Infant Orphan House, and in the Boys' Orphan House there were only enough for to-day, and there was no money in hand to buy more. In this our need T. P. C. sent a load of coals. We purpose to meet again at four this afternoon. May the Lord graciously be pleased to send help in the mean time!

Evening. The Lord has had mercy! A person bought some days since several articles, which had been given to be sold for the benefit of the orphans, and owed six pounds fifteen shillings. This morning I asked the Lord to incline his heart to bring the money, or part of it, as we were in such need. Just as I was going to meet for prayer with my fellow-laborers this afternoon, he came and brought four pounds. But our kind Father showed us still further to-day that only for the trial of our faith he had for a season withheld supplies; for there were given this evening, with Eccles. ix. 10, five pounds. There came in also nine shillings for articles which had been put into the hand of a sister, who has taken on her the service of disposing of articles which are given for sale. Thus the day which had begun in prayer, ended in praise. But there is one thing more to be recorded respecting this day, as precious or more so than what has been said: I was to-day informed that the Lord had begun to stir up several of the boys to care about their souls.

June 17. For several days past I had been very poor in reference to my own temporal necessities, as well as in reference to the orphans. To-day we were especially poor, in both respects; but our kind Father remembered not merely the need of the orphans, but gave me also some money for my own personal expenses. The same sister just referred to, who brought five pounds ten shillings sixpence for the orphans, brought me also seven pounds for myself.

June 22. To-morrow, the Lord willing, I purpose, with my wife, to accompany the three German brethren and the five German sisters to Liverpool, who purpose to sail from thence. Under these circumstances it is desirable to leave at least a little money behind. This desire of my heart the Lord has granted; for this morning D. C. gave me five pounds, and there came in by sale of articles ten shillings fivepence. In the evening a sister, who has left Bristol to-day, sent me by her mother five pounds.

During the absence of Mr. M., the wants of the orphans were supplied in a wonderful manner. To mention but one instance, at a time when there was extreme need, a poor German missionary, just embarking for a heathen land, gave six pounds ten shillings, being his all.

The following event came to his notice during his journey: —

About Oct., 1837, I sent some Bibles and forty-six copies of my Narrative to a brother in Upper Canada, who, in dependence upon the Lord for temporal supplies, is laboring as a missionary in that country. About eighteen months afterwards I heard that this box had not arrived. I had reason to think that the broker had never sent off the box. My comfort, however, was, that though this poor sinner had acted thus, yet the Lord, in his own place and way, would use the Bibles and my Narratives. Now, almost immediately after my arrival in Liverpool, a brother told me that several persons wished to hear me preach who had read my Narrative; and that he knew a considerable number had been bought by a brother, a bookseller, from pawnbrokers, and sold again; and that some also had been ordered from London when there was no more to be had otherwise. It was thus evident that the ship-broker pawned these Narratives before he absconded; but the Lord used them as I had hoped.

Aug. 1. A few days since a brother was staying with me, on his way to his father, whom he had not seen for above two years, and who was greatly opposed to him, on account of the decided steps which his son had taken for the Lord. Before this brother left, that precious promise of our Lord was brought to my mind: "If two of you shall agree on earth as touching anything that they shall ask, it shall be done for them of my Father which is in heaven." (Matt. xviii. 19.) Accordingly, I went to the brother's room, and having agreed to pray about a kind reception from his father, and the conversion of both parents, we prayed together. To-day this brother returned. The Lord has answered already one part of the prayer. The brother was most kindly received, contrary to all natural expectation. May the Lord now help us both to look for an answer to the other part of our prayer! There is nothing too hard for the Lord!

Since the publication of the last edition, the father of this brother died. He lived above ten years after Aug. 1, 1840, until he was about eighty-six years of age, and as he continued a life of much sin and opposition to the truth, the prospect with reference to his conversion became darker and darker. But at last the Lord answered prayer. This aged sinner was entirely changed, simply rested on the Lord Jesus for the salvation of his soul, and became as much attached to his believing son as before he had been opposed to him, and wished to have him about him as much as possible, that he might read the Holy Scriptures to him and pray with him.

Aug. 15. There was to-day the greatest poverty in all the three houses; all the stores were very low, as the income throughout the week has been so small. In addition to this it was Saturday, when the wants are nearly double in comparison with other days. At least three pounds were needed to help us comfortably through the day; but there was nothing towards this in hand. My only hope was in God. The very necessity led me to expect help for this day; for if none had come, the Lord's name would have been dishonored. Between twelve and one, two sisters in the Lord called on me; and the one gave me two pounds, and the other seven shillings sixpence for the orphans. With this I went to the Boys' Orphan House about one o'clock, where I found the children at dinner. Brother B. put the following note into my hand, which he was just going to send off: —

"Dear Brother,— With potatoes from the children's garden, and with apples from the tree in the playground (which apples were used for apple-dumplings), and four shillings sixpence, the price of some articles given by one of the laborers, we have a dinner. There is much needed. But the Lord has provided and will provide."

Aug. 23. Lord's day. As we have often found it to be the case, so it is again now. After the Lord has tried our faith, he, in the love of his heart, gives us an abundance, to show that not in anger, but for the glory of his name, and for the trial of our faith, he has allowed us to be poor. The Lord has kindly given to-day twelve pounds seventeen shillings.

Sept. 5. Saturday. Because there had come in so little during the last days, at least three pounds were requisite to supply the need of to-day. There was, however, not one penny in hand when the day commenced. Last evening, the laborers in the Orphan Houses, together with the teachers of the day schools, met for prayer. This morning, one of the teachers, who had a little money of his own, brought one pound five shillings sixpence. Thus we were enabled to provide for the dinner. In the afternoon all of us met again for prayer. Another teacher of the day schools gave two shillings sixpence, and one shilling came in besides. But all this was not enough. There was no dinner provided for to-morrow, nor was there any money to take in milk to-morrow, and besides this a number of other little things were to be purchased, that there might be no real want of anything. Now, observe how our kind Father helped us! Between seven and eight this evening, a sister, whose heart the Lord has made willing to take on her the service of disposing of the articles which are sent for sale, brought two pounds ten shillings sixpence, for some of the things which came a fortnight ago from Worcester, and last Wednesday from Leeds. The sister stated, that though she did not feel at all well, she had come because she had it so laid on her heart that she could not stay away.

Sept. 8. How kindly has the Lord so ordered it that for some time past the income for the school fund should have been so little, in order that thus we might be constrained to let the laborers in the day schools share our joys and our trials of faith, which had been before kept from them! But as above two years ago the Lord ordered it so that it became needful to communicate to the laborers in the Orphan Houses the state of the funds, and made it a blessing to them, so that I am now able to leave Bristol, and yet the work goes on, so, I doubt not, the brethren and sisters who are teachers in the day schools will be greatly blessed by being thus partakers of our precious secret respecting the state of the funds. Our prayer meetings have been already a blessing to us, and united us more than ever in the work. We have them now every morning at seven, and we shall continue them, the Lord helping us, till we see his hand stretched forth, not merely in giving us means for the teachers, but also for other purposes; for we need a stove in one of the school-rooms, a fresh supply of several kinds of Bibles and New Testaments, and it is desirable to have means to help missionary brethren who labor in dependence upon the Lord for the supply of their temporal necessities.

Sept. 21. To-day a brother from the neighborhood of London gave me ten pounds, to be laid out as it might be most needed. As we have been praying many days for the school, Bible and missionary funds, I took it all for them. This brother knew nothing about our work, when he came three days since to Bristol. Thus the Lord, to show his continual care over us, raises up new helpers. They that trust in the Lord shall never be confounded. Some who helped for a while may fall asleep in Jesus; others may grow cold in the service of the Lord; others may be as desirous as ever to help, but have no longer the means; others may have both a willing heart to help, and have also the means, but may see it the Lord's will to lay them out in another way; — and thus, from one cause or another, were we to lean upon man, we should surely be confounded; but, in leaning upon the living God alone, we are BEYOND *disappointment, and* BEYOND *being forsaken because of death, or want of means, or want of love, or because of the claims of other work.*

Oct. 26. Yesterday morning, when I took my hat from the rail, I found in one of my gloves a note containing a five-pound note, and the following words: "Two pounds for the orphans, the rest for dear brother and sister Muller." There came in still further yesterday two pounds twelve shillings sixpence. Thus we are again supplied for about three days.

In reference to the note which was put into my hat, containing five pounds, I just add, that I had repeatedly asked the Lord for means for our own personal expenses, previous to the reception of it, as we had but very little money for ourselves. Indeed, the very moment before I took my hat from the rail, I had risen from my knees, having again asked the Lord for means for ourselves and for the orphans.

Nov. 8. I purposed to have gone to Trowbridge yesterday, and had settled it so on Friday evening with brother ———. But no sooner had I decided to do so, than I felt no peace in the prospect of going. After having prayed about it on Friday evening and yesterday morning, I determined not to go, and I felt sure the Lord had some reason for not allowing me to feel happy in the prospect of going. I began now to look out for blessings for this day, considering that the Lord had kept me here for good to some souls. This evening I was especially led to press the truth on the consciences of the unconverted, entreating and beseeching them, and telling them also that I felt sure the Lord had, in mercy to some of them, kept me from going to Trowbridge. I spoke on Genesis vi. 1–5. Immediately after, I saw fruit of the word. An individual fully opened his heart to me. I walked about with him till about ten o'clock, even as long as I had any strength left. [About ten days afterwards, a brother told me of a poor drunkard who heard me that evening, and who since then had staid up till about twelve o'clock every night to read the Scriptures, and who had not been intoxicated since.]

At the close of these details, with reference to the year from December 9, 1839, to December 9, 1840, I make a few remarks.

1. Though our trials of faith during this year also have been many, and recurring more frequently than during any previous year, and though we have been often reduced to the greatest extremity, *yet the orphans have lacked nothing;* for they always have had good nourishing food, and the necessary articles of clothing, etc.

1. Should it be supposed by any one, in reading the plain details of our trials of faith during this year, that on account of them we have been disappointed in our expectations, or are discouraged in the work, my answer is, that

the very reverse is the fact. Such days were expected from the commencement of the work; nay, more than this, the chief end for which the Institution was established is, that the church of Christ at large might be benefited by seeing manifestly the hand of God stretched out on our behalf in the hour of need, in answer to prayer. Our desire, therefore, is, not that we may be without trials of faith, but that the Lord graciously would be pleased to support us in the trial, that we may not dishonor him by distrust.

3. This way of living brings the Lord remarkably near. He is, as it were, morning by morning inspecting our stores, that accordingly he may send help. Greater and more manifest nearness of the Lord's presence I have never had than when after breakfast there were no means for dinner, and then the Lord provided the dinner for more than one hundred persons; or when, after dinner, there were no means for the tea, and yet the Lord provided the tea; and all this without one single human being having been informed about our need. This moreover I add, that although we who have been eye-witnesses of these gracious interpositions of our Father, have not been so benefited by them as we might and ought to have been, yet we have in some measure derived blessings from them. One thing is certain, that we are not tired of doing the Lord's work in this way.

4. It has been more than once observed, that such a way of living must lead the mind continually to think whence food, clothes, etc., are to come, and so unfit for spiritual exercises. Now, in the first place, I answer that our minds are very little tried about the necessaries of life, just because the care respecting them is laid upon our Father, who, because we are his children, *not only allows* us to do so, *but will have* us to do so. Secondly, it must be remembered, that, even if our minds were much tried about the supplies for the children, and the means for the other work, yet, because we look to the Lord *alone* for these things, we should only be brought, by our sense of need, into the presence of

our Father for the supply of it; and that is a blessing, and no injury to the soul. Thirdly, our souls realize that for the glory of God, and for the benefit of the church at large it is that we have these trials of faith, and that leads again to God, to ask him for fresh supplies of grace, to be enabled to be faithful in this service.

5. My heart's desire and prayer to God is, that all believers who read this may by these many answers to prayer be encouraged to pray, particularly as it regards the conversion of their friends and relations, their own state of heart, the state of the church at large, and the success of the preaching of the gospel. Do not think, dear reader, that these things are peculiar to us, and cannot be enjoyed by all the saints. Although every child of God is not called by the Lord to establish schools and orphan houses, and to trust in the Lord for means for them; yet there is nothing on the part of the Lord to hinder, why you may not know, by experience, far more abundantly than we do now, his willingness to answer the prayers of his children. Do but prove the faithfulness of God. Do but carry your every want to him. Only maintain an *upright* heart. But if you live in sin; if you wilfully and habitually do things respecting which you know that they are contrary to the will of God, then you cannot expect to be heard by him. "If I regard iniquity in my heart, the Lord will not hear me; but verily God hath heard me; he hath attended to the voice of my prayer." Psalm lxvi. 18, 19.

6. As it regards the children of God, who by the labor of their hands, or in any business or profession, earn their bread, particularly the poorer classes of them, I give my affectionate yet solemn advice to carry into practice the principles on which this Institution is conducted as it regards not going into debt. Are you in debt? then make confession of sin respecting it. Sincerely confess to the Lord that you have sinned against Rom. xiii. 8. And if you are resolved no more to contract debt, whatever may

be the result, and you are waiting on the Lord and truly trust in him, your present debts will soon be paid. Are you out of debt? then, whatever your future want may be, be resolved, in the strength of Jesus, rather to suffer the greatest privation, whilst waiting upon God for help, than to use unscriptural means, such as borrowing, taking goods on credit, etc., to deliver yourselves. This way needs but to be tried, in order that its excellency may be enjoyed.

There are few points more which may be of interest to the believing reader, which I shall now add.

1. There have been, during this year, six day schools for poor children *entirely* supported by the funds of our Institution, all of which have been established by us.

The number of all the children that have had schooling in the day schools through the medium of the Institution, since its formation, amounts to 2,216; the number of those at present in the six day schools is 303.

These day schools have defrayed, by the payments of the children, about the sixth part of their own expenses.

2. There is one Sunday school entirely supported by the funds of the Institution.

3. There has been, since the formation of the Institution, one adult school connected with it, in which, on the Lord's day afternoons, since that time, about 150 adults have been instructed.

4. The number of Bibles and Testaments which have been circulated through the medium of our Institution, during the last year, amounts to 452 copies.

There have been circulated since March 5, 1834, 6,044 copies of the Scriptures.

5. There have been laid out, during the last year, of the funds of the Institution, £120, 10s. 2d. for missionary purposes.

6. There are at present ninety-one orphans in the three houses. The total number of the orphans who have been under our care from April 11, 1836, to Dec. 9, 1840, amounts to 129.

Without any one having been asked for anything by us, the sum of £3,937, 1s. 1d. has been given to us for the Orphan Houses, *as the result of prayer to God*, since the commencement of the work.

THE BLESSING OF THE LORD UPON THE WORK IN REFERENCE TO THE SOULS OF THE CHILDREN.

1. During the last fourteen months there have been meetings purposely for children, at which the Scriptures have been expounded to them. At these meetings an almost universal attention is manifested by them, which I thankfully ascribe to the Lord, and upon which I look as a forerunner of greater blessing.

2. During the last year three of the Sunday-school children have been received into fellowship.

3. At the end of last year there had been eight orphans received into communion; during the present year fourteen have been received; in all, twenty-two.

It was stated in the last year's Report that we were looking for fruit upon our labors as it regards the conversion of the children, as the Lord had given to us a measure of earnestness in praying for them. The Lord has dealt with us according to our expectations. But I expect far more than what we have seen. While the chief object of our work has been and is still the manifestation of the heart of God towards his children, and the reality of power with God in prayer, yet, as we hoped, and as it has been our prayer, the Lord gives to us also the joy of seeing one child after another brought to stand openly on the Lord's side. As far as my experience goes, it appears to me that believers generally have expected far too little of *present* fruit upon their labors among children. There has been a hoping that the Lord some day or other would own the instruction which they give to children, and would answer at some time or other, though after many years only, the prayers which they offer up on their behalf. Now, while such passages as Prov. xxii. 6, Eccl. xi. 1, Gal. vi. 9, 1 Cor. xv. 58, give unto us assurance not merely respecting everything which we do for the Lord, in general, but also respecting bringing up children in the fear of the Lord, in particular, that our labor is not in vain in the Lord; yet we have to guard against abusing such passages, by thinking it a matter of little moment whether we see *present* fruit or not; but, on the contrary, we should give the Lord no rest till we see present fruit, and therefore in persevering yet submissive prayer we should make known our requests unto God. I add, as an encouragement to believers who labor among children, that during the last two years seventeen other young persons or children, from the age of eleven and a half to seventeen, have been received into fellowship among us, and that I am looking out now for many more to be converted, and that not merely of the orphans, but of the Sunday and day school children. As in so many respects we live in remarkable times, so in this respect also, that the Lord is working greatly among the children in many places.

The total of the expenses connected with the objects of the Institution, exclusive of the Orphan Houses, from Nov. 19, 1839, to Nov. 19, 1840, is £622, 2s. 6½d. The balance in hand on Nov. 19, 1840, was £13, 2s. 9¾d.

The total of the expenses connected with the three Orphan Houses, from Dec. 9, 1839, to Dec. 9, 1840, is £900, 11s. 2½ d. The balance in hand on Dec. 9, 1840, was £15, 1s. 6¼d.

REVIEW OF THE YEAR 1840.

1. As to church. There are 525 at present in communion; 114 have been added during the past year, of whom 47 have been brought to the knowledge of the Lord among us.

2. As to the supply of my temporal necessities. The Lord has been pleased to send me, by the freewill offerings of the saints, £242, 8s. 11½d.[1]

---

[1] It may not be improper to state here that the little patrimony to which Mr. Muller became entitled upon the decease of his father was devoted to the purposes of charity and religion, in accordance with the principle of action indicated on page 67. This fact is not mentioned by Mr. M , but has come to the knowledge of the editor through another channel — ED.

CHAPTER XIII.

FAITH STRENGTHENED BY EXERCISE

1841.

A WANT SUPPLIED — RESOURCES EXCEEDING THE DEMAND — EVIL OF SURETY-SHIP — POWER OF CHRISTIAN LOVE — GOD'S WORD THE FOOD OF THE SOUL — PREPARATION FOR THE HOUR OF TRIAL — POVERTY — DEPENDING ONLY ON THE LIVING GOD.

JANUARY 1, 1841. During this week we have daily met for prayer, for the especial purpose of asking the Lord to give us the means of having the last year's Report printed. It is three weeks since it might have been sent to the press. We felt this now to be a matter of special importance, as, if the Report were not soon printed, it would be known that it arose from want of means. By the donations which came in during these last days for the orphans, and by ten pounds which were given to-day for the other funds, we have the means of defraying the expense of about two-thirds of the printing, and therefore a part of the manuscript was sent off, trusting that the Lord would be pleased to send in more means before two sheets are printed off; but, if not, we should then stop till we have more. Evening. There came in still further five pounds; also, ten shillings and three shillings.

Jan. 11. Monday. During the last week the Lord not only supplied us richly with all we needed for the orphans, but enabled us to put by several pounds towards printing the Report. On Saturday evening there were only three shillings sixpence left. On this account I was looking out for answers to my prayers for means, and the Lord did not disappoint me. There came in altogether yesterday nine pounds sixteen shillings fourpence. We have now enough even for the last part of the Report.

Jan. 12. To-day I have received a letter from a brother, in which he empowers me to draw upon his bankers, during this year, to the amount of one thousand pounds, for any brethren who have it in their hearts to give themselves to missionary service in the East Indies, and whom I shall consider called for this service, as far as I am able to judge. [This power lasted only for that year; but no brethren who seemed to be suitable offered themselves for this service. This is another fresh proof how much more easily pecuniary means can be obtained than suitable individuals. Indeed, in all my experience I have found it thus, that if I could only settle that a certain thing to be done was according to the will of God, the means were soon obtained to carry it into effect.]

Jan. 13. This evening I was called to the house of a brother and sister who are in the deepest distress. The brother had become surety for the debts of his son, not in the least expecting that he ever should be called upon for the payment of them; but, as his son has not discharged his debts, the father has been called upon to do so; and except the money is paid within a few days, he will be imprisoned.

How precious it is, even for this life, to act according to the word of God! This perfect revelation of his mind gives us directions for everything, even the most minute affairs of this life. It commands us, "Be not thou one of them that strike hands, or of them that are sureties for debts." Prov. xxii. 26. The way in which Satan ensnares persons, to bring them into the net, and to bring trouble upon them by becoming sureties, is, that he seeks to represent the matter as if there were no danger connected with that particular case, and that one might be sure one should never be called upon to pay the money; but the Lord, the faithful Friend, tells us in his own word that the only way "to be sure" in such a matter is "to hate suretyship." Prov. xi. 15. The following points seem to me of solemn moment for consideration, if I were called upon to become surety for another: 1. What obliges the person who wishes me to become surety for him to need a surety? Is it really a good cause in which I am called upon to become surety? I do not remember ever to have met with a case in which a plain, and godly, and in all respects scriptural matter such a thing occurred. There was generally some sin or other connected with it. 2. If I become surety, notwithstanding what the Lord has said to me in his word, am I in such a position that no one will be injured by my being called upon to fulfil the engagements of the person for whom I am going to become surety? In most instances this alone ought to keep one from it. 3. If still I become surety, the amount of money for which I become responsible must be so in my power that I am able to produce it whenever it is called for, in order that the name of the Lord may not be dishonored. 4. But if there be the possibility of having to fulfil the engagements of the person in whose stead I have to stand, is it the will of the Lord that I should spend my means in that way? Is it not rather his will that my means should be spent in another way? 5. How can I get over the plain word of the Lord, which is to the contrary, even if the first four points could be satisfactorily settled?

March 4. From February 22 up to this day our necesities in the day schools were supplied by thirteen small donations, and by a donation of eight pounds from Q. Q. To-day I received fifteen pounds. When this arrived there was not one penny in hand for the day schools, whilst two days after about seven pounds were needed. This money came from a considerable distance, and from a brother who never had assisted in this work before, whereby the Lord afresh shows how easily he can raise up new helpers.

For the encouragement of believers, who are tried by having unconverted relatives and friends, I will relate the following circumstance, the truth of which I know.

Baron Von K., who resided in my own country, the kingdom of Prussia, had been for many years a disciple of the Lord Jesus. Even about the commencement of this century, when there was almost universal darkness or even open infidelity spread over the whole continent of Europe, he knew the Lord Jesus; and when, about the year 1806, there was the greatest distress in Silesia among many thousands of weavers, this blessed man of God took the following gracious step for his Lord and Master. As the weavers had no employment, the whole continent almost being in an unsettled state on account of Napoleon's career, it seemed to him the will of the Lord that he should use his very considerable property to furnish these poor weavers with work, in order to save them from the greatest state of destitution, though in doing this there was not only no prospect of gain, but the certain prospect of immense loss. He therefore found employment for about six thousand weavers. But he was not content with this. Whilst he gave the bread which perishes, he also sought to minister to the souls of these weavers. To that end he sought to set believers as overseers over this immense weaving concern, and not only saw to it that the weavers were instructed in spiritual things, but he himself also set the truth before them. Thus it went on for a good while, till at last, on account of the loss of the chief part of his property, he was obliged to think about giving it up. But by this time this precious act of mercy had so commended itself to the government that it was taken up by them and carried on till the times altered. Baron von K. was, however, appointed director of the whole concern as long as it existed.

This dear man of God was not content with this. He travelled through many countries to visit the prisons, for the sake of improving the temporal and spiritual condition of the prisoners, and among all the other things which he sought to do for the Lord was this also in particular: He assisted poor students whilst at the university of Berlin, especially those who studied divinity, as it is called, in order to get access to them, and to win them for the Lord. One day a most talented young man, whose father lived at Breslau, where there is likewise a university, heard of the aged baron's kindness to students, and he therefore wrote to him, requesting him to assist him, as his own father could not well afford to support him any longer, having other children to provide for. A short time afterwards young T. received a most kind reply from the baron, inviting him to come to Berlin; but, before this letter arrived, the young student had heard that Baron von K. was a pietist or mystic, as true believers are contemptuously called in Germany; and as young T. was of a highly philosophical turn of mind, reasoning about everything, questioning the truth of revelation, yea, questioning, most sceptically, the existence of God, he much disliked the prospect of going to the old baron. Still, he thought he could but try, and if he did not like it, he was not bound to remain in connection with him. He arrived in Berlin on a day when there was a great review of the troops, and, being full of this, he began to speak about it to the steward of the baron. The steward, however, being a believer, turned the conversation, before the young student was aware of it, to spiritual things; and yet he could not say that it had been forced. He began another subject, and a third, but still it always came presently again to spiritual things.

At last the baron came, who received young T. in the most affectionate and familiar manner, as if he had been his equal, and as if young T. bestowed a favor on him, rather than that he was favored by the baron. The baron offered him a room in his own house, and a place at his own table, while he should be studying in Berlin, which young T. accepted. He now sought in every way to treat the young student in the most kind and affectionate way, and as much as possible to serve him, and to show him the power of the gospel in his own life, without arguing with him, yea, without speaking to him directly about his soul. For, discovering in young T. a most reasoning and sceptical mind, he avoided in every possible way getting into any argument with him, while the young student again and again said to himself, "I wish I could get into an argument with this old fool; I would show him his folly." But the baron avoided it. When the young student used to come home in the evening, and the baron heard him come, he would himself go to meet him on entering the house, would light his candle, would assist and serve him in any way he could, even to the fetching the bootjack for him, and helping him to take off his boots. Thus this lowly aged disciple went on for some time, whilst the young student still sought an opportunity for arguing with him, but wondered nevertheless how the baron could thus serve him. One evening, on the return of young T. to the baron's house, when the baron was making himself the servant as usual, he could refrain himself no longer, but burst out thus: "Baron, how can you do all this? You see I do not care about you, and how are you able to continue to be so kind to me, and thus to serve me?" The baron replied, "My dear young friend, I have learned it from the Lord Jesus. I wish you would read through the Gospel of John. Good night." The student now for the first time in his life sat down and read the word of God in a disposition of mind to be willing to learn, whilst up to that time he had never read the Holy Scriptures but with the view of wishing to find out arguments against them. It pleased God to bless him. From that time he became himself a follower of the Lord Jesus, and has been so ever since.

May 7. It has recently pleased the Lord to teach me a truth, irrespective of human instrumentality, as far as I know, the benefit of which I have not lost, though now while preparing the fifth edition for the press, more than fourteen years have since passed away. The point is this: I saw more clearly than ever that the first great and primary business to which I ought to attend every day was, to have my soul happy in the Lord. The first thing to be concerned about was not how much I might serve the Lord, how I might glorify the Lord; but how I might get my soul into a happy state, and how my inner man might be nourished. For I might seek to set the truth before the unconverted, I might seek to benefit believers, I might seek to relieve the distressed, I might in other ways seek to behave myself as it becomes a child of God in this world; and yet, not being happy in the Lord, and not being nourished and strengthened in my inner man day by day, all this might not be attended to in a right spirit. Before this time my practice had been, at least for ten years previously, as an habitual thing to give myself to prayer, after having dressed myself in the morning. *Now*, I saw that the most important thing I had to do was to give myself to the reading of the word of God, and to meditation on it, that thus my heart might be comforted, encouraged, warned, reproved, instructed; and that thus, by means of the word of God, whilst meditating on it, my heart might be brought into experimental communion with the Lord.

I began therefore to meditate on the New Testament from the beginning, early in the morning. The first thing I did, after having asked in a few words the Lord's blessing upon his precious word, was, to begin to meditate on the word of God, searching as it were into every verse, to get blessing out of it; not for the sake of the public ministry of the word, not for the sake of preaching on what I had meditated upon, but for the sake of obtaining food for my own soul. The result I have found to be almost invariably this, that after a very few minutes my soul has been led to confession, or to thanksgiving, or to intercession, or to supplication; so that, though I did not, as it were, give myself to *prayer*, but to *meditation*, yet it turned almost immediately more or less into prayer. When thus I have been for a while making confession, or intercession, or supplication, or have given thanks, I go on to the next words or verse, turning all, as I go on, into prayer for myself or others, as the word may lead to it, but still continually keeping before me that food for my own soul is the object of my meditation. The result of this is, that there is always a good deal of confession, thanksgiving, supplication, or intercession mingled with my meditation, and that my inner man almost invariably is even sensibly nourished and strengthened, and that by breakfast time, with rare exceptions, I am in a peaceful if not happy state of heart. Thus also the Lord is pleased to communicate unto me that which, either very soon after or at a later time, I have found to become food for other believers, though it was not for the sake of the public ministry of the word that I gave myself to meditation, but for the profit of my own inner man.

With this mode I have likewise combined the being out in the open air for an hour, an hour and a half, or two hours, before breakfast, walking about in the fields, and in the summer sitting for a little on the stiles, if I find it too much to walk all the time. I find it very beneficial to my health to walk thus for meditation before breakfast, and am now so in the habit of using the time for that purpose, that when I get into the open air I generally take out a New Testament of good-sized type, which I carry with me for that purpose, besides my Bible; and I find that I can profitably spend my time in the open air, which formerly was not the case, for want of habit. I used to consider the time spent in walking a loss, but now I find it very profitable, not only to my body, but also to my soul. The walking out before breakfast is of course not necessarily connected with this matter, and every one has to judge according to his strength and other circumstances.

The difference, then, between my former practice and my present one is this: Formerly, when I rose, I began to pray as soon as possible, and generally spent all my time till breakfast in prayer, or almost all the time. At all events I almost invariably began with prayer, except when I felt my soul to be more than usually barren, in which case I read the word of God for food, or for refreshment, or for a revival and renewal of my inner man, before I gave myself to prayer. But what was the result? I often spent a quarter of an hour, or half an hour, or even an hour, on my knees, before being conscious to myself of having derived comfort, encouragement, humbling of soul, etc.; and often, after having suffered much from wandering of mind for the first ten minutes, or a quarter of an hour, or even half an hour, I only then began *really to pray*. I scarcely ever suffer now in this way. For my heart being nourished by the truth, being brought into *experimental* fellowship with God, I speak to my Father and to my Friend (vile though I am, and unworthy of it) about the things that he has brought before me in his precious word. It often now astonishes me that I did not sooner see this point. In no book did I ever read about it. No public ministry ever brought the matter before me. No private intercourse with a brother stirred me up to this matter. And yet now, since God has taught me this point, it is as plain to me as anything, that the first thing the child of God has to do morning by morning is, to *obtain food for his inner man*. As the outward man is not fit for work for any length of time except we take food, and as this is one of the first things we do in the morning, so it should be with the inner man. We should take food for that, as every one must allow. Now, what is the food for the inner man? Not *prayer*, but *the word of God;* and here again, not the simple reading of the word of God, so that it only passes through our minds, just as water runs through a pipe, but considering what we read, pondering over it, and applying it to our hearts.

When we pray, we speak to God. Now, prayer, in order to be continued for any length of time in any other than a formal manner, requires, generally speaking, a measure of strength or godly desire, and the season, therefore, when this exercise of the soul can be most effectually performed is after the inner man has been nourished by meditation on the word of God, where we find our Father speaking to us, to encourage us, to comfort us, to instruct us, to humble us, to reprove us. We may therefore profitably meditate, with God's blessing, though we are ever so weak spiritually; nay, the weaker we are, the more we need meditation for the strengthening of our inner man. There is thus far less to be feared from wandering of mind than if we give ourselves to prayer without having had previously time for meditation. I dwell so particularly on this point because of the immense spiritual profit and refreshment I am conscious of having derived from it myself, and I affectionately and solemnly beseech all my fellow-believers to ponder this matter. By the blessing of God, I ascribe to this mode the help and strength which I have had from God to pass in peace through deeper trials, in various ways, than I had ever had before; and after having now above fourteen years tried this way, I can most fully, in the fear of God, commend it. In addition to this I generally read, after family prayer, larger portions of the word of God, when I still pursue my practice of reading regularly onward in the Holy Scriptures, sometimes in the New Testament and sometimes in the Old, and for more than twenty-six years I have proved the blessedness of it. I take, also, either then or at other parts of the day, time more especially for prayer.

How different, when the soul is refreshed and made happy early in the morning, from what it is when, without spiritual preparation, the service, the trials, and the temptations of the day come upon one!

Oct. 1. When I had again not one penny in hand for the necessities of this day, there was brought to me this morning ten shillings for the orphans, which had been sent from Kensington. In the paper which contained the money, was written: "*Your Heavenly Father* knoweth that ye have need of *these* things." "Trust in the Lord." This word of our Lord is to me of more value than many bank notes. About five minutes later I received from an Irish sister ten pounds, through her banker in London. I mention here, as a point particularly to be noticed, that after the season of comparative abundance had come to an end in September, the Lord did not *at once* allow us to be so sharply tried as we were afterwards. He dealt in the same gentle way with us three years before, when the trials of faith in this part of the work first commenced.

Nov. 2. At a time of the greatest poverty one pound was sent by a lady from Birmingham. About half an hour afterwards I received ten pounds from a brother who had saved up one hundred and fifty pounds, and put it into a savings-bank, but who now sees that to devote this money to the promotion of the work of God tends more to the glory of the name of Jesus than to retain it in the savings-bank upon interest for a time of sickness or old age; for he is assured that should such times come, the same Lord, who has hitherto cared for him whilst in health and strength and able to work, will also care for him then. The same brother gave me three pounds a fortnight since. These ten pounds came in very seasonably; for, though we had been able to provide for the absolute necessities of to-day, yet there was want in many respects, especially as a boy is just going out as an apprentice, who needs tools and an outfit.

Nov. 14. When we met again this afternoon for prayer, we had reason to praise, for the Lord had sent in means. This morning were given to me five pounds, and six shillings had come in by sale of articles.

Nov. 15. Last Friday brother Craik and I had a meeting for inquirers and candidates for fellowship. We saw eight, and had to send away ten whom we could not see, our strength being quite gone after we had seen the eight, one after another. This evening we saw seven, and had to send away three.

Nov. 16. The last four days we have daily met for prayer, there being no means to pay the teachers in the day schools. Besides this, we need a stove in one of the school-rooms; also some Bibles and tracts. To-day I received two pounds from a brother at Exmouth.

Dec. 9. We are now brought to the close of the sixth year of this part of the work, *having only in hand the money which has been put by for the rent;* but during the whole of this year we have been supplied with all that was needed.

During the last three years we had closed the accounts on this day, and had, a few days after, some public meetings, at which, for the benefit of the hearers, we stated how the Lord had dealt with us during the year, and the substance of what had been stated at those meetings was afterwards printed for the benefit of the church at large. This time, however, it appeared to us better to delay for a while both the public meetings and the publishing of the Report. Through grace we had learned to lean upon the Lord only, being assured that if we never were to speak or write one single word more about this work, yet should we be supplied with means, as long as he should enable us to depend on himself alone. But whilst we neither had had those public meetings for the purpose of exposing our necessity, nor had had the account of the Lord's dealings with us published for the sake of working thereby upon the feelings of the readers, and thus inducing them to give money, but only that we might by our experience benefit other saints; yet it might have appeared to some that in making known our circumstances we were actuated by some such motives. What better proof, therefore, could we give of our depending upon the living God alone, and not upon public meetings or printed reports, than that, *in the midst of our deep poverty*, instead of being glad for the time to have come when we could make known our circumstances, we still went on quietly for some time longer, without saying anything? We therefore determined, as we sought and still seek in this work to act for the profit of the saints generally, to delay both the public meetings and the Reports for a few months. *Naturally* we should have been, of course, as glad as any one to have exposed our poverty at that time; but *spiritually* we were enabled to delight even then in the prospect of the increased benefit that might be derived by the church at large from our acting as we did.

CHAPTER XIV.

WALKING IN DARKNESS.

1841 — 1842.

"GOD'S WAY LEADS INTO TRIAL"—GROUNDS OF THANKFULNESS—PROTRACTED DARKNESS—CAST DOWN, BUT NOT DESTROYED—TRUST IN GOD COMMENDED—THE MEANS OF ITS ATTAINMENT—REVIEW OF THE WORK.

DECEMBER 15, 1841. From Nov. 12 to this day my fellow-laborers in the church and I have seen thirty inquirers and candidates for fellowship, and some of them we have seen repeatedly. How can we sufficiently praise the Lord for still continuing to use us in his service?

Dec. 18. Saturday morning. There is now the greatest need, and only fourpence in hand, which I found in the box at my house; yet I fully believe the Lord will supply us this day also with all that is required. — Pause a few moments, dear reader. Observe two things. We acted *for God* in delaying the public meetings and the publishing of the Report; but *God's way leads into trial, so far as sight and sense are concerned. Nature* always will be tried *in God's ways.* The Lord was saying by this poverty, " I will now see whether you truly lean upon me and whether you truly look to me." Of all the seasons that I had ever passed through since I had been living in this way, *up to that time,* I never knew any period in which my faith was tried so sharply as during the four months from Dec. 12, 1841, to April 12, 1842. But observe further: We might even now have altered our minds with respect to the public meetings and publishing the Report; *for no one knew our determination, at this time*, concerning this point. Nay, on the contrary, we knew with what delight very many children of God were looking forward to receive further accounts. But the Lord kept us steadfast to the conclusion at which we arrived under his guidance. — Now to return to Saturday, Dec. 18. Evening. The Lord has been very kind to us this day. In the course of the morning six shillings came in. We had thus, with what provisions there were in hand, all that was needed for the dinner, but no means to provide for the next meal in the afternoon. A few minutes after the laborers had met together for prayer this morning, there was given to one of them a sovereign for himself. By means of this all that was needed for tea could be procured. When we again met in the evening for prayer, we found that the supplies amounted to two pounds eight shillings twopence, — enough for all that was required to-day. But one thing more is to be noticed respecting this day. I was informed that three more of the orphans have been recently brought to the knowledge of the truth. We have now been meeting daily for prayer during the last five weeks, and thus the Lord has not merely heard our prayers respecting the funds, but has also blessed these children.

Dec. 23. This is now the sixth week that the laborers in the **day** schools and Orphan Houses have daily met for prayer. Several precious answers we have already received since we began to meet, as it regards pecuniary supplies, fresh instances of conversion among the children, etc. One of our petitions has been that the Lord would be pleased to furnish us with means for a stove at Callowhill Street school-room. But, though we had often mentioned this matter before the Lord, he seemed not to regard our request. Yesterday afternoon, while walking in my little garden, and meditating and praying, I had an unusual assurance that the time was now come when the Lord would answer our request, which arose partly from my being able to believe that *he would* send the means, and partly from the fact that the answer could no longer be delayed without prayer having failed in this matter, as we could not assemble the children again after the Christmas vacation, without there being a stove put up. And now, dear reader, observe: This morning I received from A. B. twenty pounds, and we have thus much more than is required for a stove.

REVIEW OF THE YEAR 1841.

1. In reading over my journal, I find that the Lord has given me, during this year, many precious answers to prayer, in addition to those which have been recorded in the previous part of the Narrative. I mention the following for the encouragement of the reader: 1. One of the orphan boys needed to be apprenticed. I knew of no suitable believing master who would take an in-door apprentice. I gave myself to prayer, and brought the matter daily before the Lord I marked it down among the subjects for which I would daily ask the Lord; and at last, though from May 21 to September I had to pray about the matter, the Lord granted my request; for in September I found a suitable place for him. 2. On May 23 I began to ask the Lord that he would be pleased to deliver a certain sister in the Lord from the great spiritual depression under which she was suffering; and after three days the Lord granted me my request. 3. On June 15 I began to ask the Lord to deliver a brother at a distance, from the great spiritual nervousness in which he found himself shut up, which not only distressed him exceedingly, and in a great measure hindered him in his service towards the world and the church, but which in consequence was also a trial to the saints who knew and valued this dear brother. This petition I brought many times before the Lord. The year passed away, and it was not granted. But yet at last this request also has been granted to me and to the many dear saints who I know prayed for this dear brother; for though he was for some years in this state, it is now [in 1845] two years and more since he has been quite restored. 4. On June 15 I also began to ask the Lord daily in his mercy to keep a sister in the Lord from insanity, who was then apparently on the very border of it; and I have now [in 1845] to record to his praise, after nearly four years have passed away, that the Lord has kept her from it. 5. During this year I was informed about the conversion of one of the very greatest sinners

that I had ever heard of in all my service for the Lord. Repeatedly I fell on my knees with his wife, and asked the Lord for his conversion, when she came to me in the deepest distress of soul, on account of the most barbarous and cruel treatment that she received from him in his bitter enmity against her for the Lord's sake, and because he could not provoke her to be in a passion, and *she would not* strike him again, and the like. At the time when it was at at its worst I pleaded especially on his behalf the promise in Matthew xviii. 19 · · Again I say unto you, that if two of you shall agree on earth as touching anything that they shall ask, it shall be done for them of my Father which is in heaven." And now this awful persecutor is converted. 6. On May 25 I began to ask the Lord for greater real spiritual prosperity among the saints among whom I labor in Bristol than there ever yet had been among them; and now I have to record to the praise of the Lord that truly he has answered this request; for, considering all things, at no period has there been more manifestation of grace, and truth, and spiritual power among us, than there is now while I am writing this for the press [1845].

2. The state of the church with reference to numbers. There are 572 at present in communion, 88 having been added during the past year, of whom 30 have been brought to the knowledge of the Lord among us.

3. The Lord's goodness as to my temporal supplies during this year. He has been pleased to give me by freewill offerings of the saints, £238, 11s. 1¾d.

Jan. 3, 1842. This evening we had a precious public prayer meeting. When the usual time for closing the meeting came, it appeared to me that there was a desire to continue to wait upon the Lord. I therefore proposed to the brethren that those who had bodily strength, time, and a desire for waiting still longer upon the Lord, would do so. At least thirty remained, and we continued till after ten in prayer, whilst several brethren prayed. I never knew prayer more really in the Spirit. I experienced for myself unusual nearness to the Lord, and was enabled to ask in faith, nothing doubting.

Jan. 4. As we have often found it to be the case, so it is now. After a season of more than usual poverty, comes a time of more than usual abundance. To-day the same brother who has been spoken of under November 3, and who has drawn his money out of the savings-bank to spend it for the Lord, sent twenty pounds more of it. There came in also from Guernsey one pound, and one pound seven shillings besides. I am now able to order oatmeal from Scotland, buy materials for the boys' clothes, order shoes, etc. Thus the Lord has been pleased to answer *all* our requests with respect to the pecuniary necessities of the orphans, which we have brought before him in our prayer meetings during the last seven weeks. We have thus had of late an abundance, but the expenses have been great also; for within the last twenty-five days I have paid out above one hundred pounds.

Feb. 8. By what came in yesterday and the day before, the need of yesterday was supplied, and there is enough in all the houses for the meals of to-day; but in none of the houses have we been able to take in any bread; and as yesterday also but little could be taken in, there will not remain any for to-morrow; nor is there money enough to take in milk to-morrow morning. There are likewise coals needed in two houses. Indeed, so far as I know, these three years and seven months, since first the funds were exhausted, we were never in greater poverty; and if the Lord were not to send means before nine o'clock to-morrow morning, his name would be dishonored. But I am fully assured that he will not leave us. — Evening. The Lord has not yet been pleased to send us what is needed for to-morrow, but he is given us a fresh proof that he is mindful of us. Between four and five o'clock this afternoon were sent nine plum cakes, which a sister had ordered to be baked as a treat for the orphans. These cakes were an encouragement to me to continue to look out for futher supplies. There were also found in the boxes at the Orphan Houses two shillings and a penny halfpenny, and one shilling fourpence came in for stockings. These little donations are most precious, but they are not enough to meet the need of to-morrow; yea, before nine o'clock to-morrow morning we need more money to be able to take in the milk. Truly, we are poorer than ever; but through grace my eyes look not at the empty stores and the empty purse, but to the riches of the Lord only.

Feb. 9. This morning I went between seven and eight o'clock to the Orphan Houses, to see whether the Lord had sent in anything. When I arrived there, he had just two or three minutes before sent help. A brother, in going to his house of business this morning, had gone already about half a mile, when the Lord was pleased to lay the orphans upon his heart. He said, however, to himself, I cannot well return now, but will take something this evening; and thus he walked on. Nevertheless, he could not go on any further, but felt himself constrained to go back, and take to brother R. B., at the Boys' Orphan House, three sovereigns. [The donor himself stated this to me afterwards.] Thus the Lord in his faithfulness helped us. Help was never more truly needed, for our poverty was never greater; nor did the help of the Lord ever come more manifestly from himself; for *the brother was gone on a good distance, it was between seven and eight o'clock in the morning, and it was so short a time before money would have been needed.* Consider this, beloved reader, and with us praise the Lord for his goodness. Praise him particularly that he enabled us to trust in him in this trying hour. There came in besides, to-day, seven shillings sixpence.

Feb 12. Saturday. Never since the funds were for the first time exhausted had there come in less during any week than during this. We were only able to supply the absolute necessities; but this we were enabled to do. When the meal-times came, the Lord always provided what was needful, and, considering the great distress there is now almost everywhere, our dear orphans are very well provided for. Now this day began not only without there being anything in hand, but our stores were greatly reduced, and we had to procure provisions for two days. One of the laborers gave five shillings in the morning, to provide the means to take in the milk. I collected together some pamphlets, which had been given for sale, to dispose of them, and they were sold about eleven o'clock for four shillings. There came in also by sale of stockings three shillings, and twelve shillings were paid on behalf of one of the orphans. Thus we were provided with means to procure a dinner, and had a *little* towards purchasing bread, but by no means enough. All the laborers were together in prayer from half-past eleven till one, and we separated comfortably, with the purpose of meeting again in the evening. When I came home there was given to me an old broken silver pencil-case, which, though worth very little, I took as a fresh proof that our Father was mindful of our need. When we met again this evening, we found that three shillings sixpence had come in by sale of stockings, and sixpence for two Reports. As all this was not enough, a few old and needless articles were disposed of for four shillings, also the broken pencil-case for sixpence. I say *needless* articles, for other articles it did not seem right to us to dispose of, in order that the Lord's own deliverance might be manifest. A laborer was also still further able to give seven shillings of his own. To one of the laborers two shillings had been owed by a certain individual for more than a twelvemonth, which being paid just now, and given by him for the orphans, came in most seasonably. Thus we had one pound eighteen shillings sixpence, as much as was needful to procure provisions till after breakfast on Monday morning. However, the Lord helped still further. Between eight and nine this evening, after we had been together for prayer, and had now separated, some money was given to one of the laborers for himself, by which means he was able to give nine shillings, so that altogether two pounds seven shillings sixpence had come in this day. This has been, of all the weeks, during the last three years and seven months, one of the most trying. so far as it regards the trial of faith. Thanks to the Lord who has helped us this day also! Thanks to him for enabling us already this morning, when we met for prayer, to praise him for the deliverance which we were sure he would work.

Feb. 16. This morning there was now again only sufficient money in hand to take in milk at two of the houses; but as a laborer was able to give six shillings sixpence, we had sufficient for the milk, and had also enough, with the provisions that were in the houses, to provide for the dinner. Nothing more came in in the course of the morning, nor was I able to make inquiries how matters stood. In the afternoon, between three and four o'clock, having once more besought the Lord to send us help, I sat peacefully down to give myself to meditation over the word, considering that that was now my service, though I knew not whether there was a morsel of bread for tea in any one of the houses, *but being assured that the Lord would provide.* For, through grace, my mind is so fully assured of the faithfulness of the Lord, that, in the midst of the greatest need, I am enabled in peace to go about my other work. Indeed, did not the Lord give me this, which is the result of trusting in him, I should scarcely be able to work at all; for it is now comparatively a rare thing that a day comes when I am not in need for one or the other part of the work. Scarcely had I sat down to meditate, when a note was sent to me from the Orphan Houses, in which brother R. B., master of the Orphan boys, had written thus: "On visiting the sisters in the Infant and Girls' Orphan Houses, I found them in the greatest need. There was not bread in one of the houses for tea this evening, and the six shillings sixpence were scarcely enough to supply what was needed for the dinner. I therefore opened the box in the Boys' Orphan House, and most unexpectedly found one pound in it. Thus, through the kindness of the Lord, we were again abundantly supplied as it regards present necessities." In the evening the Lord, in his love and faithfulness, stretched out his hand still further. I had expounded at the meeting a part of John xi. The last words on which I spoke were, "Said I not unto thee that if thou wouldest believe thou shouldest see the glory of God?" When the meeting was over, as a fresh proof of the truth of this word, a note was given to me in which a sick sister sent me five pounds for the orphans.

Feb. 21. Since Saturday evening came in one pound eight shillings elevenpence. There were also sent from Plymouth a piece of blond, a piece of quilling net. and eleven pairs of children's stockings, for sale. Thus we were supplied with means for that which was requisite for the beginning of this day; but, as our stores had been so reduced at the end of last week there was not enough for tea this afternoon. Four o'clock had now come, one hour before the usual tea-time, when a brother from Somersetshire came to see the Orphan Houses, and put a sovereign into each of the boxes. Our great need soon brought out the money, and thus we were supplied. [Observe! The brother, as he himself told me a few days after in the course of conversation, had but little time, and therefore rather hastily went over the houses. Had he stayed long and conversed much, as might have been the case, his donations would not have been in time for the tea.] There came in one shilling besides, by needlework done by the children.

Feb. 25. Greater than now our need had never been. Our trials of faith have never been so sharp as during this week. Indeed, so much so, that most of the laborers felt to-day considerably tried. Yet neither this day has the Lord suffered us to be confounded. Through a remarkable circumstance one of the laborers obtained some money this morning, so that all the need of to-day could be amply met.

Feb. 26. My prayer this morning was in particular

that the Lord would be pleased now to look in pity upon us, and take off his hand. Indeed, for several days my prayer has been that he would enable us to continue to trust in him, and not lay more upon us than he would enable us to bear. This is now again Saturday. There having been given yesterday a rich supply to the matrons, I knew that not so much as usual would be required *this* Saturday; still, I thought that one pound ten shillings would be needed. Between ten and eleven o'clock this morning a parcel came from Clapham, containing two pounds two shillings, with two frocks, two petticoats, two chemises, two pinafores, and six handkerchiefs, all new. Thus we were richly supplied for to-day, for only one pound ten shillings were needed.

March 2. This evening were sent, by order of an Irish sister, thirty-three and a half pounds of woollen yarn. Respecting this donation it is to be remarked that last Saturday we had asked the Lord, in our prayer meeting, that he would be pleased to send us means to purchase worsted, in order that the boys might go on with their knitting.

March 9. At a time of the greatest need, both with regard to the day schools and the orphans, so much so that we could not have gone on any longer without help, I received this day ten pounds from a brother who lives near Dublin. The money was divided between the day schools and the Orphan Houses. The following little circumstance is to be noticed respecting this donation. As our need was so great, and my soul was, through grace, truly waiting upon the Lord, I looked out for supplies in the course of this morning. The post, however, was out, and no supplies had come. This did not in the least discourage me. I said to myself, the Lord can send means without the post, or even now, though the post is out, by this very delivery of letters he may have sent means, though the money is not yet in my hands. It was not long after I had thus spoken to myself when, according to my hope in God, we were helped; for the brother who sent us the ten pounds, had this time directed his letter to the Boys' Orphan House, whence it was sent to me.

March 17. From the 12th to the 16th had come in four pounds five shillings elevenpence halfpenny for the orphans. This morning our poverty, which now has lasted more or less for several months, had become exceedingly great. I left my house a few minutes after seven to go to the Orphan Houses to see whether there was money enough to take in the milk, which is brought about eight o'clock. On my way it was especially my request that the Lord would be pleased to pity us, even as a father pitieth his children, and that he would not lay more upon us than he would enable us to bear. I especially entreated him that he would now be pleased to refresh our hearts by sending us help. I likewise reminded him of the consequences that would result, both in reference to believers and unbelievers, if we should have to give up the work because of want of means, and that he therefore would not permit its coming to nought. I moreover again confessed before the Lord that I deserved not that he should continue to use me in this work any longer. While I was thus in prayer, about two minutes' walk from the Orphan Houses, I met a brother who was going at this early hour to his business. After having exchanged a few words with him, I went on; but he presently ran after me, and gave me one pound for the orphans. Thus the Lord speedily answered my prayer. Truly, it is worth being poor and greatly tried in faith for the sake of having day by day such precious proofs of the loving interest which our kind Father takes in everything that concerns us. And how should our Father do otherwise! He that has given us the greatest possible proof of his love which he could have done, in giving us his own Son, surely he will with him also freely give us all things. It is worth also being poor and greatly tried in faith, if but thereby the hearts of the children of God may be comforted and their faith strengthened, and if but those who do not know God, and who may read or hear of his dealings with us, should be led thereby to see that faith in God is more than a mere notion, and that there is indeed reality in Christianity. In the course of this day there came in still further thirteen shillings.

March 19. Saturday. As it has often been the case on Saturdays, so it was this day in particular. We began the day in very great poverty, as only seven shillings had come in since the day before yesterday. There was not one ray of light as to natural prospects. The heart would be overwhelmed at such seasons, were there not an abundance of repose to be found by trusting in God. The trial having continued so long, and our poverty having now come to such a degree that it was necessary we should have help in order that the name of the Lord might not be dishonored, I had proposed to my fellow-laborers that we should set apart this day especially for prayer. We met accordingly at half-past ten in the morning. By that time had come in four shillings sixpence, seven shillings sixpence, and ten shillings. In the afternoon we met again at three, when ten shillings came in. In the evening, at seven, we met once more, there being yet about three shillings needed to procure all that was required. This also we received, and even three shillings more than was actually needed came in, just when we were about to separate.

April 12. We were never in greater need than to-day, perhaps never in so much, when I received this morning one hundred pounds from the East Indies. It is impossible to describe the real joy in God it gave me. My prayer had been again this morning particularly that our Father would pity us, and now at last send larger sums. I was not in the least surprised or excited when this donation came, for I took it as that *which came in answer to prayer, and had been long looked for.*

May 6. Only three pounds ten shillings twopence halfpenny had been received since the 2d, on which account there would have been only enough means in hand to provide for the breakfast to-morrow morning, when in this our fresh need we received eighty-six pounds, two pair of gold ear-rings, a brooch and two rupees.

May 10. To-day, in closing the accounts, we have left, at the end of this period of seventeen months, in which we have been so often penniless, the sum of sixteen pounds eighteen shillings tenpence halfpenny for the orphans, and forty-eight pounds twelve shillings five and one fourth pence for the other objects of the Scriptural Knowledge Institution.

The time now seemed to us to have come, when, for the profit of the church at large, the Lord's dealings with us, with reference to the various objects of the Scriptural Knowledge Institution, should be made known by publishing another Report. For, whilst we, on purpose, had delayed it at this time five months longer than during the previous years, and that during a period when we were in deeper poverty than during any previous time; yet, as from the commencement it had appeared to me important from time to time to make known the Lord's dealings with us, so I judged it profitable still to seek to comfort, to encourage, to exhort, to instruct, and to warn the dear children of God by the printed accounts of the Lord's goodness to us.

Though our trials of faith during these seventeen months lasted longer and were sharper than during any previous period, yet during all this time the orphans had everything that was needful in the way of nourishing food, the necessary articles of clothing, etc. Indeed, I should rather at once send the children back to their relations than keep them without sufficient maintenance.

I desire that all the children of God who may read these details may thereby be led to increased and more simple confidence in God for everything which they may need under any circumstances, and that these many answers to prayer may encourage them to pray, particularly as it regards the conversion of their friends and relations, their own progress in grace and knowledge, the state of the saints whom they may know personally, the state of the church of Christ at large, and the success of the preaching of the gospel. Especially, I affectionately warn them against being led away by the device of Satan, to think that these things are peculiar to me, and cannot be enjoyed by all the children of God; for though, as has been stated before, every believer is not called upon to establish orphan houses, charity schools, etc., and trust in the Lord for means, yet all believers are called upon, in the simple confidence of faith, to cast all their burdens upon him, to trust in him for everything, and not only to make everything a subject of prayer, but to expect answers to their petitions which they have asked according to his will and in the name of the Lord Jesus. Think not, dear reader, that I have *the gift of faith*, that is, that gift of which we read in 1 Cor. xii. 9, and which is mentioned along with "the gifts of healing," "the working of miracles," " prophecy," and that on that account I am able to trust in the Lord. *It is true* that the faith which I am enabled to exercise is altogether God's own gift; it is true that he alone supports it, and that he alone can increase it; it is true that moment by moment I depend on him for it, and that if I were only one moment left to myself my faith would utterly fail; but *it is not true* that my faith is that gift of faith which is spoken of in 1 Cor. xii. 9. It is the self-same faith which is found in *every believer*, and the growth of which I am most sensible of to myself; for by little and little it has been increasing for the last six and twenty years.

This faith which is exercised respecting the Orphan Houses, and my own temporal necessities, shows itself in the same measure, for instance, concerning the following points: I have never been permitted to doubt during the last twenty-seven years that my sins are forgiven, that I am a child of God, that I am beloved of God, and that I shall be finally saved, because I am enabled by the grace of God to exercise faith upon the word of God, and believe what God says in those passages which settle these matters (1 John v. 1; Gal. iii. 26; Acts x. 43; Romans x. 9, 10; John iii. 16, etc.). Further, at the time when I thought I should be insane, though there was not the least ground for thinking so, I was in peace; because my soul believed the truth of that word, "We know that all things work together for good to them that love God." Rom. viii. 28. Further: When my brother in the flesh and my dear aged father died, and when concerning both of them I had no *evidence* whatever that they were saved (though I dare not say that they are lost, for I know it not), yet my soul was at peace, perfectly at peace, under this great trial, this exceedingly great trial, this trial which is one of the greatest perhaps which can befall a believer. And what was it that gave me peace? My soul laid hold on that word, "Shall not the Judge of all the earth do right?" This word, together with the whole character of God, as he has revealed himself in his holy word, settled all questionings. I believed what he has said concerning himself, and I was at peace, and have been at peace ever since, concerning this matter. Further: When the Lord took from me a beloved infant, my soul was at peace, perfectly at peace; I could only weep tears of joy when I did weep. And why? Because my soul laid hold in faith on that word, "Of such is the kingdom of heaven." Matthew xix. 14. Further: When sometimes all has been dark, exceedingly dark, with reference to my service among the saints, judging from natural appearances; yea, when I should have been overwhelmed indeed in grief and despair had I looked at things after the outward appearance: at such times I have sought to encourage myself in God, by laying hold in faith on his almighty power, his unchangeable love, and his infinite wisdom, and I have said to myself,

God is able and willing to deliver me, if it be good for me; for it is written, "He that spared not his own Son, but delivered him up for us all, how shall he not with him also freely give us all things?" Rom. viii. 32. This it was which, being believed by me through grace, kept my soul in peace. Further: When, in connection with the Orphan Houses, day schools, etc., trials have come upon me which were far heavier than the want of means; when lying reports were spread that the orphans had not enough to eat, or that they were cruelly treated in other respects, and the like; or when other trials, still greater, but which I cannot mention, have befallen me in connection with this work, and that at a time when I was nearly a thousand miles absent from Bristol, and had to remain absent week after week; at such times my soul was stayed upon God; I believed his word of promise which was applicable to such cases; I poured out my soul before God, and arose from my knees in peace, because the trouble that was in the soul was in believing prayer cast upon God, and thus I was kept in peace, though I saw it to be the will of God to remain far away from the work. Further: When I needed houses, fellow-laborers, masters and mistresses for the orphans or for the day schools, I have been enabled to look for all to the Lord, and trust in him for help.

Dear reader, I may seem to boast; but, by the grace of God, I do not boast in thus speaking. From my inmost soul I do ascribe it to God alone that he has enabled me to trust in him, and that hitherto he has not suffered my confidence in him to fail. But I thought it needful to make these remarks, lest any one should think that my depending upon God was a particular gift given to me, which other saints have no right to look for; or lest it should be thought that this my depending upon him had *only to do with the obtaining of* MONEY *by prayer and faith.* By the grace of God I desire that my faith in God should extend towards EVERYTHING, the smallest of my own temporal and spiritual concerns, and the smallest of the temporal and spiritual concerns of my family, towards the saints among whom I labor, the church at large, everything that has to do with the temporal and spiritual prosperity of the Scriptural Knowledge Institution, etc. Dear reader, do not think that I have attained in faith (and how much less in other respects!) to that degree to which I might and ought to attain; but thank God for the faith which he has given me, and ask him to uphold and increase it. And lastly, once more, let not Satan deceive you in making you think that *you* could not have the same faith, but that it is only for persons who are situated as I am. When I lose such a thing as a key, I ask the Lord to direct me to it, and I look for an answer to my prayer; when a person with whom I have made an appointment does not come, according to the fixed time, and I begin to be inconvenienced by it, I ask the Lord to be pleased to hasten him to me, and I look for an answer; when I do not understand a passage of the word of God, I lift up my heart to the Lord, that he would be pleased, by his Holy Spirit, to instruct me, and I expect to be taught, though I do not fix the time when, and the manner how it should be; when I am going to minister in the word, I seek help from the Lord, and while I, in the consciousness of natural inability as well as utter unworthiness, begin this his service, I am not cast down, but of good cheer, because I look for his assistance, and believe that he, for his dear Son's sake, will help me. And thus in other of my temporal and spiritual concerns I pray to the Lord, and expect an answer to my requests; and may not *you* do the same, dear believing reader? Oh! I beseech you do not think me an extraordinary believer, having privileges above other of God's dear children, which they cannot have; nor look on my way of acting as something that would not do for other believers. Make but trial! Do but stand still in the hour of trial, and you will see the help of God, if you trust in him. But there is so often a forsaking the ways of the Lord in the hour of trial, and thus the *food for faith*, the means whereby our faith may be increased, is lost. This leads me to the following important point. You ask, How may I, a true believer, have my faith strengthened? The answer is this: —

I. "Every good gift and every perfect gift is from above, and cometh down from the Father of lights, with whom is no variableness, neither shadow of turning." James i. 17. As the increase of faith is a good gift, it must come from God, and therefore he ought to be asked for this blessing.

II. The following means, however, ought to be used: 1. *The careful reading of the word of God, combined with meditation on it.* Through reading of the word of God, and especially through meditation on the word of God, the believer becomes more and more acquainted with the nature and character of God, and thus sees more and more, besides his holiness and justice, what a kind, loving, gracious, merciful, mighty, wise, and faithful being he is, and, therefore, in poverty, affliction of body, bereavement in his family, difficulty in his service, want of a situation or employment, he will repose upon the *ability* of God to help him, because he has not only learned from his word that he is of almighty power and infinite wisdom, but he has also seen instance upon instance in the Holy Scriptures in which his almighty power and infinite wisdom have been actually exercised in helping and delivering his people; and he will repose upon the *willingness* of God to help him, because he has not only learned from the Scriptures what a kind, good, merciful, gracious, and faithful being God is, but because he has also seen in the word of God how in a great variety of instances he has proved himself to be so. And the consideration of this, if *God has become known to us through prayer and meditation on his own word*, will lead us, in general at least, with a measure of confidence to rely upon him; and thus the reading of the word of God, together with meditation on it, will be one especial means to strengthen our faith.

2. As, with reference to the growth of every grace of the Spirit, it is of the utmost importance that we seek to maintain an upright heart and a good conscience, and, therefore, do not knowingly and habitually indulge in those things which are contrary to the mind of God, so it is also particularly the case with reference to the *growth in faith*. How can I possibly continue to act faith upon God, concerning anything, if I am habitually grieving him, and seek to detract from the glory and honor of him in whom I profess to trust, upon whom I profess to depend? All my confidence towards God, all my leaning upon him in the hour of trial, will be gone, if I have a guilty conscience, and do not seek to put away this guilty conscience, but still continue to do things which are contrary to the mind of God. And if, in any particular instance, I cannot trust in God, because of the guilty conscience, then my faith is weakened by that instance of distrust; for faith with every fresh trial of it either increases by trusting God, and thus getting help, or it decreases by not trusting him; and then there is less and less power of looking simply and directly to him, and a habit of self-dependence is begotten or encouraged. One or other of these will always be the case in each particular instance. Either we trust in God, and in that case we neither trust in ourselves, nor in our fellow-men, nor in circumstances, nor in anything besides; or we DO trust in one or more of these, and in that case do NOT trust in God.

3. If we, indeed, desire our faith to be strengthened, we should not shrink from opportunities where our faith may be tried, and, therefore, through the trial, be strengthened. In our natural state we dislike dealing with God alone. Through our natural alienation from God we shrink from him, and from eternal realities. This cleaves to us more

or less, even after our regeneration. Hence it is that, more or less, even as believers, we have the same shrinking from standing with God alone, from depending upon him alone, from looking to him alone; and yet this is the very position in which we ought to be, if we wish our faith to be strengthened. The more I am in a position to be tried in faith with reference to my body, my family, my service for the Lord, my business, etc., the more shall I have opportunity of seeing God's help and deliverance; and every fresh instance in which he helps and delivers me will tend towards the increase of my faith. On this account, therefore, the believer should not shrink from situations, positions, circumstances, in which his faith may be tried, but should cheerfully embrace them as opportunities where he may see the hand of God stretched out on his behalf, to help and deliver him, and whereby he may thus have his faith strengthened.

4. The last important point for the strengthening of our faith is, that we let God work for us, when the hour of the trial of our faith comes, and do not work a deliverance of our own. Wherever God has given faith, it is given, among other reasons, for the very purpose of being tried. Yea, however weak our faith may be, God will try it; only with this restriction, that as, in every way, he leads us on gently, gradually, patiently, so also with reference to the trial of our faith. At first our faith will be tried very little in comparison with what it may be afterwards; for God never lays more upon us than he is willing to enable us to bear. Now, when the trial of faith comes, we are naturally inclined to distrust God, and to trust rather in ourselves, or in our friends, or in circumstances. We will rather work a deliverance of our own, somehow or other, than simply look to God and wait for his help. But if we do not patiently wait for God's help, if we work a deliverance of our own, then at the next trial of our faith it will be thus again, we shall be again inclined to deliver ourselves; and thus,

with every fresh instance of that kind, our faith will decrease; whilst, on the contrary, were we to stand still in order to see the salvation of God, to see his hand stretched out on our behalf, trusting in him alone, then our faith would be increased, and in every fresh case in which the hand of God is stretched out in our behalf in the hour of the trial of our faith, our faith would be increased yet more. Would the believer, therefore, have his faith strengthened, he must, especially, *give time to God*, who tries his faith in order to prove to his child, in the end, how willing he is to help and deliver him, the moment it is good for him.

I now return, dear reader, to the Narrative, giving you some further information with reference to the seventeen months from Dec. 10, 1840, to May 10, 1842, as it respects the Orphan Houses, and other objects of the Scriptural Knowledge Institution for Home and Abroad, besides the facts of which mention has been already made.

During this period, also, 1. Two Sunday schools were entirely supported by the funds of the Institution. 2. There were two adult schools, one for females, and one for males, entirely supported during these seventeen months, in which on two evenings of the week the males, and on two evenings the females, were instructed quite gratuitously, in reading and writing, and were furnished with books and writing materials gratuitously. There were, during these seventeen months, 344 adults taught in these two schools, and on May 10, 1842, the number under instruction amounted to 110. 3. There were, during these seventeen months, also six day schools entirely supported by the funds of the Institution, three for boys and three for girls. On May 10, 1842, the number of children who attended these day schools was 363; and the total number who, from the formation of the Institution, March 5, 1834, up to May 10, 1842, had been instructed in the day schools, which are supported by the funds of the Institution, amounts to

2,616. 4 During these seventeen months, 798 copies of the Holy Scriptures were circulated, and from the commencement of the Institution, up to May 10, 1842, 6,842 copies. 5. During these seventeen months was spent for missionary purposes the sum of £126, 15s. 3d. of the funds of the Institution, whereby assistance was rendered to the work of God in Jamaica, in Australia, in Canada, and in the East Indies. 6. At the commencement of these seventeen months, *i. e.*, on Dec. 10, 1840, a new object was begun, the circulation of such publications as may be beneficial, with the blessing of God, to both unbelievers and believers. We laid out for this object during these seventeen months the sum of £62, 17s. 4d., for which 22,190 such little publications were purchased, and of which number 19,609 were actually given away. 7. There were received into the three Orphan Houses 15 orphans, who, together with those who were in the houses on Dec. 10, 1840, make up 106 in all. Of these, five girls were sent out to service, two boys and one girl were apprenticed, one girl was removed by a lady who had placed her for a time under our care, and one was sent back to his relations, as he was injurious to the other children.

There were on May 10, 1842, 96 orphans in the three houses, *i. e.*, 30 in the Girls' Orphan House, 37 in the Infant Orphan House, and 29 in the Boys' Orphan House. Besides this, three apprentices were supported by the funds of the Institution; so that the total number was 99. The number of orphans who were under our care from April, 1836, to May 10, 1842, amounts to 144.

I notice further, in connection with the Orphan Houses, that, *without any one having been asked for anything by me,* the sum of £5,276, 14s. 8d. was given to me from the beginning of the work up to May 10, 1842, *as the result of prayer to God.*

The total of the expenditure for the various objects of the Institution, exclusive of the Orphan Houses, during these seventeen months, amounted to £710, 11s. 5d.; the total of the income amounted to £746, 1s. 0½d. The total of the expenditure for the three Orphan Houses, from Dec. 10, 1840, to May 10, 1842, amounted to £1,333, 15s. 2¾d.; the total of the income amounted to £1,339, 13s. 7d.

CHAPTER XV.

PROSPERITY.

1842 — 1843.

ABUNDANT SUPPLIES — RESTING ON THE WRITTEN WORD — "SEEKING AND FINDING" — ERRONEOUS IMPRESSIONS REMOVED — PERSEVERING AND PREVAILING PRAYER ANSWERED — "LENGTHENING THE CORDS AND STRENGTHENING THE STAKES" — A FOURTH ORPHAN HOUSE.

JUNE 3, 1842. For several days past I had not been particularly led to pray for means for the orphans. Last evening, however, I did so, as we had now again no money in hand, there having come in only ten pounds two shillings twopence during the last five days; and in answer to my request two pounds nineteen shillings sixpence came in this morning.

For several months succeeding the last date, means continued to flow in, without interruption, as they were needed. There was no excess of means, nor was there any lack. On Dec. 1, 1842, Mr. Müller writes: —

Nothing had come in, except five shillings for needlework. The laborers had nothing to give, except one of them one shilling sixpence; yet this little supplied the absolute need, which was only milk. We were unable to take in the usual quantity of bread. Should it be said that the not taking in the usual quantity of bread would at once prove to the bakers that we are poor, my reply is, that that does not follow, because bread has often been sent as a present, as may be seen in the list of articles, given for the orphans, at the end of the printed Reports. But perhaps it may be asked, Why do you not take the bread on credit? What does it matter whether you pay immediately for it, or at the end of the month, or the quarter, or the half year? Seeing that the Orphan Houses are the work of the Lord, may you not trust in him that he will supply you with means to pay the bills which you contract with the butcher, baker, grocer, etc., as the things which you purchase are needful? My reply is this: 1. If the work in which we are engaged is indeed the work of God, then he whose work it is is surely able and willing to provide the means for it. 2. But not only so, he will also provide the means *at the time when they are needed.* I do not mean that he will provide them when *we think* that they are needed; but yet that when there is real need, such as the necessaries of life being required, he will give them; and on the same ground on which we suppose we do trust in God to help us to pay the debt which we now contract, we may and ought to trust in the Lord to supply us with what we require at present, so that there may be no need for going into debt. 3. It is true, I might have goods on credit, and to a very considerable amount; but, then, the result would be, that the next time we were again in straits, the mind would involuntarily be turned to further credit which I might have, instead of being turned to the Lord, and thus faith, which is kept up and strengthened only by being EXERCISED, would become weaker and weaker, till at last, according to all human probability, I should find myself deeply in debt, and have no prospect of getting out of it. 4. Faith has to do with the word of God, — rests upon the written word of God, but there is no promise that he will pay our debts. The word says rather, "Owe no man anything;" whilst there is the promise given to his children, "I will never leave thee nor forsake thee," and, "Whosoever believeth on him shall not be confounded." On this account we could not say, *upon the ground of the Holy Scriptures*, Why do you not trust in God that he will supply you with means to pay your debts which you contract in his service for the necessities of the orphans? 5. The last reason why we do not take goods on credit is this: The chief and primary object of the work was not the temporal welfare of the children, nor even their spiritual welfare, blessed and glorious as it is, and much as, through grace, we seek after it and pray for it; but the first and primary object of the work was, *to show before the whole world and the whole church of Christ, that even in these last evil days the living God is ready to prove himself as the living God, by being ever willing to help, succor, comfort, and answer the prayers of those who trust in him:* so that we need not go away from him to our fellowmen, or to the ways of the world, seeing that he is both able and willing to supply us with all we can need in his service.

From the beginning, when God put this service into my heart, I had anticipated trials and straits; but knowing, as I did, the heart of God, through the experience of several years previously, I also knew that he would listen to the prayers of his child who trusts in him, and that he would not leave him in the hour of need, but listen to his prayers, and deliver him out of the difficulty, and that then, this being made known in print for the benefit of both believers and unbelievers, others would be led to trust in the Lord. We discern, therefore, more and more clearly that it is for the church's benefit that we are put into these straits, and if therefore in the hour of need we were to take goods on credit, the first and primary object of the work would be completely frustrated, and no heart would be further strengthened to trust in God; nor would there be any longer that manifestation of the special and particular providence of God which has hitherto been so abundantly shown through this work, even in the eyes of unbelievers, whereby they have been led to see *that there is after all reality in the things of God,* and many, through these printed accounts, have been truly converted. For these reasons, then, we consider it our precious privilege, as heretofore, to continue to wait upon the Lord only, instead of taking goods on credit, or borrowing money from some kind friends when we are in need. Nay, we purpose, as God shall give us grace, to look to him only, though morning after morning we should have nothing in hand for the work, yea, though from meal to meal we should have to look to him; being fully assured that he who is now (1845) in the tenth year feeding these many orphans, and who has never suffered them to want, and that he who is now (1845) in the twelfth year carrying on the other parts of the work, without any branch of it being stopped for want of means, will do so for the future also. And here I do desire, in the deep consciousness of my natural helplessness and dependence upon the Lord, to confess that through the grace of God my soul has been in peace, though day after day we have had to wait for our daily provisions upon the Lord; yea, though even from meal to meal we have been required to do this.

Dec. 16. Nothing has come in. Three shillings fivepence, which one of the laborers was able to give, was all we had. At six o'clock this evening, our need being now very great, not only with reference to the Orphan Houses, but also the day schools, etc., I gave myself, with two of the laborers, to prayer. There needed some money to come in before eight o'clock to-morrow morning, as there was none to take in milk for breakfast (the children have oatmeal porridge with milk for breakfast), to say nothing about the many other demands of to-morrow, being Saturday. Our hearts were at peace, while asking the Lord, and assured that our Father would supply our need. WE HAD SCARCELY RISEN FROM OUR KNEES when I received a letter, containing a sovereign for the orphans, half of which was from a young East India officer, and the other half the produce of the sale of a piece of work which the sister who sent the money had made for the benefit of the orphans. She wrote, "I love to send these little gifts. They so often come in season." Truly, thus it was at this time. About five minutes later I received from a brother the promise of fifty pounds for the orphans, to be given during the next week; and a quarter of an hour after that, about seven o'clock, a brother gave me a sovereign, which an Irish sister in the Lord had left this day, on her departure for Dublin, for the benefit of the orphans. How sweet and precious to see thus so manifestly the willingness of the Lord to answer the prayers of his needy children!

Dec. 19. Our need, with reference to the school fund, had been great during the last three weeks, though we had received as much as the teachers absolutely required. Now, however, it was very great, as one brother especially needed to have several pounds within a day or two, and three other teachers also required supplies. It had in addition to this been much in my heart to send some money to several brethren who labor in foreign lands, in dependence upon the Lord only for their pecuniary supplies; but I had been kept from doing so for want of means. On these accounts, therefore, I gave myself again especially to prayer this morning, when, *within a quarter of an hour* after I had risen from my knees, I received the order for one hundred pounds, which I was at liberty to use as need required.

REVIEW OF THE YEAR 1842.

1. As to the church. There are 601 at present in communion; 73 have been added during the past year, of whom 27 have been brought to the knowledge of the Lord among us.

2. As to the supply of my temporal necessities, the Lord has been pleased to send me £329, 16s.

Feb 11, 1843. We had one pound fourteen shillings towards the expenses of this day. But as this was not enough, I asked the Lord still further for help, and, behold, this morning's post brought me a post-office order for two pounds from Stafford, of which one pound seven shillings sixpence are for the orphans. Thus we have three pounds one shilling sixpence, which is quite enough for this day.

Admire with me, my dear reader, if you know the Lord, his seasonable help. Why does this post-office order not come a few days sooner or later? Because the Lord would help us by means of it, and therefore influences the donor just then, and not sooner nor later, to send it. Surely, all who know the Lord, and who have no interest in disowning it, cannot but see his hand in a remarkable manner in this work. Nor will the godly and simple-minded reader say, "There is no difference between this way of proceeding, on the one hand, and going from individual to individual, asking them for means, on the other hand; for the writing of the Reports is just the same thing." My dear reader, there is a great difference. Suppose that we are in need. Suppose that our poverty lasts for some weeks, or even some months, together. Is there not, in that case, a difference between asking the Lord only from day to day, without speaking to any human being not connected directly with the work about our poverty, on the one hand, and writing letters or making personal application to benevolent individuals for assistance, on the other hand? Truly, there is a great difference between these two modes. I do not mean to say that it would be acting against the precepts of the Lord to seek for help in his work by personal and individual application to *believers* (though it would be in direct opposition to his will to apply to *unbelievers*, 2 Cor. vi. 14–18); but *I* act in the way in which I do for the benefit of the church at large, cheerfully bearing the trials, and sometimes the deep trials, connected with this life of faith (which, however, brings along with it also its precious joys), if by any means a part at least of my fellow-believers might be led to see the reality of dealing with God only, and that there is such a thing as the child of God having power with God by prayer and faith. That the Lord should use for so glorious a service one so vile, so unfaithful, so altogether unworthy of the least notice as I am, I can only ascribe to the riches of his condescending *grace*, in which he takes up the most unlikely instruments, that the honor may be *manifestly* his.

Should Satan seek to whisper into your ears, Perhaps the matter is made known, after all, when there is need (as it has been once said about me at a public meeting in a large town, that when we were in want I prayed *publicly* that the Lord would send help for the orphans, which is entirely false); I say, should it be said that I took care that our wants were made known, I reply: Whom did I ask for anything these many years since the work has been going on? To whom did I make known our wants, except to those who are closely connected with the work? Nay, so far from wishing to make known our need, for the purpose of influencing benevolent persons to contribute to the necessities of the Institution under my care, I have even refused to let our circumstances be known, after having been asked about them, when, on simply saying that we were in need, I might have had considerable sums. Some instances of this have been given in the former part of this Narrative. In such cases I refused in order that the hand of God only might be manifest; for that, and not the money, nor even the ability of continuing to carry on the work, is my especial aim. And such self-possession has the Lord given me, that in the times of the deepest poverty, whilst there was nothing at all in hand, and whilst we had even from meal to meal to wait upon the Lord for the necessities of more than one hundred persons, when a donation of five pounds or ten pounds, or more, has been given to me, the donors could not have read in my countenance whether we had much or nothing at all in hand. But enough of this. I have made these few remarks, beloved reader, lest by any means you should lose the blessing which might come to your soul through reading the account of the Lord's faithfulness and readiness to hear the prayers of his children.

March 8. On Oct. 25, 1842, I had a long conversation with a sister in the Lord, who opened her heart to me. On leaving me I told her that my house and my purse were hers, and that I should be glad if she would have one purse with me. This I said because I judged that at some future time it might prove a comfort to her in an hour of trial, having at the same time, to judge from a circumstance which had occurred two days before, every reason to believe that she had not five pounds of her own. This sister, after I had said so, readily took me at my word, and said, I shall be glad of it, adding presently that she had five hundred pounds. The moment I heard that, I drew back, and said that had I known that she had any money I should not have made her this offer, and then gave her my reason why I supposed she had no property at all. She then assured me that she possessed five hundred pounds, and that she had never seen it right to give up this money, else she would have done so; but that, as God had put this sum into her hands without her seeking, she thought it was a provision which the Lord had made for her. I replied scarcely anything to this; but she asked me to pray for her with reference to this matter. This whole conversation about the money occupied but very few minutes, and it all took place after the sister had risen and was on the point of leaving me. After she was gone, I asked the Lord if he would be pleased to make this dear sister so happy in himself, and enable her so to realize her true riches and inheritance in the Lord Jesus, and the reality of her heavenly calling, that she might be constrained, by the love of Christ, cheerfully to lay down this five hundred pounds at his feet. From that time I repeated this my request before the Lord *daily*, and often two, three, or four times a day;

but not a single word or line passed between me and this sister on the subject, nor did I even see her; for I judged that it would be far better that she retained this money, than that by persuasion she should give it up, and afterwards perhaps regret the step she had taken, and thereby more dishonor than honor be brought on the name of the Lord. After I had thus for twenty-four days daily besought the Lord on behalf of this sister, I found her one day, on returning home, at my house, when she told me that she wished to see me alone. She then said to me that from the time she had last conversed with me she had sought to ascertain the Lord's will with reference to the five hundred pounds, and had examined the Scriptures and prayed about it, and that she was now assured that it was the will of the Lord she should give up this money. After she had told me this, I exhorted her to count well the cost, and to do nothing rashly, lest she should regret the step she had taken, and to wait at least a fortnight longer before she carried out her intention. Thus we separated. On the eighteenth day after this conversation, I received the following letter: —

DEAR BROTHER. —
I believe the Lord has not permitted you to grow weary of remembering me, but that he has still enabled you to bear me upon your heart in his presence. All is well with me, dear brother. Your petitions have been heard and answered; I am happy and at peace. The Lord has indeed manifested his tender care of and his great love towards me in Jesus, in inclining my heart cheerfully to lay *all* I have hitherto called my own at his feet. It is a high privilege.

I write in haste to ask you, as we have *now* one purse, to receive the money at a bank in Bristol. I will direct it to be sent in my name, to be delivered into your hands, etc.

As this whole circumstance is related only for the profit of the reader, and as I knew that the sister still had my letters on the subject in her possession, I wrote to her, requesting her to send them to me, at the time when I published the last account about the Orphan Houses, etc., and extracts of them were given in the last Report, in so far as they might refer to the subject or tend to edification. These extracts are here reprinted. My reply to the above was this: —

BRISTOL, Dec 6, 1842

MY DEAR SISTER: —

Your letter found me in peace, and did not in the least surprise me. Dealing with God is a reality. Saints have power with him through Jesus. It is now forty-two days since you first mentioned this matter to me. I cannot but admire the wisdom of God and his love to you in allowing me to speak to you as I did [*i. e*, offering her to have one purse with me, when I thought she had no earthly possessions at all], that thus this great privilege might be bestowed on you to give up this little sum for him. Since that hour I have daily prayed for you, and often thrice or more in the course of the day, that the Lord would make you so happy in himself and help you with such faith to lay hold on all which he has given you in Jesus, that you might be constrained by love cheerfully to lay down this little sum at his feet. Thus I prayed again at six o'clock this morning for you. Nor have I had the least doubt from the commencement that the Lord did hear my prayer; yea, so fully have I been assured that I had the petition, that again and again I have thanked him that he had answered my prayer, before I saw you eighteen days since, and before your letter came this morning. Moreover, I have been fully assured, since you were last here, that he was carrying on his work in your soul with reference to this matter, and that no subtle suggestions of Satan, nor educational prejudices, nor misinterpretations of the Scriptures, were able to prevail; for I had asked the Lord by his Spirit to overcome them in you, and that, if a brother's word should be needed, he would be pleased to incline your heart to write to me; and as no letter came, I felt fully confident you were going forward in this matter in peace. When I had seen you this day six weeks, and learned about this little sum, *I determined never to say or write to you another word on the subject, but to leave you in the hands of the Lord.* Thus I purposed again during the last eighteen days; *for it was not the money given up,* that I cared for in you, *but the money given up unto the Lord, and from right motives.* On this very account I advised you to wait one fortnight longer, though you had come to the conclusion; but now, having done so, and seeing that you are fully purposed in the Lord to be poor in this world indeed, that the more abundantly you may enjoy his riches, his inexhaustible riches, I change my advice. My word now, beloved sister, is this " Whatsoever thy hand findeth to do, do it with thy might," and " If ye know these things, happy are ye if ye do them." Delay then no longer, even as also you have no desire to delay; and the Lord will bless you abundantly in doing so, *inasmuch as you do it unto him* As you desire to intrust me with this money, I do not refuse it, knowing many ways to lay it out for him, etc. [Then only follows the direction how the money is to be paid into my banker's hands.]

On Dec. 18, 1842, I received a reply to my letter, which answer was begun to be written on Dec. 8th, but finished on the 16th. I give a few extracts of the letter: —

Since I last saw you, dear brother, I have not had the slightest doubt as to what I ought to do. The word of God has been so clear to me on this head, that I have been kept resting on it, and, in answer to your prayers, no temptation has been allowed to *prevail*, indeed, I think I may add to *arise*. But I feel that temptations *may* come, and that I may in seasons of trial not always have faith to be able to rejoice in this privilege. My heart is so deceitful, and my faith so weak, that I shall greatly need your prayers still Will you, then, if the Lord enables you, pray that I may never offend my Father by regretting in the *least* measure this act of obedience, which he has by his grace inclined me to carry out? *Before I ever saw you* I had asked the Lord to make me willing to give this little sum into your hands, if it were his will I should, but his time to make me willing had not then come; even then I had in a measure given it to you, having written a paper, desiring in case I should fall asleep in Jesus, that you might get possession of it. I had it signed by two witnesses, and I always carried it about with me when I travelled, sealed, and directed to you. When I wrote this, I little thought what grace the Lord had in store for me. You will forgive my being thus tedious, but I am sure you will praise the Lord with me for his gracious dealings with me, etc.

At the end of this letter, which was finished on Dec. 16, the sister tells me that unexpectedly a hindrance had arisen to her having possession of the money, so that it was not likely it could be paid over to me till about the end of January, 1843.

When this letter came, it would have been *naturally* a great disappointment to me, as the sister had told me in a previous letter that the money should be paid into my hands, and as just at that time in a variety of ways it was desirable that I should have considerable sums. The Lord, however, enabled me to immediately lay hold on that word, " We know that all things work together for good to them that love God" (Rom. viii. 28), and my soul was in peace, though we had only enough money in hand to provide for one or at the most for two days the necessary provisions in the Orphan Houses. It was but the next day, Dec. 19, 1842, when I received one hundred pounds from A. B., and on Dec. 22, I received fifty pounds from a brother in Bristol, besides other donations; so that within one week after I had had grace to delight myself in the will of God, he gave me about two hundred pounds, whereby I was able to meet all the heavy expenses of replenishing the stores, etc., on account of which I should *naturally* have been tried in the payment of the money being delayed.

In reply to the letter which I received from this sister on Dec. 18, I wrote another on Dec. 31, 1842, of which I give an extract on this subject: —

I have continued to pray for you, or rather the Lord has enabled me every day once, twice, thrice, or even more, to remember you. The burden of my prayer still has been, that he would be pleased to make you very happy in himself, and enable you to enter into the inheritance which awaits you; further, that you may not be permitted in the least to regret the step which you have taken, but rather consider it a privilege to be permitted to give this little sum back to him who gave it to you, and who gave himself for you With reference to the delay, I cannot but rejoice. This gives you abundant opportunity to ponder the matter, and afterwards to state to any (who, judging as those who know not how rich the saints are, might blame you) that you did not do the thing in haste. I consider this delay to be for the furtherance of the honor of the

Lord. You know my advice to you, to wait at least a fortnight. That you have seen much of your unfaithfulness, etc., I consider to be an especial blessing which the Lord has bestowed upon you, lest this step you have taken should become a snare to you. Humblings last our whole life. Jesus came not to save *painted* but *real* sinners; but he *has* saved us, and will surely make it manifest. I have a passage laid on my heart for you; read the whole of it carefully: 2 Cor. viii. 1–9, especially verse 9.

Day after day now passed away and the money did not come. The month of January was come to an end, and February also, and the money had not come. Thus more than one hundred and twenty days were gone by, whilst day by day I brought my petition before the Lord that he would bless this sister, keep her steadfast in her purpose, and intrust me with this money for his work in my hands. Amidst it all my heart was assured, judging from the earnestness which he had given me in prayer, and that I had only desired this matter to the praise of his name, that in his own time he would bring it about. *But I never wrote one single line to this sister on the subject all this time.* At last, on the one hundred and thirty-fourth day since I had *daily* besought the Lord about this matter, on March 8, 1843, I received a letter from the sister, informing me that the five hundred pounds had been paid into the hands of my bankers.

And now I only give a few lines of a letter which I received on July 3, 1844, from the sister who gave this donation, together with my letters for which I had asked her, in order that I may show her state of mind on the subject, after she had had it more than twenty months before her, and after she had for sixteen months actually given up the money. She writes thus: "I am thankful to say that I have never for one moment had the slightest feeling of regret, but it is *wholly* of the Lord's abounding grace. I speak it to his praise."

On March 31, 1843, I called at the Orphan Houses to

make certain arrangements, and one of the sisters told me by the way that she had been asked by Miss G., who with her father occupied the house No. 4 Wilson Street, to let me know that they wished to give up their house, if I would like to take it; but she had replied that it was of no use to tell me about it, for she was sure that I had no thought of opening another Orphan House. When I came home, this matter greatly occupied my mind. I could not but ask the Lord again and again whether he would have me to open another Orphan House, and whether the time was now come that I should serve him still more extensively in this way. The more I pondered the matter, the more it appeared to me that this was the hand of God moving me onwards in this service. The following remarkable combination of circumstances struck me in particular: 1. There are more applications made for the admission of orphans, especially of late, than we are at all able to meet, though we fill the houses as much as the health of the children and of the laborers will possibly admit. 2. If I did take another house for orphans, it would be most desirable it should be in the same street where the other three are, as thus the labor is less, and in times of great need we are near together for prayer, the distribution of the money, etc. But since the third Orphan House was opened, in Nov. 1837, there never has been one of the larger houses in the street to be let. 3. There are about fifteen children in the Infant Orphan House, whom it would have been well some time ago to have removed to the house for the older girls, had there been room; but when a vacancy happened to occur in that house, there were generally several waiting to fill it up, so that unintentionally the female children in the Infant Orphan House remained where they were; but this is not well, nor is it according to my original intention; for the infants were intended only to be left till they are seven years old, and then to be removed to the houses for older boys and girls. This my original plan could be executed better for the future, and at once for the present, were I to open another Orphan House. 4. I know two sisters who seem suitable laborers for this fourth Orphan House, and who have a desire thus to be engaged. 5. There are three hundred pounds remaining of the five hundred pounds which I so lately received. This money may be used for the furnishing and fitting up of a new Orphan House. So much money I have never had in hand at any one time during the last five years. This seemed to me a remarkable thing, in connection with the four other reasons. 6. The establishing of a fourth Orphan House, which would increase our expenses several hundred pounds a year, would be, after we have gone for five years almost uninterruptedly through trials of faith, a plain proof that I have not regretted this service, and that I am not tired of this precious way of depending upon the Lord from day to day; and thus the faith of other children of God might be strengthened.

But most important, yea, decidedly conclusive as these points were, yet they did not convince me that I ought to go forward in this service, if the Spirit's leadings were not in connection with them. I therefore gave myself to prayer. I prayed day after day, *without saying anything to any human being*. I prayed two and twenty days without even mentioning it to my dear wife. On that very day, when I did mention it to her, and on which I had come to the conclusion, after three weeks' prayer and consideration in the fear of God, to establish another Orphan House, I received from A. B. fifty pounds. What a striking confirmation that the Lord will help, though the necessities should increase more and more! At last, on the twenty-fourth day, having been now for several days fully assured that God would have me go forward in this service, I went to inquire whether Mr. and Miss G. still wished to give up the house. But here I found an apparent hindrance. Having heard no wish expressed on my part to take the house, and the sister in the Orphan Houses, with whom Miss

G. had communicated, not having given her the least reason to think that I should do so, Mr. and Miss G. had altered their plans, and now purposed to remain in the house. However, I was to call again in a week, when I should receive an answer. I was not in the least discomforted by this obstacle. "Lord, if *thou* hast no need of another Orphan House, *I* have none," was the burden of my prayer. I was willing to do God's will, yea, to delight myself in his will. And just on this very ground, because I knew I sought not my own honor, but the Lord's; because I knew I was not serving myself, but the Lord, in this thing; and because I knew that with so much calm, quiet, prayerful, self-questioning consideration I had gone about this business, and had only after many days, during which I had been thus waiting upon the Lord, come to the conclusion that it was the will of God I should go forward in this service. For these reasons I felt sure, notwithstanding what Mr. and Miss G. had told me, that I should have the house. I also especially judged that thus it would be, *because I was quite in peace* when I heard of the obstacle; a plain proof that I was not in self-will going on in this matter, but according to the leading of the Holy Ghost; for if according to my natural mind I had sought to enlarge the work, I should have been excited and uncomfortable when I met with this obstacle. After a week I called again on Mr. G. And now see how God had wrought! On the same day on which I had seen Mr. G., he went out and met with a suitable house, so that when I came the second time, he was willing to let me have the one which he then occupied in Wilson Street; and as the owner accepted me as a tenant, all the difficulties were removed, so that after the first of June we began fitting up the house, and in July the first orphans were received.

Mr. M. having been invited by several Christians in Germany to visit that, his native land, and to labor there for the promulgation of scriptural truth and the advancement of religion, as well as to publish a German translation of his Narrative, felt that it was his duty to accede to the request. In answer to prayer, he received ample means for his journey, for the support of the orphans during his absence, and for the publication of the Narrative. He left Bristol on the 9th of August, 1843, and returned on March 6, 1844. During the journey he was greatly aided by Providence in the purposes of his mission, and saw much fruit of his labors.

CHAPTER XVI.

STEWARDSHIP.

1844.

EARTHLY AND HEAVENLY TREASURES — SEEKING THE KINGDOM OF GOD — FELLOWSHIP WITH THE FATHER — THE CHRISTIAN MERCHANT — EXAMPLES — MISTAKES.

IN concluding this portion of my Narrative, I would add some hints on a few passages of the word of God, both because I have so very frequently found them little regarded by Christians, and also because I have proved their preciousness, in some measure, in my own experience; and therefore wish that all my fellow-saints may share the blessing with me.

I. In Matt. vi. 19–21, it is written: "Lay not up for yourselves treasures upon earth, where moth and rust doth corrupt, and where thieves break through and steal; but lay up for yourselves treasures in heaven, where neither moth nor rust doth corrupt, and where thieves do not break through nor steal: for where your treasure is, there will your heart be also." Observe, dear reader, the following points concerning this part of the divine testimony:

1. It is the Lord Jesus, our Lord and Master, who speaks this as the lawgiver of his people, — he who has infinite wisdom and unfathomable love to us, who therefore both knows what is for our real welfare and happiness, and who cannot exact from us any requirement inconsistent with that love which led him to lay down his life for us.

2. His counsel, his affectionate entreaty, and his commandment to us his disciples is, "Lay not up for yourselves treasures upon earth." The meaning obviously is,

that the disciples of the Lord Jesus, being strangers and pilgrims on earth, *i. e.*, neither belonging to the earth nor expecting to remain in it, *should not seek to increase their earthly possessions*, in whatever these possessions may consist. This is a word for poor believers as well as for rich believers; it has as much a reference to putting shillings into the savings-bank as to putting thousands of pounds into the funds, or purchasing one house or one farm after another. It may be said, But does not every prudent and provident person seek to increase his means, that he may have a goodly portion to leave to his children, or to have something for old age, or for the time of sickness, etc.? My reply is, it is quite true that this is the custom of the world. But whilst thus it is in the world, and we have every reason to believe ever will be so among those that are of the world, and who therefore have their portion on earth, we disciples of the Lord Jesus, being born again, being the children of God, not nominally, but really, being truly partakers of the divine nature, being in fellowship with the Father and the Son, and having in prospect " an inheritance incorruptible, and undefiled, and that fadeth not away " (1 Peter i. 4), ought in every respect to act differently from the world, and so in this particular also. If we disciples of the Lord Jesus seek, like the people of the world, after an increase of our possessions, may not those who are of the world justly question whether we believe what we say, when we speak about our inheritance, our heavenly calling, our being the children of God, etc.? Often it must be a sad stumbling-block to the unbeliever to see a professed believer in the Lord Jesus acting in this particular just like himself. Consider this, dear brethren in the Lord, should this remark apply to you

3. Our Lord says about the earth that it is a place " where moth and rust doth corrupt and where thieves break through and steal." All that is of the earth, and in any way connected with it, is subject to corruption, to change, to disso

lution. There is no reality, or substance, in anything else but in heavenly things. Often the careful amassing of earthly possessions ends in losing them in a moment by fire, by robbery, by a change of mercantile concerns, by loss of work, etc.; but suppose all this were not the case, still, yet a little while, and thy soul shall be required of thee; or, yet a little while, and the Lord Jesus will return; and what profit shalt thou then have, dear reader, if thou hast carefully sought to increase thy earthly possessions?

4 Our Lord, however, does not merely bid us not to lay up treasure upon earth; for if he had said no more, this his commandment might be abused, and persons might find in it an encouragement for their extravagant habits, for their love of pleasure, for their habit of spending everything they have, or can obtain, *upon themselves*. It does not mean, then, as is the common phrase, that we should " live up to our income;" for he adds, " But lay up for yourselves treasures in heaven." There is such a thing as laying up as truly in heaven as there is laying up on earth; if it were not so, our Lord would not have said so. Just as persons put one sum after another into the bank, and it is put down to their credit, and they may use the money afterwards: so truly the penny, the shilling, the pound, the hundred pounds, the ten thousand pounds, *given for the Lord's sake, and constrained by the love of Jesus*, to poor brethren, or in any way spent in the work of God, he marks down in the book of remembrance, he considers as laid up in heaven. *The money is not lost, it is laid up in the bank of heaven,* yet so, that whilst an earthly bank may break, or through earthly circumstances we may lose our earthly possessions, the money which is thus secured in heaven cannot be lost. But this is by no means the only difference. I notice a few more points: Treasures laid up on earth bring along with them many cares; treasures laid up in heaven never give care. Treasures laid up on earth never can afford spiritual joy; treasures laid up in heaven bring along with

them peace and joy in the Holy Ghost even now. Treasures laid up on earth, in a dying hour cannot afford peace and comfort, and when life is over they are taken from us; treasures laid up in heaven draw forth thanksgiving that we were permitted and counted worthy to serve the Lord with the means with which he was pleased to intrust us as stewards, and when this life is over we are not deprived of what was laid up there, but when we go to heaven we go to the place where our treasures are, and we shall find them there. Often we hear it said, when a person has died, he died worth so much. But whatever be the phrases common in the world, it is certain that a person may die worth fifty thousand pounds sterling, as the world reckons, and yet that individual may not possess, in the sight of God, one thousand pounds sterling, because *he was not rich towards God*, he did not lay up treasure in heaven. And so, on the other hand, we can suppose a man of God falling asleep in Jesus, and his surviving widow finding scarcely enough left behind him to suffice for the funeral, who was nevertheless *rich towards God:* in the sight of God he may possess five thousand pounds sterling; he may have laid up that sum in heaven. Dear reader, does your soul long to be rich towards God, to lay up treasures in heaven? The world passes away, and the lust thereof. Yet a little while and our stewardship will be taken from us. At present we have the opportunity of serving the Lord with our time, our talents, our bodily strength, our gifts, and also with our property; but shortly this opportunity may cease. Oh, how shortly may it cease! Before ever this is read by any one, I may have fallen asleep; and the very next day after you have read this, dear reader, you may fall asleep; and, therefore, whilst we have the opportunity, let us serve the Lord.

5. The Lord lastly adds: "For where your treasure is, there will your heart be also." Where should the heart of the disciple of the Lord Jesus be, but in heaven? Our calling is a heavenly calling, our inheritance is a heavenly

inheritance, and reserved for us in heaven; our citizenship is in heaven; but if we believers in the Lord Jesus lay up treasures on earth, the necessary result of it is, that our hearts will be upon earth; nay, the very fact of our doing so proves that they are there! Nor will it be otherwise, till there be a ceasing to lay up treasures upon earth. The believer who lays up treasures upon earth may, at first, not live openly in sin, he in a measure may yet bring some honor to the Lord in certain things; but the injurious tendencies of this habit will show themselves more and more, whilst the habit of laying up treasures in heaven would draw the heart more and more heavenward; would be continually strengthening his new, his divine nature, his spiritual faculties, because it would call his spiritual faculties into use, and thus they would be strengthened; and he would more and more, whilst yet in the body, have his heart in heaven, and set upon heavenly things; and thus the laying up treasures in heaven would bring along with it, even in this life, precious spiritual blessings as a reward of obedience to the commandment of our Lord.

II. The next passage, on which I desire to make a few remarks, is Matt. vi. 33: "But seek ye first the kingdom of God and his righteousness; and all these things shall be added unto you." After our Lord, in the previous verses, had been pointing his disciples "to the fowls of the air," and "the lilies of the field," in order that they should be without carefulness about the necessaries of life, he adds: "Therefore take no thought (literally, be not anxious), saying, What shall we eat? or, What shall we drink? or, Wherewithal shall we be clothed? (for after all these things do the Gentiles seek;) for your heavenly Father knoweth that ye have need of all these things." Observe here particularly that we, the children of God, should be different from the nations of the earth, from those who have no Father in heaven, and who therefore make it their great business, their first anxious concern, what they shall eat, and what they shall drink, and wherewithal they shall be clothed. We, the children of God, should, as in every other respect, so in this particular also, be different from the world, and prove to the world that we believe that we have a Father in heaven who knoweth that we have need of all these things. The fact that our Almighty Father, who is full of infinite love to us his children, and who has proved to us his love in the gift of his only-begotten Son, and his almighty power in raising him from the dead, knows that we have need of these things, should remove all anxiety from our minds. There is, however, one thing that we have to attend to, and which we *ought* to attend to, with reference to our temporal necessities; it is mentioned in our verse: "But seek ye first the kingdom of God and his righteousness." The great business which the disciple of the Lord Jesus has to be concerned about (for this word was spoken to disciples, to professed believers) is, to seek the kingdom of God, *i. e.*, to seek, as I view it, after the external and internal prosperity of the church of Christ. If, according to our ability, and according to the opportunity which the Lord gives us, we seek to win souls for the Lord Jesus, that appears to me to be seeking the *external prosperity* of the kingdom of God; and if we, as members of the body of Christ, seek to benefit our fellow-members in the body, helping them on in grace and truth, or caring for them in any way to their edification, that would be seeking the *internal prosperity* of the kingdom of God. But in connection with this we have also "to seek his righteousness," which means (as it was spoken to disciples, to those who have a Father in heaven, and not to those who were without), to seek to be more and more like God, to seek to be inwardly conformed to the mind of God. If these two things are attended to (and *they imply also that we are not slothful in business*), then do we come under that precious promise: "And all these things (that is, food, raiment, or anything else that is needful for this present life) shall be added unto you." It is not *for* attending to these two things that we obtain the blessing, but *in* attending to them.

I now ask you, my dear reader, a few questions in all love, because I do seek your welfare, and I do not wish to put these questions to you without putting them first to my own heart. Do you make it your primary business, your first great concern, to seek the kingdom of God and his righteousness? Are the things of God, the honor of his name, the welfare of his church, the conversion of sinners, and the profit of your own soul, your chief aim? Or does your business, or your family, or your own temporal concerns, in some shape or other *primarily* occupy your attention? If the latter be the case, then, though you may have all the necessaries of life, yet could you be surprised if you had them not? Remember that the world passeth away, but that the things of God endure forever.

I never knew a child of God, who acted according to the above passage, in whose experience the Lord did not fulfil his word of promise, "All these things shall be added unto you."

III. The third portion of the divine testimony on which I desire to throw out a few hints, is in 1 John i. 3: "And truly our fellowship is with the Father, and with his Son Jesus Christ." Observe,

1. The words "fellowship," "communion," "coparticipation," and "partnership," mean the same.

2. The believer in the Lord Jesus does not only obtain forgiveness of all his sins, as he does through the shedding of the blood of Jesus, by faith in his name; does not only become a righteous one before God, through the righteousness of the Lord Jesus by faith in his name; is not only begotten again, born of God, and partaker of the divine nature, and therefore a child of God and an heir of God; but he is also in fellowship or partnership with God. Now, so far as it regards God, and our standing in the Lord

Jesus, we have this blessing once for all; nor does it allow of either an increase or a decrease. Just as God's love to us believers, his children, is unalterably the same, whatever may be the manifestations of that love; and as his peace with us is the same, however much our peace may be disturbed; so it is also with regard to our being in fellowship or partnership with him: it remains unalterably the same so far as God is concerned. But then,

3. There is an *experimental* fellowship, or partnership, with the Father and with his Son, which consists in this: that all which we possess in God, as being the partners or fellows of God, is brought down into our daily life, is enjoyed, experienced, and used. This *experimental* fellowship, or partnership, allows of an increase or a decrease, in the measure in which faith is in exercise, and in which we are entering into what we have received in the Lord Jesus. The measure in which we enjoy this *experimental* fellowship with the Father and with the Son is without limit; for without limit we may make use of our partnership with the Father and with the Son, and draw by prayer and faith out of the inexhaustible fulness which there is in God.

Let us now take a few instances in order to see the practical working of this *experimental* fellowship, or partnership, with the Father and with the Son. Suppose there are two believing parents who were not brought to the knowledge of the truth until some years after the Lord had given them several children. Their children were brought up in sinful, evil ways, whilst the parents did not know the Lord. Now the parents reap as they sowed. They suffer from having set an evil example before their children, for their children are unruly and behave most improperly. What is now to be done? Need such parents despair? No. The first thing they have to do is, to make confession of their sins to God, with regard to neglecting their children whilst they were themselves living in sin, and then to remember that they are in partnership with God, and therefore to be of good courage, though they are in themselves still utterly insufficient for the task of managing their children. They have in themselves neither the wisdom, nor the patience, nor the long-suffering, nor the gentleness, nor the meekness, nor the love, nor the decision and firmness, nor anything else that may be needful in dealing with their children aright. But their heavenly Father has all this. The Lord Jesus possesses all this. And they are in partnership with the Father, and with the Son, and therefore they can obtain by prayer and faith all they need out of the fulness of God. I say by *prayer* and *faith*, for we have to make known our need to God in prayer, ask his help, and then we have *to believe* he will give us what we need. Prayer alone is not enough. We may pray never so much, yet, if we do not believe that God will give us what we need, we have no reason to expect that we shall receive what we have asked for. So then these parents would need to ask God to give them the needful wisdom, patience, long-suffering, gentleness, meekness, love, decision and firmness, and whatever else they may judge they need. They may in humble boldness remind their heavenly Father that his word assures them that they are in partnership with him, and, as they themselves are lacking in these particulars, ask him to be pleased to supply their need; and then they have *to believe* that God will do it, and they shall receive according to their need.

Another instance: Suppose I am so situated in my business that day by day such difficulties arise that I continually find that I take wrong steps by reason of these great difficulties. How may the case be altered for the better? In myself I see no remedy for the difficulties. In looking at myself I can expect nothing but to make still further mistakes, and, therefore, trial upon trial seems to be before me. And yet I need not despair. The living God is my partner. *I have not sufficient wisdom to meet these difficul-*

ties so as to be able to know what steps to take, but *he* is able to direct me. What I have, therefore, to do, is this: in simplicity to spread my case before my heavenly Father and my Lord Jesus. The Father and the Son are my partners. I have to tell out my heart to God, and to ask him, that, as he is my partner, and I have no wisdom in myself to meet all the many difficulties which continually occur in my business, he would be pleased to guide and direct me, and to supply me with the needful wisdom: and then I have *to believe* that God will do so, and go with good courage to my business, and *expect* help from him in the next difficulty that may come before me. *I have to look out* for guidance, *I have to expect* counsel from the Lord; and as assuredly as I do so, I shall have it, I shall find that I am not nominally, but really, in partnership with the Father and with the Son.

Another instance: There is a father and mother with seven small children. Both parents are believers. The father works in a manufactory, but cannot earn more than ten shillings per week. The mother cannot earn anything. These ten shillings are too little for the supply of nourishing and wholesome food for seven growing children and their parents, and for providing them with the other necessaries of life. What is to be done in such a case? Surely not to find fault with the manufacturer, who may not be able to afford more wages, and much less to murmur against God, but the parents have in simplicity to tell God, their partner, that the wages of ten shillings a week are not sufficient in England to provide nine persons with all they need, so as that their health be not injured. They have to remind God that he is not a hard master, not an unkind being, but a most loving Father who has abundantly proved the love of his heart in the gift of his only begotten Son. And they have in childlike simplicity to ask him that either he would order it so that the manufacturer may be able to allow more wages; or that he (the Lord) would find them another place, where the father would be able to earn more; or that he would be pleased, somehow or other, as it may seem good to him, to supply them with more means. They have to ask the Lord, in childlike simplicity, again and again for it, if he does not answer their request at once; and they have *to believe* that God, their Father and partner, will give them the desire of their hearts. They have *to expect* an answer to their prayers; day by day they have *to look out* for it, and to repeat their request till God grants it. As assuredly as they *believe* that God will grant them their request, so assuredly it shall be granted.

Thus, suppose I desired more power over my besetting sins; suppose I desired more power against certain temptations; suppose I desired more wisdom, or grace, or anything else that I may need in my service among the saints, or in my service towards the unconverted: what have I to do but to make use of my being in fellowship with the Father and with the Son? Just as, for instance, an old faithful clerk, who is this day taken into partnership by an immensely rich firm, though himself altogether without property, would not be discouraged by reason of a large payment having to be made by the firm within three days, though he himself has no money at all of his own, but would comfort himself with the immense riches possessed by those who so generously have just taken him into partnership: so should we, the children of God and servants of Jesus Christ, comfort ourselves by being in fellowship, or partnership, with the Father, and with the Son, though we have no power of our own against our besetting sins; though we cannot withstand temptations, which are before us, in our own strength; and though we have neither sufficient grace nor wisdom for our service among the saints, or towards the unconverted. All we have to do is, to draw upon our partner, the living God. By prayer and faith we may obtain all needful temporal and spiritual help and blessings. In all simplicity have we to tell out our heart before God, and then we have to believe that he will give to us according to our need.

But *if we do not believe* that God will help us, could we be at peace? The clerk, taken into the firm as partner, *believes* that the firm will meet the payment, though so large, and though in three days it is to be made, and it is this that keeps his heart quiet, though altogether poor himself. We have to believe that our infinitely rich partner, the living God, will help us in our need, and we shall not only be in peace, but we shall actually find that the help which we need will be granted to us. Let not the consciousness of your entire unworthiness keep you, dear reader, from believing what God has said concerning you. If you are indeed a believer in the Lord Jesus, then this precious privilege, of being in partnership with the Father and the Son, is yours, though you and I are entirely unworthy of it. If the consciousness of our unworthiness were to keep us from believing what God has said concerning those who depend upon and trust in the Lord Jesus for salvation, then we should find that there is not one single blessing, with which we have been blessed in the Lord Jesus, from which, on account of our unworthiness, we could derive any settled comfort or peace.

IV. There is one other point, which, in connection with several portions of the word of God which bear on the subject, I desire to bring before the believing reader, and it refers to the "scriptural way of overcoming the difficulties with which the believer now meets who is engaged in a business, trade, profession, or any earthly calling whatever, which arise from competition in business, too great a number of persons being occupied in the same calling, stagnation of trade, and the like." The children of God, who are strangers and pilgrims on earth, have at all times had difficulty in the world, for they are not *at* home, but *from* home; nor should they, until the return of the Lord Jesus, expect it to be otherwise with them. But whilst this is true, it is also true that the Lord has provided us in all our difficulties with something in his own word to meet them. All difficulties may be overcome by acting according to the word of God. At this time I more especially desire to point out the means whereby the children of God who are engaged in any earthly calling may be able to overcome the difficulties which arise from competition in business, too great a number of persons being occupied in the same calling, stagnation of trade, and the like.

1. The first thing which the believer who is in such difficulties has to ask himself is, *Am I in a calling in which I can abide with God?* If our occupation be of that kind that we cannot ask God's blessing upon it, or that we should be ashamed to be found in it at the appearing of the Lord Jesus, or that it *of necessity* hinders our spiritual progress, then we must give it up, and be engaged in something else; but in few cases only this is needful. Far the greater part of the occupations in which believers are engaged are not of such a nature as that they need to give them up in order to maintain a good conscience, and in order to be able to walk with God, though, perhaps, certain alterations may need to be made in the manner of conducting their trade, business, or profession. About these parts of our calling which may need alteration, we shall receive instruction from the Lord if we indeed desire it, and wait upon him for it, and expect it from him.

2. Now suppose the believer is in a calling in which he can abide with God, the next point to be settled is, "*Why do I carry on this business, or why am I engaged in this trade or profession?*" In most instances, so far as my experience goes, which I have gathered in my service among the saints during the last fifteen years and a half [*i. e.*, in 1845], I believe the answer would be, "I am engaged in my earthly calling that I may earn the means of obtaining the necessaries of life for myself and family." Here is the chief error from which almost all the rest of

the errors which are entertained by children of God, relative to their calling, spring. It is no right and scriptural motive to be engaged in a trade or business or profession *merely* in order to earn the means for the obtaining of the necessaries of life for ourselves and family, *but we should work because it is the Lord's will concerning us.* This is plain from the following passages: 1 Thess. iv. 11, 12; 2 Thess. iii. 10–12; Eph. iv. 28. It is quite true that, in general, the Lord provides the necessaries of life by means of our ordinary calling; but that that is not THE REASON why we should work, is plain enough from the consideration that if our possessing the necessaries of life depended upon our ability of working, we could never have *freedom from anxiety*, for we should always have to say to ourselves, And what shall I do when I am too old to work, or when by reason of sickness I am unable to earn my bread? But if, on the other hand, we are engaged in our earthly calling because *it is the will of the Lord concerning us that we should work*, and that thus laboring we may provide for our families, and also be able to support the weak, the sick, the aged, and the needy, then we have good and scriptural reason to say to ourselves, Should it please the Lord to lay me on a bed of sickness, or keep me otherwise by reason of infirmity, or old age, or want of employment, from earning my bread by means of the labor of my hands, or my business, or my profession, he will yet provide for me. Because we who believe are servants of Jesus Christ, who has bought us with his own precious blood, and are not our own, and because this our precious Lord and Master has commanded us to work, therefore we work: and *in doing so* our Lord will provide for us, but whether in this way or any other way he is sure to provide for us, for we labor in obedience to him; and if even a just earthly master gives wages to his servants, the Lord will surely see to it that we have our wages, if, in obedience to him, we are engaged in our calling, and not for our own sake.

How great the difference between acting according to the word of God and according to our own natural desires, or the customs of the world, will be plain, I trust, by the following case: Suppose I were engaged in some useful trade. Suppose I had the certain human prospect that within the next three months my labor would bring me in nothing, for certain reasons connected with the state of mercantile affairs. As a man of the world I should say, I shall not work at all, because my labor will not be paid; but as a Christian, who desired to act according to God's holy word, I ought to say, My trade is useful to society, and I will work notwithstanding all human prospects, because the Lord Jesus has commanded me to labor; from him, and not from my trade, I expect my wages. In addition to this, the Christian ought also to say, Idleness is a dreadful snare of the devil; he has especial opportunity to get an advantage over the children of God when they are unoccupied; and therefore, I will work though I have no human prospect of obtaining payment for my labor, but shall get only the cost price of the material, and shall have to give my work for nothing. Moreover, the Christian ought to say, Though, according to *human* probability, I shall have to labor for nothing during the next three months, yet I will work, because the Lord may speedily alter the state of things, contrary to all human expectation; but whether he be pleased to do so or not, I labor because I am the Lord's, bought by his precious blood, and he commands me to labor.

But there are motives still lower than to be engaged in our earthly calling merely that we may earn the means of obtaining the necessaries of life, why even Christians, true children of God, may be engaged in their calling, such as, to obtain a certain sum of money, and then to retire from business and to live upon the interest; or to provide something for old age; or to obtain a certain amount of property, without intending to give up business. If it be unscriptural to be engaged in our calling merely even for the sake of earning the means for procuring the necessaries of life for ourselves and family, how much more unbecoming that a child of God should be engaged in his calling for the sake of any of the last-mentioned reasons.

This second point, then, Why do I carry on this business? Why am I engaged in this trade or profession? ought first to be settled in the fear of God, and according to the revealed will of God; and if we cannot say, in honesty of heart, I do carry on my business, I am engaged in my trade or art, or profession, as a servant of Jesus Christ, whose I am, because he has bought me with his precious blood, and he has commanded me to work, and therefore I work, — I say, if we cannot say this in honesty of heart, but must confess that we work on account of lower motives, such as that we may earn our bread, or on account of still lower motives, and such as are altogether unbecoming a child of God, who is not of the world, but of God, such as to obtain a certain sum of money in order to be able to live on the interest without having to work or to provide something for old age, or to obtain a certain amount of property without intending to give up business; — if these are our motives for being engaged in our calling, I say, can we be surprised that we meet with great difficulties in our business, and that the Lord in his abounding love to us, his erring children, does not allow us to succeed? But suppose this second point is scripturally settled, and we can honestly say that because we are servants of Jesus Christ we are occupied as we are; we have further to consider, —

3. Whether we carry on our business, or are engaged in our trade, art, or profession, *as stewards* of the Lord. To the child of God it ought not to be enough that he is in a calling in which he can abide with God, nor that he is engaged in his calling because it is the will of his Lord and Master that he should work, but he should consider

himself in his trade, business, art, or profession, only as the *steward* of the Lord with reference to his income. The child of God has been bought with the precious blood of the Lord Jesus, and is altogether his property, with all that he possesses, his bodily strength, his mental strength, his ability of every kind, his trade, business, art, or profession, his property, etc.; for it is written, "Ye are not your own; for ye are bought with a price." 1 Cor. vi. 19, 20. The proceeds of our calling are therefore not our own in the sense of using them as our natural heart wishes us to do, whether to spend them on the gratification of our pride, or our love of pleasure, or sensual indulgences, or to lay by the money for ourselves or our children, or to use it in any way as we *naturally* like; but we have to stand before our Lord and Master, whose *stewards* we are, to seek to ascertain his will, how he will have us use the proceeds of our calling.

But is this indeed the spirit in which children of God generally are engaged in their calling? It is but too well known that it is not the case. Can we then wonder at it, that even God's own dear children should so often be found greatly in difficulty with regard to their calling, and be found so often complaining about stagnation or competition in trade, or the difficulties of the times, though there have been given to them such precious promises as, "Seek ye first the kingdom of God, and his righteousness, and all these things shall be added unto you;" or, "Let your conversation (disposition or turn of mind) be without covetousness; and be content with such things as ye have: for he hath said, I will never leave thee, nor forsake thee." Heb. xiii. 2. Is it not obvious enough that when our heavenly Father sees that we his children do or would use the proceeds of our calling, *as our natural mind* would desire, that he either cannot at all intrust us with means, or will be obliged to decrease them? No wise and really affectionate mother will permit her infant to play with a razor, or with fire, however much the child may desire to have them; and so the love and wisdom of our heavenly Father will not, cannot, intrust us with pecuniary means, *except it be in the way of chastisement, or to show us finally their utter vanity,* if he sees that we do not desire to possess them as *stewards* for him, in order that we may spend them as he may point out to us by his Holy Spirit, through his word.

In connection with this subject, I give a few hints to the believing reader on three passages of the word of God. In 1 Cor. xvi. 2, we find it written to the brethren at Corinth, "Upon the first day of the week let every one of you lay by him in store, as God has prospered him." A contribution for the poor saints in Judea was to be made, and the brethren at Corinth were exhorted to put by for it, *every Lord's day,* according to the measure of success which the Lord had been pleased to grant them in their calling during the week. Now, ought not the saints in our day also to act according to this word? There is no passage in the word of God why we should not do so, and it is altogether in accordance with our pilgrim character, not only once or twice, or four times a year, to see how much we can afford to give to the poor saints, or to the work of God in any way, but to seek to settle it weekly. If it be said, I cannot ascertain how much I have gained in the course of the week by my business, and therefore I cannot give accordingly; my reply is this, Seek, dear brethren, as much as possible, to bring your business upon such a footing as that you may be able, as nearly as possible, to settle how much you have earned in your calling in the course of the week. But suppose you should be unable to settle it exactly to the shilling or pound, yet you will know pretty well how it has been with you during the week, and therefore, *according to your best knowledge,* contribute on the coming Lord's day towards the necessities of the poor saints, and towards the work of God, as he, after your having sought his guidance, may lead you.

Perhaps you say, the weeks are so unlike; in one week I may earn three or even ten times as much as in another week, and if I give according to my earnings from my calling during a very good week, then how are such weeks, when I earn scarcely anything, or how are the bad debts to be met? How shall I do when sickness befalls my family, or when other trials productive of expense come upon me, if I do not make provision for such seasons? My reply is, 1. I do not find in the whole New Testament one single passage in which either directly or indirectly exhortations are given to provide against deadness in business, bad debts, and sickness, by laying up money. 2. Often the Lord is obliged to allow deadness in business, or bad debts, or sickness in our family, or other trials which increase our expenses, to befall us, because we do not, as his *stewards*, act *according to stewardship*, but as if we were owners of what we have, forgetting that the time has not yet come when we shall enter upon *our possessions;* and he does so in order that, by these losses and expenses, our property which we have collected may be decreased, lest we should altogether set our hearts again upon earthly things, and forget God entirely. His love is so great, that he will not let his children quietly go their own way when they have forsaken him; but if his loving admonitions by his Holy Spirit are disregarded, he is obliged in fatherly love to chastise them. A striking illustration of what I have said we have in the case of Israel nationally. The commandment to them was, to leave their land uncultivated in the seventh year, in order that it might rest, and the Lord promised to make up for this deficiency by his abundant blessing resting upon the sixth year. However, Israel acted not according to this commandment, no doubt saying, in the unbelief of their hearts, as the Lord had foretold, "What shall we eat in the seventh year? Behold, we shall not sow, nor gather in our increase." Levit. xxv. But what did the Lord do? He was determined the land should have rest, and as the Israelites did not willingly give it, he sent them for seventy years into captivity, in order that thus the land might have rest. See Levit. xxvi. 33–35. Beloved brethren in the Lord, let us take heed so to walk as that the Lord may not be obliged by chastisement to take a part of our earthly possessions from us in the way of bad debts, sickness, decrease of business, and the like, because we would not own our position as *stewards*, but act as *owners*, and keep for ourselves the means with which the Lord had intrusted us, not for the gratification of our own carnal mind, but for the sake of using them in his service and to his praise.

It might also be said by a brother whose earnings are small, should *I* also give according to my earnings? They are already so small that my wife can only with the greatest difficulty manage to make them sufficient for the family. My reply is, Have you ever considered, my brother, that the very reason why the Lord is obliged to let your earnings remain so small may be the fact of your spending everything upon yourselves, and that if he were to give you more you would only use it to increase your own family comfort, instead of looking about to see who among the brethren are sick, or who have no work at all, that you might help them, or how you might assist the work of God at home or abroad? There is a great temptation for a brother whose earnings are small to put off the responsibility of assisting the needy and sick saints, or helping on the work of God, and to lay it upon the few rich brethren and sisters with whom he is associated in fellowship, and thus rob his own soul!

It might be asked, How much shall I give of my income? The tenth part, or the fifth part, or the third part, or one half, or more? My reply is, God lays down no rule concerning this point. What we do we should do cheerfully and not of necessity. But if even Jacob, with the first dawning of spiritual light (Genesis xxviii. 22), promised to God the tenth of all he should give to him, how much ought we believers in the Lord Jesus to do for him: we, whose calling is a heavenly one, and *who know distinctly* that we are children of God, and joint heirs with the Lord Jesus! Yet do all the children of God give even the *tenth* part of what the Lord gives them? That would be two shillings per week for the brother who earns one pound, and four shillings to him who earns two pounds, and two pounds per week to him whose income is twenty pounds per week.

In connection with 1 Cor. xvi. 2, I would mention two other portions: 1. "He which soweth sparingly shall reap also sparingly; and he that soweth bountifully shall reap also bountifully." 2 Cor. ix. 6. It is certain that we children of God are so abundantly blessed in Jesus, by the grace of God, that we ought to need no stimulus to good works. The forgiveness of our sins, the having been made forever the children of God, the having before us the Father's house as our home;—these blessings ought to be sufficient motives to constrain us in love and gratitude to serve God abundantly all the days of our life, and cheerfully also to give up, as he may call for it, that with which he has intrusted us of the things of this world. But whilst this is the case, the Lord nevertheless holds out to us in his holy word motives why we should serve him, deny ourselves, use our property for him, etc., and the last-mentioned passage is one of that kind. The verse is true, both with reference to the life that is now, and that which is to come. If we have been sparingly using our property for him, there will have been little treasure laid up in heaven, and therefore a small amount of capital will be found in the world to come, so far as it regards reaping. Again, we shall reap bountifully if we seek to be rich towards God, by abundantly using our means for him, whether in ministering to the necessities of the poor saints, or using otherwise our pecuniary means for his work. Dear brethren, these things are realities! Shortly, very shortly, will come the reaping-time, and then will be the question whether we shall reap sparingly or bountifully.

But while this passage refers to the life hereafter, it also refers to the life that now is. Just as now *the love of Christ* constrains us to communicate of that with which the Lord intrusts us, so will be the present reaping, both with regard to spiritual and temporal things. Should there be found, therefore, in a brother, the want of entering into his position as being merely a *steward* for the Lord in his calling, and should he give no heed to the admonitions of the Holy Ghost to communicate to those who are in need or to help the work of God, then can such a brother be surprised that he meets with great difficulties in his calling, and that he cannot get on? This is according to the Lord's word. He is *sowing sparingly*, and he therefore *reaps sparingly*. But should *the love of Christ* constrain a brother, out of the earnings of his calling, to sow bountifully, he will even in this life reap bountifully, both with regard to blessings in his soul, and with regard to temporal things. Consider in connection with this the following passage, which, though taken from the Book of Proverbs, is not of a Jewish character, but true concerning believers under the present dispensation also: "There is that scattereth, and yet increaseth; and there is that withholdeth more than is meet, but it tendeth to poverty. The liberal soul shall be made fat; and he that watereth shall be watered also himself." Prov. xi. 24, 25.

In connection with 1 Cor. xvi. 2, I would also direct my brethren in the Lord to the promise made in Luke vi. 38: "Give, and it shall be given unto you; good measure, pressed down, and shaken together, and running over, shall men give into your bosom. For with the same measure that ye mete withal it shall be measured to you again." This refers evidently to the present dispensation, and evidently in its primary meaning to temporal things. Now let any one, *constrained by the love of Jesus*, act according to this passage; let him on the first day of the week communicate as the Lord has prospered him, and he will see that the Lord will act according to what is contained in this verse. If pride constrain us to give, if self-righteousness make us liberal, if natural feeling induce us to communicate, or if we give whilst we are in a state of insolvency, not possessing more perhaps than ten shillings in the pound, were our creditors to come upon us; then we cannot expect to have this verse fulfilled in our experience; nor should we give at any time for the sake of receiving again from others, according to this verse; but if indeed *the love of Christ constrain us* to communicate according to the ability which the Lord gives us, then we shall have this verse fulfilled in our experience, though this was not the motive which induced us to give. Somehow or other the Lord will abundantly repay us, through the instrumentality of our fellow-men, what we are doing to his poor saints, or in any way for his work, and we shall find that in the end we are not losers, even with reference to temporal things, whilst we communicate liberally of the things of this life with which the Lord has intrusted us.

Here it might be remarked, But if it be so that even in this life, and with regard to temporal things, it is true that " to him that gives shall be given, good measure, pressed down, and shaken together, and running over," and that " he which soweth bountifully shall reap also bountifully," then in the end the most liberal persons would be exceedingly rich. Concerning this remark we have to keep in mind, that the moment persons were to begin to give for the sake of receiving more back again from the Lord, through the instrumentality of their fellow-men, than they have given; or the moment persons wish to alter their way, and no more go on sowing bountifully, but sparingly, in order to increase their possessions, whilst God is allowing them to reap bountifully, the river of God's bounty toward them would no longer continue to flow. God had supplied them abundantly with means, because he saw them act as *stewards* for him. He had intrusted them with a little which they had used for him, and he therefore intrusted them with more; and if they had continued to use the much also for him, he would have still more abundantly used them as instruments to scatter abroad his bounties. The child of God must be willing to be a channel through which God's bounties flow, both with regard to temporal and spiritual things. This channel is narrow and shallow at first, it may be; yet there is room for some of the waters of God's bounty to pass through. And if we cheerfully yield ourselves as channels for this purpose, then the channel becomes wider and deeper, and the waters of the bounty of God can pass through more abundantly. Without a figure, it is thus: At first we may be only instrumental in communicating five pounds, or ten pounds, or twenty pounds, or fifty pounds, or one hundred pounds, or two hundred pounds per year, but afterwards double as much; and, if we are still more faithful in our stewardship, after a year or two four times as much, afterwards perhaps eight times as much, at last perhaps twenty times or fifty times as much. We cannot limit the extent to which God may use us as instruments in communicating blessing, both temporal and spiritual, if we are willing to yield ourselves as instruments to the living God, and are content to be *only instruments, and to give him all the glory.*

But with regard to temporal things it will be thus, that if indeed we walk according to the mind of God in these things, whilst more and more we become instruments of blessing to others, we shall not seek to enrich ourselves, but be content, when the last day of another year finds us still in the body, to possess no more than on the last day of the previous year, or even considerably less, whilst we have been, however, in the course of the year, the instruments of communicating largely to others, through the means with which the Lord had intrusted us. As to my own soul, by the grace of God, it would be a burden to me that however much my income in the course of the year might have been, I were increasing in earthly possession; for it would be a plain proof to me that I had not been acting as a *steward* for God, and had not been yielding myself as a channel for the waters of God's bounty to pass through. I also cannot but bear my testimony here, that in whatever feeble measure God has enabled me to act according to these truths for the last fifteen years [this was written in 1845], I have found it to be profitable, most profitable to my own soul; and as to temporal things, I never was a loser in doing so, but I have most abundantly found the truth in 2 Cor. ix. 6, and Luke vi. 38, and Prov. xi. 24, 25, verified in my own experience. I only have to regret that I have acted so little according to what I have now been stating; but my godly purpose is, by the help of God, to spend the remainder of my days in practising these truths more than ever; and I am sure that when I am brought to the close of my earthly pilgrimage, either in death, or by the appearing of our Lord Jesus, I shall not have the least regret in having done so; and I know that, should I leave my dear child behind, the Lord will abundantly provide for her, and prove that there has been a better provision made for her than her father could have made, if he had sought to insure his life or lay up money for her.

Before leaving this part of the subject, I mention to the believing reader, that I know instance upon instance in which what I have been saying has been verified, but I will only mention the following: I knew many years ago a brother as the manager of a large manufactory. Whilst in this capacity he was liberal, and giving away considerably out of his rather considerable salary. The Lord repaid this to him; for the principals of the establishment, well knowing his value to their house of business, gave him now and then, whilst he thus was liberally using his means for the Lord, very large presents in money. In process of time, however, this brother thought it right to begin business on his own account, in a very small way. He still continued to be liberal, according to his means, and God prospered him, and prospered him so that now, whilst I am writing, his manufactory is as large as the one which he formerly managed, or even larger, though that was a very considerable one. And sure I am that if this brother shall be kept by God from setting his heart upon earthly things, and from seeking more and more to increase his earthly riches, but shall delight himself in being used as a *steward* by God, cheerfully communicating to the needs of God's poor children, or to his work in other ways, and doing so not sparingly, but bountifully, the Lord will intrust him more and more with means; if otherwise, if he shut up his hands, seek his own, wish to obtain sufficient property that he may be able to live on his interest, then what he has to expect is that God will shut up his hands, he will meet with heavy losses, or there will be an alteration in his affairs for the worse, or the like.

I also mention two other cases, to show that the Lord increases our ability of communicating temporal blessings to others if we distribute according to the means with which he has intrusted us, though we should not be in a trade or business or profession. I know a brother who many years ago saw it right not only to spend his interest for the Lord, but also the principal, as the Lord might point out to him opportunities. His desire was not, as indeed it ought never to be, to get rid of his money as fast as possible, yet he considered himself a steward for the Lord, and was therefore willing, as his Lord and Master might point it out to him, to spend his means. When this brother came to this determination, he possessed about twenty thousand pounds sterling. According to the light and grace which the Lord had been pleased to give, he afterwards acted, spending the money for the Lord, in larger or smaller sums, as opportunities were pointed out to him by the Lord. Thus the sum more and more decreased, whilst the brother steadily pursued his course, serving the Lord with his property, and spending his time and ability also for the Lord, in service of one kind or another among his children. At last, the twenty thousand pounds were almost entirely spent, when at that very time the father of this very brother died, whereby he came into the possession of an income of several thousand pounds a year. It gives joy to my heart to be able to add, that this brother still pursues his godly course, living in the most simple way, and giving away perhaps ten times as much as he spends on himself or family. Here you see, dear reader, that this brother, using faithfully for the Lord what he had been intrusted with at first, was made steward over more; for he has now more than one third as much in a year coming in as he at first possessed altogether.

I mention another instance: I know a brother to whom the Lord has given a liberal heart, and who bountifully gave of that over which the Lord had set him as steward. The Lord, seeing this, intrusted him with still more, for through family circumstances he came into the possession of many thousand pounds, in addition to the considerable property he possessed before. I have the joy of being able to add also concerning this brother, that the Lord continues to give him grace to use his property as a steward for God, and that he has not been permitted to set his heart upon his riches, through the very considerable increase of his property, but that he continues to live as the steward of the Lord, and not as the owner of all this wealth.

And now, dear reader, when the brethren to whom I have been referring are brought to the close of their earthly pilgrimage, will they have one moment's regret that they have used their property for the Lord? Will it be the least particle of uneasiness to their minds, or will their children be the worse for it? Oh, no! The only regret they will have concerning this matter will be, that they did not serve the Lord still more abundantly with their property. Dear reader, let us each in our measure act in the same spirit. Money is really worth no more than as it is used according to the mind of the Lord; and life is worth no more than as it is spent in the service of the Lord.

Whilst the three points mentioned — 1. That our calling must be of that nature that *we can abide in it with God;* 2. That unto the Lord we should labor in our calling, as *his servants,* because he has bought us with his blood, and because he will have us to labor; 3. That as *stewards* we should labor in our calling, because the earnings of our calling are the Lord's and not our own, as he has bought us with his blood; — I say, whilst these three points are particularly to be attended to in order that the Lord's blessing may rest upon our calling, and we be prospering in it, there are, nevertheless, some other points to be attended to, which I mention in love to my brethren in the Lord, by whom they may be needed.

4. The next point is, that *a believer in the Lord Jesus should do nothing in his calling which is purely for the sake of attracting the world;* such as, for instance, fitting up his shop or rooms of business in the most costly manner. I do not in the least mean to say that his shop or rooms of business should not be clean, orderly, and of such a character as that there may be no positive hindrance in persons going there. All the *needful* conveniences that are expected may be there, and ought to be there. But if any child of God seek to have the front of his shop, or the interior of his shop, or of his place of business, fitted up in a most expensive way, simply for the sake of attracting attention, then let him be aware that, just in so far as he is trusting in these things, he is not likely to succeed in his calling, because he puts the manner of fitting up the shop in the room of trust in the Lord. Such things the

Lord may allow to succeed in the case of an unbeliever, but they will not prosper in the case of a child of God, except it be in the way of chastisement, just as the Lord gave to Israel in the wilderness the desire of their hearts, but sent leanness into their souls. Should any brother have fallen into this error, the first thing he has to do, when the Lord has instructed him concerning this point, is to make confession of sin, and, as far as it can be done, to retrace his steps in this particular. If this cannot be done, then to cast himself upon the mercy of God in Christ Jesus.

5. Of the same character is to seek to attract the attention of the world by "boasting advertisements," such as "no one manufactures so good an article," "no one sells this article so cheap," " we sell the best article in the city," etc. Suppose these statements were quite correct, yet they are unbecoming for a child of God, who has the living God to care for him and to provide for him, and therefore needs not to make use of such boasting, whereby he may seek to insure custom to himself and keep it from others. The law of love is, " Whatsoever ye would that men should do to you, do ye even so to them." Matt. vii. 12. Now, what do I wish in this particular that others should do to me, but that they should not seek to keep away persons from dealing with me; but if I use such like expressions in my advertisements as have been mentioned, what do they imply but that I wish all people should come to me, and deal with me? If, however, already under the old covenant it was said, "Thou shalt not covet," how much more sinful and altogether unbecoming is it for us, children of God, who are in fellowship with the Father and the Son, to make use of such means in order to insure to ourselves pecuniary advantages! But, however much the Lord may allow a man of the world to prosper in using such means, they are only hindrances to the child of God to getting on in his calling, because the Lord sees that they are substituted instead of

trust in himself; and should the Lord for a season allow his child apparently to be benefited by them, it will only be for his chastisement and connected with leanness in his soul. Therefore, my brethren in the Lord, I beseech you to put away all these things out of your calling, lest you should be hindering instead of furthering your real welfare.

6. Likewise of a similar character is the following point, which God may suffer to be a real hindrance to his children in their calling; it is, To seek the very best, and therefore the most expensive, situations which can be had in a town or city. Now, I do by no means intend to say, that in our trade, business, art, or profession, we should seek the most obscure, retired, out-of-the-way place possible, and say, "God will provide, and I need not mind in what part of the town I carry on my calling." There are most assuredly certain things to be considered. The persons who are likely to buy the articles I sell, or employ me, are to be considered, and I have not to say, it matters nothing to me whether I make them come a mile or two to my house, or to the most dirty and disagreeable part of the town; this would be the extreme in the other way. But whilst there is a certain consideration to be used with reference to those who may employ us in our calling, yet if the trust of the child of God respecting temporal prosperity is in the fact that he lives in the best situation, the Lord will surely disappoint him. He will have to pay a very high rent for the best situation, and yet not succeed, because his trust is in the best situation. He is substituting it for dependence upon the living God for customers. He is robbing his soul, not only in not taking the customers as from the hands of the Lord, but he is also obliging his heavenly Father, in the very love of his heart, to cause him to be disappointed, because he is not trusting in him. If the child of God were saying and acting thus: the best situation would cost me fifty pounds a year more rent than one which is not really inconvenient for my customers, nor in an improper

neighborhood, and the like; this fifty dollars I dedicate unto the Lord, to be paid in instalments for his work or his poor saints, whenever the rent-day comes; such a brother would find himself to be no loser, if this indeed were done in dependence upon the Lord, and constrained by the love of Jesus. But if the fifty pounds more are paid for rent, and yet the living God, in the very love of his heart, should be obliged to withhold prosperity from his child in his calling, because he sees that he is laying undue stress upon the situation of the house, then not only the fifty pounds extra rent per year are lost, but also that which the Lord is obliged to withhold from his child besides, in order to teach him the lesson; and thus year after year, by our own fault, we may have scarcely anything to give for the work of God.

7. The next obstacle to prosperity in our calling which I now would mention is, That children of God often use such expressions as these with reference to their calling: "This is our busy time," or "This is our dead time;" which implies that they do not day after day deal with God about their calling, but that they ascribe their having much or little to do to circumstances, or to times and seasons. That the people of the world should do so is not to be wondered at; but that the children of God should act thus, who in the most minute affairs of life should seek the help of God, and deal with God about them, is a matter of sorrow to the spiritual mind, and is altogether unbecoming saints. But what is the result? The Lord, according to the expectations of his children, allows them to be without employment, because they say, "This is our dead season." "He did not many mighty works there because of their unbelief," contains a truth which comes in here. But what is the right way of looking at the matter? It is this: the child of God should say, though generally about this time of the year there is little employment to be expected, looking at it naturally, just as want of employment is neither

good for the outward nor inward man, and as I only desire employment to serve God in my business, to have to give to those who are in need, or help in other ways the work of God, I will now give myself to prayer for employment, for I can by prayer and faith as a child of God obtain blessings from my heavenly Father, though not in the ordinary course of things. If thus the child of God were to say and to act, he would soon have employment in his calling, except the Lord meant to use his time otherwise in his work, which he would point out to him.

8. A further reason why God may be obliged to resist children of God in their business, may be this, that they with the greatest carefulness seek to obtain persons for their shop who are considered "good salesmen," *i. e.*, persons who have such persuasive ways, as that they gain an advantage over the customers and induce them not only to buy articles for which they ask, whether suitable or not, but that they also induce them to buy articles which they did not at all intend to buy when they came to the shop. Concerning this I notice, in the first place, that if the child of God puts his dependence upon the "good salesmen," let him not be surprised if his heavenly Father should be obliged to disappoint him, because he sees his child lean upon the arm of flesh, instead of trusting in the living God; and therefore the business does not succeed. Further, it is altogether wrong for a child of God to induce the customers, by means of such men or women who have a persuasive tongue, to purchase articles whether they suit or not, and whether they are needed or not. This is no less than defrauding persons in a subtle way, or leading them into the sin of purchasing beyond their means, or at least spending their money needlessly. However such sinful tricks may be allowed to prosper in the case of a man of the world, in the case of a child of God they will not prosper, except God allow them to do so in the way of chastisement, whilst leanness and wretchedness are

brought into the soul. I knew a case of this kind where it was the whole bent of the mind of a professed believer to obtain such "good salesmen," and where even a Jew was kept outside the shop, walking up and down, to induce persons to come in and buy, and yet that same professed believer failed twice in his business.

9. Another evil with reference to business, and why children of God do not get on in their calling, is, that they enter upon business often without any capital at all, or with too little. If a believer has no capital at all, or only a very small capital, in comparison with what his business requires, then ought he not to say this to himself: "If it were my heavenly Father's will that I should enter upon business on my own account, then would he not somehow or other have intrusted me with the needful means? And since he has not, is it not a plain indication that for the present I should remain a journeyman (or shopman, or clerk, as the case may be)?" In a variety of ways the means might come. For instance, a legacy might be left to him, or money might be given to him by a brother in the Lord for that very purpose, or a brother or sister might propose to the individual to lend him money, yet so that if he were unable to pay it again they would not consider him their debtor. But if in some such way the Lord did not remove the hindrance, and the brother would still go into business, he would, through the bill system and other things connected with the want of capital, not only bring great distress into his mind, and subject himself to the possibility of at last being unable to pay his creditors, whereby dishonor would be brought upon the name of the Lord, but he likewise could not be surprised (as he went into business contrary to the will of God, since he pointed out to him that he was not to do so for want of means) if he should find that he cannot get on, and that the blessing of God manifestly is wanting. In such a case as this, if it can be done, the retracing our

steps is the best thing we can do; but often this cannot be done, as others are involved in the matter, and then we have to make acknowledgment of our sin, and seek God's merciful help to bring us into a right position.

10. But suppose all these nine previous points were attended to, and we neglected *to seek God's blessing upon our calling,* we need still not be surprised if we met with difficulty upon difficulty, and could not get on at all. It is not enough that we seek God's help for that which manifestly is of a spiritual character; but we should seek his help and blessing by prayer and supplication for all our ordinary concerns in life, and if we neglect doing so we shall surely suffer for the neglect. "Trust in the Lord with all thine heart; and lean not unto thine own understanding. In all thy ways acknowledge **him,** and he shall direct thy paths." Prov. iii. 5, 6.

Though these few remarks are written by one who never was in business himself, yet the truths therein set forth have been learned by him in the school of God, and he has had them abundantly confirmed through his pastoral labors during the last fifteen years and a half. [This was written in 1845.]

CHAPTER XVII.

REAPING BOUNTIFULLY.

1845 — 1846.

AN UNEXPECTED REQUEST — DELIBERATION — A GREAT UNDERTAKING — RELIANCE ON THE RESOURCES OF THE LIVING GOD — AN ANSWER EXPECTED AND RECEIVED — PRAYER FOR FAITH AND PATIENCE — FURTHER PROOFS OF DIVINE FAVOR — THE BLESSEDNESS OF DEVISING LIBERAL THINGS.

I BEGAN the service of caring for children who are bereaved of *both* parents, by death, born in wedlock, and are in destitute circumstances, on Dec. 9, 1835. For nearly ten years I had never had any desire to build an Orphan House. On the contrary, I decidedly preferred spending the means which might come in for present necessities, and desired rather to enlarge the work according to the means which the Lord might be pleased to give. Thus it was till the end of October, 1845, when I was led to consider this matter in a way in which I had never done before.[1] The occasion of my doing so was this: On Oct. 30, 1845, I received from a gentleman, who lived in the street where the four Orphan Houses were, a polite and friendly letter, in which he courteously stated to me that the inhabitants in the adjoining houses were in various ways inconvenienced by the Orphan Houses being in Wilson Street. He left to myself the judgment of the case.

This letter I received on Thursday morning, Oct. 30, 1845. Being very much occupied that week, I had scarcely any time to consider the matter. On Monday morning, however, Nov. 3, I set apart some hours for the prayerful con-

---

[1] The reader will not fail to remark the striking illustration afforded, in the present chapter, of the truth stated in Chapter XVI., that God rewards the right use of means of benevolence by affording the means of enlarged usefulness. — ED.

sideration of the subject, and after I had besought the Lord to guide me to a right decision, I wrote down the reasons which appeared to me to make it desirable that the Orphan Houses should be *removed* from Wilson Street, and also the reasons *against removing*. As far as they are suitable for being stated in print they were these: —

I. REASONS FOR REMOVING FROM WILSON STREET.

1. The neighbors feel themselves inconvenienced by the noise of the children in the play-hours. This complaint is neither without foundation, nor unjust; for many persons are very much inconvenienced by the noise of children, and those living close by the Orphan Houses must be so during the play-hours, even though the noise be only of that kind that one could not at all find fault with the dear children on account of it. I should myself feel it trying to my head to live next door to the Orphan Houses, on that account. I therefore ought to do to others as I should wish to be done by. This point had never before appeared to me in so serious a light.

2. The greatness of the number of the inmates in the houses had several times prevented the drains from acting properly, and thus has a few times affected the water in one or two of the neighbors' houses. With reference to these two reasons as it regards those living near the Orphan Houses, these words, "Let not your good be evil spoken of" (Rom. xiv. 16), and "Let your moderation (*i. e.*, yieldingness) be known unto all men" (Philip. iv. 5), seemed to me two important portions of the word of God to be acted out in this matter.

But in addition to the reasons for removing the Orphan Houses from Wilson Street, on account of the unavoidable occasional inconvenience that comes upon the neighbors, there appeared now to me, when once I was led to consider seriously the reasons for removing the Institution from Wilson Street, other reasons for doing so, in connection with the work itself, which had occurred to me before, but never in so strong a light as now, when the subject was brought more immediately before me by the letter in which I was politely requested to remove the Orphan Houses from Wilson Street. These reasons are: —

1. We have no proper play-grounds in Wilson Street. There is one play-ground, which, however, is only large enough for the children of *one house* at a time; but as there are children in *four* houses who ought to have the benefit of it, we cannot arrange so that all the children have the full benefit of that play-ground, as the meals the school-hours, the weather, and other hindrances interfere. The dear orphans ought, I know, to be trained in habits of industry, but children are children, and need to be treated as such; and they should, on account of their health, have the full benefit of a play-ground. But this they cannot have in Wilson Street; and to take them out into the fields for the benefit of bodily exercise, as we have been in the habit of doing, is often very inconvenient.

2. We have no ground for cultivation near the Orphan Houses, and hence there must be more walking for the children, on account of using proper means for keeping them, with the blessing of God, in health, than is in other respects good for them; because frequent walks easily beget in children habits of idleness, which would be especially felt when boys are apprenticed. But this difficulty cannot be obviated by remaining in Wilson Street, and renting a piece of land somewhere else for cultivation; for to get the children ready and conduct them to the piece of ground not only takes a good deal of time, but is connected with other great inconveniences, yea, with insurmountable difficulties, so that we found it needful to give up a small piece of ground which we once rented for about two years for the orphan boys, at a distance of about half

a mile from Wilson Street. Thus, by removing from Wilson Street, and obtaining premises surrounded by land for cultivation, we should be able to procure a most important moral benefit for the children, by having the opportunity more fully than we now have of training them in habits of industry, besides giving to the boys occupation which is more suitable for them than knitting, which is now the only employment they have, besides making their beds, cleaning the house, and attending to the cooking of their meals. Moreover, this would be occupation in the open air, which not only would bring into exercise the use of their limbs, but also make walking for the sake of health almost entirely needless.

3. If we were to remove from Wilson Street, and obtain premises in the country, we might have all the washing done at home, which now, for want of room, can be only done in part. Thus the girls also would have more laborious work at home, a point of great importance for them, so that they would not feel so much the hardships connected with going out to service.

4. The situation of Wilson Street is *perhaps* scarcely bracing enough for strengthening the constitution of the orphans, most of whom, being the offspring of very diseased parents, require a very invigorating place of abode.

5. The present situation is *certainly* not desirable for the teachers, especially as, when their hours of work are over, they have no garden or fields next to the house immediately to go into for a little refreshment of their body; and for some of them it is too far to go to fields where they might have a bracing air.

6. In times of sickness we are too confined in the houses in Wilson Street. If there were less than thirty children in each house, the average expenses of each child would be too great, it being desirable, as the arrangements are now, that there should not be less than three laborers in each

house; and yet, if there are thirty children in each house, we are too full in time of sickness, as we have not a single spare room in any of the houses. Now, though the Lord has during all these years most mercifully helped us through such seasons, yet it has not been without inconvenience, and without also, perhaps, having more of the children in one room, at such times, than on account of health it is desirable.

7. Even ordinarily, when there is no sickness, it would be desirable to have more room.

There are no premises to be had in Bristol, or in the immediate neighborhood, where we could have these advantages; *for I have been looking about in all directions for this purpose during the last ten years.* But suppose there were a large house to be had in one part of the city, and a second a mile off, and a third and a fourth in other directions, such houses, on account of our peculiar position in the work, would not do. For in seasons of need the distance of the several houses would render it very inconvenient for the laborers to meet together for prayer, to divide the means that may be in hand, etc. Besides, when in seasons of other peculiar difficulties, connected with the work, I wished to meet all my fellow-laborers, there would arise great difficulty by their being divided in different parts of the city. It would also thus be very inconvenient to persons who wish to see the work, to go from place to place, in order to have a view of all the Orphan Houses. But this is not all. The more I have considered the matter, the more am I now persuaded that no ordinary large houses, built for private families, and therefore only calculated to accommodate ten or fifteen persons at most for any length of time in them, will do for charitable institutions of any considerable size, as no ordinary house, except built on purpose, furnishes the proper advantages of ventilation, *a point so needful for the health of the inmates in a charitable institution.* There seemed to me, therefore, to remain nothing but to build premises for the purpose.

II. REASONS FOR REMAINING IN WILSON STREET.

1. God *hitherto* has pointed out the spot most plainly. At the commencement of the work, in 1835, no other house was to be had but No. 6 Wilson Street. Afterwards, when in 1836 the Infant Orphan House was on the point of being opened, again I was looking about in all directions, and saw many houses, but found none that was suitable, till all at once, most unlooked for, the occupiers of No. 1 Wilson Street were desirous of immediately leaving that house, and I was able thus to rent it. When in 1837, I was on the point of opening the Boys' Orphan House, I looked about again for a house in all directions; for I knew not at that time, what I have since learned by experience, that it was so important that all the houses should be near together. After seeking long in vain, I at last found a very large house, not far from Wilson Street, which I rented; but when the occupiers of the houses in the neighborhood heard that that house had been let for a charitable institution, they threatened the owner with an action, which led him to request me to give up the agreement, which, of course, I did immediately. At last, most unexpectedly, after having looked about in vain in all directions, the occupiers of No. 3 Wilson Street offered it to me, and I rented it for the orphan boys. Lastly, in the year 1843, when I was led to see it to be the will of God to go forward in this work, and to establish the Girls' Orphan House No. 2, for older girls, one particular feature in the matter was, that the house No. 4 in Wilson Street had been offered to me, without being sought after, when there had not been, for about six years, one single large house to be let in that street.

[But though *hitherto* God has pointed out Wilson Street

as being the spot where the work should be carried on, may not *now* the time have come for removing?]

2. Perhaps we might also rent Nos. 2, 5, and 7, in Wilson Street, and use two out of those three houses for Orphan Houses, and one of them for an infirmary in the case of sickness.

[But then, I said to myself, would not the objection, which the neighbors on the opposite side of the street might make, on account of the noise of the children in their play-hours, etc., remain? Also the drains would be still more unsuitable, not being constructed for so many inmates; and to alter them would be a heavy expense. The play-ground would be still less sufficient, if two new houses were added. Lastly, there was no reason to think that we could rent Nos. 2, 5, and 7.]

3. There are these three great objections against building: The considerable sum which is required, and which could be spent for present use upon the orphans. The pilgrim character of the Christian seems lost in building. The time that it will necessarily take in making arrangements for it.

[Do not all these objections only hold good, I said to myself, if I were *needlessly* to set about building? If I could rent premises, which are really in every way suitable for the work, and I *preferred* building, then those objections would apply to the case; but when one is *forced* to it, it is no more than erecting a large building, because there may be eight hundred children of God in fellowship who have been hitherto renting a meeting-place, but for certain reasons are obliged to leave it, and cannot rent another. Such could not be accused of needlessly spending money in building instead of renting; nor could it be justly said that they have *on that account* given up the pilgrim character; nor would it be time wasted if some individuals were to make arrangements about the building of that meeting-place. Therefore these three objections just mentioned, which had been *for ten years strongly in my own mind*, were removed when once I saw plainly that nothing remained but to build.]

After I had spent a few hours in prayer and consideration over the subject, I began already to see that the Lord would lead me to build, and that his intentions were not only the benefit of the orphans and the better ordering of the whole work, but also the bearing still further testimony that he *could* and *would* provide *large* sums for those who need them and trust in him for them; and besides, that he would enlarge the work, so that, if I once did build a house, it might be large enough to accommodate three hundred orphans, with their teachers and other overseers and servants needful for the work. Concerning this latter point, I think it important to remark, that during no period had the number of the applications for the admission of orphans been greater than just before I was led to think about building, so that it was quite painful to me not to be able to comply with the wishes of all the many persons who applied for the admission of orphans. There were many waiting for admission, particularly orphan boys.

In the afternoon of November 3, 1845, I laid the matter before my fellow-laborers in the church (eight in number), to get their judgment, whether I ought not to leave Wilson Street, and to build. All judged that I ought to leave Wilson Street, and none saw reasons against building.

On Nov. 4 my dear wife and I began to meet for prayer about this matter, and purposed to do so morning by morning. We asked God for clearer light concerning the particular points connected with the subject; and being assured that it was his will that I should build, I began asking the Lord for means.

On Nov. 7 I judged, having considered the matter more fully, that sufficiently large premises to furnish all needful accommodation for three hundred children (from their earliest days up to fifteen or sixteen years old), together with a sufficiently large piece of ground in the neighborhood of Bristol, for building the premises upon, and the remainder for cultivation by the spade, would cost at least ten thousand pounds. I was not discouraged by this, but trusted in the living God.

We continued meeting for prayer morning by morning for fifteen days, but not a single donation came in; yet my heart was not discouraged. The more I prayed, the more assured I was that the Lord would give the means. Yea, as fully assured was I that the Lord would do so, as if I had already seen the new premises actually before me. This assurance arose not from some vague, enthusiastical feeling, the mere excitement of the moment, but, 1. From the reasons already related, and especially from the commandment contained in Philip. iv. 5. For I saw that I should not act according to the mind of our Lord Jesus if I did not, as soon as I could, remove the orphans from Wilson Street, as it had been stated to me, in the letter above referred to, that their living there was an annoyance to some of the inhabitants in that street. 2. This assurance that I should build an Orphan Home arose further from the whole way in which the Lord had been pleased to lead me in connection with the Scriptural Knowledge Institution for Home and Abroad since its beginning on March 5, 1834, *i. e.*, he has been leading me forward as by an unseen hand, and enlarging the work more and more from its commencement, and, generally, without my seeking after it, and bringing things so clearly before me that I could not but see that I ought to go forward. 3. Lastly and chiefly, this, my assurance that I should build unto the Lord this house of mercy, arose also particularly from this, that having strictly examined my heart as to the motives for doing so, I found that, as before God, I could say that my only motives were his honor and glory, and the welfare of the church of Christ at large, the real temporal and spiritual welfare of destitute orphans, and the welfare of all those who might take care of them, in the building to be erected. And finding that, after praying again and again about the matter, I still remained in perfect peace, I judged it assuredly to be the will of God that I should go forward.

On Nov. 15 brother R. C. arrived, to labor for a little while in Bristol. I communicated to him my position with reference to having to remove the orphans from Wilson Street, and I had his judgment also as to its being of God that I should *build*. This dear brother's judgment greatly encouraged me. His visit was to me of great help in this particular, especially in stirring me up yet more to bring everything in connection with this matter before God. He also laid it on my heart to seek direction from God with reference to the plan of the building. He said, " You must ask help of God to show you the plan, so that all may be according to the mind of God."

Up to Dec. 9 thirty-five days had passed away, whilst I was day by day waiting upon God for means for this work, and not a single penny had been given to me. Nevertheless, this did not in the least discourage me, but my assurance that God, in his own time and in his own way, would give the means, increased more and more. The portion which came in course of my meditation on the New Testament was the beginning of the epistle of James. More than at any period in my life was I struck with these verses: " My brethren, count it all joy when ye fall into divers temptations (*i. e.*, trials) ; knowing this, that the trying of your faith worketh patience. But let patience have her perfect work, that ye may be perfect and entire, wanting nothing." James i. 2-4. It was especially the last verse, " But let patience have her perfect work," etc., which I found of exceeding great importance with reference to the building of the Orphan House. It led out my soul in prayer day after day, to ask the Lord to increase my faith, and to sustain my patience. I had these verses so impressed upon my heart that I could not but think that God meant particularly to bless me by them, with regard to the work before me, and that I should especially need patience as well as faith.

On the thirty-sixth day after having begun to pray, Dec. 10, 1845, I received one thousand pounds towards the building of the Orphan House. This is the largest donation that I had received up to that time for the Scriptural Knowledge Institution; but when I received it I was as calm, as quiet, as if I had only received one shilling. For my heart was looking out for answers. Day by day I was expecting to receive answers to my prayers. Therefore, having faith concerning the matter, this donation did not in the least surprise me. Yea, if five thousand pounds or ten thousand pounds had been given to me, instead of one thousand pounds, it would not have surprised me.

Dec. 13. On the thirty-ninth day my sister-in-law, who had been for some weeks absent in London, and who had now returned to Bristol, told me that she had met a gentleman in London, who, having quite recently read with deep interest the Narrative of the Lord's dealings with me, wished to know as many particulars about the work in my hands as he could. Being told by my sister-in-law that I purposed to build an Orphan House, he, an architect, offered to make the plan, and superintend the building *gratuitously*. Unsolicited, he pressed this matter upon her with deep and lively interest. I hear also that he is a Christian. The fact that this offer comes *unsolicited*, and from a Christian architect, shows especially the hand of God. This is the *second* proof that God will help me in this matter.

Dec. 23. This is now the fiftieth day since I have come to the conclusion to build, and the forty-ninth day since we have been daily waiting upon God for help. Nothing more has come in since Dec. 10, not even one penny. This morning I have been particularly encouraged by the consideration that the Lord has sent me the one thousand pounds, and the promise from that pious architect, whom I have never seen, and of whose name I am as yet in ignorance, *not to mock me, but as an earnest that he will give all that is needed.*

It seems desirable that we should have a large piece of ground, at least six or seven acres. This piece of ground must be in the vicinity of Bristol: 1. In order that the Orphan House may be accessible to me, as my place at present is fixed by my other work in Bristol. 2. That the laborers in the Institution and the orphans may be able to attend our meetings, at least on the Lord's day. For if meetings were held on purpose in the Orphan House, either the laborers or the children would not be benefited by them in that measure in which it is desirable. 3. That the inhabitants of Bristol may have the benefit of seeing with their own eyes this work of God, which is so manifestly his, and not mine. 4. That strangers who pass through Bristol may have easy access to it, for the same reason. But then, such a piece of ground near Bristol, where there is just now such an inordinate desire for building, in the way of speculation, would cost, in all human probability, between two and three thousand pounds. Then the building itself, however plain, would not cost less than from six to eight thousand pounds, being for three hundred orphans, besides all their overseers, teachers, and assistants. In addition to this, the fitting up and furnishing the house for all these between three and four hundred inmates would not cost less than fifteen hundred pounds more. This is indeed a large sum of money which I need; but my hope is in God. I have not sought after this thing. It has not begun with me. God has altogether unexpectedly, by means of the letter before mentioned, led me to it. Only the day before I received the letter, I had no more thought about *building* premises for the accommodation of the orphans than I had had during the ten previous years. My especial prayer is that God would continue to me *faith* and *patience*. If he shall be pleased to help me in faith and patience to continue to wait on him, help will surely come.

Dec. 24. No further donation yet. But my hope in God is unshaken. He most assuredly will help. I have on purpose not issued any circular in connection with this matter, in order that the hand of God may be the more manifest. To some persons residing in or out of Bristol I have spoken about my intention of building, when conversation led to it. Through this, if the Lord please, he can make it known to others, and thus send means for the building fund. Or he can send in such an abundance of means for the work which is already in existence, that from that abundance there might be a rich surplus towards the building fund. But howsoever God may help, I do desire to see his hand made most manifest. There will be, no doubt, many trials connected with this enlargement of the field of labor (for if with the one hundred and thirty orphans there has been so much trial of faith, what is to be expected when the number is three hundred); and therefore I desire to see as clearly as daylight that God himself is leading me onward.

Dec. 29. This is the fifty-sixth day since I came to the conclusion to build, and the fifty-fifth since I have been day by day waiting upon God concerning it. Only that one donation had come in till this evening, when I received fifty pounds. This donation is exceedingly precious to me, not only because I am sure it is most cheerfully given, nor even because of its largeness, but because it is another precious proof that God will bring about the matter, else he would not give me these earnests. All *my* business therefore is, to continue in faith and patience to wait upon God. My assurance has been more and more increasing that God will build for himself a large Orphan House in this city, to show to the inhabitants, and to all who may read and hear about it, what a blessed thing it is to trust in him. Of late I have seen, by God's grace, more and more, how entirely unworthy I am of being used by God for this glorious and honorable service, and I can only say

"Lord, here is thy servant, if thou art pleased to use such a one as I am."

Dec 30, 1845. This morning I came, in course of my reading, to the commencement of the book of Ezra. I was particularly refreshed by the two following points contained in the first chapter, in applying them to the building of the Orphan House: 1. Cyrus, an *idolatrous* king, was used by God to provide the means for building the temple at Jerusalem: how easy therefore for God to provide ten thousand pounds for the Orphan House, or even twenty or thirty thousand pounds, if needed! 2. The people were stirred up by God to help those who went up to Jerusalem. Thus it is a small matter for him to put it into the hearts of his children to help me, in desiring to build this house of mercy unto his name. This meditation I had before breakfast. After family prayer in the morning, I had again my usual season for prayer about the building, and at this time it was particularly coupled with thanksgiving for the fifty pounds received last evening, and with entreating blessings on the donor. This evening I received one thousand pounds towards the building fund. When I received this donation I was as calm, yea as perfectly calm, as if I had received a single penny, because, by God's grace, I have faith in him, and therefore I am looking for answers to my prayers, and am sure that God will give every shilling that is needed.

Jan. 2, 1846. This evening I received from Bideford eleven shillings toward the building fund.

Having asked the Lord to go before me, I went out to-day to look for a piece of ground. The armory which is to be sold had been several times mentioned to me as a suitable place. I did not think so, yet I thought I ought at least to look at it. Having seen it and been confirmed in my judgment about its unsuitableness, I asked the Lord whether I should turn towards the city or towards Stapleton. I felt led to go towards the city, and saw immediately after some fields near the armory. After having made inquiry to whom they belonged, I have been led to write this evening to the owner of them, asking him whether he is disposed to sell them, etc. I am now quietly waiting the Lord's pleasure. If his time has come to answer our requests as to a suitable piece of land, I shall be glad; if it is not yet come, I desire that "patience may have her perfect work, being perfect and entire, wanting nothing."

Jan. 8. This evening I received a reply to my letter. The owner of those fields writes, that, if he did sell them, it would be only for building land, and therefore they will be too dear.

Jan. 9. Went this morning once more to see those fields, which seem very suitable. Met there Mr. L., a land agent, who told me that they would be nearly a thousand pounds per acre, and therefore too dear. I asked Mr. L. to inform me if he should hear of any suitable land for sale.

Jan. 31. It is now eighty-nine days since I have been daily waiting upon God about the building of an Orphan House. The time seems to me now near when the Lord will give us a piece of ground, and I told the brethren and sisters so this evening, after our usual Saturday evening prayer meeting at the Orphan House.

Feb. 1. A poor widow sent to-day ten shillings.

Feb. 2. To-day I heard of suitable and cheap land on Ashley Down.

Feb. 3. Saw the land. It is the most desirable of all I have seen. There was anonymously put into an orphan box at my house a sovereign, in a piece of paper on which was written, "The New Orphan House."

Feb. 4. This evening I called on the owner of the land on Ashley Down, about which I had heard on the 2d, but he was not at home. As I, however, had been informed that I should find him at his house of business, I went there, but did not find him there either, as he had *just before* left. I might have called again at his residence at a later hour, having been informed by one of the servants that he would be sure to be at home about eight o'clock; but I did not do so, judging that there was the hand of God in my not finding him at either place: and I judged it best therefore, not to force the matter, but to "let patience have her perfect work."

Feb. 5. Saw this morning the owner of the land. He told me that he awoke at three o'clock this morning and could not sleep again till five. While he was thus lying awake his mind was all the time occupied about the piece of land respecting which inquiry had been made of him for the building of an Orphan House, at my request; and he determined with himself that, if I should apply for it, he would not only let me have it, but for one hundred and twenty pounds per acre, instead of two hundred pounds, the price which he had previously asked for it. How good is the Lord! The agreement was made this morning, and I purchased a field of nearly seven acres, at one hundred and twenty pounds per acre.

Observe the hand of God in my not finding the owner at home last evening! The Lord meant to speak to his servant first about this matter, during a sleepless night, and to lead him *fully* to decide before I had seen him.

Feb. 8. I wrote the day before yesterday to the architect, who has offered his help gratuitously.

Feb. 11. Received from a sister in the Lord five pounds. Received also from the architect the following reply to my letter: —

MY DEAR SIR: —

It will afford me a gratification, beyond what I can communicate by letter, to lend you the helping hand in the labor of love you are engaged in, and I shall esteem it a very great privilege being allowed to exercise my abilities as an architect and surveyor in the erection of the building you propose to erect for the orphans. I really do mean what I say, and, if all is well, by the blessing of God, I will *gratui-*

tously furnish you with plans, elevations, and sections, with specification of the work, so that the cost may be accurately estimated. I will also make you an estimate and superintend the works for you *gratuitously*, etc.

The total amount which has been given for the building fund, up to June 4, 1846, is two thousand seven hundred and ten pounds three shillings five and a half pence. This is only a small part of what will be needed; but, by the grace of God, I am in perfect peace, being fully assured that God in his own time will send the whole sum which is required. Many and great have already been the exercises of faith and patience since I first began to give myself to prayer about this work, and still greater they may be, before it is accomplished; but God, in the riches of his grace, will help me through them all. It is now (June 4, 1846) two hundred and twelve days since I first began to pray about this work, and day after day, since then, have I been enabled to continue to wait upon God, and I am more than ever assured that, notwithstanding all my exceeding great unworthiness, God will condescend to use me, to build this house. Had it been the excitement of the moment, the difficulties which have already come upon me in connection with this work (and which are not stated here, on account of their occupying too much room) would have overwhelmed me; but as God himself, I trust, led me to this work, so he has helped me, and does help me, and I doubt not will help me to the end.

The house is intended to be built so as to accommodate one hundred and forty orphan girls above seven years of age, eighty orphan boys above seven, and eighty male and female orphans from their earliest days, till they are seven years old, together with all the overseers and teachers, etc., that may be needed. The infants, after having passed the age of seven, will be removed into the different departments for older boys and girls.

Before leaving this period, it may be proper to recur to the following miscellaneous points, respecting the Scriptural Knowledge Institution for Home and Abroad, with reference to the period from July 14, 1844, to May 26, 1846.

1. During the whole of this period four day schools, with 278 children in them, were *entirely* supported by the funds of the Institution. Three day schools besides were *assisted*. The number of children that were taught in the day schools, entirely supported by the funds of the Institution, from March 5, 1834, to May 26, 1846, amounts to 3,983. During the period from July 14, 1844, to May 26, 1846, £628, 19s. 4¼d. was spent on all the schools, which were either entirely or in part supported by the funds of the Scriptural Knowledge Institution. Further during this period there were also entirely supported a Sunday school with 80 children, and an adult school with 60 persons attending it. The total number of the adult scholars who received instruction, from the formation of this Institution to May 26, 1846, is 1,146.

2. During this period were circulated 269 Bibles and 171 Testaments; and 5,079 Bibles and 3,528 Testaments were circulated from the commencement of the work up to May 26, 1846. From July 14, 1844, to May 26, 1846, £40, 7s. 10d were expended of the funds of the Institution on this object.

3. From July 14, 1844, to May 26, 1846, was laid out for foreign and home missions the sum of £595, 7s. 9d. During no period previously was so much of the funds of this Institution spent on missionary work, which arose from the fact that the more I corresponded with brethren who labored in the word and doctrine in foreign lands, the more I saw how much they stood in need of assistance, and thus, my heart having been led out in prayer to God on their behalf, that he would be pleased to send me means, whereby I might be able to assist them, he was pleased to do so. This led me to the purpose, as God should give me grace, to be still more mindful of them in future, and to seek to be able still more to assist them. The same was the case with regard to those brethren who labor in England, but who have no salary or stipend, but trust in the living God for the supply of their daily necessities; I did long to help such brethren, and had no doubt that God would enable me to do so.

4. There was laid out for the circulation of tracts from July 14, 1844, to May 26, 1846, the sum of £56, 6s. 9½d., for which 52,003 such

little publications were bought, which, with 5,315 in hand on July 14, 1844, makes 57,318, of which number 40,565 were circulated. The total number circulated from Nov. 19, 1840, to May 26, 1846, amounts to 99,647.

5. There were received into the four Orphan Houses, from July 14, 1844, to May 26, 1846, 30 orphans, who, together with those who were in the four houses on July 14, 1844, make up 151 in all.

On May 26, 1846, there were 121 orphans in the four houses. Besides this, six apprentices were still supported by the funds of the Institution, so that the total number was 127. The number of the orphans who were under our care from April, 1836, to May 26, 1846, amounts to 213.

I notice further the following points in connection with the Orphan Houses:

1. *Without any one having been personally applied to for anything by me*, the sum of £13,275, 6s. 9¾d. was given to me *as the result of prayer to God*, from the commencement of the work up to May 26, 1846. This sum includes the £2,710, 3s. 5½d. which, up to June 4, 1846, were given towards the building fund. (It may be interesting to the reader to know that the total amount which was given as free contributions, for the other objects, from the commencement of the work up to May 26, 1846, amounts to £4,833,18s. 10¾d; and that which came in by the sale of Bibles and tracts, and by the payments of the children in the day schools, amounts to £2,097, 18s 2½d.) 2. Besides this, also a great variety and number of articles of clothing, furniture, provisions, etc , were given for the orphans, as has been stated in the printed reports. The total expenditure for the orphans from July 14, 1844, to May 26, 1846, was £2,732, 14s. 1½d., and for the other objects, £1,325, 7s. 7¼d.

In conclusion, I cannot but mention to the praise of the Lord concerning this period, that four of the Sunday-school children were admitted to communion. Likewise three more of the orphans were received into church fellowship; so that up to that time, altogether, thirty-two of the orphans had been admitted. I also mention with peculiar joy, and as a matter for thankfulness, that of those who were apprenticed or sent out to service, from July 14, 1844, to May 26, 1846, ten were believers, most of whom had been for several years in fellowship before they were sent out to service. But whilst we desire to receive these instances as precious encouragements from the Lord to continue our service, we cannot but believe, judging from the many prayers the Lord gives us for the children and adults under our care and instruction, that that which we *see* is but an earnest of a far larger harvest in the day of Christ's appearing.

Dec. 31, 1844. Since brother Craik and I came to Bristol, 982 believers have been received into communion. During this year 73 have been received.

The Lord has been pleased to give me during this year £267, 6s. 9d.

To this is to be added that for the first two months and six days of this year, my expenses, and those of my dear wife, during our stay in Germany, were met, as also our travelling expenses back, as stated in another part of my Narrative. Also during the whole of this year a Christian lady gave to our dear child board and schooling without any remuneration, — a present worth to us not less than fifty pounds. On this point I cannot help making a few remarks: I had clearly seen it to be the will of God that my daughter should be brought up at school, and not at home. My reasons for it were these: 1. My dear wife, though well qualified to instruct our daughter, so far as knowledge goes, was unable, on account of being engaged as my wife in a variety of things connected with the Lord's service, to give herself uninterruptedly to this work; and to do it partially we judged to be injurious to our daughter. 2. I had seen instances in which a home education for an only child had turned out very badly. 3. I judged that the mixing with other children would be beneficial to our daughter, provided that intercourse was under proper oversight; as thus a child is in early life introduced into a little world, and things do not all at once come upon a young person, when at last obliged to leave the parental roof. 4. But that which most of all led me to this decision was, that as in the church of Christ the Lord has qualified the members of the body for the performance of certain work, and all have not the same gift and service, so, in the same way, certain believers are called and qualified above others for instructing children, and give themselves to this particular service, and that, therefore, I ought to make use of the qualifications of such, and of their having given their whole time to this particular service. These reasons led us to place our daughter at school, instead of educating her at home, and we have never had cause to regret the step we took, but, on the contrary, have had abundant reason to praise God for it. I have purposely made these remarks, as I am fully aware that some believers have different views on this subject, and I desire to serve them with the measure of light and experience I have obtained.

After our daughter had been at school for half a year, I asked for the account, when it was stated to me by the Christian lady in whose establishment she was that she had a pleasure in educating her gratuitously. However, as I pressed the matter, I obtained the account. It was paid, but the exact sum was returned to me anonymously, which, of course, I found out at once to be from the Christian sister at whose school my daughter was. From that time I could never more obtain the account, though my dear child was about six years longer at school. I refer to this point for this especial reason: God had laid it on my heart to care about poor destitute orphans. To this service I had been led to give myself; he, in return, as a recompense, even for this life, took care that my own beloved child should have a very good education, free of expense to me. I was able and well able to pay for her education, and most willing to do so; but the Lord gave it gratuitously; thus also showing how ready he is abundantly to help me, and to supply my wants.

Having learned that the brethren in Germany were led away by false teachers, and having received, in answer to prayer, five hundred pounds, for the expenses of his journey thither, Mr. M. left Bristol July 19, 1845, and, after laboring in word and doctrine in Germany, he returned to Bristol Oct. 11, 1845.

Perhaps the reader may ask, What has been the result of this labor in Germany? My reply is, God only knows The day of Christ will declare it. Judging from the constant labor in prayer during eight months before I went the second time, and day by day while I was on the Continent, and day by day for a long time after my return, I am warranted to expect fruit, and I do expect it. I expect abundant fruit in the day of Christ's appearing. In the mean time my comfort is that two hundred and twenty thousand tracts have been circulated, many of which, through the providence of God, found their way not only into the darkest places of the continent of Europe, but went also to America and Australia. Further: four thousand copies of my Narrative, in German, are almost all circulated. And again, the publishing of my Narrative in German led me to do the same in French, which was accomplished about three years later. Further: these tracts were reprinted at Hamburg and at Cologne, and are circulated by other Christians; in addition to which, my having published them in Germany led me to get them stereotyped in England, and they continue to be circulated in many countries.

Dec. 31, 1845. There have been received into communion 53 during this year, and 1,055 since the commencement of our coming to Bristol.

During this year the Lord has been pleased to give to me £433, 19s. 1¾d. To this is to be added that my dear child had again during the whole of this year her education free at a boarding-school, as stated at the close of the last year, whereby I saved about fifty pounds. Also, my travelling expenses to and from Germany, and other expenses connected with my service in Germany, were paid out of the £500 pounds to which reference has been made. Adding these two items to £433, I had at least £500.

April 29, 1846. To-day my beloved wife and myself had the inexpressibly great joy of receiving a letter from our beloved daughter, while we are staying in the Lord's service at Chippenham, in which she writes that she has now found peace in the Lord Jesus. Thus our prayers are turned into praises. About eighteen months before this I began especially to pray for the conversion of my dear child, and the Lord soon after seems to have begun to work in her heart.

CHAPTER XVIII.

FAITH CONFIRMED BY PROSPERITY.

1846 — 1848

THE SPIRIT OF SUPPLICATION BESTOWED AND PRAYER ANSWERED — THE TIME OF MAN'S NEED AND OF GOD'S BOUNTY — FAITH NOT SHAKEN — DEALING ONLY WITH GOD — THE NEEDED AMOUNT FURNISHED — PERPETUAL "NEED" — NOT WEARY IN GOD'S WORK — JOY IN ANSWERED PRAYER — FOUR REQUESTS GRANTED — "CONTINUING INSTANT IN PRAYER" — THE BUILDING COMMENCED — PERSONAL HISTORY — A MARKED DELIVERANCE.

IN the following chapter, Mr. Müller has grouped together, under the appropriate heads, the leading events connected with each of the departments of the work of the Lord in his hands.

I. ASSISTANCE TO THE MISSIONARY LABORERS.

During no former period since undertaking to send aid to laborers at home and abroad was I intrusted by the Lord with such large sums as during the one to which this chapter refers. I had never had more need of pecuniary supplies than during those two years, on account of the many pressing calls; but, at the same time, I had the exceeding great joy and privilege of being able to respond to them in such a way as I had never before been allowed to do. These remarks apply to all the various objects of the Institution, but especially to the supplies for brethren who labor at home and abroad in word and doctrine without being connected with any society, or without having any regular salary for preaching the word.

On May 26, 1846, after the accounts had been closed, a

check for one hundred pounds was given to me, the application of which was left to my disposal. I put half the amount to the fund for these objects, and half to the orphan fund. When the accounts were closed, there were ninety-one pounds four shillings elevenpence three farthings in hand for these objects, to which these fifty pounds were added; therefore I began this period with more means than I had had in hand at any time previously at the beginning of a fresh period; and as was its beginning, so was the continuance. It has often struck me that one especial reason why, on the whole, I was allowed to have so little trial with regard to means for the work during those two years, in comparison with former times, may have been, that thereby the Lord would say that he was willing to give what would be needed, when once the new Orphan House should be built, though the expenses would be about two thousand five hundred pounds a year more than they were before.

June 4, 1846. To-day was given to me, *just when I rose from my knees*, after having asked the Lord for more means, especially for missionary purposes, the sum of one hundred and fifty pounds, with the request to use of it fifty pounds for the orphans, fifty pounds for laborers in England, and fifty pounds for laborers abroad.

From the commencement of this Institution, on March 5, 1834, it had been my desire to employ part of the funds, with which I might be intrusted, in aiding missionary brethren in foreign lands, who are not supported by any regular salary; and for several years I had likewise had the desire to assist brethren, laboring in similar circumstances, in Great Britain and Ireland. The Lord also had given me the great privilege to assist such brethren more or less during the time that this Institution had been in operation; but especially he began during the two years to which this chapter refers to allow me to do so in a far greater degree than before. I knew it to be a fact that many brethren who preach the word, without having any salary for doing so, or property to live upon, were in need. Now it might be said that such brethren ought to trust in God; that, if they preach Jesus as the only hope for the salvation of sinners, they ought to set them a good example by trusting themselves in God for the supply of their temporal necessities, in order that unconverted persons thereby might be led to trust in the Lord Jesus alone for the salvation of their souls. This is true, quite true. Preachers of the precious good news of salvation to every sinner who puts his trust in the merits of the Lord Jesus, ought indeed themselves to depend upon God, their Lord and Father, for the supply of their temporal necessities; but I also felt that I, as their brother, ought to seek to help them as far as lay in me. To this I set myself more than ever after the beginning of the year 1846, as I knew, that, from particular causes, there was an especial call to help such brethren; and as my own means would go but a little way, I gave myself to more earnest prayer than ever for such brethren. The result was, that, during the two years of this period, the Lord so answered my *daily* supplications with regard to this particular, that I was honored to send nearly three times as much to home and foreign laborers as during any previous period of the same length. One thousand five hundred and fifty-nine pounds eleven shillings sixpence were spent in this way, by which twenty-one brethren were assisted who labored in foreign lands, and nineteen who labored in Great Britain and Ireland. Large as this sum is, in comparison with what I had been able to do in this particular in former years, yet it is small, very small, in comparison with what my heart desired to be able to do for these forty brethren. It has frequently, yea almost always, so happened, that the assistance which God has allowed me to send to such brethren has come to them *at a time of great need.* Sometimes *they had no money at all left.* Sometimes *even their last provisions were almost consumed,* when I sent them supplies. Some of them are fathers of large families, or have sickly wives and children; some were once well off in this world, but for Christ's sake have become poor; and some have had for Christ's sake their all taken from them. Is it not an honor to help such brethren? I could fill hundreds of pages by giving extracts from the letters of the dear brethren to whom I have sent help, and they would be greatly to the edification of the reader; but I do not feel free to do so. As I have not only been laboring for these brethren in prayer that God would intrust me with means and allow me the privilege of helping them, but as I have also asked God to direct me especially to send to those who might be in particular need, in case I could not help them all; and as I have sought by an encouraging word to strengthen their hands in God; I have great reason to believe that these dear brethren have not only been helped by these pecuniary supplies in a temporal point of view, but also that the fact of God sending them help in their extremity has tended to refresh and strengthen their hearts, and to lead them more and more to trust in him.

March 7, 1847. Often of late had I entreated the Lord that he would be pleased to condescend to use me still further as a steward, in allowing me to send help to the many dear brethren whom I know laboring at home and abroad without any salary, the need of many of whom I knew. Under these circumstances, I received this morning one hundred and fifty pounds with the following lines: —

DEAR BROTHER: —

I have great pleasure in sending you one hundred pounds on account of laborers in the Lord's vineyard at home and abroad, and fifty pounds for other work in your hands.

Yours very affectionately,

* * *

April 5. I have been praying day by day, ever since I was able during the last month to send about one hundred and thirty pounds to home and foreign laborers, that the Lord would be pleased soon again to give me means for them, on account of their great need; indeed, all our means were so exhausted, that I had only just enough for to-morrow evening to meet the weekly expenses connected with the six day schools, when this morning I received one hundred and twenty-five pounds for these objects. Almost immediately after this donation had been given to me, I received a letter from Demerara about the great need among the brethren who labor there, by which intelligence the seasonable help just received has become still more precious to me.

May 26, 1848. By the Lord's faithful love I have been enabled to meet all the heavy expenses connected with *these objects* during the last two years, amounting to nearly two thousand and six hundred pounds, and at the same time owe no one anything, and have a balance of five pounds nineteen shillings sevenpence halfpenny left in hand.

II. *THE SUPPORT OF THE ORPHANS.*

Jan. 20, 1847. For the whole of this period since May 26, 1846, therefore nearly eight months, when the accounts were closed, we have had always an abundance of means, and for the greater part of the time about two hundred pounds in hand. The sum of one thousand sixty-five pounds has come in for the orphans in less than eight months, to which is to be added the balance of eighty-five pounds four shillings ninepence three farthings in hand when the accounts were closed. Invariably I have thus been able to give to the matrons of the four Orphan Houses the money in advance, which was required for the necessities of one week. But now, after having paid away last evening forty-five pounds five shillings for the house-keeping of a week in advance and for other expenses, the money which remains in hand is needed for rent, and oatmeal, which has been ordered from Scotland. This morning therefore I gave myself particularly to prayer with regard to means for present use for the orphans. How blessed to have the living God to go to! Particularly precious to know him in these days of wide-spread distress! Potatoes are too dear for food for the orphans at this time. The rice, which we have substituted instead of them, is twice as dear as usual; the oatmeal more than twice as dear, and the bread one-half dearer than usual. But the riches of God are as great as ever. He knows that our expenses are great. He knows that a little will not do in these days, when provisions are so dear, as there are about one hundred and fifty persons to be provided for, including teachers and apprentices. My soul is at peace. — Evening. About noon I received from a pious physician the following note, with a check for five pounds: —

MY DEAR SIR: —

I send you something towards buying bread for the orphans. The dearness of food must be felt by many; but the Lord in judgment is, nevertheless, gracious. He will sustain. I am your sincere friend and well-wisher,

* * * *

March 9. This evening, Tuesday, I find that since last Tuesday evening again forty-four pounds one shilling sixpence three farthings have come in. How good is the Lord in helping me week after week through the heavy expenses, especially in this season of deep distress and dearness of provisions! To his praise I can say we have lacked nothing all this winter. Whilst preparing these extracts from my journal for the press, I remember to have heard the following remarks made with reference to the time about which I am just now writing, I mean the season of dearth during the winter of 1846-7: "I wonder how it is now with the orphans? If Mr. Müller is now able to provide for them as he has, we will say nothing." When I heard such like remarks I said nothing except this: "We lack nothing;" or, "God helps us." Should this fall into the hands of any who have had such thoughts, let them remember that it is the very time for *faith* to work, when *sight* ceases. The greater the difficulties, the easier for *faith*. As long as there remain certain natural prospects, faith does not get on even as easily (if I may say so) as when all natural prospects fail. It is true that during the time of the dearth our expenses were considerably greater than usual; it is also true that many persons, who otherwise might have given, were unable to do so, or had their surplus directed into other channels, such as Ireland, etc.; but the gold and silver are the Lord's. To him we made our prayer. In him we put our trust. And he did not forsake us. *For we went as easily through that winter as through any winter since the work had been in existence.* Nor could it be otherwise; for God had at this very time an especial opportunity of showing the blessedness of trusting in him. Seek, dear reader, more and more to put your trust in him for everything, and you will, even concerning this life, find it most precious so to do.

May 11. This evening I have been able to meet all the expenses connected with house-keeping during the coming week, through what has come in since May 4, but at the same time I have nothing left. Hitherto the children have lacked nothing. Never were provisions nearly so dear since the commencement of the work as they are now. The bread is almost twice as much as eighteen months ago, the oatmeal nearly three times as much as formerly, the rice more than double the usual price, and no potatoes can be used on account of the exceedingly high price.

May 30. Lord's-day morning. I have just now received, in our great need, when there was not sufficient in hand to meet the necessities of to-morrow, six pounds six shillings, from a Christian gentleman of title at Zurich in Switzerland, a distance of about one thousand miles. What a most seasonable help! Thus I am able to send all the remainder of the supplies which are needed till Tuesday evening.

In these days of straitness the question would naturally arise, If, when you have only to care for one hundred and thirty orphans, you are so poor, what will you do when there are three hundred, for whom you are just on the point of building a house? And, further, Is it not an indication not to increase the work, seeing you are now so poor with only about one third of the number of orphans which you purpose to receive into the new Orphan House? I am not tried, however, with such thoughts; for I know that, 1. Only for the trial of my faith, as heretofore, the Lord allows me now again to be poor. Never at any time have the expenses been so great for the work as from May 26, 1846, to May 26, 1847; but also never has so much come in in the same space of time during any other period of this work. 2. It is for the profit of the church at large that I have now again to pass through these days of poverty. 3. It is as easy for the Lord to supply me with all the means that the work will require when once the new Orphan House is opened, as it is for him to give me what I need now, though the expenses in all likelihood will then be two thousand five hundred pounds a year more than they are at present.

Oct. 19. I left Bristol with my dear wife, partly because both of us much needed change of air, and partly because I had a great desire to labor in the word for a few weeks in Westmoreland and Cumberland. I was not able to leave more means than enough for about three days for house-keeping expenses. But I could not have stayed in Bristol, though there had been nothing at all in hand; my hope was that God would help during my absence. During all the time of my stay at Bowness in Westmoreland, from Oct. 20 to Nov. 20, there was day by day, with the exception of the first three days after my departure, need to wait upon God for daily supplies for the orphans. In consequence of this, *every donation, without exception, which was received during my absence, came in most seasonably.* Partly on account of my health, and partly on account of opportunities for service in Westmoreland and elsewhere, I did not feel it right to return to Bristol sooner than I did, though there was such great poverty; nor could I have done anything in Bristol which I could not do in Westmoreland, as it regards procuring means, since prayer and faith are all the means I make use of to obtain supplies when we are in need.

Dec. 23. The need of to-day was eleven pounds. This sum the Lord gave me thus: Last evening I received one pound, together with a pair of trousers and gaiters, and a remnant of fustian for the orphans. But as I knew how much there would be needed to-day, I waited further upon the Lord this morning for help, and, in ONE MINUTE after I had risen from my knees, I received a letter from Liverpool with ten pounds for the orphans. The donor writes: " I have had the enclosed ten-pound note in my drawer for some time, intending to send it to you for the orphans; but my time is so occupied that at a suitable time when at my desk I have overlooked it. I now, however, inclose it," etc. How seasonable this help! How exactly *to the very shilling* what is needed to-day! How remarkable that *just now* this donor in Liverpool is led to send the ten pounds which had been, according to his own words, for some time in his drawer for the purpose of sending it! All this abundantly proves *the most minute and particular providence* of God, and his readiness to answer the supplications of his children.

Dec. 31, 1847. The last day of another year had now come. Great and many had been the mercies of God to me this year in every way, particularly also in connection with the orphans; but now I had again nothing for to-day, except two shillings which are in one of the boxes in my house. I was, however, by God's grace, able to look out for supplies for this last day of another year also, being fully assured that the Lord would not confound me. And thus it has been, according to my expectation; for, before I was called on for money, I received one hundred pounds, which were left to me to apply to any part of the Lord's service where there seemed the most need.

Feb. 2, 1848. This morning on my walk before breakfast, I felt myself led out of my usual track into a direction in which I had not gone for some months. In stepping over a stile I said to myself: "Perhaps God has a reason even in this." About five minutes afterwards I met a Christian gentleman who gave me two sovereigns for the orphans, and then I knew the reason why I had been led this way.

Feb. 3. The reader might say, "*You are continually in need. No sooner is the one demand met, than another comes. Do you not find it a trying life, and are you not tired of it?*" My reply is, it is true I am more or less continually in need in connection with this work. And if I were to tell out all my heart to the reader concerning it, he would have still more reason to say that I am continually in need. For what I have here written is almost exclusively about the way in which God has been pleased to supply me with *money* for carrying on the work; but I do deliberately state that this, much as it might appear to one or the other, is by no means the chief thing that I stand in need of from day to day. I will just hint at a few other things. Sickness among the children, very difficult and tedious cases, in which, notwithstanding all the means which are used, month after month, yea, year after year, the children remain ill. Nothing remains but either to keep them, or to send them to the Parish Union, to which they belong, as they have no relatives able to provide for them. The very fact of having cared for them and watched over them for years only endears them the more to us, and would make it the more trying to send them back to their parish. This is a "need" which brings me to God. Here is prayer required, not only for means which such sick children call for, but for guidance and wisdom from on high.

Sometimes children are to be placed out as servants or apprentices. A suitable place is needed, or else they had better remain under our care. The obtaining of this suitable place is a "need" indeed. It is more difficult to be obtained than money. Sometimes for many weeks have I had to wait upon God to have this "need" supplied; but he has always at last helped. Sometimes great has been my "need" of wisdom and guidance in order to know how certain children ought to be treated under particular circumstances; and especially how to behave towards certain apprentices or servants who were formerly in the Orphan Houses. A "need" in this respect is no small thing; though I have found that in this and in all other matters, concerning which I was in "need," I have been helped, provided I was indeed able to wait patiently upon God. That word, "Godliness is profitable unto all things, having promise of the life that now is and of that which is to come" (1 Tim. iv. 8), I have in times almost without number found to be true in my own experience.

Further, when one or the other of the laborers needed to leave the work on account of health, or for other reasons, I have been at such times in far greater "need" than when I required money for the various objects of the Institution. I could only have such "need" supplied by waiting upon God. I could do nothing but speak to my heavenly Father about this matter, and he has always helped. One of the greatest difficulties connected with this work is to obtain suitable godly persons for it; so many things are to be taken into the account. Suitable age, health, gift, experience, love for children, true godliness, a ready mind to serve God in the work and not themselves, a ready mind to bear with the many trials and difficulties connected with it, a manifest purpose to labor, not for the sake of the remuneration, but to serve God in their work; surely, to obtain godly persons, in whom these qualifications even in some measure are found combined, is not an easy matter. Not that any one will suppose me to mean that I am looking out for perfect fellow-laborers. Not that any one will suppose that my fellow-laborers are referred to by me as if they were without weaknesses, deficiencies, and failings. I am myself far, very far from being without weaknesses, deficiencies, and failings. Moreover, I never expect to find fellow-laborers for this work who have not their weaknesses; but *this I do mean to say*, that the work of God in my hands is of that character, and, by God's grace, is really carried on with such a true purpose to serve God thereby (however much I and my fellow-laborers may fail), that it is with me a matter of deep moment to find truly suitable individuals for it, in whom, as much as possible, the above qualifications should be found united. And, however much there may be wanting, this is more and more my aim, that I may obtain *such* helpers; and hence it can be easily perceived how great my "need" must be again and again on this very account. I do here especially advise that if any should apply in future for situations in connection with this work, they would keep these remarks before them; for, by God's grace, it is my purpose never to give to any persons a situation in connection with the Institution, if they are not suitable for it according to the light which God gives me.

Further, that the laborers work happily together among themselves, and that I go on happily in service with them; that I be their servant, on the one hand, and yet, on the other, maintain the place which God has given me in this work; surely, if any one carefully looks at this, he will at once see that there is a difficulty and a "need" far greater than any that is connected with *money*. Oh, how these matters lead one to call upon God! How they continually make one sensible of one's "need!" Truly, I am in need, in continual need. I might refer to many more points, in connection with this work, in which I am more or less continually in "need;" but I will only mention one. It is now many years since I have made my boast in the living God in so public a manner by my publications. On this account Satan unquestionably is waiting for my halting, and if I were left to myself I should fall a prey to him. Pride, unbelief, or other sins would be my ruin, and lead me to bring a most awful disgrace upon the name of Jesus. Here is then a "need," a great "need." I do feel myself in "need," in great "need," even to be upheld by God; for I cannot stand for a moment if left to myself. Oh that none of my dear readers might admire me, and be astonished at my faith, and think of me as if I were beyond unbelief! Oh that none of my dear readers might think that I could not be puffed up by pride, or in other respects most awfully dishonor God, and thus at last though God has used me in blessing hitherto to so many, become a beacon to the church of Christ! No, I am as weak as ever. I need as much as ever to be upheld as to faith and every other grace. I am therefore in "need," in great "need;" and therefore help me, dear Christian reader, with your prayers.

I allow, then, most fully that I am in continual "need." This is the case with regard to money matters, because the work is now so large. A few hundred pounds go but a little way. There have often been weeks when my demands have been several hundred pounds a week, and it can therefore easily be supposed that, even if large donations come in, they do not last long. But whilst I allow this, I desire that the Christian reader may keep in mind that there are other necessities, and even greater ones than those connected with *money*. Should, however, the reader say that he thinks "*I must find this a very trying life, and that I must be tired of it,*" I beg to state that he is entirely mistaken. I do not find the life in connection with this work a trying life, but a very happy one. It is impossible to describe the abundance of peace and heavenly joy that often has flowed into my soul by means of the fresh answers which I have obtained from God, after waiting upon him for help and blessing: and the longer I have had to wait upon him, or the greater my need was, the greater the enjoyment when at last the answer came, which has often been in a very remarkable way, in order to make the hand of God the more manifest. I do therefore solemnly declare that I do not find this life a trying life, but a very happy one, and I am consequently not in the least tired of it. Straits and difficulties I expected from the very beginning. Before I began this service I expected them; nay, the chief object of it was, that the church at large might be strengthened in faith, and be led more simply, habitually, and unreservedly to trust in the living God, by seeing his hand stretched out in my behalf in the hour of need. I did, therefore, expect trials, great trials and straits; but cheerfully, for the glory of God, and the profit of God's dear children, did I desire to pass through them, if only the saints might be benefited by the dealings of God with me. The longer I go on in this service, the greater the trials of one kind or another become; but at the same time the happier I am in this my service, and the more I am assured that I am engaged as the Lord would have me to be. How then could I be tired of carrying on the work of God on such principles as I do?

III. *THE NEW ORPHAN HOUSE ON ASHLEY DOWN.*

Up to May 26, 1846, £2,710, 3s. 5½d. had been received toward building the new Orphan House.

July 4, 1846. For about three months my faith and patience have been exceedingly tried about the field which I have purchased for the building of the Orphan House, as the greatest difficulties arose about my possessing the land after all; but, by God's grace, my heart was kept in peace, being fully assured that if the Lord were to take this piece of land from me *it would be only for the purpose of giving me a still better one; for our heavenly Father never takes any earthly thing from his children except he means to give them something better instead.* But in the midst of all this great trial of faith I could not but think, judging from the way in which God so manifestly had given me this piece of land, that the difficulties were only allowed *for the trial of my faith and patience.* And thus it was. Last evening I received a letter by which all the difficulties were removed, and now, with the blessing of God, in a few days the conveyance will be made out.

July 6. The reason why, for several months, there had come in so little for the building fund, appeared to me this, that we did not need the money at present; and that when it was needed, and when my faith and patience had been sufficiently tried, the Lord would send more means. And thus it has proved; for to-day was given me the sum of two thousand and fifty pounds, of which two thousand pounds are for the building fund, and fifty pounds for present necessities.

It is impossible to describe my joy in God when I received this donation. I was neither excited nor surprised; for *I look out* for answers to my prayers. *I believe that God hears me.* Yet my heart was so full of joy that I could only *sit* before God, and admire him, like David in 2 Sam. vii. At last I cast myself flat down upon my face, and burst forth in thanksgiving to God, and in surrendering my heart afresh to him for his blessed service.

July 21. This morning a gentleman from Devonshire, on his way to London, called on me. When he came I was just in prayer, having, among other matters, brought also before the Lord the following points: 1. I had been asking him for some supplies for my own temporal necessities, being in need. 2. I had asked him for more means for the building fund, and besought him to hasten the matter, on account of the inhabitants in Wilson Street, on account of the welfare of the children and those who have the oversight of them in the Orphan Houses, and lastly that I might be able to admit more orphans, the number of applications being so great. 3. I had also asked the Lord for means for present use for the orphans, as the outgoings are so great. 4. I had asked for means for the other objects. When I saw this gentleman from Devonshire, he gave me twenty pounds, of which ten pounds are to be used for the building fund, five pounds for present use of the orphans, two pounds for brother Craik and myself, and the remaining three pounds were left to my disposal, which I applied to the other objects of the Scriptural Knowledge Institution. Thus I received, *at the very moment that I had been asking God*, FOUR answers to my prayers.

Nov. 19. I am now led more and more to importune the Lord to send me the means which are requisite in order that I may be able to commence the building. Because, 1. It has been for some time past publicly stated in print that I consider it is not without ground that some of the inhabitants of Wilson Street consider themselves inconvenienced by the Orphan Houses being in that street, and I long therefore to be able to remove the orphans from thence as soon as possible. 2. I become more and more convinced that it would be greatly for the benefit of the children, both physically and morally, with God's blessing, to be in such a position as they are intended to occupy, when the new Orphan House is built. And, 3. Because the number of very poor and destitute orphans, that are waiting for admission, is so great, and there are constantly fresh applications made. Now whilst, by God's grace, I would not wish the building to be begun one single day sooner than it is his will; and whilst I firmly believe that he will give me, in his own time, every shilling which I need; yet I also know that he delights in being earnestly entreated, and that he takes pleasure in the continuance in prayer, and in the importuning him, which so clearly is to be seen from the parable of the widow and the unjust judge. Luke xviii. 1–8. For these reasons I gave myself again particularly to prayer last evening that the Lord would send further means, being also especially led to do so in addition to the above reasons, because there had come in but little comparatively since the 29th of last month. This morning between five and six o'clock I prayed again, among other points, about the building fund, and then had a long season for the reading of the word of God. In the course of my reading I came to Mark xi. 24: "What things soever ye desire, when ye pray, believe that ye receive them, and ye shall have them." The importance of the truth contained in this portion I have often felt and spoken about; but this morning I felt it again most particularly, and, applying it to the new Orphan House, said to the Lord: "Lord, I believe that thou wilt give me all I need for this work. I am sure that I shall have all, because I believe that I receive in answer to my prayer." Thus, with the heart full of peace concerning this work, I went on to the other part of the chapter, and to the next chapter. After family prayer I had again my usual season for prayer with regard to all the many parts of the work, and the various necessities thereof, asking also blessings upon my fellow-laborers, upon the circulation of Bibles and tracts, and upon the precious souls in the adult school, the Sunday schools, the six day schools, and the four Orphan Houses. Amidst all the many things I again made my requests about means for the building. And now observe: About five minutes after I had risen from my knees, there was given to me a registered letter, containing a check for three hundred pounds, of which two hundred and eighty pounds are for the building fund, ten pounds for my own personal expenses, and ten pounds for brother Craik. The Lord's holy name be praised for this precious encouragement, by which the building fund is now increased to more than six thousand pounds.

Dec. 9. It is now four hundred days since day after day I have been waiting upon God for help with regard to the building of the Orphan House; but as yet he keeps me still in the trial of faith and patience. He is still saying, as it were, "Mine hour is not yet come." Yet he does sustain me in continuing to wait upon him. By his grace my faith is not in the least shaken; but I am quite sure that he, in his own time, will give me everything which I need concerning this work. *How* I shall be supplied with the means which are yet requisite, and *when,* I know not; but I am sure that God will help me in his own time and way. In the mean time I have abundant reason to praise God that I am not waiting on him in vain; for since this day twelvemonth he has given me, in answer to prayer, a most suitable piece of ground, and six thousand three hundred and four pounds for the building fund, and about two thousand seven hundred pounds for present use for the work, so that altogether I have received, since this day twelvemonth, solely in answer to prayer, the sum of nine thousand pounds. Surely, I am not waiting upon the Lord in vain! By his help, then, I am resolved to continue this course unto the end.

Dec. 22. To-day I have again a precious proof that *continuing* to wait upon the Lord is not in vain. During this month comparatively little had come in for the building fund; yet, by God's grace, I had been enabled, as before, yea, even with more earnestness perhaps than before, to make known my requests unto God, being more and more convinced that I ought to seek by earnest prayer soon to be able to begin the building. In addition to this I had also especially besought the Lord to give me means for missionary brethren, and also for brethren who labor in the word in various parts of England and Ireland, as all my means for them were now gone. I had also been waiting upon God for means to order a fresh stock of tracts. I had lastly again and again besought the Lord to give me means for the poor saints in Bristol, of whom there are many, and whose need is now particularly great. Now to-day the Lord has granted me precious answers to my requests concerning these various objects, for I received this morning one thousand pounds, with these words: " I send you some money, part of which you can apply to the orphans and the other objects of your Institution, according to their need, and the rest you can put to the building fund. At the present price of provisions your expenses must be large for the orphans. Please also take twenty-five pounds for your own need."

Jan. 25, 1847. The season is now approaching when building may be begun. Therefore with increased earnestness I have given myself unto prayer, importuning the Lord that he would be pleased to appear on our behalf, and speedily send the remainder of the amount which is required, and I have increasingly, of late, felt that the time is drawing near when the Lord will give me all that which is requisite for commencing the building. All the various arguments which I have often brought before God I brought also again this morning before him. It is now fourteen months and three weeks since day by day I have uttered my petitions to God on behalf of this work. I rose from my knees this morning in full confidence not only that God *could*, but also *would*, send the means, and that soon Never, during all these fourteen months and three weeks, have I had the least doubt that I should have all that which is requisite. And now, dear believing reader, rejoice and praise with me. About an hour after I had prayed thus, there was given to me the sum of two thousand pounds for the building fund. Thus I have received altogether £9,285, 3s. 9½d. towards this work. I cannot describe the joy I had in God when I received this donation. It must be known from experience in order to be felt. Four hundred and forty seven days I have had to wait upon God before the sum reached the above amount. How great is the blessing which the soul obtains by *trusting in God*, and *by waiting patiently!* Is it not manifest how precious it is to carry on God's work in this way, even with regard to the obtaining of means? From Dec. 10, 1845, to Jan. 25, 1847, being thirteen months and a half, I have received, solely in answer to prayer, nine thousand two hundred and eighty-five pounds. Add to this what came in during that time for present use for the various objects of the Institution and the total is about twelve thousand and five hundred pounds, entirely the fruit of prayer to God. Can it be said, therefore, with good ground, that this way of carrying on the work of God may do very well in a limited and small way, but it would not do on a large scale? The fact brought out here contradicts such statements.

June 23. This day the Lord in his great goodness, by a donation of one thousand pounds for the building fund, has again encouraged my heart abundantly to trust in him for all that which I shall yet need to meet the remainder of the expenses connected with the fitting up and furnishing the new Orphan House, etc.

April 29, 1848. The total amount which I have received for the building fund is £11,062, 4s. $11\frac{1}{2}$d. This sum enables me to meet all the expenses connected with the purchase of a piece of land and with the erection of the house. I stated before that I did not mean to commence the building until I had all the means requisite for it; and this intention was carried out. It was not until I had a sufficient amount of means to meet all the sums required for the various contractors that a single thing was done; but when I once had as much as was required for them, I did not consider it right to delay any longer, though I saw then clearly, and have since seen still more clearly, that I should need yet a considerable sum to complete the work. For whilst in every respect the building will be most plain and inexpensive, yet, it being intended to be the abode of three hundred orphans, with all their teachers and overseers, it necessarily must be a very large building, and was therefore found to be even somewhat more expensive than I had thought, as the whole (including fittings and furniture) cannot be accomplished for less than fourteen thousand five hundred pounds, towards which the Lord has already given me, as stated, eleven thousand and sixty-two pounds four shillings elevenpence halfpenny. The sum still needed is required for all the ordinary fittings, the heating apparatus, the gas fittings, the furnishing the whole house, making three large play-grounds, and a small road, and for some additional work which could not be brought into the contracts. I did not think it needful to delay commencing the building, though several thousand pounds more would be required, as all these expenses needed not to be met till many months after the beginning of the building.

The work of the building commenced on July 5, 1847. Six hundred and seven days I sought the help of God day by day, before we came so far as to be able to commence the building; yet at last he gave me the desire of my heart.

IV. MISCELLANEOUS POINTS RESPECTING THE SCRIPTURAL KNOWLEDGE INSTITUTION FOR HOME AND ABROAD.

1. During the whole of this period six day schools, with 330 children, were supported by the funds of the Institution; two Sunday schools were entirely supported by it, and a third one was occasionally assisted Again, four from among the Sunday-school children were, during these two years, received into church fellowship. The total number of the children who received instruction in the day schools of the Institution, from its commencement up to May 26, 1848, amounted to 4,519. The number of the adult scholars who were instructed during this period in the adult school, which was supported by the funds of the Institution, amounted to 292; and the total number of adults who had instruction from March 5, 1844, to May 26, 1848, was 1,438. The total of the expenses connected with all these schools, during these two years, amounted to £886, 1s. 11½d.

2. During this period were circulated 649 Bibles and 232 New Testaments. There were circulated from March 5, 1834, up to May 26,

1848, 5,746 Bibles and 3,760 New Testaments. During this period, £74, 9s. 10d. were expended of the Funds of the Institution on this object.

3 From May 26, 1846, to May 26, 1848, were expended of the funds of the Institution on missionary objects, £1,559, 11s 6d , whereby 43 laborers in the gospel, at home and abroad, were assisted.

4. During this period 64,021 tracts were circulated, and the sum of £63, 1s. 5d was expended on this object of the funds of the Institution. The total number of tracts circulated from Nov. 19, 1840, to May 26, 1848, amounted to 163,668.

5. There were received into the four Orphan Houses from May 26, 1846, to May 26, 1848, 51 orphans, who, together with those who were in the four houses on May 26, 1846, made up 172 in all.

On May 26, 1848, there were 122 orphans in the four houses. The number of the orphans under our care from April, 1836, to May 26, 1848, was 264. The total amount of expenditure in connection with the support of the orphans from May 26, 1846, to May 26, 1848, was £3,223, 5s. 11d.

I notice, in connection with the Orphan Houses, that *without any one having been personally applied to for anything by me*, the sum of £24,771, 19s 8¼d was given to me *as the result of prayer to God*, from the commencement of the work up to May 26, 1848. This sum includes the £11,062, 4s. 11½d., which, up to May 26, 1848, had been given towards the building fund. It may be interesting to the reader to know that the total amount which was given as free contributions for the other objects, from the commencement of the work up to May 26, 1848, was £7,060, 14s 1¾d.; and that which came in by the sale of Bibles and tracts, and by the payment of the children in the day schools, amounted to £2,373, 3s. 7½d

V. *PERSONAL HISTORY.*

Dec. 31, 1846. During this year there have been received into fellowship 66. The Lord has been pleased to give me during this year £399, 2s. 11d To this is again to be added what I have enlarged on in a former chapter, that during the whole of this year also my daughter was, free of all expenses, at a boarding-school, worth about fifty pounds.

In November, 1847, I had a most remarkable deliverance, which, to the praise of the Lord, is here recorded, as it is a further illustration of how the Lord watches over his children.

I was laboring for a little while at Bowness and Keswick in the ministry of the word, in October and November. When at Keswick, I stayed with my dear wife in a large boarding-house, in which, however, we were then alone, except a single gentleman. Just before we left Keswick, on the morning of Nov. 24, I heard that the gentleman, lodging in the same house, had shot himself during the night, but was not quite dead. We had not heard the report of the pistol, it being a very stormy night and the house large. Two days after, I received from a Christian brother at Keswick the following information respecting the transaction:

KESWICK, Nov. 25, 1847.

DEAR MR. MULLER:—

The tender and Almighty care of our loving Father was never more over *you*, and indeed over all of us, than in your stay at Mrs. ———'s. Mr ——— was quite deranged for two or three days before you left. Without any control, he had been walking about his room for the last two days and nights, with loaded pistols in his hands. Furthermore, he had taken into his head that you were going to kill him. How gracious of God that he spread his wings over you and over dear Mrs. Muller, so that Satan could not break through the fence, to hurt even a hair of your heads! Speaking after the manner of men, there was nothing to have hindered him coming into the room, where we were all at tea,[1] and firing amongst us; but the Lord was our refuge and fortress, and preserved us from danger, which we knew not of. He shot himself in the neck and breast, but is not dead. He has a strait-waistcoat on. I assisted in cutting his clothes off, and in other little offices needed at such a time, and told him of Christ's love in dying for poor sinners. "I know it," he said He shot himself the first time about three o'clock in the morning, and again about seven. What a scene his room presented: pistols lying in gore; bloody knives, lancets, and razors strewed about the floor, etc.

I add an extract from a second letter, written by the same Christian brother, because it shows still further how

[1] The evening before my departure I had invited a number of believers to tea, to spend some time together in prayer, reading the Holy Scriptures, and in intercourse on spiritual subjects.

very merciful the Lord was to us at that time, in protecting us.

Mr. ———— is still alive, and has been removed by his friends into Yorkshire. It appears, insanity is in his family, his father being at this time in an asylum. It is evident that he had the pistols in his pockets, but of this no one knew until after the occurrence took place. I do not know what time of night you went to bed, but I judge it was about ten. If so, it was at ten o'clock Mr. ———— came down from his bedroom, after having been there six hours. It was a mercy you did not meet him, as it is plain that he had loaded pistols on his person.

Dec. 31, 1847. There have been received into fellowship, during this year, 39; and altogether, since Mr. Craik and I began laboring in Bristol, 1,157, besides the 68 whom we found in fellowship. During this year the Lord has been pleased to give me £412, 18s. 8½d. To this is again to be added the free education of my dear daughter at a boarding-school, worth to us at least fifty pounds.

In April, 1848, I was enabled, by the help of the Lord, to complete all the arrangements for the publication of the Narrative of the Lord's dealings with me, in the French language; and about September of the same year, the book appeared, under the following title: "Exposé de quelques-unes des dispensations de Dieu envers Georges Müller. Paris, librairie Protestante, Rue Tronchet, 2."

CHAPTER XIX.

CONTINUED MERCIES.

1848 — 1850.

HUMBLE BEGINNINGS — **DEVISING LIBERAL THINGS** — THE ORPHANS PROVIDED FOR — A MEMORABLE DAY — MONEY "AT INTEREST" — MEANS FROM AN UNEXPECTED SOURCE — THE PROGRESS OF THE NEW ORPHAN HOUSE — MEANS PROVIDED FOR ITS COMPLETION — INEXPRESSIBLE DELIGHT IN GOD — REVIEW OF THE TWO YEARS PAST.

ON the 26th of May, 1848, I had on hand for the Bible, tract, missionary, and school funds of the Scriptural Knowledge Institution, five pounds nineteen shillings sevenpence one farthing; a sum so small, that, without the help of God, I could not have gone on even for a few days; for during this period our average expenditure for one single day, merely for this part of the work, was as much as the whole balance left in hand. Now see how God carried me through, in meeting the expenditure of the thousands of pounds which were laid out for these objects, irrespective of the orphan work, from May 26, 1848, to May 26, 1850.

On the very next day, after the accounts were closed, May 27, 1848, I received from Westmoreland five pounds, being the first donation during this period towards this part of the work, of which sum one half was intended by the donor for the current expenses of the orphans, and the other half for these objects. On the following day, May 28, were anonymously put into the chapel boxes for missions one shilling sixpence, and twopence. Now it happened so that all the expenses, connected with these objects, during the first two days amounted only to about three pounds, which I was able to meet by what had come in and the balance left in hand; and on May 29 I received one hundred pounds. As the application of this sum was left to me, I took one-half of it for the orphans, and the other half for these objects. Thus I was supplied with means to meet the expenses which came on me the following day. May 30, when I had to pay the weekly salaries of the teachers in the day schools.

June 9. Great has been my desire, and many have been my prayers to God, that he would be pleased to condescend to use me still further, in allowing me the privilege of helping brethren who labor in the word and doctrine at home and abroad, without any salary, as I have been able to do but very little for them comparatively during the last four months. Now at last, in answer to my prayers, I have received this morning one hundred and sixty pounds for home and foreign laborers. The Lord may see it needful, for the trial of our faith, to seem for a season not to regard our supplications; yet, if we patiently and believingly continue to wait upon him, it will be manifest, in his own time and way, that we did not call upon him in vain.

Nov. 9. Only a few shillings were left in my hands on Tuesday evening, the 7th instant, towards the weekly salaries of the teachers, for the coming week. Also, almost all the tracts are again gone, and it is nearly four weeks since I paid out the last money I had in hand for missionary objects. As to this latter point, my heart had been especially longing to be able to send again help to home and foreign laborers, knowing how very great the need of many is. Thus I was situated with regard to means, when I received to-day one thousand pounds.

Since March 5, 1834, I have received above forty-four thousand pounds altogether [up to May 26, 1850, only]; and so has the Lord enlarged the work and helped me that during the last three years I have had the privilege of paying away in his service, in connection with this work, about twenty-five thousand pounds; nor have I had during this period, in any one instance, to meet a payment without being previously provided by the Lord with means for it. If it pleased the Lord to condescend to use me further in this way, he could so order it that even a still larger field of labor were intrusted to me, which would require still greater sums. Truly, it must be manifest to all simple-hearted children of God, who will carefully read the accounts respecting this Institution, that he is most willing to attend to the supplications of his children, who in their need cry to him; and to make this manifest is the great object I aim at, through the means of this Institution.

Jan. 2, 1850. The new year commences, even as to this part of the work, with new mercies. There were given to me one hundred and sixty pounds, to be used as might be most needed.

Jan. 30. During this month I had been especially led to send much assistance to home and foreign laborers. Also in other respects the expenses for *these* objects had been considerable. On this account the funds for them had been reduced to about eighty pounds when I received this evening four hundred and fifty pounds, of which the donor kindly wished me to take fifty pounds for my own personal expenses, to give to brother Craik fifty pounds, and to use the other as might be most needed.

When the accounts were closed, on May 26, 1848, I had on hand for the orphans a balance of one pound ten shillings three and three-fourths pence. With this amount then we began, whilst day by day above one hundred and thirty persons were to be provided for in the four Orphan Houses in Wilson Street.

On the very next day, after the accounts were closed, May 27, 1848, I received from Westmoreland five pounds, half of which sum was intended by the donor for the orphans, and half for the other objects. This donation I took as an earnest out of the hands of the living God, that during the whole of this period also he would provide for these many orphans, as he had done in former years.

Nov. 9. Up to date the wants of the orphans have been supplied as heretofore. Yesterday only five shillings sixpence came in. To-morrow more money will be needed for house-keeping In this our poverty I received this morning one thousand pounds. The money being left to my disposal as it might be most needed, I took of it six hundred pounds for the building fund, three hundred pounds for missionary purposes and the circulation of Bibles and tracts, and one hundred pounds for present use for the orphans. I have thus the means which are yet needed for this week's house-keeping expenses, besides being able to meet other heavy expenses which are before me next week.

Feb. 20, 1849. For three months and ten days, since Nov. 9, 1848, the donations had always come in so that we abounded during the whole period, there having been always fresh donations received before all the money in hand was disbursed. The total amount that came in during this period was four hundred and sixty-nine pounds fourteen shillings tenpence. Now to-day there was no money in hand for advancing the amount needed for the next week's house-keeping. All the money in hand was due for rent, and therefore unavailable, as I never go into debt for anything. In this our need there was given to me this afternoon the sum of two hundred pounds, which was left to my disposal for fitting up the new Orphan House, or for any of the objects in connection with the Scriptural Knowledge Institution that might be in need. As, however, I have all the means for fitting up and furnishing the new Orphan House, as far as I know, and as there is no money in hand for the present use of the orphans, I took one hundred pounds for that object.

March 9. The new Orphan House is now nearly ready. On this account we have to get in large supplies for the children's clothes. Within the last few days I have ordered

THE FIRST ORPHAN HOUSE, ASHLEY DOWN

thousands of yards of material for this purpose, and thousands more will need to be ordered, besides providing a stock of many other things. For this large sums are needed. Under these circumstances I received to-day a donation of three hundred pounds, to be used for the building fund, or the current expenses of the various objects, just as it might be most required. As I judge that we have all that is needed for the fitting up and furnishing of the house, and as there is more in hand than usual for the missionary objects, the circulation of Bibles and tracts, and for the various schools, and as we have only about sixty pounds for present use for the orphans, towards meeting all the heavy expenses before us, I took the whole of this donation for the orphans, as the donor has kindly left the disposal of the money entirely to me. This donation coming in just now has been an exceedingly great refreshment to my spirit; for it is at the commencement of the great increase of our expenses, in connection with the three hundred orphans, instead of one hundred and twenty, like an earnest from God that he will supply us also with means when the demands for the three hundred will be more than twice as great as they are now. Through this donation I have means to meet all the expense which will be incurred in getting in for the new establishment the stores of provisions, soap, material for clothes, haberdashery, and of the many other articles of which it would be desirable to buy our supplies on wholesale terms. The Lord be praised for his kindness!

June 18. To-day, as the fruit of the prayers of three years and seven months, the children began to be moved from the four Orphan Houses in Wilson Street, Bristol, into the new Orphan House.

June 23. Saturday Evening. This has been indeed a week of great and many and peculiar mercies. All the orphans with their teachers and overseers have been moved into the new Orphan House during Monday, Tuesday, Wednesday, and Thursday; so that there are now about one hundred and forty persons under one roof. The Lord has most signally helped. As I had for more than three years sought the help of God concerning all matters connected with the new Orphan House. I did expect his help in this particular also; but he has done beyond my expectations. Though only the day before yesterday the last children were moved in, there is already such a measure of order established in the house, by the help of God, as that things can be done by the minute hands of the timepieces. His name is to be praised for this, and my soul does magnify him for his goodness! Also with regard to temporal supplies for the dear orphans, the Lord has been exceedingly kind. On the second day of receiving the children, there were sent twenty pounds. On the third day, an individual who walked with me through part of the house said, "These children must consume a great deal of provisions," and, whilst saying it, took out of his pocket a roll of Bank of England notes to the amount of one hundred pounds, and gave them to me for the orphans. On the very same evening I had also sent for the orphans a very large cask of treacle, and for their teachers and overseers six loaves of sugar. Also a cooper made gratuitously two large new casks for treacle. On the next day I received information that about one thousand pounds of rice had been purchased for the orphans, which should be sent. Besides this, several small donations have come in. So bountifully has the Lord been pleased to help of late, that I have not only been able to meet all the extraordinary heavy expenses connected with moving the orphans from Wilson Street into the new Orphan House, filling the stores of the new Orphan House, etc.; but I have more than five hundred pounds in hand to begin house-keeping in the new Orphan House. How true that word that those that trust in the Lord shall not be confounded! After all the many and long-continued seasons of great trial of faith within these thirteen years and two months, during which the orphans were in Wilson Street, the Lord dismisses us from thence in comparative abundance. His holy name be praised for it!

Aug. 30. Received a fifty-pound note with these words: "I send you herewith a fifty-pound note, half for the missions, half for the orphans, unless you are in any personal need; if so, take five pounds for yourself. This will be the last large sum I shall be able to transmit to you. Almost all the rest is already *out at interest*." I took half of this fifty pounds for the orphans, and half for missionaries. The writer sold some time since his only earthly possession, and sent me at different times sums of one hundred and twenty pounds, of one hundred pounds, of fifty-five pounds, of fifty pounds, and of twenty pounds for the work of the Lord in my hands. When he says, therefore, "the rest is already *out at interest*," he means that he has given it away for the Lord, which indeed both for time and eternity is the very best way of using the means with which the Lord may be pleased to intrust us, in so far as, considering in the fear of God all our various claims and duties and relationships, we may do so. As this is written for the spiritual profit of the reader, I cannot but add to this extract from my journal under Aug. 30, 1849, that since that time I have received other donations from the same donor, and much larger still. He used for God the means with which he was pleased to intrust him, and, contrary to this brother's expectation, the above fifty pounds was not the last large donation; for it pleased God soon after to intrust him with another considerable sum, which he again used for the Lord. This did not at all surprise me; for it is the Lord's order that, in whatever way he is pleased to make us his stewards, whether as to temporal or spiritual things, if we are indeed acting as *stewards*, and not as *owners*, he will make us stewards over *more*.

I also cannot help noticing the remarkable coincidence that, at the time that God visited this land with the cholera, in 1849, I had so much room for the reception of orphans,

The Lord was pleased to allow me the joy and sweet privilege of receiving altogether twenty-six children, from ten months old and upward, who lost their parents in the cholera *at that time*, and many besides, since then, who were bereaved of their parents through this fearful malady.

At the time when I last referred to the *progress* of the new Orphan House, it was being built. A part of it was already roofed in, and the remainder was to be roofed not many weeks afterwards. But how much did there yet remain to be done in other respects! A building so considerable as to contain about three hundred large windows would require, even after it was finished, an immense amount of labor to be fitted up and furnished for three hundred and thirty persons. Then, after this was done, the settling in of the orphans and their teachers, and other overseers, needed still more abundant help. Further, the obtaining of suitable helpers for this part of the work was indeed no small matter. Lastly, though the Lord had been pleased to give me already above eleven thousand pounds for the new Orphan House, yet I needed several thousand pounds more, in order to bring the whole into such a state as might render the building fit for the reception of the orphans. And now, in looking back, and finding that I not only was helped in *all* these matters, but also *in every one of them* far beyond my largest expectations, does it not become me to say to those who love the Lord Jesus, and into whose hands this account may fall: "Oh, magnify the Lord with me, and let us exalt his name together!" Each one of the foregoing difficulties which still existed on the 26th of May, 1848, was so great, that if only one of them had remained, and I had not been helped, what would have been the result? But while the prospect before me would have been overwhelming had I looked at it *naturally*, I was never, even for once, permitted to question what would be the end. For as, from the beginning, I was sure *that it was the will of God* that I should go to the work of building for him this large Orphan

House, so also, from the beginning, I was as certain that the whole would be finished as if the building had been already before my natural eyes, and as if the house had been already filled with three hundred destitute orphans. I was therefore of good courage in the midst of an overwhelming pressure of work yet to be done, and very many difficulties yet to be overcome, and thousands of pounds yet needed; and I gave myself still further to prayer, and sought still further to exercise faith on the promises of God. And now the work is done, the difficulties are overcome, all the money that was needed has been obtained, and even more than I needed; and, as to helpers in the work, I have obtained even beyond my expectations and prayers. Nearly seven years have passed away (1856) since the new Orphan House was opened, and about three hundred and thirty persons sit down in it day by day to their meals.

Up to May 26, 1848, I had received altogether towards meeting the expenses connected with the building of the new Orphan House the sum of eleven thousand and sixty-two pounds four shillings elevenpence halfpenny.

Nov. 9. To-day the Lord has helped still more abundantly. I have received a donation of one thousand pounds, to be used for the building fund and the present necessities of the work generally, as the various objects of the Institution might require it.

Jan. 17, 1849. The time is now near when further steps are to be taken to fit up and furnish the house, as more than two thirds of the rooms are all but ready. Under these circumstances I have prayed the more earnestly, day by day, that the Lord would be pleased to give me the means which are yet needed; and as my heart has been assured from the beginning, and all through these three years and two months, since I first began to pray about this subject, that God would in every way help me in this work, so I have also been particularly satisfied that he would be pleased to provide the means which may be required to meet all the heavy expenses which yet remain to be met. Now, to-day I have had again a precious answer to my daily supplications with reference to this work; for I received this evening six hundred pounds, concerning which it were desired that brother Craik and myself should each take of it fifty pounds for ourselves; the remaining five hundred pounds was left entirely to my disposal; yet an especial reference was made to the heavy expenses connected with fitting up and furnishing the new Orphan House, towards which I might, either in part or entirely, take this sum.

Feb. 12. The new Orphan House is now almost entirely finished. In six weeks, with the help of God, all will be completed. On this account I have been during the last fortnight much occupied in making the necessary arrangements for fitting it up and furnishing it; but the more I have been occupied about this, the more I have seen how large a sum the whole of the fittings and the furniture will require; and this consideration has led me still more earnestly of late to entreat the Lord that he would be pleased to give me the means which may yet be needed for the completion of the whole. Under these circumstances a brother in the Lord came to me this morning, and after a few minutes' conversation gave me two thousand pounds, concerning which sum he kindly gave me permission to use it for the fitting up and furnishing of the new Orphan House, or for anything else needed in connection with the orphans. I have placed the whole of this sum, at least for the present, to the building fund. It is impossible to describe the real joy I had in God when I received this sum. I was calm, not in the least excited, able to go on immediately with other work that came upon me at once after I had received the donation; but inexpressible was the delight which I had in God, who had thus given me the full answer to my thousands of prayers.

I have thus given a few out of the hundreds of donations, varying from one farthing to two thousand pounds, as specimens, to show how the Lord was pleased to furnish me with the means. The total amount which came in for the building fund was fifteen thousand seven hundred and eighty-four pounds eighteen shillings tenpence.

After all the expenses had been met for the purchase of the land, the conveyance of the same, the enrolment of the trust-deeds in chancery, the building, fitting up, and furnishing of the New Orphan House, there remained a balance of seven hundred and seventy-six pounds fourteen shillings threepence three farthings, affording a manifest proof that the Lord can not only supply us with all we need in his service, simply in answer to prayer, but that he can also give us even more than we need.

During the whole of the two years ending May 26, 1850, five day schools, with 329 children in them, were entirely supported by the funds of this Institution, and some pecuniary assistance was rendered to four other day schools. Also a Sunday school, with 168 children, was entirely supported, and another was occasionally assisted. Lastly, an adult school, with 106 adult scholars, was supported during this period. There were expended on these various schools £851, 1s 5½d, during these two years. The number of all the children that were taught in the day schools, through the medium of this Institution, from March 5, 1834, to May 26, 1850, amounted to 5,114; the number of those in the Sunday schools amounted to 2,200, and the number of the persons in the adult school to 1,737. In all, 9,051.

From May 26, 1848, to May 26, 1850, were circulated 719 Bibles, and 239 New Testaments. There were expended on this object, during this period, of the funds of the Institution, £104, 15s. 11d. There were circulated altogether from March 5, 1834, to May 26, 1850, 6,465 Bibles, and 3,999 New Testaments.

From May 26, 1848, to May 26, 1850, were spent £2,574, 16s. 6d. of the funds of the Institution for missionary objects, whereby forty preachers of the gospel in British Guiana, the East Indies, Switzerland, France, Germany, Canada, Scotland, Ireland, and England, were assisted.

The reader will notice how greatly this object of the Institution was increased during the last four years previous to May 26, 1850. This arose from the fact that, in the early part of 1846, the need of certain brethren who labored in the word and doctrine came before me, and God laid them on my heart to labor for them in prayer, in order that I might obtain means from him for such brethren to a greater extent than I had done before. Ever since then the Lord has been pleased increasingly to use me in this way. For from May 26, 1846, to May 26, 1848, there was spent for that object nearly three times as much as during any former period of the same length; and during the period from May 26, 1848, to May 26, 1850, I was not only allowed to do as much as before, but to expend even £1,016, 5s more than during the former period, notwithstanding all the many heavy additional expenses for the various other objects of the Institution.

It is my sweet privilege to state that the labors of many of these forty servants of the Lord, whom I assisted, were especially owned of God during these two years. There took place very many conversions through their instrumentality.

From May 26, 1848, to May 26, 1850, the sum of £184, 9s. 4½d. was expended on the circulation of tracts. There were circulated during this period 130,464 tracts. The total number which was circulated from Nov. 19, 1840, up to May 26, 1850, amounted to 294,128.

From July 24, 1849, up to May 26. 1850, altogether 170 orphans were received, from ten months old and upwards. On May 26, 1850, there were, therefore, 275 orphans in the new Orphan House; and with the teachers, overseers, nurses, and in door and out-door servants, etc , the whole number of persons connected with the establishment was 308 The total number of orphans who were under our care from April, 1836, up to May 26, 1850, was 443.

Without any one having been personally applied to for anything by me, the sum of £33,868, 11s. 1¼d. was given to me for the orphans, *as the result of prayer to God,* from the commencement of the work up to May 26, 1850. It may be also interesting to the reader to know that the total amount which was given as free contributions, for the other objects, from the commencement of the work up to May 26, 1850, amounted to £10,531, 3s. 8¾d ; and that which came in by the sale of Bibles and tracts, and by the payments of the children in the schools, up to May 26, 1850, amounted to £2,707, 9s. 8½d.

The total for the current expenses for the orphans from May 26, 1848, to May 26, 1849, was £1,559, 6s. 9d , and the total of the current expenses for them from May 26, 1849, to May 26, 1850, was only £2,665, 13s. 2¾d., *i. e.,* only about £1,100 more than the previous year.

As to matters connected with my own personal affairs, from May 26, 1848, to May 26, 1850:—

Dec. 31, 1848 During this year the Lord was pleased to give me £474, 17s. 7d. To this is again to be added, for this year also, as before stated, the free education of my daughter at a boarding-school, worth at least £50.

Dec. 31, 1849. The Lord sent me, during the past year, £413, 2s. 4d

CHAPTER XX.

A NEW VICTORY OF FAITH.

1850 — 1851.

PAST MERCIES AN ENCOURAGEMENT TO NEW UNDERTAKINGS — A HOUSE FOR SEVEN HUNDRED ORPHANS PROPOSED — WALKING BY FAITH — COUNSEL SOUGHT FROM GOD — THE PURPOSE FORMED — DELIGHT IN THE MAGNITUDE AND DIFFICULTY OF THE DESIGN.

DECEMBER 5, 1850. It is now sixteen years and nine months this evening since I began the Scriptural Knowledge Institution for Home and Abroad. This Institution was in its beginning exceedingly small. Now it is so large that I have not only disbursed, since its commencement, about fifty thousand pounds sterling, but that also the current expenses, after the rate of the last months, amount to above six thousand pounds a year. I did "open my mouth wide," this very evening fifteen years ago, and the Lord has filled it. The new Orphan House is now inhabited by three hundred orphans; and there are altogether three hundred and thirty-five persons connected with it. My labor is abundant. The separation from my dear wife and child is great, on account of my being the greater part of the day at the new Orphan House; sometimes also by night. But notwithstanding all this, I have again and again thought about laboring more than ever in serving poor orphans. Within the last ten days this matter has much occupied my mind, and for the last five days I have had much prayer about it. It has passed through my mind to build another Orphan House, large enough for seven hundred orphans, so that I might be able to care for one thousand altogether. The points which have led me to this thought are: 1. The many distressing cases of children bereaved of *both* parents, who have no helper. I have received two hundred and seven orphans within the last sixteen months, and have now seventy-eight waiting for admission, without having vacancies for any. I had about sixty children waiting for admission about sixteen months since, so about two hundred and thirty children have been applied for within these sixteen months.

The thoughts about enlarging the orphan work have not arisen on account of an abundance of money having lately come in; for I have had of late to wait for about seven weeks upon God, whilst little, very little comparatively, came in, *i. e.*, about four times as much was going out as came in; and, had not the Lord previously sent me large sums, we should have been distressed indeed.

Lord, how can thy servant know thy will in this matter? Wilt thou be pleased to teach him?

Dec. 26. Twenty-one days have elapsed since I wrote the preceding paragraph. Every day since then I have continued to pray about this matter, and that with a goodly measure of earnestness, by the help of God. There has passed away scarcely an hour during these days in which, whilst awake, this matter has not been more or less before me; but all without even a shadow of excitement. I converse with no one about it. Hitherto have I not even done so with my dear wife. From this I refrain still, and deal with God alone about the matter, in order that no outward influence and no outward excitement may keep me from attaining unto a clear discovery of his will. I have the fullest and most peaceful assurance that he will clearly show me his will. This evening I have had again an especial solemn season for prayer, to seek to know the will of God. But whilst I continue to entreat and beseech the Lord that he would not allow me to be deluded in this business, I may say that I have scarcely any doubt remaining on my mind as to what will be the issue, even that I should go forward in this matter. As this, however, is one of the most momentous steps that I have ever taken, I judge that I cannot go about this matter with too much caution, prayerfulness, and deliberation. I am in no hurry about it. I could wait for years, by God's grace, were this his will, before even taking one single step towards this thing, or even speaking to any one about it; and, on the other hand, I would set to work to-morrow, were the Lord to bid me do so. This calmness of mind, this having no will of my own in the matter, this only wishing to please my heavenly Father in it, this only seeking his and not my honor in it, — this state of heart, I say, is the fullest assurance to me that my heart is not under a fleshly excitement, and that if I am helped thus to go on I shall know the will of God to the full. But, while I write thus, I cannot but add, at the same time, that I do crave the honor and the glorious privilege to be more and more used by the Lord. I have served Satan much in my younger years, and I desire now with all my might to serve God during the remaining days of my earthly pilgrimage. I am forty-five years and three months old. Every day decreases the number of days that I have to stay on earth. I therefore desire with all my might to work. There are vast multitudes of orphans to be provided for. About five years ago a brother in the Lord told me that he had seen, in an official report, that there were at that time six thousand young orphans in the prisons of England. My heart longs to be instrumental in preventing such young orphans from having to go to prison. I desire to be used by the Lord as an instrument in providing all the necessary temporal supplies, not only for the three hundred now under my care, but for seven hundred more. I desire to alleviate yet further the sufferings of poor dying widows, when looking on their helpless orphans about to be left behind. I desire yet further to assist poor persons to whom destitute orphans are left, and who are unable to provide for them. I desire to be allowed to provide scriptural instruction for a thousand orphans, instead of doing so for three hundred. I desire to expound the Holy Scriptures regularly to a thousand orphans, instead of doing so to three hundred. I desire that thus it may be yet more abundantly manifest that God is still the hearer and answerer of prayer, and that he is the living God now, as he ever was and ever will be, when he shall, simply in answer to prayer, have condescended to provide me with a house for seven hundred orphans, and with means to support them. This last consideration is the most important point in my mind. The Lord's honor is the principal point with me in this whole matter; and just because that is the case, if he would be more glorified by my not going forward in this business, I should, by his grace, be perfectly content to give up all thoughts about another Orphan House. Surely, in such a state of mind, obtained by thy Holy Spirit, thou, O my heavenly Father, wilt not suffer thy child to be mistaken, much less to be deluded! By the help of God I shall continue further, day by day, to wait upon him in prayer concerning this thing till he shall bid me act.

Jan. 2, 1851. A week ago I wrote the preceding paragraph. During this week I have still been helped, day by by, and more than once every day, to seek the guidance of the Lord about another Orphan House. The burden of my prayer has still been, that he in his great mercy would keep me from making a mistake. During the last week the Book of Proverbs has come in the course of my Scripture reading, and my heart has been refreshed, in reference to this subject, by the following passages: "Trust in the Lord with all thine heart; and lean not unto thine own understanding. In all thy ways acknowledge him, and he shall direct thy paths." Prov. iii. 5, 6. By the grace of God I do acknowledge the Lord in my ways, and in this thing in particular; I have therefore the comfortable assurance that he will direct my paths concerning this part of my service, as to whether I shall be occupied in it or not. Further:

"The integrity of the upright shall preserve them; but the perverseness of fools shall destroy them." Prov. xi. 3. By the grace of God I am upright in this business. My honest purpose is to get glory to God. Therefore I expect to be guided aright. Further: "Commit thy works unto the Lord, and thy thoughts shall be established." Prov. xvi. 3. I do commit my works unto the Lord; I therefore expect that my thoughts will be established. My heart is more and more coming to a calm, quiet, and settled assurance that the end will be that the Lord will condescend to use me yet further in the orphan work. Here, Lord, is thy servant!

Jan. 14. Twelve days have passed away since I wrote the last paragraph. I have still day by day been enabled to wait upon the Lord with reference to my enlarging the orphan work. I have been during the whole of this period also in perfect peace, which is the result of seeking in this thing only the Lord's honor and the temporal and spiritual benefit of my fellow-men. Without an effort could I, by his grace, put aside all thoughts about this whole affair, could I be only assured that it is the will of God that I should do so; and, on the other hand, at once would I go forward, if he would have it to be so. I have still kept this matter entirely to myself. Though it is now about seven weeks since day by day, more or less, my mind has been exercised about it, and since I have daily prayed concerning it, yet not one human being knows of it. As yet I have not mentioned it even to my dear wife, in order that thus, by quietly waiting upon the Lord, I might not be influenced by what might be said to me on the subject. This evening I have particularly set apart for prayer, beseeching the Lord once more not to allow me to be mistaken in this thing, and much less to be deluded by the devil. I have also sought to let all the reasons *against* building another Orphan House, and all the reasons *for* doing so, pass before my mind; and I now, for the sake of clearness and definiteness, write them down.

Reasons AGAINST *establishing another Orphan House for Seven Hundred Orphans.* — 1. Would not this be going beyond my measure *spiritually?* according to that word: "For I say, through the grace given unto me, to every man that is among you, not to think of himself more highly than he ought to think; but to think soberly, according as God has dealt to every man the measure of faith." Rom. xii. 3. Answer: If the Lord were to leave me to myself, the tenth part of the difficulties and trials which befall me now in connection with the various objects of the Scriptural Knowledge Institution for Home and Abroad would be enough to overwhelm me; but, whilst he is pleased to sustain me, I am able day by day to pass on peacefully, and am carried through one difficulty after the other: and thus, by God's help, even with my present measure of faith, if continued to me, I should be enabled to bear up under other difficulties and trials; but I look for an increase of faith with every fresh difficulty through which the Lord is pleased to help me.

2. Would it not be going beyond my measure *naturally*, with reference to mental and bodily strength? Answer: Of all the objections against establishing another Orphan House, there is none that weighs more with me than this one; I might say, it is the only real difficulty. This, however, too, I am enabled to put aside and to overcome thus: By husbanding my strength, by great order, by regular habits, by lightening the work as much as possible, by using every help that I can, I have been enabled to get through a vast quantity of work. My immense correspondence of about three thousand letters a year I have been enabled to accomplish without a secretary. The whole management and direction and the whole vast correspondence of the Scriptural Knowledge Institution has devolved upon myself alone these sixteen years and ten months, and I have been thinking that, by seeking for an efficient secretary, and an efficient clerk, and an inspector of the schools,

I might, with God's help, accomplish yet more, though much of what I have been doing hitherto would need to be be done by others. There have been several other arrangements brought before my mind, since I have been exercised about this matter, whereby, with the blessing of God, the work might be lightened. I should certainly need efficient helpers to carry out the plans before me; but with such, I, as director, might be enabled, by God's help, to accomplish yet more.

3. There must be a limit to my work and service. Answer: That is true, and if I were quite sure that the present state of the Scriptural Knowledge Institution were to be the limit, I would at once lay aside this thing; but I am not sure that I am come as yet to God's limit. All these sixteen years and ten months the work has been constantly progressing, and the Lord has helped me continually; and now my mind is just in the same way exercised as when, fifteen years ago, I began the orphan work, and as when, thirteen years ago, I enlarged the orphan work, and as when, seven years and nine months since, I still further enlarged the orphan work, and as when, five years and two months since, I was led to decide on building the new Orphan House. Under these circumstances, having been helped through all these difficulties, and seeing such a vast field of usefulness before me, and as I have so many applications for the admission of very destitute orphans, I long to be used still further, and cannot say, that as yet the Lord has brought me to his limit.

4. Is it not like "tempting God," to think of building another Orphan House for seven hundred more orphans? Answer: "Tempting God" means, according to the Holy Scriptures, to limit him in any of his attributes. I, by his grace, do not wish to limit his power or his willingness to give to me, his poor servant, simply in answer to prayer, all the means and every other help and blessing which I shall need to build another large Orphan House.

5. You will not get the means for building and fitting up so large an Orphan House; and, even if you did, how will you, *at the same time*, get the means for carrying on the work which already exists? Answer: Looking at the matter *naturally*, this is indeed a weighty objection.

The new Orphan House, with its three hundred orphans only, cost about fifteen thousand pounds to build and to fit up and furnish; and still the expenses are not all met even now. It will, in all probability, cost several hundred pounds yet. And this large sum was needed, though the style of the building is most simple, and though the field in which it was built was comparatively cheap. After this rate, a building to accommodate seven hundred orphans, with the necessary ground attached to it for the cultivation of the vegetables used in the Institution, could not be less than thirty-five thousand pounds. Now, looking at it naturally, where is this great sum to come from? Though I looked at all my friends who have given hitherto, and several have done so very liberally, yet I should have no natural prospect whatever that I should receive this amount; especially if it be kept in mind that I should need six or seven thousand pounds besides, every year, for carrying on *that which is already in existence*. I might, therefore, well tremble, looking at the matter naturally, and say, I shall never have the money for this intended Orphan House for seven hundred children; for where is this large sum of thirty-five thousand pounds to come from? And even if I were to get the money, will not persons, in giving means for such a building fund, take it away from what they might have given me for carrying on the work which exists already? But whilst thus, *naturally*, I have no hope of succeeding, I am not in the least discouraged *spiritually*; for by faith in the living God I say this: He has the power to give me these thirty-five thousand pounds, and much more were it needed; and he has the power, in the mean time, to give me also all the large sums required, week after week, for meeting the current expenses for the present state of the work. Moreover, I delight in the greatness of the difficulty as it respects the large sum needed for building and fitting up such an establishment; for I desire to be most fully assured, from the very outset, that I go forward in this matter according to the Lord's bidding. If so, he will give me the means; if not, I shall not have them. Nor do I mean to apply to any one personally for pecuniary help, but purpose to give myself to prayer for means, as heretofore.

6. Suppose, now, you were even to succeed in getting this large Orphan House built, how will you be able to provide for seven hundred other orphans? Answer: There is much weight in this objection, looking at it *naturally*. I am too much a man of business, and too much a person of calm, quiet, cool calculation, not to feel its force. And indeed, were I only to look at the thing *naturally*, I should at once be ready to own that I am going too far; for the increase of expenditure for the support of these seven hundred other orphans could not be less than eight thousand pounds a year more, so that the current expenses of the Scriptural Knowledge Institution, reckoning its present state, and including those eight thousand pounds, would be about fifteen thousand pounds a year. Now I am free to own that I have no human prospect of obtaining such a sum year by year. But while matters stand thus, looking at them *naturally*, I see no difficulty at all in them *spiritually*. If according to the will of God I am enabled to go about this intended second Orphan House; and if, under his help, I shall be enabled to finish it; he will surely provide for those who are gathered together in it as long as he shall be pleased to enable me to trust in him for supplies. And here I look back upon the way in which the Lord has led me and dealt with me. When, about seventeen years ago, I took up, in dependence upon the living God for means, two charity schools, with which the **Scriptural**

Knowledge Institution commenced (and this involved an expense of less than one hundred pounds a year), I had no certain prospect of being able to meet even that small sum; but God so helped me that I had shortly *six* charity schools. He helped me then, also, and enabled me to meet all their expenses. When, fifteen years ago, I began the orphan work, which was connected with far heavier expenses, I had still less prospect, according to natural reason, of being able to meet *them;* but I trusted in God, and he helped me, and he not only enabled me to meet the current expenses of thirty orphans in the first house rented for them, but enabled me also soon to open another for thirty-six more, and I was also enabled to meet all those expenses; for as I had begun in faith in the living God, and not in putting my trust in my brethren in Christ, so I was not confounded. After I had gone on some time with these orphans in the two rented houses, about thirteen years ago the Lord was pleased greatly to encourage me and to increase my faith by a donation of five hundred pounds for the orphans; for up to that period I had never received more than one hundred pounds at once. But this kind donor, a stranger to me up to that time, suggested to me the propriety of investing this sum and using only the interest of it, as I could not expect to have the orphans supported for a continuance in the way they had been till then; for that such institutions must depend upon regular subscriptions or funded property, otherwise they could not go on. As, however, this was only a friendly hint, and no condition under which the money was given, I took this five hundred pounds towards fitting up a third house, for the reception of thirty more orphans. From that time the work has been increasing more and more, till it has come to what it is at present. Now, suppose I had said, seventeen years ago, looking at matters according to natural reason, "The two charity schools are enough, I must not go any further;" then the work would have stopped there. Or, if I had had a little more trust in my exertions or my friends, I might have taken at the utmost one or two steps further. Instead of this, however, I looked in no degree whatever at things according to my natural fallen reason, and I trusted not in the circle of my Christian friends, but in the living God; and the result has been that there have been since 1834 ten thousand souls under our instruction in the various day schools, Sunday schools, and adult schools; several hundred orphans have been brought up, and many of them from their very tenderest infancy; several hundred thousand tracts and many thousand copies of the Word of God have been circulated; about forty preachers of the gospel at home and abroad have been, for several years, assisted in connection with the Scriptural Knowledge Institution; and a house has been built and fitted up for the accommodation of three hundred destitute orphans, each of whom has neither father nor mother. How blessed therefore is it to trust in God, and in him alone, and not in circumstances nor friends! There is, however, one thing which I must record here, because it has taken place since I last wrote in my journal on this subject, on January 2. It is this. During these twelve days I have received for the various object of the Scriptural Knowledge Institution, in smaller donations, sixty-four pounds fifteen shillings sixpence two farthings, also a donation of one hundred and fifty pounds, and one of three thousand pounds. Is not this a plain proof that God is both able and willing to help simply in answer to prayer? Is not human reason confounded by such instances? When I first began to write these exercises of my mind about another Orphan House, I knew not that, on January 4, I should receive a donation of three thousand pounds; yet I was fully assured that God was able to support one thousand orphans as easily as he did the thirty whom I first received in a rented house. Does he not, however, tell me by all this,—Go forward, my servant, and I will help thee?

7. But, it might be said, suppose you were able by prayer to obtain this large sum for building a house for seven hundred other orphans; and suppose you were able to provide for them during your lifetime,— what would become of this Institution after your death? Answer: I am quite familiar with this objection. I have heard it many times as a reason against the way of obtaining the means for the Scriptural Knowledge Institution, simply by trusting in God, without any funded property, and without looking to regular subscribers; but my reply is this. My business is, with all my might to serve my own generation; in doing so, I shall best serve the next generation, should the Lord Jesus tarry. Soon he may come again; but if he tarry, and I have to fall asleep before his return, I shall not have been altogether without profit to the generation to come, were the Lord only to enable me to serve my own generation. Suppose this objection were a sound one, I ought never to have commenced the orphan work at all, for fear of what might become of it after my death, and thus all the hundreds of destitute children without father and mother, whom the Lord has allowed me to care for during the last fifteen years, would not have been taken up by me. The same argument was again and again used to Franké my esteemed countrymen, who at Hallé, in Prussia, commenced, about A. D. 1696, the largest charitable establishment for poor children that, as far as I know, exists in the world. He trusted in God alone. He went on trusting in God alone. And God helped him throughout abundantly. Simply by trust in the living God, the Institutions, resembling a large street rather than a house, were erected, and about two thousand children instructed in them. For about thirty years all was going on under his own eye, until 1727, when it pleased God to take his servant to himself. At his death these Institutions were directed by his truly pious son-in-law. It is true that, at the latter part of the last century, and during the first part of the present,

there was little real vital godliness in these Institutions; still, they were a temporal blessing to many tens of thousands of young persons even then. So then for several tens of years they were carried on in a truly godly way, after Franké's death, and when afterwards there was but little real vital godliness found in these schools, yet tens of thousands of children were benefited at least for this life. Now these Institutions have existed already one hundred and fifty years, and are in existence still; and, if the Lord Jesus tarry, are likely, humanly speaking, to exist hereafter, as they have existed hitherto. Suppose, then, that dear man of God, A. H. Franké, had listened to the suggestions of unbelief, and said, I must not undertake this work, for what will become of it after my death? — then all the blessing which spiritually resulted from it to thousands, and all temporal benefits which have resulted from it to hundreds of thousands, would have been lost. I add, however, this. The new Orphan House has been placed in the hands of eleven trustees, and has been properly enrolled in chancery, and so, also, should God condescend to honor me further in building for him this intended house for seven hundred orphans, it would likewise be placed in the hands of trustees and enrolled in chancery. I say one word in conclusion on this subject: let every one take heed lest, in caring about what will become of the next generation, he forget to serve his own generation. The latter, each one should seek to do with his might, and thus it should be with each succeeding generation; then, though we be dead, yet should we be speaking. A. H. Franké is long since gone to his rest, but he spoke to my soul in 1826, and he is speaking to my soul now; and to his example I am greatly indebted in having been stirred up to care about poor children in general, and about poor orphans in particular.

8. The last objection which has occurred to my own mind is, that, by building another Orphan House, I should

be in danger of being lifted up. Answer: I should be in danger of it indeed; and so I am in great danger, even were I not in the least degree to go forward. Yea, the tenth part of the honor which the Lord has condescended to bestow upon me, and the tenth part of service with which he has been pleased to intrust me, would be enough, if I were left to myself, exceedingly to puff me up. I cannot say that hitherto the Lord has kept me humble; but I can say that hitherto he has given me a hearty desire to give to him all the glory, and to consider it a great condescension on his part that he has been pleased to use me as an instrument in his service. I do not see, therefore, that fear of being lifted up ought to keep me from going forward in this work; but that I have rather to beseech the Lord that he would be pleased to give me a lowly mind, and never suffer me to rob him of the glory which is due to him alone.

Reasons FOR *establishing another Orphan House for Seven Hundred Orphans.* — 1. The many applications for the admission of destitute orphans which continue to be made, I consider as a call from God upon me to do all that is in my power to provide a home and scriptural education for a still greater number of orphans. Nothing but positive inability to go forward ought to keep me standing still, whilst I have almost daily fresh entreaties to receive orphans. Since I began writing on this subject in my journal, thirty more orphans have been applied for, from two years old and upward. I cannot refuse to help, as long as I see a door open, and opened by God, as I consider, to help them.

2. The moral state of the poor-houses greatly influences me to go forward. I have heard it again and again, from good authority, that children, placed at the Unions, are corrupted, on account of the children of vagrants, and other very bad young people, who are in such places; so that many poor relatives of orphans, though unable to provide for them, cannot bear the idea of their going there,

lest they should be corrupted. I therefore judge that, even for the sake of keeping orphans of poor yet respectable people from being obliged to mix with the children of vagabonds, I ought to do, to my utmost power, all I can to help them. For this reason, then, I purpose, in dependence upon the living God, to go forward and to establish another Orphan House for seven hundred destitute children, who are bereaved of both parents. When I write thus about the poor-houses, I do not wish to be understood in the way of reproof; for I know not how these matters could be altered; but I simply state the fact that thus it is.

3. In this my purpose I am the more confirmed, since I know it to be a fact that the Orphan Houses already in existence in the kingdom are by no means sufficient to admit *even the most deserving and distressing cases*, and far less all that it would be well to provide for. Moreover, there is great difficulty connected with the admission of an orphan into most of the ordinary orphan establishments, on account of the votes which must be obtained, so that *really* needy persons have neither time nor money to obtain them. Does not the fact that there were six thousand young orphans in the prisons of England about five years ago call aloud for an extension of orphan institutions? By God's help I will try to do what I can to keep poor orphans from prison.

4. In this purpose I am still further encouraged by the great help which the Lord has hitherto given me in this blessed service. When I look at the small beginning, and consider how the Lord has helped me now for more than fifteen years in the orphan work; and when I consider how he has been pleased to help me through one great difficulty after another; and when I consider, especially, how, as with an unseen hand, I might say almost against my will and former desires and thoughts, he has led me on from one step to another, and has enlarged the work more and more, — I say, when I review all this, and compare with it

my present exercise of mind, I find the great help, the uninterrupted help which the Lord has given me for more than fifteen years, a great reason for going forward in this work. And this, trusting in him, I am resolved to do.

5. A further reason for going forward in this service I see in the experience which I have had in it. From the smallest commencement up to the present state of the establishment, with its three hundred orphans, all has gone through my own hands. In the work itself I obtained the experience. *It* has grown *with the work*. I have been the sole director of the work, under God, from its smallest commencement. Now this is not an every-day case. No committee member of a society, no president or vice-president of an institution, except they had been situated as myself, could have this experience. Coupled with this is the measure of gift which the Lord has been pleased to give me for such work, and for the exercise of which I am responsible to him. These things, in connection with the former reasons, it appears to me, are a call from God to go forward in a greater degree than ever in this work.

6. The spiritual benefit of still more orphans is another especial reason with me why I feel called to go forward. The orphans who have been under my care hitherto were almost all the children of parents who were naturally weak in body, if not consumptive. The very fact of a child being deprived of *both* parents when four, five, six, or seven years old, shows that, except the parents lost their lives by casualty, they were constitutionally weak. On this account, young orphans, generally speaking, require particular care as to their health. In this respect I desire to care for them; but there is more than that to be attended to. I further heartily desire to keep them from the corrupting and demoralizing effect of the lowest sort of children in the streets and courts and Unions. But I desire more for them than mere decency and morality; I desire that they should be useful members of society, and that the prisons of the

United Kingdom should not be filled with poor, destitute, and homeless orphans; and we bring them up, therefore, in habits of industry, and seek to instruct them in those things which are useful for the life that now is. But I desire more than this for the orphans. I cannot be satisfied with anything concerning them short of this, that their souls be won for the Lord. For this reason I long to have them from their early days, yea, the younger the better, under my care, that thus, under the care of godly nurses and teachers, they may be brought up from their earliest days in the fear of the Lord. Now, as this is the chief and primary aim concerning the dear orphans, even the salvation of their souls through faith in the Lord Jesus, I long to be more extensively used than hitherto, even that I may have a thousand of them instead of three hundred under my care.

7. But there is one point which weighs more strongly with me than even the last-mentioned one. It is this: When I began the orphan work more than fifteen years ago, it was for the definite and especial purpose that, by means of it, the unconverted might see, through the answers of prayer that I received in connection with it, that there is verily reality in the things of God; and that the children of God might have their faith strengthened by means of it, and might be encouraged, in all simplicity, to deal with God under every circumstance, and trust in him at all times. But if this would be answered in a measure by the state in which the orphan work has been in former times, and more so by what it has been since the erection of the new Orphan House, it would be still more so, by the blessing of God, by my going forward in it to a far greater degree than before. This point, even the glory of God in the manifestation of his readiness to hear prayer, has weighed especially and supremely with me in purposing to enlarge the orphan work.

8. Lastly, I am peaceful and happy, spiritually, in the

prospect of enlarging the work, as on former occasions when I had to do so. This weighs particularly with me as a reason for going forward. After all the calm, quiet, prayerful consideration of the subject for about eight weeks, I am peaceful and happy, spiritually, in the purpose of enlarging the field. This, after all the heart-searching which I have had and the daily prayer to be kept from delusion and mistake in this thing, and the betaking myself to the word of God, would not be the case, I judge, had not the Lord purposed to condescend to use me more than ever in this service.

I, therefore, on the ground of the objections, answered, and these eight reasons FOR enlarging the work, come to the conclusion that it is the will of the blessed God that his poor and most unworthy servant should yet more extensively serve him in this work, which he is quite willing to do.

Up to this day, Jan. 25, 1851, I have not spoken to one human being about it. As yet, even my dear wife knows not about it. I purpose to keep the matter still for some time entirely to myself, dealing with God alone about it, in order that no outward excitement may be in the least degree a stimulus to me. I still pray to be kept from mistake and delusion in this thing; not that I think I am mistaken or deluded,—quite the reverse,—but yet I would distrust myself and cling to God, to be kept from mistakes and delusions.

Jan. 31. For several weeks past I have now had no doubt that the Lord would have me to serve him in the erection and fitting up of another Orphan House for seven hundred orphans, and I am quite decided on doing so, under his help; and I am now quiet about it, not because I have the least misgiving in my own mind, but because I know that it is most suitable that I should still for some time continue to deal quietly with God alone about it.

March 5. Nearly five weeks have passed away since I

wrote the last paragraph, and my mind has not been once during this time, even for a moment, in uncertainty as to what I ought to do. It is now about fifteen weeks since I have been especially praying about this subject, and three months since I began first to write on the subject in my journal, and about ten weeks since I have had any doubts as to what is the will of the Lord concerning this service. I believe that, altogether unworthy though I am of this great honor, he will condescend to use me further and more extensively than before in caring for destitute children who are bereaved of both parents. And this I purpose to do.

May 24. From the time that I began to write down the exercises of my mind on Dec. 5, 1850, till this day, ninety-two more orphans have been applied for, and seventy-eight were already waiting for admission before. But this number increases rapidly, as the work becomes more and more known.

On the ground of what has been recorded above, I purpose to go forward in this service, and to seek to build, to the praise and honor of the living God, another Orphan House, large enough to accommodate seven hundred orphans.

When I published these exercises of my mind, and made known my purpose respecting the intended Orphan House for seven hundred orphans, in the Twelfth Report of the Scriptural Knowledge Institution, the following particulars were added to what has been stated : —

1. All this time, though now six months have elapsed, since I first began to be exercised about this matter, I have never once been led to ask the Lord for means for this work, but have only continued day by day, to seek guidance from him as to whether I should undertake it or not.

2. The means requisite to accomplish the building and fitting up of a house which shall be really suitable for my intended purposes, though the building be quite simple, can-

not be less than thirty-five thousand pounds, including fifteen or twenty acres of land round the building for cultivation by the spade, in order to obtain out of our own grounds all the vegetables which are so important to the health of the children.

3. I do not mean to begin the building until I have the means requisite in hand, just as was the case with regard to the new Orphan House. If God will condescend to use me in building for him another Orphan House (as I judge he will) he will give me the means for it. Now, though I have not on my own mind any doubt left that it is his will that I should do so, which has been stated again and again in the preceding pages; yet there is one point still wanting for confirmation, and that is, that he will also furnish me, without personal application to any one, with all the means requisite for this new part of my service. I am the more needing also to my own soul this last of all the proofs that I have not been mistaken (as I firmly believe I have not been), in order to have unquestionable assurance that, whatever trials hereafter might be allowed to befall me in connection with this work, I did not at my own bidding and according to my own natural desire undertake it, but that it was under the guidance of God. The greatness of the sum required affords me a kind of secret joy; for the greater the difficulty to be overcome, the more will it be seen, to the glory of God, how much can be done by prayer and faith; and also because, when God himself overcomes our difficulties for us, we have, in this very fact, the assurance that we are engaged in his work, and not in our own.

CHAPTER XXI.

UNVARYING PROSPERITY.

1850 — 1852.

DESIRES FOR MORE ENLARGED USEFULNESS GRATIFIED — A LARGE DONATION ANTICIPATED AND RECEIVED — REVIEW OF 1851 — PERSONAL EXPERIENCE — BUILDING FUND FOR THE SECOND NEW ORPHAN HOUSE — DOUBT RESISTED — WAITING ON GOD NOT IN VAIN — REVIEW OF 1852.

AT the commencement of the year beginning with May, 1850, it was my purpose to seek help from the Lord that I might be able, in a still greater degree than before, to assist brethren who labor in the gospel at home and abroad, in dependence upon God for their temporal supplies, and to labor more than ever in the circulation of the Holy Scriptures, and of simple gospel tracts.

June 11. By the sums which came in within the first fifteen days of this period I was able to begin to carry out the purpose I had formed; and as the Lord enabled me, without anxious reckoning, to go on giving out as he was pleased to intrust me with means, so again he sent further supplies before all was gone. It is a point of great importance in the divine life not to be anxiously reckoning about the morrow, nor dealing out sparingly on account of possible future wants which never may come; but to consider that the *present* moment to serve the Lord only is ours, and that the morrow may never come to *us*.

April 20, 1851. During the whole of the current year, up to this date, the Lord has so abundantly supplied me with means that there came not one single case before me in which it would have been desirable to help, according to the measure of light given to me, or to extend the work, without my having at the same time ample means for doing so. In the midst of the great depression of the times, which was so generally felt, and on account of which, humanly speaking, I also might have been exceedingly tried for want of means, I, on the contrary, at no period of the work for the seventeen years previous had a greater abundance of means. I do on purpose lay stress upon this because I desire that it may become increasingly known that there is no easier, no better, and no happier way in the end than God's way, and this in particular also with regard to the obtaining of means *simply in answer to prayer, without personal application to any one.*

At the beginning of the year I had more in hand for the orphans than for many years before under similar circumstances, the balance for current expenses on May 26, 1850, being one hundred and fifty pounds seven shillings tenpence. Yet, much as this was in comparison with what the balance had generally been before, how small was the amount in reality! About three hundred persons were connected with the new Orphan House, who day by day were to be provided with all they needed, besides several apprentices who also were still to be supported. On this account the one hundred and fifty pounds in hand would only furnish that which was needed for about fifteen days, as the average expenses of the orphan work alone were about ten pounds daily. Place yourself, therefore, dear reader, in my position. Three hundred persons daily at table, and one hundred and fifty pounds in hand! Looking at it naturally, it is enough to make one tremble; but trusting in the living God, as by his grace I was enabled to do, I had not the least trial of mind, and was assured that God would as certainly help me as he had done fourteen years before, when the number of the orphans was only the tenth part as large.

Jan. 4, 1851. This very day the Lord has given me a

most precious proof that he delights in our having large expectations from him. I have received this evening the sum of three thousand pounds, being the largest donation which I have had as yet. I now write again that I expect far larger sums still, in order that it may be yet more and more manifest that there is no happier, no easier, and no better way of obtaining pecuniary means for the work of the Lord than the one in which I have been led. How great my joy in God is, on account of this donation, cannot be described; but it is not in the least coupled with excitement. I take this donation out of the hands of the living God; I continually look for his help, and am perfectly assured that I shall have it, and therefore is my soul calm and peaceful, without any excitement, though the donation is so large. This donation is, however, like a voice from heaven speaking to me concerning a most deeply important matter respecting which I am seeking guidance from the Lord, the building of another Orphan House.

May 26. I am brought to the close of this period. The work is more and more enlarging. During the last month I have paid out for the orphans more than four hundred and fifty pounds, and for the other objects more than five hundred pounds, being nearly one thousand pounds during one month; and yet I have a greater balance left in hand, through the Lord's kindness, than at the close of any of the previous periods.

From May 26, 1850, to May 26, 1851, there were four day schools in Bristol, with 286 children in them, *entirely supported* by the funds of the Institution; and three others in Devonshire, Gloucestershire, and Norfolk, with 180 children in them, were *assisted*. Further, one Sunday school in Bristol, with 184 children, was entirely supported, and two others in Devonshire and Gloucestershire, with 213 children, were assisted. Lastly, an adult school in Bristol, with 90 persons in it, was entirely supported. The expenses connected with all these various schools were, during this period, £379, 17s. From the formation of the Institution, on March 5, 1834, up to May 26, 1851, there were 5,343 children in the various day schools in Bristol alone, 2,379 in the Sunday school, and 1,896 persons in the adult school, besides the thousands in the schools out of Bristol which were assisted.

There were expended during this period, out of the funds of the Institution, on the circulation of the Holy Scriptures, £150, 16s. 5d. There were 345 Bibles sold, and 899 given away; and 30 New Testaments sold, and 413 given away, during this period. From March 5, 1834, to May 26, 1851, there were circulated 7,709 Bibles and 4,442 New Testaments.

During this year were spent of the funds of the Institution, for missionary objects, the sum of £2,000, 11s. 1d. By this sum forty-five laborers in the word and doctrine in various parts of the world were to a greater or less degree assisted. The total amount of £2,000 was sent to these forty-five servants of the Lord Jesus in 264 different sums.

During this period £358, 7s. 3d. were expended on the circulation of tracts, and 303,098 tracts and little books were circulated. I was permitted to send out more tracts than *during the whole of the previous ten years taken together*. Nor must it be withheld from the reader, as matter for thankfulness, that the Lord was pleased to allow me to hear again and again of instances of conversion, by means of the distribution of these tracts during this period

On May 26, 1850, there were 275 orphans in the new Orphan House on Ashley Down, Bristol. On May 26, 1851, there were 300 orphans in the new Orphan House The total number of orphans who were under our care from April, 1836, to May 26, 1851 is 488. There came in altogether during this year £4,102, 14s. 9¼d. for the support of the orphans, and £3,640, 9s 1¾ d. for the other objects; and, after having met to the full every demand with reference to the orphans, the balance of £970, 13s 11¾d. remained in hand. Also, after having entered into every door which the Lord was pleased to set before me respecting the other objects, and to do far more than during any one year previously, the balance of £809, 10s. 6d remained in hand on May 26, 1851. Verily we do not trust in the Lord in vain!

Without any one having been personally applied to for anything by me, the sum of £38,018, 4s. 6½d. was given to me for the orphans *as the result of prayer to God* from the commencement of the work May 26, 1851. It may be also interesting to the reader to know that the total amount which was given as free contributions for the other objects from the commencement of the work to May 26, 1851. amounted to £13,988, 11s. 9¼d. and that which came in by the sale of

Bibles and tracts, and by the payments of the children in the day schools, amounted to $2,890, 9s 11¾d.

It pleased the Lord greatly to gladden our hearts by the working of his Holy Spirit among the orphans during this period.

Dec. 31, 1850. During this year there have been received into fellowship 57, and altogether, from the time that brother Craik and I began to labor in Bristol, 1,313. The Lord has been pleased to give me, for my personal expenses, £402, 4s. 5d.

May 26, 1851. The reader will remember that I stated in a previous chapter that I purposed, not in dependence upon my Christian friends, nor in dependence upon former donors, but alone in dependence upon the living God, to enlarge the orphan work. Before I brought before the public what I purposed to do, I gave the record of the exercises of my mind on this subject to a valued Christian friend to read, the only one who, besides my family, knew anything of this my intention before it came before the public. I did this particularly in order that, after I had been waiting for several months in secret upon God for guidance and direction concerning it, I might also have the counsel of a prayerful, judicious, and cautious man of God. When this brother returned the manuscript, he spoke to me words of encouragement concerning this purpose, and gave me a half sovereign towards the building fund for this house for seven hundred destitute orphans. This was the first donation, which I received on May 13, 1851, and which, I confess, was a great refreshment and encouragement to me, the more so as it came from so cautious a brother, and after I had been for several months, through secret prayer, assured that I should go forward.

On May 28, 1851, my intention became publicly known, and in the evening of May 29 I received from a Christian lady a sovereign towards the building fund.

June 1. A brother in the Lord, who gives his donations with the letter "P.," gave me ten shillings. I also received a sovereign. This evening I received still further four half crowns, with very encouraging words and expressions of joy that I have been led to this purpose of building another Orphan House for seven hundred more orphans. There came to hand, also anonymously, three shillings. Ditto an old shilling, a small American coin, and two shillings. Also from a Christian servant in Clifton two shillings sixpence.

June 21. Twenty-four days have now passed away since I have been enabled, day by day, to wait with a goodly measure of earnestness and in faith upon the Lord for means; but as yet only a little above twenty-eight pounds has come. But I am not discouraged. The less there comes in, the more earnestly I pray, the more I look out for answers, and the more assured I am that the Lord, in his own time, after he has tried my faith, will send me larger sums, and, at last, all I need.

Aug. 12. Day by day I am waiting upon the Lord for means for this object, and generally more than once a day am I bowing my knees before God with reference to it. Moreover, of late I have been enabled, with increasing earnestness, to beseech the Lord that he would be pleased to send in means for the building fund. My soul has been all along at peace, though only so little, as yet, comparatively, has come in (in all, one hundred and twenty seven pounds nineteen shillings sixpence); and though Satan has in the most subtle way sought to shake my confidence, and to lead me to question whether, after all, I had not been mistaken concerning this whole matter. Yet, though he has aimed after this, to the praise of God I have to confess that he has not been allowed to triumph. I have especially besought the Lord of late that he would be pleased to refresh my spirit by sending in some large donation for this part of the work. Under these circumstances I received this morning five hundred pounds for the new building. I was not in the least excited. I look out for means. *Even that very moment*, when I received this donation, I was looking out for means, for large donations; and I should not have been surprised if five thousand pounds had come in or more. The Lord be praised for this precious encouragement, which has still further quickened me for prayer!

March 17, 1852. Day by day I am waiting upon God for means. With full confidence, both as to the power of the Lord to give me the means, and likewise his willingness, I am enabled to continue to wait. But he is pleased to exercise my faith and patience, and especially has this been the case of late. Not more than twenty-seven pounds eleven shillings have come in during the last four weeks for the building fund. Yet, amidst it all, by the help of God, my heart has been kept looking to the Lord, and expecting help from him. Now to-day my heart has been greatly refreshed by a donation of nine hundred and ninety-nine pounds thirteen shillings fivepence. I cannot describe to any one how refreshing this donation is to my spirit. After having been for weeks, day by day, waiting upon the Lord, and receiving so little comparatively, either for current expenses or for the building fund, this answer to many prayers is exceedingly sweet to my spirit.

May 20. There remained in hand from the *former* building fund the balance of £776, 14s. 4¾d., which I added to the *present* building fund, so that on the evening of May 26, 1852, I had altogether £3,530, 9s. 0¼d.

Supplies for the School, Bible, Missionary, and Tract Fund, sent in answer to prayer from May 26, 1851, to May 26, 1852. — At no time during the past eighteen years did I begin a new period with so much money in hand as was the case at the commencement of this. These was a balance of £809, 10s. 6d. left for *these* objects. Long before this balance was expended, however, the Lord was pleased to send in further supplies; so that during all the year there did not come before me one single instance in which, according to my judgment, it would have been desirable to help forward schools or missionary objects, or the circulation of the Holy Scriptures and tracts, but I had always the means in hand for doing so.

Supplies for the Support of the Orphans sent in answer to prayer from May 26, 1851, *to May* 26, 1852 — When this period commenced I had in hand for the current expenses for the orphans £970, 13s 11¾d. We had never had so large a balance for the other objects at the commencement of any new period as was the case at the commencement of this, and so it was also with regard to the orphan work. But though there was this large balance to begin with, dependence upon God was still required day by day, as the *pecuniary* help is only a very small part of that which is needed; and even as to means, this sum would not have lasted long, had the Lord not sent in further supplies. This, however, he did; and thus it was that while there were other trials, varied and many, yet, as to means, we experienced scarcely any difficulty at all.

During the period from May 26, 1851, to May 26, 1852, there were *entirely supported* by the funds of the Institution four day schools in Bristol, with 248 poor children in them, and three others in Devonshire, Monmouthshire, and Norfolk, were *assisted*. Further, one Sunday school in Bristol, with 243 children, was entirely supported, and two others in Devonshire and Gloucestershire, with 230 children, were assisted. Lastly, one adult school in Bristol, with 120 adult scholars, was entirely supported during this period. From March 5, 1834, up to May 26, 1852, there were 5,525 children in the day schools in Bristol, 2,600 in the Sunday school, and 2,033 grown-up persons in the adult school. There were expended of the funds of the Institution, for these various schools, during this period, £360, 1s. 9d.

During this period, there were expended of the funds of the Institution £207, 3s. 1d for the purpose of circulating the Holy Scriptures, especially among the very poorest of the poor. There were issued during this period 1,101 Bibles and 409 New Testaments. There were altogether circulated from March 5, 1834, up to May 26, 1852, 8,810 Bibles, and 4,851 New Testaments.

During this year there was spent of the funds of the Institution, for missionary objects, the sum of £2,005, 7s 5d. By this sum fifty-one laborers in the word and doctrine, in various parts of the world, were to a greater or less degree assisted.

There was laid out for the circulation of tracts, from May 26, 1851, to May 26, 1852, the sum of £356, 11s. 3½d. There were circulated during the year 489,136 tracts.

The total number of tracts which were circulated from the beginning up to May 26, 1852, was 1,086,366.

On May 26, 1851, there were 300 orphans in the new Orphan House on Ashley Down, Bristol. From that day up to May 26, 1852, there were admitted into it 27 orphans. The total of the expenses connected with the support of the orphans, from May 26, 1851, to May 26. 1852, was £3,035, 3s. 4d. The total number of orphans who were under our care from April, 1836, to May 26, 1852, was 515

Without any one having been personally applied to for anything by me, the sum of £42,970, 17s. 6d. was given to me for the orphans *as the result of prayer to God* from the commencement of the work up to May 26, 1852. It may be also interesting to the reader to know that the total amount which was given as free contributions, for the other objects, from the commencement of the work up to May 26, 1852, amounted to £15,976, 10s. 6¼d.; and that which came in by the sale of Bibles and tracts, and by the payments of the children in the day schools, amounted to £3,073, 1s. 9¾d. Besides this, also, a great variety and number of articles of clothing, furniture, provisions, etc., were given for the use of the orphans.

Several of the orphans who left the establishment during this year went away as believers, having been converted some time before they left; one also who died gave very decided evidence of a true change of heart by faith in our Lord Jesus; several who in former years were under our care, as we heard during this year, took their stand openly on the Lord's side, and dated their first impressions to the instructions received whilst under our care; and lastly, of those under our care, there were not a few whose spiritual state gave us joy and comfort. Thus, amidst many difficulties and trials and some discouragements, we had abundant cause to praise God for his goodness, and to go forward in the strength of the Lord.

Dec. 31, 1851. During this year the Lord was pleased to give me, for my personal expenses £465, 13s. 1¾d.

CHAPTER XXII.

REAPING IN JOY.

1852 — 1854.

EXPECTING GREAT THINGS FROM GOD — MUNIFICENT DONATION — INCREASING USEFULNESS OF THE SCRIPTURAL KNOWLEDGE INSTITUTION — ACCESS TO GOD THROUGH FAITH IN CHRIST — A VOICE FROM MOUNT LEBANON — BENEFIT OF WAITING GOD'S TIME — CAREFUL STEWARDSHIP — FAITH, THE ONLY RELIANCE — "THIS POOR WIDOW HATH CAST IN MORE THAN THEY ALL" — GREATER ACHIEVEMENTS OF FAITH ANTICIPATED — COUNSEL TO TRACT DISTRIBUTORS — A NEW AND SEVERE TRIAL OF FAITH.

ON May 26, 1852, there were in hand toward the erection of the second new Orphan House three thousand five hundred and thirty pounds nine shillings sixpence and one farthing. Donations varying in amount from three hundred pounds to fourpence continued to be received in answer to prayer. On the 4th of Jan. 1853, Mr. M. writes: —

From London two shillings sixpence. Day by day I have now been waiting upon God for means for the building fund for more than nineteen months, and almost daily I have received something in answer to prayer. These donations have been, for the most part, small, in comparison with the amount which will be required for the completion of this object; nevertheless, they have shown that the Lord, for the sake of his dear Son, listens to my supplications, and to those of my fellow-laborers and helpers in the work; and they have been precious encouragements to me to continue to wait upon God. I have been for many months assured that the Lord, in his own time, would give larger sums for this work; but for this I have been more and more earnestly entreating him during the last months. Now at last he has abundantly refreshed my spirit, and answered my request. I received to-day, the promise that, as *the joint donation of several Christians*, there should be paid me a donation of eight thousand and one hundred pounds, for the work of the Lord in my hands.

It is impossible to describe the spiritual refreshment which my heart received through this donation. Day by day, for nineteen months, I had been looking out for more abundant help than I had had. I was fully assured that God would help me with larger sums; yet the delay was long. See how precious it is to wait upon God! See how those who do so are not confounded! Their faith and patience may long and sharply be tried; but in the end it will most assuredly be seen that those who honor God he will honor, and will not suffer them to be put to shame. The largeness of the donation, whilst it exceedingly refreshed my spirit, did not in the least surprise me; *for I expect* GREAT *things from God*. Have I been boasting in God in vain? Is it not manifest that it is most precious in every way to depend upon God? Do I serve God for naught? Is it not obvious that the principles on which I labor are not only applicable to the work of God *on a small scale*, but also, as I have so many times affirmed during the past nineteen years, *for the most extensive operations for God?*

During the year ending May 26, 1853, nine thousand and one pounds three shillings were received toward the building fund, making the present amount of that fund twelve thousand five hundred and thirty-one pounds twelve shillings one farthing.

For the various objects of the Scriptural Knowledge Institution, viz., for school, missionary, Bible, and tract purposes, I had to expend during the year from May, 1852, to May, 1853, about six hundred pounds per month, or above seven thousand pounds in all; but I had sufficient to meet every demand; and over and above I was helped by the Lord to increase the building fund nine thousand pounds. The current expenses of the Institution were never so great during the previous nineteen years; but the extent of its operations, and the means which the Lord was pleased to send in, were also never so great.

You see, dear reader, that we are richly recompensed for our waiting upon God. You perceive the readiness of his heart to listen to the supplications of his children who put their trust in him. If you have never made trial of it, do so now. But in order to have your prayers answered, you need to make your requests unto God on the ground of the merits and worthiness of the Lord Jesus. You must not depend upon your own worthiness and merits, but solely on the Lord Jesus, as the ground of acceptance before God, for your person, for your prayers, for your labors, and for everything else. Do you really believe in Jesus? Do you verily depend upon him alone for the salvation of your soul? See to it well that not the least degree of your own righteousness is presented unto God as a ground of accepttance. But then, if you believe in the Lord Jesus, it is further necessary, in order that your prayers may be answered, that the things which you ask God should be of such a kind that God can give them to you, because they are for his honor and your real good. If the obtaining of your requests were not for your real good, or were not tending to the honor of God, you might pray for a long time without obtaining what you desire. The glory of God should be always before the children of God, in what they desire at his hands; and their own spiritual profit, being so intimately connected with the honor of God, should never be lost sight of in their petitions. But now, suppose we are believers in the Lord Jesus, and suppose we make our requests unto God, depending alone on the Lord Jesus as the ground of having them granted; suppose also, that, so far as we are able honestly, and uprightly to judge, the obtaining of our requests would be for our real spiritual good, and for the honor of God; we yet need, lastly, to *continue* in prayer until the blessing is granted unto us. It is not enough to begin to pray, nor to pray aright; nor is it enough to continue *for a time* to pray; but we must patiently, believingly, continue in prayer until we obtain an answer; and, further, we have not only *to continue* in prayer unto the end, but we have also *to believe* that God does hear us, and will answer our prayers. Most frequently we fail *in not continuing* in prayer until the blessing is obtained, and *in not expecting* the blessing. As assuredly as in any individual these various points are found united together, so assuredly will answers be granted to his requests.

During the year 1852–53, the expense of the support of the orphans was fully met by unsolicited donations. Two or three particulars only will be given.

June 29, 1852. To-day I received one of the most remarkable donations which I ever had. I give the whole account, without the name of the dono

LYONS, June 24, 1852.

DEAR BROTHER IN CHRIST: -

It is now several years that I read with great interest, and I hope with some benefit to my soul, the account of your labors and experiences. Ever since then your work was the object of many thoughts and prayers, and I gave many copies of your book to Christian friends. One of them has read it in Syria, on Mount Lebanon, where he is for commercial business; and, whilst praying for you and your dear orphans, the Lord put it in his heart to send you two pounds, to which my husband added two others, and we beg you to accept that small offering in the name of the Lord. If you have published anything of the Lord's dealings with you since the year 1844, we shall be very happy to receive it. You could forward it to Messrs. * * * *, London, for * * * * of Lyons. And now, dear brother, may the grace and peace of the Lord rest on you and your dear home's inhabitants.

I have had donations from Australia, the East Indies, the West Indies, the United States, Canada, from the Cape of Good Hope, from France, Switzerland, Germany, Italy, etc.; and now comes also this donation from Mount Lebanon, with the prayer of a Christian brother whose name I never heard nor know even now. See, dear reader, this is the way in which the Lord has helped me in this precious service for twenty-two years. With my fellow-laborers, or without them, and they without me, our prayers are offered up unto the Lord for help, and he is pleased, for Jesus' sake, to listen to our supplications, and to influence the hearts of some of his children, known to us or not, to send us help. The donors may be rich or poor; they may live near, or at a distance of more than ten thousand miles; they may give much or little; they may have often given before, or never; they may be well known to us, or not at all: in these and many other things there may be constant variations; but God continually helps us; we are never confounded. And why not? Simply because we are enabled by the grace of God to put our trust in him for what we need.

Oct. 9. This morning Luke vii. came in the course of my reading before breakfast. While reading the account about the centurion and the raising from death of the widow's son at Nain, I lifted up my heart to the Lord Jesus thus: "Lord Jesus, thou hast the same power now. Thou canst provide me with means for thy work in my hands. Be pleased to do so." About half an hour afterwards I received two hundred and thirty pounds fifteen shillings; also one shilling. These two hundred and thirty pounds fifteen shillings were left at my disposal, as most needed. I took one-half for the current expenses for the orphans, and the other half for the other objects. I am now amply provided for meeting the demands of this day.

The joy which such answers to prayer afford cannot be

described. I was determined to wait upon God only, and not to work an unscriptural deliverance for myself. I have thousands of pounds for the building fund; but I would not take of it because it was once set apart for that object. There is also a legacy of one hundred pounds for the orphans two months overdue, in the prospect of the payment of which the heart might be naturally inclined to use some money from the building fund, to be replaced by the legacy money when it comes in; but I would not thus step out of God's way of obtaining help. At the very time when this donation arrived, I had packed up one hundred pounds which I happened to have in hand, received for the building fund, in order to take it to the bank, as I was determined not to touch it, but to wait upon God. My soul does magnify the Lord for his goodness!

This last paragraph is copied out of my journal, written down at the time. I add a few words more to the last sentences.

The natural mind is ever prone *to reason*, when we ought *to believe;* to be *at work*, when we ought to be *quiet;* to go our own way when we ought steadily to walk on in God's ways, however trying to nature. When I was first converted, I should have said, What harm can there be to take some of the money which has been put by for the building fund? God will help me again after some time with means for the orphans, and then I can replace it. Or, there is this money due for the legacy of one hundred pounds. This money is quite sure; may I not, therefore, on the strength of it, take some of the money from the building fund, and, when the legacy is paid, replace the money which I have taken? From what I have seen of believers, I know that many would act thus. But how does it work, when we thus anticipate God, by going our own way? We bring, in many instances, guilt on our conscience; but if not, we certainly weaken faith instead of increasing it; and each time we work thus a deliverance of our own we find it more and more difficult to trust in God, till at last we give way entirely to our natural fallen reason, and unbelief prevails. How different, if one is enabled to wait God's own time, and to look alone to him for help and deliverance! When at last help comes, after many seasons of prayer it may be, and after much exercise of faith and patience it may be, how sweet it is, and what a present recompense does the soul at once receive for trusting in God, and waiting patiently for his deliverance! Dear Christian reader, if you have never walked in this path of obedience before, do so now, and you will then know experimentally the sweetness of the joy which results from it.

Oct. 12. By sale of rags and bones twelve shillings sixpence. I copy literally from the receipt book. We seek to make the best of everything. As a steward of public money, I feel it right that even these articles should be turned into money; nor could we expect answers to our prayers if *knowingly* there were any waste allowed in connection with this work. For just because the money is received from God, simply in answer to prayer only, therefore it becomes us the more to be careful in the use of it.

From Dec. 20, 1852, to Jan. 4, 1853, we had nothing in advance of our wants. Means came in only as they were required for pressing needs. But on the 4th January, we received, as stated under another head, the largest donation I ever had, of which I took six hundred pounds for the support of the orphans. These facts I state, in order to give a practical illustration that those are entirely mistaken who suppose that the work is now *no longer* a work of faith, as it used to be in former years. It is true, we have now a larger income than we used to have in the years 1838, 1839, and 1840; but it is also true that our expenses are three times as great. We have no regular income now, even as we had not then. We ask no human being now for help; even as we did not then. We depend alone upon God, by his grace; even as we did then. Who is there in the whole world who will state that I ever asked him for help in this orphan work, from its commencement, on Dec. 9, 1835, up till now? Now, as we have no funds to live upon; as we have no regular subscribers or donors upon whom we could depend; as we never ask help from man, but God alone; and as, finally, we never did go into debt for this work, nor do we now: why is it not now a work of faith, as formerly? Will those who say it is not, place themselves in the position in which I was, when, at the close of the year 1852, I had not two pounds left, and about three hundred and thirty persons were day by day to be provided for, with all they need, and prove whether it is now anything else than a work of faith? But perhaps I have said too much about this. For every one, except those who are *determined* not to see, will have no difficulty in perceiving that now, as formerly, one could only be kept from being overwhelmed in such a position by looking day by day to the Lord, and that not merely for pecuniary supplies, but for help under the numberless difficulties which continually are met with in such a work.

How can I sufficiently praise, and adore, and magnify the Lord for his love and faithfulness in carrying me thus from year to year through this his service, supplying me with all I need in the way of means, fellow-laborers, mental strength, and, above all, spiritual support! But for his help and support I should be completely overpowered in a very short time; yet, by his help I go on, and am very happy, spiritually, in my service; nor am I now generally worse in health than I was twenty years ago, but rather better.

During the year 1852-53, there were four day schools, with 235 children in them, entirely supported by the funds of the Institution. Further, one Sunday school in Bristol, with 150 children, was entirely supported, and three others in Devonshire, Somersetshire, and Gloucestershire, with 280 children, were assisted. Lastly, one adult school, with 103 adult scholars, was entirely supported by the funds of the Institution There were under our care, from March 5, 1834, to May 26, 1853, in the various day schools 5,686 children, in the Sunday schools 2,673 children, and in the adult school 2,132 persons. There were expended of the funds of the Institution during this year, for the various schools, £349, 12s. 11d.

During this year there were laid out of the funds of the Institution, on the circulation of the Holy Scriptures, £431, 5s. 1½d , and there were circulated 1,666 Bibles and 1,210 New Testaments There were circulated from March 5, 1834, up to May 26, 1853, 10,476 Bibles, and 6,061 New Testaments.

For several years past this part of the work has appeared more and more important to me on account of the fearful attempts which have been made by the powers of darkness to rob the church of Christ of the Holy Scriptures. I have on this account sought to embrace every opportunity to circulate the Holy Scriptures in England, Ireland, Canada, British Guiana, the East Indies, China, Australia, etc. Every open door which the Lord was pleased to set before me in these or other parts of the world, I have joyfully entered; yea, I have counted it a privilege, indeed, to be permitted of God to send forth his Holy Word. Many servants of Christ, in various parts of the world, have assisted me in this service, through whose instrumentality copies of the Holy Scriptures have been circulated.

During this year there were spent of the funds of the Institution for missionary objects £2,234, 2s. 6d. By this sum fifty-four laborers in the word and doctrine, in various parts of the world, were to a greater or less degree assisted.

There was laid out for the circulation of tracts, from May 26, 1852, to May 26, 1853, the sum of £555, 16s. 7½d.; and there were circulated within this year 733,674 tracts.

The total number of tracts which were circulated up to May 26, 1853, was 1,820,040. From Nov. 19, 1840, to May 10, 1842, the first period that the circulation of tracts was in operation in connection with the Scriptural Knowledge Institution for Home and Abroad, there were circulated 19,609; from May 26, 1851, to May 26, 1852, 489,136; and during this period 733,674.

At the beginning of this period there were 300 orphans in the new Orphan House on Ashley Down, Bristol. During the year there were admitted into it 13 orphans, making 313 in all. The total number of orphans who were under our care from April, 1836, to May 26, 1853, was 528.

Without any one having been personally applied to for anything by me, the sum of £55,408, 17s. 5¾d. was given to me for the orphans, as the result of prayer to God, from the commencement of the work up to May 26, 1853. It may be also interesting to the reader to know that the total amount which was given for the other objects, from the commencement of the work up to May 26, 1853, amounted to £19,163, 14s. 1½d.; and that which came in by the sale of Bibles and tracts, and by the payments of the children in the day schools, amounted to £3,490, 7s. 1¾d. Besides this, also, a great variety and number of articles of clothing, furniture, provisions, etc., were given *for the use* of the orphans.

The expenses in connection with the support of the 300 orphans and the apprentices during this year were £4,453, 15s. 1½d.

Dec. 31, 1852. During this year there have been received into fellowship 35 believers. The Lord has been pleased to give unto me £445, 8s. 8½d.

My brother-in-law, Mr. A. N. Groves, of whom mention has been made in the first part of this Narrative, as having been helpful to me by his example when I began my labors in England in 1829, in that he, without any visible support, and without being connected with any missionary society, went with his wife and children to Bagdad, as a missionary, after having given up a lucrative practice of about one thousand five hundred pounds per year, returned in autumn 1852, from the East Indies, a third time, being exceedingly ill. He lived, however, till May 20, 1853, when, after a most blessed testimony for the Lord, he fell asleep in Jesus in my house.

I have already stated that on May 26, 1853, I had on hand toward building premises large enough for the accommodation of 700 children, the sum of £12,531, 12s. 0¼d.

A single circumstance will illustrate the widely diverse sources from which donations are received, as well as the great disparity in amount.

Jan. 17, 1854. From S. R. and E. R., two poor factory girls, near Stroud, 1s. 7d. This day I also received the

the Lord in my hands, £5,207, to be disposed of as I might consider best.

The whole amount received for the new Orphan House, during the year closing May 26, 1854, was £5,285, 17s. 5d., which made the total of £17,816, 19s. 5¼d. in hand on May 26, 1854.

During this year the current expenses for the various objects of the Scriptural Knowledge Institution for Home and Abroad amounted to £7,507, 0s. 11½d., being £471, 8s. 11d. more than during any previous year; yet the Lord not only enabled me to meet them all, but to add the sum of £5,285, 7s. 5d. to the building fund.

There is yet a large sum required before I shall be enabled to build another house for 700 orphans; nor have I now, any more than at the first, any natural prospect of obtaining what is yet needed; but my hope is in the living God. When I came to the conclusion that it was the will of God that I should build another Orphan House, I had not only no natural prospect of obtaining the £35,000 which would be needed for this object, but also I had no natural prospect of being able to provide for the necessities of the three hundred orphans already under my care. Three years have elapsed since then, and I have had all I needed for them, amounting to about £10,500; and £17,816, 19s. 5¼d. I have received for the building fund. May I not well trust in the Lord for what is yet needed for the building fund? By his grace I will do so, and delight in doing so; for I know that at last all my prayers will be turned into praises concerning this part of the service.

There is one point which is particularly an encouragement to me to go on waiting upon the Lord for the remainder of the means which are required, viz.: applications for the admission of orphans *continue* to be made. On May 26, 1853, there were 480 orphans waiting for admission. Since then 181 more have been applied for, making in all

661. These children are from three months old and upwards, and all bereaved of both parents by death.

During the year now under review I received the following donation for the missionary laborers, under circumstances of peculiar interest.

On Aug. 9, 1853, I received a letter from a Christian brother, accompanied with an order for eighty-eight pounds two shillings sixpence on his bankers, of which three pounds two shillings sixpence were the proceeds of an orphan box in a meeting-place of believers, and eighty-five pounds from a poor widow who had sold her little house, being all her property, and who had put ninety pounds, the total amount of what she had received, into that orphan box two months before, on June 9, 1853. In this box the money had been for some time, without its being known, till the orphan box was opened, and the ninety pounds with a few lines without name were found in it. As, however, the fact of her intending to sell the little house, and her intention of sending me the money for the Lord's work had been known to the brother who sent me the money, he did not feel free to send it to me without remonstrating with her through two brethren, whom he sent with the money, offering it again to her; for he knew her to be very poor, and feared that this might be an act of excitement, and therefore be regretted afterwards. These brethren could not prevail on her to receive back the money, but they did *persuade* her to receive back five pounds of the amount, and then the brother referred to felt no longer free to keep the money from me, and hence sent me the eighty-five pounds.

On the receipt of this, I wrote at once to the poor godly widow, offering her the travelling expenses for coming to Bristol, that I might have personal intercourse with her; for I feared lest this should be an act of excitement, and the more so, as she had received back five pounds of years of age, came to Bristol, and told me in all simplicity how that ten years before, in the year 1843, she had purposed that if ever she should come into the possession of the little house in which she lived with her husband, she would sell it, and give the proceeds of it to the Lord. About five years afterwards her husband died, and she, having no children, nor any one having particular claim upon her, then sought to dispose of her little property, as had been her mind all those years before. However, one difficulty after another prevented her being able to effect a sale. At last she felt in particular difficulty on account of her inability to pay the yearly ground-rent of the little house and garden, and she asked the Lord to enable her to sell the property, in order that she might be able to carry out her desire which she had had for ten years, to give to him the proceeds of this her possession. He now helped her. The house was sold, the money paid, and she put the whole ninety pounds into the orphan box for me, being assured that the Lord would direct me how best the money might be used for him. I still questioned her again and again, to find out whether it was not excitement which had led her to act as she had done; but I not only saw that her mind had been fully decided about this act for ten years before, but that she also was able to answer from the word of God all the objections which I purposely made, in order to probe her, whether she had intelligently and from right motives acted in what she had done. At last I was fully satisfied that it was not from impulse, nor under excitement, that she had given the money. I next stated to her something like this: "You are poor, and you are about sixty years old, therefore decreasing in strength, and may you not therefore keep this money for yourself?" Her reply was, as nearly as I remember, something like this: "God has always provided for me, and I have no doubt he will do so in future also. I am able to work and as a nurse, or in any other way." What could I say against this? This is just what a child of God would say, and should say. But the greatest of all the difficulties to the accepting of the eighty-five pounds remained in my mind, and I state it, as I relate the whole for the profit of the reader. It was this. The house had been sold for ninety pounds. The whole amount had been put into the box, but, on the persuasion of those two brethren who were requested to remonstrate with this widow, she had been induced to take back five pounds out of the ninety pounds. I therefore said to myself, might she not be willing, after a time, to take back the whole ninety pounds; how, therefore, can I feel happy in accepting this money? On this account I particularly laid stress upon this point, and told her that I feared she might regret her act altogether after some time, as she had taken back these five pounds. I now learned the circumstances under which she had been induced to take back these five pounds.

The two brethren who had called on her for the purpose of pointing out to her the propriety of receiving back again the ninety pounds, or part of it, told her that Barnabas sold his land, but afterwards lived with others on that which he and others had thrown into the common stock, and that, therefore, she might receive at least part of the ninety pounds back again, if she would not take the whole. She then said to herself that, "as a child of God, she might take the children's portion," and, as she had given to God these ninety pounds, she might receive five pounds back again. She told me that she considered the brethren had shown her from the Holy Scriptures what she might do, and therefore she had taken these five pounds. I did not myself agree with the judgment of those brethren who had said this (as there is no evidence that Barnabas ever was supported out of the common stock, the proceeds of the sale of houses and lands, out of which the poor widow, lest she should at once be induced to give me these five pounds also. She had, however, these five pounds untouched, and showed them to me; and before she left she would make me take one pound for the benefit of the orphans, which I did not refuse, as I had no intention of keeping the eighty-five pounds. She also gave me a sixpence for the orphans, which some one had given her for herself, a few days before.

I now asked her, as this matter concerning the retaining of the five pounds was satisfactorily explained, as far as it respected her own state of heart, what she wished me to do with the money, in case I saw it right to keep it. Her reply was that she would leave that with me, that God would direct me concerning it; but that, if she said anything at all about it, she should most like it to be used for the support of brethren who labor in the word without any salary, and who hazard their lives for the name of Christ. She wished *me* to have a part of the money; but this I flatly refused, lest I should be evil spoken of in this matter. I then offered to pay her travelling expenses, as she had come to me, which she would not accept, as she did not stand in need of it. In conclusion, I told her that I would now further pray respecting this matter, and consider what to do concerning it. I then prayed with this dear, godly woman, commended her to God, separated from her, and have not seen her since.

I waited from Aug. 9, 1853, to March 7, 1854, when I wrote to her offering her back again the whole eighty-five pounds, or a part of it. On March 9, 1854, just seven months after I received the money, and just nine months after she had actually given it, and ten years and nine months after she had made the resolution to give her house and garden to God, I heard from her stating that she was of the same mind as she had been for years. I therefore disposed of the money, to aid such foreign missionary brethren as, according to the best of my knowledge, resembled most the class of men whom she wished to assist.

The reasons why I have so minutely dwelt upon this circumstance are: 1. If, as a steward of the bounties of the children of God, I should be blamed for receiving from a poor widow almost literally her all, it may be seen in what manner I did so. To have refused on March 9, 1854, also, would be going beyond what I should be warranted to do. 2. I desired, also, to give a practical illustration that I only desire donations in God's way. It is not the money only I desire; but the money received in answer to prayer, in God's order. 3. This circumstance illustrates how God helps me often in the most unexpected manner. 4. I have also related this instance that there may be a fresh proof that even in these last days the love of Christ is of constraining power, and may work mightily, as in the days of the apostles. I have witnessed *many* such instances as this, in the twenty years during which I have been occupied in this my service. Let us give thanks to God for such cases, and let us seek for grace rather to imitate such godly men and women, than think that they are going too far.

I cannot, however, dismiss this subject, without commending this poor widow to the prayers of all who love our Lord Jesus, that she may be kept humble, lest, thinking highly of herself, on account of what she has been able to do, by the grace of God, she should not only lose blessing in her own soul, but this circumstance should become a snare to her. Pray also, believing reader, that she may never be allowed to regret what she has done for the Lord.

After giving in detail the sources and manner of supply for the maintenance of the orphans during twenty-four days, Mr. M. adds: —

The particular end why I have been so minute, is, *to show*

that the work is now, as much as ever, a work carried on entirely in dependence upon the living God, who alone is our hope, to whom alone we look for help, and who never has forsaken us in the hour of need. There is, however, one thing different with reference to this year, when compared with former years, and that is, that, while our trials of faith during this year were just as great as in previous years, the amount needed in former times was never so great as during this year, especially as the bread during the greater part of this year was about twice as dear as for several years before.

But then, it may be said, If you have had this trial of faith, with these three hundred orphans, why do you seek to build another Orphan House for seven hundred more, and thus have a thousand to care for? Will you not have still greater trials of faith?

My reply is: 1. God has never failed me all the twenty years of this my service. 2. I am going on as easily now, with three hundred orphans, as with thirty, the number with which I commenced. Their number is ten times as large as it was at the first; but God has always helped me. 3. Trials of faith were anticipated, yea, were one chief end of the work, for the profit of the church of Christ at large. 4. I had courage given me to go forward, solely in dependence upon God, being assured that he would help me; yet I waited in secret upon him for six months before I made this my intention known, in order that I might not take a hasty step; and I have never regretted my having gone forward. 5. But it needs to be added that the very abundance which the Lord gave me at the time, when my mind was exercised about this matter, was a great confirmation to me that I had not mistaken his mind. And even during this year, how great has been his help; for the income for the work altogether has been twelve thousand seven hundred and eighty-five pounds fifteen shillings sevenpence halfpenny. I am, therefore, assured that the Lord will, in his own time, not only allow me to build another Orphan House, but that he will also, when he shall have been pleased to fill it, find the means to provide for these children.

During this year four day schools, with 202 children, were *entirely supported* by the funds of the Institution. Further, one Sunday school in Bristol, with 137 children, was *entirely supported*, and three others in Devonshire, Somersetshire, Gloucestershire, with 300 children, were *assisted*. Lastly, one adult school, with 154 adult scholars, was *entirely* supported. The total amount which was spent during this year in connection with these schools was £359, 15s. 10½d. The number of all the children who were under our care merely in the schools which were *entirely* supported by this Institution, from March 5, 1834, to May 26, 1854, was 5,817 in the day schools, 2,748 in the Sunday schools, and 2,315 persons in the adult school.

During this year were expended on the circulation of the Holy Scriptures, of the funds of the Institution, £433, 2s. 9d. There were circulated during this year 1,890 Bibles and 1,288 New Testaments; and from the commencement of the work up to May 26, 1854, 12,366 Bibles and 7,349 Testaments.

During this year there was spent of the **funds of the Institution**, for missionary objects, the sum of £2,249, 10s 8½d. By this sum fifty-six laborers in the word and doctrine, in various parts of the world, were to a greater or less degree assisted.

During this year the Lord was pleased to bless again abundantly the labors of many of those servants of Christ who were assisted through the funds of this Institution, and this has been the case in foreign countries as well as at home.

There was laid out for the circulation of tracts, from May 26, 1853, to May 26, 1854, the sum of £563, 5s. 0½d ; and there were circulated 869,636 tracts.

The total number of all the tracts which were circulated from the beginning up to May 26, 1854, was 2,689,676.

We desire to be grateful to the Lord that during no period previously we were enabled to circulate more tracts, and more copies of the Holy Scriptures, and to aid to a greater degree missionary labors, than during this period; yet we would not rest in that. It is the blessing of the Lord upon our labors which we need, which we desire, and

If any of the Christian readers are in the habit of circulating tracts, and yet have never seen fruit, may I suggest to them the following hints for their prayerful consideration. 1. Seek for such a state of heart, through prayer and meditation on the Holy Scriptures, as that you are willing to let God have all the honor, if any good is accomplished by your service. If you desire for yourself the honor, yea, though it were in part only, you oblige the Lord, so to speak, to put you as yet aside as a vessel not meet for the Master's use. One of the greatest qualifications for usefulness in the service of the Lord is a heart truly desirous of getting honor for him. 2. Precede all your labors with earnest, diligent prayer; go to them in a prayerful spirit; and follow them by prayer. Do not rest on the number of tracts you have given. A million of tracts may not be the means of converting one single soul; and yet how great, beyond calculation, may be the blessing which results from one single tract. Thus it is also with regard to the circulation of the Holy Scriptures, and the ministry of the word itself. Expect, then, everything from the blessing of the Lord, and nothing at all from your own exertions. 3. And yet, at the same time, labor, press into every open door, be instant in season and out of season, as if everything depended upon your labors. This, as has been stated before, is one of the great secrets in connection with successful service for the Lord: to work, as if everything depended upon our diligence, and yet not to rest in the least upon our exertions, but upon the blessing of the Lord. 4. This blessing of the Lord, however, should not merely be sought in prayer, but it should also be *expected, looked for, continually looked for;* and the result will be that we shall surely have it. 5. But suppose that, for the trial of our faith, this blessing were for a long time withheld from our sight; or suppose, even, that we should have to fall asleep before we see much good resulting from our labors; yet will our labors, if carried on in such a way and spirit as has been stated, be at last abundantly owned, and we shall have a rich harvest in the day of Christ.

At the beginning of this period there were 300 orphans in the new Orphan House on Ashley Down, Bristol. During the year there were admitted into it 30 orphans, making 330 in all. The total number of orphans who were under our care from April, 1836, to May 26, 1854, was 558.

The expenses during this year for the support of the orphans were £3,897, 2s. 0½.

Without any one having been personally applied to for anything by me, the sum of £64,591, 6s. 11¼d. was given to me for the orphans, *as the result of prayer to God*, from the commencement of the work up to May 26, 1854. It may be also interesting to the reader to know that the total amount which was given for the other objects, from the commencement of the work up to May 26 1854, amounted to £22,268, 2s 11¼d ; and that which came in by the sale of Bibles and tracts, and by the payments of the children in the day schools, from the commencement up to May 26, 1854, amounted to £3,989, 4s. 5¾d.

Our labors continued to be blessed among the orphans. We saw also again fruit of our labors, during this year, with regard to orphans who formerly were under our care.

In July, 1853, it pleased the Lord to try my faith in a way in which before it had not been tried. My beloved daughter, an only child, and a believer since the commencement of the year 1846, was taken ill on June 20. This illness, at first a low fever, turned to typhus. On July 3 there seemed no hope of her recovery. Now was the trial of faith. But faith triumphed. My beloved wife and I were enabled to give her up into the hands of the Lord. He sustained us both exceedingly. But I will only speak about myself. Though my only and beloved child was brought near the grave, yet was my soul in perfect peace, satisfied with the will of my heavenly Father, being assured that he would only do that for her and her parents which in the end would be the best.

She continued very ill till about July 20, when restoration began. On Aug. 18 she was so far restored that she could be removed to Clevedon, for change of air, though exceedingly weak. It was then fifty-nine days since she was first taken ill.

While I was in this affliction, this great affliction, besides being at peace, as far as the Lord's dispensation was concerned, I also felt perfectly at peace with regard to the cause of the affliction. When in August, 1831, the hand of the Lord was heavily laid on me in my family, as related in the first part of this Narrative, I had not the least hesitation in knowing that it was the Father's rod, applied in infinite wisdom and love for the restoration of my soul from a state of lukewarmness. At this time, however, I had no such feeling. Conscious as I was of my manifold weaknesses, failings, and shortcomings, so that I too would be ready to say with the Apostle Paul, "O wretched man that I am!" yet I was assured that this affliction was not upon me in the way of the fatherly rod, but for the trial of my faith. Persons often have, no doubt, the idea respecting me, that all my trials of faith regard matters connected with money, though the reverse has been stated by me very frequently; now, however, the Lord would try my faith concerning one of my dearest earthly treasures, yea, next to my beloved wife, the dearest of all my earthly possessions. Parents know what an only child, a beloved child, is, and what to believing parents an only child, a believing child, must be. Well, the Father in heaven said, as it were, by this his dispensation, Art thou willing to give up this child to me? My heart responded, As it seems good to thee, my heavenly Father. Thy will be done. But as our hearts were made willing to give back our beloved child to him who had given her to us, so he was ready to leave her to us, and she lived. "Delight thyself also in the Lord; and he shall give thee the desires of thine heart." Psalm xxxvii. 4. The desires of my heart were, to retain the beloved daughter, if it were the will of God; the means to return her were, to be satisfied with the will of the Lord.

Of all the trials of faith that as yet I have had to pass through, this was the greatest; and, by God's abundant mercy, I own it to his praise, I was enabled to delight my self in the will of God; for I felt perfectly sure that if the Lord took this beloved daughter, it would be best for her parents, best for herself, and more for the glory of God than if she lived: this better part I was satisfied with; and thus my heart had peace, perfect peace, and I had not a moment's anxiety. Thus would it be under all circumstances, however painful, were the believer exercising faith.

Dec. 31, 1853. During this year the Lord was pleased to give me £638, 11s. 8½d

CHAPTER XXIII.

THREE YEARS OF PROSPERITY.

1854 — 1857.

THE SITE SELECTED — SIX THOUSAND ORPHANS IN PRISON — HOW TO ASK FOR DAILY BREAD — REVIEW OF TWENTY-FOUR YEARS — "TAKE NO THOUGHT FOR THE MORROW" — INSURANCE AGAINST BAD DEBTS.

DURING the year ending May 26, 1855, Mr. M. received toward the erection of the second new Orphan House five thousand two hundred and forty-two pounds eighteen shillings threepence, and the whole sum on hand for this object amounted to twenty-three thousand and fifty-nine pounds seventeen shillings eightpence one farthing. After recording the amount thus obtained, he adds: —

I judged that, though I had not such an amount of means in hand as I considered necessary before being warranted to begin to build, yet that I might make inquiries respecting land. Accordingly, I applied in the beginning of February for the purchase of two fields which join the land on which the new Orphan House is built. On these two fields I had had my eye for years, and had purposed to endeavor to purchase them whenever I might be in such a position, as to means for the building fund, that it would be suitable to do so. I found, however, that, according to the will of the late owner of these fields, they could not be sold *now*. Thus my prospects were blighted. When I obtained this information, though *naturally* tried by it and disappointed, I said, by *God's grace* to myself, " The Lord has something better to give me, instead of these two fields;" and thus my heart was kept in peace. But when now the matter was fully decided that I could not obtain those fields, which had appeared to me so desirable for the object, the question arose, what I was to do for the obtaining of land. Under these circumstances some of my Christian friends again asked, as they had done before, why I did not build on the ground which we have around the new Orphan House. My reply was, as before, that it could not be done: 1. Because it would throw the new Orphan House for nearly two years into disorder, on account of the building going on round about it. 2. There would not be sufficient room without shutting in the present house to a great extent. 3. That, as the new Orphan House stands in the centre of our ground, there would not be sufficient room on any of the sides for the erection of a building so large as would be required. I was, however, led to consider whether there was any way whereby we could accomplish the building on the ground belonging to the new Orphan House. In doing so, I found that, — 1. By having a high temporary boundary made of old boards, the building ground could be entirely distinct from the present establishment. 2. By building on an entirely different plan from that of the present house, we should not only have room enough; but that, also, 3. The present house would not be so inclosed that the health of the inmates of the establishment would thereby be injured.

But there was in connection with this another point which now came under consideration in addition to the particulars already mentioned: it was this. Though for four years past I had never had a doubt as to its being the will of God that I should build accommodation for seven hundred more orphans; yet, at the same time, I had for a long time seen the desirableness of having two houses instead of one, for the seven hundred orphans. This previously formed judgment of having two houses for three

THE SECOND ORPHAN HOUSE, ASHLEY DOWN.

hundred and fifty orphans in each, or four hundred in the one, and three hundred in the other, led me now to see whether there could be another house built on each side of the present new Orphan House; and I judged, from measuring the ground, that there was no objection to this plan. I then called in the aid of architects, to survey the ground and to make a rough plan of two houses, one on each side, and it was found that it could be accomplished. Having arrived thus far, I soon saw that we should not only save expense by this plan in various ways, but especially that thus the direction and inspection of the whole establishment would be much more easy and simple, as the buildings would be so near together. This, indeed, on being further considered, soon appeared to be a matter of such importance, that if even land could be had but a quarter of a mile off, the difficulties would be greatly increased thereby. At the same time I found that we still should retain so much land for cultivation by the spade as would furnish some out-door employment for many boys, and would produce such kind of vegetables as are the most important for young children, to be had fresh out of the ground; or that we could easily *rent* a piece of ground near for that purpose, though it could not be *bought*.

The result, then, to which I have arrived at present is this: that having seen what could be accomplished on the ground which we have already, I decided to build, without any further delay than was necessary for preparing the plans, at the south side of the new Orphan House, another house for four hundred children. The plans are now ready, and in a very short time, God willing, *i. e.*, as soon as all the necessary preliminary arrangements can be made, the building will commence, which I think will be in the early part of July of the present year (*i. e.*, 1855).

This house is intended for four hundred female orphans, bereaved of both parents, from their *earliest* days until they can be placed out in service. With regard to the other house for three hundred orphans, to be built at the north side of the new Orphan House, nothing definitely can be stated at present. There is enough money in hand to build, fit up, and furnish the house for four hundred orphans, and it is expected that something will be left; but there is not sufficient money in hand, at present, to warrant the commencement of the building of both. As soon, however, as there is, I shall be delighted to take active measures with regard to that for three hundred orphans also. I do not ask persons to help me with their means. I speak to the Lord about my need in prayer, and I do not wait upon him in vain. At the same time I feel it right to state that there is a loud and an abundant call for caring for destitute orphans. On May 26, 1854, I had six hundred and two waiting for admission, each bereaved of both parents by death. Since then, one hundred and ninety-seven more have been applied for, making in all, seven hundred and ninety-nine. Of these I have been able to receive only thirty-nine during the past year, and forty-five who were waiting for admission have been otherwise provided for, or have died since application was made for them; so that still seven hundred and fifteen orphans are waiting for admission, from three months old and upward. But this number, I state unhesitatingly, would be much larger, had not very many persons refrained from making application because they judged it would be of no use, as there are already so many waiting for admission. Indeed, there is every reason to believe that there are many tens of thousands of destitute orphans in this country. And what provision is there in the way of orphan establishments, it may be asked. At the last census, in 1851, there were in England and Wales thirty-nine orphan establishments, and the total number of orphans, provided for through them, amounted only to three thousand seven hundred and sixty-four; but at the time the new Orphan House was being built there were about six thousand young orphans in the prisons of England. To prevent their going to prison, to prevent their being brought up in sin and vice, yea, to be the honored instrument to win their souls for God, I desire, by his help, to enlarge the present establishment so as to be able to receive one thousand orphans; and individuals who have purposed not to live for time but for eternity, and to look on their means as in the light of eternity, will thus have an opportunity of helping me to care for these children. It is a great honor to be allowed to do anything for the Lord; therefore, I do not press this matter. We can only give to him of his own; for all we have is his. When the day of recompense comes, the regret will only be that we have done so little for him, not that we have done too much.

During the year from May, 1854, to May, 1855, ample means were provided, in answer to prayer only, for the maintenance of the orphans, and for the various purposes of the Scriptural Knowledge Institution. The following statement exhibits the results of Mr. Müller's labors during the year under review: —

During this year four day schools in Bristol, with 184 children in them, were *entirely supported* by the funds of the Institution; and several other day schools in Devonshire, Cornwall. Suffolk, Ireland, and Scotland, were *assisted* with copies of the Holy Scriptures. Further, one Sunday school in Bristol, with 158 children, was *entirely supported*, and seven others in Cornwall, Devonshire, Somersetshire, and Gloucestershire, with about 400 children in them, were *assisted*. Lastly, one adult school, with 133 adults, was entirely supported during this year. The amount expended during this year, on these various schools, was £338, 2s. 5d.

In connection with all these various schools, I would suggest the following important matter for prayer. From March, 1834, to May 26, 1855, there were 5,936 children in the day schools. In the adult schools there were 2,459 persons. The number of the Sunday-school children amounted to 2,817. Thus, without reckoning the orphans, 11,232 souls were brought under *habitual* instruction in the things of God in these various schools; besides the many thousands in the schools in various parts of England, Ireland, Scotland, British Guiana, the West Indies, the East Indies, etc., which were to a greater or less degree assisted.

The total sum which was expended during the twenty-one years, from March 5, 1834, to May 26, 1855, in connection with the schools, which were either entirely or in part supported by the funds of this Institution, amounted to £7,204, 12s. 8¼d.

The number of Bibles, New Testaments, and portions of the Holy Scriptures, which were circulated from May 26, 1854, to May 26, 1855, is as follows : —

Bibles sold, 693. Bibles given away, 890. Testaments sold, 950. Testaments given away, 748. Copies of the Psalms sold, 82. Other small portions of the Holy Scriptures sold, 136.

There were circulated from March 5, 1834, to May 26, 1855, through the medium of this Institution, 13,949 Bibles, 9,047 New Testaments, 188 copies of the Psalms, and 789 other small portions of the Holy Scriptures.

The total amount of the funds of this Institution spent on the circulation of the Holy Scriptures from March 5, 1834, to May 26, 1855, is £3,389, 10s. 1d. The amount spent during this year, £476, 12s. 3d.

During this year there was spent of the funds of the Institution, for missionary objects, the sum of £2,081, 3s. 2d. By this sum fifty-seven laborers in the word and doctrine, in various parts of the world, were to a greater or less degree assisted.

The total amount of the funds of the Institution spent on missionary operations, from March 5, 1834, to May 26, 1855, was £16,115, 0s. 5½d.

There was laid out for tracts, from May 26, 1854, to May 26, 1855, the sum of £624, 8s. 4d ; and there were circulated within this year 895,034 tracts and books.

The total number of all the tracts and books which were circulated from the beginning up to May 26, 1855, was 3,584,710.

The total amount of means expended on this object, from Nov. 19, 1840, to May 26, 1855, was £2,868, 15s. 6¾d.,

At the commencement of this period there were 298 orphans in the new Orphan House on Ashley Down, Bristol. During the year there were admitted into it 39 orphans.

The expenses for the orphans during this year were £4,304, 4s. 7½d.

Without any one having been personally applied to for anything by me, the sum of £74,132, 6s. 10¾d. was given to me for the orphans, *is the result of prayer to God*, from the commencement of the work up to May 26, 1855, which sum includes the £15,055, 3s. 2¼d., which was the cost of the building, fitting up and furnishing of the present new Orphan House, and the £23,059, 17s. 8¼d., which was in hand on the 26th May, 1855, for the building fund, and the £116, 17s. 8½d., the balance for the current expenses. It may also be interesting to the reader to know that the total sum which was given for the other objects, from the commencement of the work up to May 26, 1855, amounted to £25,239, 8s. 10¾d. and that which came in by the sale of Bibles and tracts, and by the payments of the children in the day schools, from the commencement, amounted to £4,531, 12s. 10¾d. Besides this also a great variety and number of articles of clothing, furniture, provisions, etc., were given *for the use* of the orphans.

I have the joy of being able to state that we have great cause for thankfulness in that in the midst of many difficulties our labors among the orphans continue to be blessed, and that especially again and again instances now come before us in which those who were formerly under our care declare themselves on the Lord's side.

Besides being able to meet the expenses for the orphans and the other objects, amounting altogether to £7,832, 7s. 0½d., during this year I was able to add to the building fund £5,242, 18s. 3d. The total income during the year was £13,054, 14s. 4d.

Dec. 31, 1854. During this year there have been received into fellowship 61.

The Lord has been pleased to give me during this year £697, 11s. 5d.

One or the other of my readers may be ready to exclaim, six hundred and ninety-seven pounds eleven shillings fivepence! What a large sum! Not one out of a hundred ministers has such a large salary, nor one out of twenty clergymen such a good living! Should you, esteemed reader, say so, my reply is: Indeed, mine is a happy way for the obtaining of my temporal supplies; but if any one desires to go this way, he must,—

1. Not *merely say* that he trusts in God, but must *really do so*. Often individuals profess to trust in God, but they embrace every opportunity where they may directly or indirectly be able to expose their need, and thus seek to induce persons to help them. I do not say it is wrong to make known our wants; but I do say it ill agrees with **trust in God to expose our wants for the sake of inducing**

persons to help us. God will take us at our word. If we say we trust in him, he will try whether we *really* do so, or only *profess* to do so; and if *indeed* we trust in him, we are satisfied to stand with him alone.

2. The individual who desires to go this way must be willing to be rich or poor, as the Lord pleases. He must be willing to know what it is to have an abundance or scarcely anything. He must be willing to leave this world without any possessions.

3. He must be willing to take the money in God's way. not merely in large sums, but in small. Again and again have I had a single shilling given or sent to me. To have refused such tokens of Christian love would have been ungracious.

4. He must be willing to live as the Lord's steward. If any one were to begin this way of living, and did not communicate out of that which the Lord gives to him, but hoard it up, or if he would live up to his income, as it is called, then the Lord, who influences the hearts of his children to help him with means, would soon cause those channels to be dried up. How it came that my already good income still more increased so as to come to what it is, I have stated in the early part of this volume; it was when I determined that, by God's help. *his* poor and *his* work should more than ever partake of my means. From that time the Lord was pleased more and more to intrust me with means for my own purse.

Various reasons might have kept me from publishing these accounts; but I have for my object in writing the glory of God, and therefore I delight in thus showing what a loving Master I serve, and how bountifully he supplies my necessities; and I write for the comfort and encouragement of my fellow-believers, that they may be led to trust in God more and more, and therefore I feel it due to them to state how, even with regard to this life, I am amply provided for, though that is not what I seek after.

Up to May 26, 1856, the total income for the building fund was £29,297, 18s. 11½d., so that only about £5,700 more will be required, as far as I am able to see, in order to accomplish to the full my purpose respecting the accommodation for 700 more orphans.

During the year 1855–1856, the wants of the orphans, as well as the demands of the missionary, Bible, tract, and school work, were supplied more amply than ever before, and a blessing rested upon all these departments of labor, as will appear from the following statement: —

During this year four day schools, with 203 children, were *entirely supported* by the funds of the Institution; and nine day schools were assisted with copies of the Holy Scriptures. Further, one Sunday school, with 158 children, was *entirely supported*, and eight others were *assisted*. Lastly, one adult school, with 158 adult scholars, was *entirely supported*, and two other adult schools, in Kent and Norfolk, were *assisted* with books. The amount which was spent during this year, in connection with these schools, was £348, 5s 11¼d.; and the sum total expended during the last twenty-two years, in connection with the schools which were either entirely or in part supported by the funds of this Institution, amounts to £7,552, 18s. 7½d. The number of all the children who were under our care, merely in the schools which were *entirely* supported by this Institution, from March 5, 1834, to May 26, 1856, was 6,104 in the day schools, 2,911 in the Sunday schools, and 2,611 persons in the adult school. Thus, without reckoning the orphans, 11,626 have been brought under habitual instruction in the things of God in these various schools; besides the many thousands in the schools in various parts of England, Ireland, Scotland, British Guiana, the East Indies, etc., which have been to a greater or less degree assisted.

During this year were expended on the circulation of the Holy Scriptures, of the funds of this Institution, £496, 10s. There were circulated during this year 2,175 Bibles, 1,233 New Testaments, 119 copies of the Psalms, and 155 other small portions of the Holy Scriptures. There have been circulated since March 5, 1834, through the medium of this Institution, 16,124 Bibles, 10,280 New Testaments, 307 copies of the Psalms, and 944 other small portions of the Holy

Scriptures. The sum total spent on the circulation of the Holy Scriptures, since March 5, 1834, is £3,886, 0s. 1d.

During this year there were spent, of the funds of the Institution, for missionary objects, £2,501, 9s. 1d. By this sum sixty-one laborers in the word and doctrine, in various parts of the world, were to a greater or less degree assisted.

The sum total which has been expended on missionary operations, of the funds of the Institution, since March 5, 1834, is £18,616, 9s 6½d.

There was laid out for the circulation of tracts, from May 26, 1855, to May 26, 1856, the sum of £791, 1s. 0½d., and there were circulated 812,970 tracts and books. The sum total which has been expended on this object since Nov. 19, 1840, amounts to £3,659, 16s. 7¼d. The total number of all the tracts and books which have been circulated since Nov. 19, 1840, is 4,397,680.

At the beginning of this period there were 297 orphans in the new Orphan House. During the past year there have been admitted into it 25 orphans. The total number of orphans who have been under our care since April, 1836, is 622.

Without any one having been personally applied to for anything by me, the sum of £84,441, 6s. 3¼d. has been given to me for the orphans *as the result of prayer to God* since the commencement of the work, which sum includes the £15,055, 3s. 2¼d which was the cost of the building, fitting up, and furnishing of the present new Orphan House, and the £29,297, 18s. 11½d. received up to May 26, 1856, for the building fund, and the £167, 18s 11¾d., the balance of the current expenses. The total sum which has been given for the other objects since the commencement of the work amounts to £28,904, 11s. 3¾d ; and that which has come in by the sale of Bibles and tracts, and by the payments of the children in the day schools, from the commencement up to May 26, 1856, amounts to £5,145, 17s.

Dec. 31, 1855. During this year the Lord has been pleased to give me £726, 16s. 2¼d.

May 26, 1856. Yesterday evening it was twenty-four years since I came to labor in Bristol. In looking back upon this period, as it regards the Lord's goodness to my family and myself, the Scriptural Knowledge Institution, and the saints among whom I seek to serve him, I exclaim, What has God wrought! I marvel at his kindness, and yet I do not; for such is his manner; and, if it please him that I remain longer on earth, I expect, not fewer manifestations of his love, but more and more.

Since my beloved friend and fellow-laborer and I first came to Bristol, 1,586 believers have been received into fellowship, which number, with the 68 we found in communion, makes 1,654. But out of that number 252 have fallen asleep, 53 have been separated from fellowship, 145 have left us, some, however, merely through circumstances and in love, and 510 have left Bristol; so that there are only 694 remaining in communion.

By the contributions received during the year 1856-7, the whole amount on hand for the new buildings was raised to thirty-one thousand eight hundred seventeen pounds one shilling and elevenpence. For the Bible, tract, and missionary work, and for schools, Mr. M. had the pleasure of receiving and of expending eight hundred and twenty-nine pounds more than in the previous year. For the support of the orphans all means were so abundantly provided that at the end of the year there was on hand a balance of one thousand four hundred and eighty-nine pounds.

The following incident illustrates the author's reliance upon God for his own future support.

On Oct. 12, 1856, was sent to me a check for one hundred pounds, with the request of the donor to receive this for myself, as the beginning of raising a fund for my support when advanced in years, and for that of my family. This very kind and well-intended proposal by the donor, who since has died, appeared to me as a subtle temptation laid for me, though far from being intended so by him, to depart from the principles on which I had been acting for twenty-six years previously, both regarding myself and the orphan work. I give the account of this circumstance fully, as it may be profitable to one or other of the readers.

**** Oct. 11, 1856.

DEAR SIR —

In admiration of the services which you have rendered to poor orphans and mankind in general, I think it right that some provision should be made for yourself. I think it right to send you one hundred pounds, as a beginning to form a fund, which I hope many good Christians will add to, * * * * for the maintenance of you and your family, if your own labors should be unequal to it, and I hope you will lay out this as a beginning accordingly. May God bless you and your labors, as he has hitherto done everything connected with your Institutions.

I am, dear sir,

* * * *

By God's grace I had not a moment's hesitation as to what to do. While I most fully appreciated the great kindness of the donor, I looked upon this as being permitted by God as a temptation to put my trust in something else than himself, and I therefore sent the following letter in reply : —

BRISTOL, Oct. 12, 1856.

MY DEAR SIR : —

I hasten to thank you for your kind communication, and to inform you that your check for one hundred pounds has safely come to hand.

I have no property whatever, nor has my dear wife; nor have I had one single shilling regular salary as minister of the gospel for the last twenty-six years, nor as the director of the Orphan House and the other objects of the Scriptural Knowledge Institution for Home and Abroad. When I am in need of anything, I fall on my knees, and ask God that he would be pleased to give me what I need; and he puts it into the heart of some one or other to help me. Thus all my wants have been amply supplied during the last twenty-six years, and I can say, to the praise of God, I have lacked nothing. My dear wife and my only child, a daughter of twenty-four years, are of the same mind with me. Of this blessed way of living none of us are tired, but become day by day more convinced of its blessedness.

I have never thought it right to make provision for myself, or my dear wife and daughter, except in this way, that when I saw a case of need, such as an aged widow, or a sick person, or a helpless infant, I would use my means freely which God had given me, fully believing that if either myself, or my dear wife or daughter, at some time or other, should be in need of anything, God would richly repay what was given to the poor, considering it as lent to himself.

Under these circumstances I am unable to accept your kindness of the gift of one hundred pounds *towards making a provision for myself and family;* for so I understand your letter. Any gift given to me, unasked for, by those who have it in their heart to help me to supply my personal and family expenses, I thankfully accept; or any donation given to me for the work of God in which I am engaged, I also thankfully accept, as a steward for the orphans, etc.; but your kind gift seems to me especially given to *make a provision for myself,* which I think would be displeasing to my heavenly Father, who has so bountifully given me my daily bread hitherto. But should I have misunderstood the meaning of your letter, be pleased to let me know it. I hold the check till I hear again from you.

In the mean time, my dear sir, however you meant your letter, I am deeply sensible of your kindness, and daily pray that God would be pleased richly to recompense you for it, both temporally and spiritually.

I am, dear sir,

Yours very gratefully,
GEORGE MULLER.

Two days after I received a reply, in which the donor desired me to use the one hundred pounds for the support of the orphans, for which object I gladly accepted this sum. The day after that I received another one hundred pounds from the same donor, and four days after that one hundred pounds more, all for the support of the orphans, and all from an individual whom I have never seen.

In the following words is contained a useful lesson to persons engaged in business: —

Feb. 24, 1857. Received five pounds as a thank-offering to the Lord for preservation from making bad debts the past year. Has it ever occurred to the reader that the Lord only can preserve any one engaged in business from making bad debts? Has it also occurred to the reader that often the Lord is obliged, because we do not use for him, as good stewards, that with which he has been pleased to intrust us, to allow bad debts to be made? Consider these things, dear Christian reader, you who are engaged in business. If you were engaged in mercantile affairs, connected with hundreds of thousands of pounds, you may, by the help of God, be preserved year after year from making bad debts, though several millions of pounds should be turned in the course of a few years, provided you keep before you that you are the Lord's steward, and carry on business for him; whilst, on the other hand, thousands of pounds may be lost in one single year, out of only a comparatively small business, because he who carries it on " withholds more than is meet, and therefore it tends to poverty," the Lord being obliged by bad debts (as they are called), which he uses as one of his rods, to deprive his servants of that which was not used aright.

The review of the year ending May, 1857, presents us with the following results: —

There have been during this period four day schools *entirely supported* by the funds of this Institution. There are at present in these four day schools 181 children.

In addition to the entire support of these four day schools, six schools were assisted with money, or books, or copies of the Holy Scriptures, or both money and books.

There was one Sunday school, in which there were 175 children, *entirely supported* by the funds of this Institution; and six others were *assisted*

There has been, since the formation of the Institution, one adult school connected with it, the expenses of which have been *entirely* borne by the Institution, and in which, since March 5, 1834, altogether 2,699 adults have been instructed. The number at present on the books is 72.

There were also two other adult schools *assisted* during the past year.

The total amount of means which has been expended during the last twenty-three years in connection with the schools, which have been either entirely or in part supported by the funds of this Institution, amounts to £7,938, 13s. 4d.

The number of Bibles, Testaments, and portions of the Holy Scriptures, which have been circulated since May 26, 1856, is as follows: —

Bibles sold, 601. Bibles given away, 1,476. Testaments sold, 829. Testaments given away, 393. Copies of the Psalms sold, 151. Other small portions of the Holy Scriptures sold, 316.

There have been circulated since March 5, 1834, through the medium of this Institution, 18,201 Bibles, 11,502 Testaments, 458 copies of the Psalms, and 1,260 other small portions of the Holy Scriptures.

The total amount of the funds of this Institution spent on the circulation of the Holy Scriptures, since March 5, 1834, is £4,407, 7s. 2½d. The amount spent during the past year, £521, 7s. 1½d.

Some time since a brother in the Lord wrote to me that he had it in his heart to visit from house to house, in a large manufacturing town in Yorkshire, and, if possible, to supply each house with a tract, and to seek out persons who were destitute of copies of the Holy Scriptures. I supplied him, therefore, with 10,000 gospel tracts and 30 Bibles, and subsequently with 127 more Bibles, and finally with 10,000 more tracts and 74 Bibles.

The third object of this Institution is, to aid missionary efforts.

During the past year has been spent of the funds of the Institution for this object, the sum of £3,177, 17s. 11½d. By this sum seventy four laborers in the word and doctrine, in various parts of the world, have been to a greater or less degree assisted.

The year before last I had been enabled to spend on this part of the work more than during any previous year; but the last year I was, by God's help, enabled not only to disburse for this object as much as during the previous year, but £676, 8s. 10½d. more. For this privilege I feel grateful; yet I long to be permitted by the Lord to do much more still. But whilst it has been a source of joy to me to be able to assist seventy-four servants of Christ in many parts of the world, that which was far more than this a cause of thankfulness, was, that almost week by week, and often repeatedly in the same week, I had refreshing intelligence from the brethren whom I sought to help.

The letters of these brethren exhibit the fact that the aid conveyed through Mr. M. was most timely, coming often in the hour of sore need. They also give assurance that their labors had been singularly blessed to the conversion of the heathen, and of the ignorant and deluded among whom they preached.

The total amount of the funds of the Institution which has been spent on missionary operations, since March 5, 1834, is £21,794, 7s. 6d.

There has been laid out for tracts, from May 26, 1856, to May 26, 1857, the sum of £975, 18s. 7½d ; and there have been circulated within the last year 1,313,301 tracts and books. The sum total which has been expended on this object, since Nov. 19, 1840, amounts to £4,635, 15s. 2¾d

The total number of all the tracts and books which have been circulated since Nov. 19, 1840, is 5,710,981.

Letters from those to whom tracts were sent for distribution, convey the intelligence that in very many instances the tracts were blessed to the conversion of sinners.

At the commencement of the last period there were 299 orphans in the new Orphan House on Ashley Down, Bristol. During the past year there were admitted into it 30 orphans, making 329 in all. When the last Report was published, there were 847 orphans waiting for admission. Since then 231 more destitute orphans, bereaved of both parents by death, and some only a few weeks old, have been applied for to be admitted, making 1,078 in all. Of these 1,078 we were only able to receive 30, as has been stated, and 58 either died or were otherwise provided for, as their relatives or friends have informed us so that there are still 990 waiting for admission. Christian reader, think of these 990 destitute orphans, bereaved of both parents! I have now, however, before me the most pleasant prospect, if the Lord permit, of being able to receive 400 of them in about three months, and also of being permitted to build the third house for 300 more.

Without any one having been personally applied to for anything by me, the sum of £92,175, 4s 2½d has been given to me for the orphans, *as the result of prayer to God,* since the commencement of the work, which sum includes the £15,055, 3s. 2¼d. which was the cost of the building, fitting up, and furnishing of the present new Orphan House, and the £31,817, 1s. 11d., which had been received up to May 26, 1857, for the building fund, and the £1,489, 7s. 9d , the balance of the current expenses. It may also be interesting to the reader to know that the total amount which has been given for the other objects, since the commencement of the work, amounts to £33,293, 9s. 10¼d.; and that which has come in by the sale of Bibles, since the commencement, amounts to £2,080, 9s. 10½d.; by sale of tracts, £1,778, 2s. 5d.; and by the payments of the children in the day schools, from the commencement. £2,066, 13s. 4½d.

The Lord is pleased to continue to allow us to see fruit in connection with the orphan work, with reference to those who are *now* under our care, and we hear still again and again of cases in which those who were *formerly* under our care have been led to declare themselves openly for the Lord, besides those in whom we saw the work of grace manifestly begun before they left the **Orphan House.**

CHAPTER XXIV.

SUMMARY.

1857 — 1860.

THE HOUSE FOR FOUR HUNDRED OPENED — PRAYER MORE THAN ANSWERED — THE RESORT IN TROUBLE — AN OUTPOURING OF THE SPIRIT ON THE ORPHANS — LAND FOR A NEW BUILDING PURCHASED — "BUT ONE LIFE TO SPEND FOR GOD" — SCATTERING, YET INCREASING" — A MEMORABLE YEAR — THE GERM OF THE IRISH REVIVAL — LETTER FROM AN ORPHAN — THE FRUIT OF SIX MONTHS' PRAYER — THE RESULTS OF THE WORK — REVIVAL AMONG THE ORPHANS.

NOVEMBER 12, 1857. The long looked-for and long prayed-for day had now arrived when the desire of my heart was granted to me, to be able to open the house for four hundred additional orphans. Much had I labored in prayer and active engagements to accomplish what was to be done previously; and now things were so far advanced as that the new house was ready for use; and a few days after we began to receive the children into it. How precious this was to me, such will be able to enter into, who, having day by day prayed for a blessing for seven years, and often repeatedly on the same day, at last obtain the desire of their heart. Yet this blessing came not unexpectedly to me, but had been looked for, and had, in the full assurance of faith, been expected to be obtained in God's own time.

Dec. 3. A donor has sent me above fifty £5 notes, one every month. Another donor, with an income of only £400 per annum, has sent me one donation of £10, or £15, or £20, after the other, during this year and former years, so that from this donor *I have had about £130 during this one year.*

Another donor has sent me £30, £50, or even £100 again

and again, for several years past. Thus the Lord, by smaller or larger amounts, oft repeated, or given only once or twice, helps me. Thousands of donors have contributed towards this work during the past twenty-four years; though a great part of the income, *perhaps one-half or more, has come from about one hundred donors only.*

Feb. 17, 1858. As far as I am able to judge, I have now all I require in the way of pecuniary means for the third house also, so that I am able to accomplish the full enlargement of the orphan work to one thousand orphans.

By the conclusion of the year under consideration, Mr. M. had received, from all sources, thirty-five thousand three hundred and thirty-five pounds nine shillings threepence toward the new Orphan Houses, " being actually three hundred and thirty-five pounds nine shillings threepence more than I had been from the commencement praying for."

The following circumstance, connected with the maintenance and care of the orphans, exhibits the reliance placed upon prayer and faith for relief in every exigency: —

Towards the end of November, 1857, I was most unexpectedly informed that the boiler of our heating apparatus at the new Orphan House No. 1, leaked very considerably, so that it was impossible to go through the winter with such a leak. Our heating apparatus consists of a large cylinder boiler, inside of which the fire is kept, and with which boiler the water pipes which warm the rooms are connected. Hot air is also connected with this apparatus. This now was my position. The boiler had been considered suited for the work of the winter; the having had ground to suspect its being worn out, and not to have done anything towards its being replaced by a new one, and to have said I will trust in God regarding it, would be careless presumption, but not **faith in God. It would be the counterfeit of faith.**

The boiler is entirely surrounded by brickwork; its state, therefore, could not be known without taking down the brickwork; this, if needless, would be rather injurious to the boiler than otherwise; and, as, year after year, for eight winters, we had had no difficulty in this way, we had not anticipated it now. But suddenly and most unexpectedly, at the commencement of the winter, this difficulty occurred. What then was to be done? For the children, especially the younger infants, I felt deeply concerned that they might not suffer through want of warmth. But how were we to obtain warmth? The introduction of a *new* boiler would, in all probability, take many weeks. The *repairing* of the boiler was a questionable matter, on account of the greatness of the leak; but, if not, nothing could be said of it, till the brick-chamber in which the boiler, with Hazard's patent heating apparatus, is inclosed, was, at least in part, removed; but that would, at least as far as we could judge, take days, and what was to be done in the meantime to find warm rooms for three hundred children? It naturally occurred to me to introduce temporary gas stoves, but, on further weighing the matter, it was found that we should be unable to heat our very large rooms with gas except we had very many stoves, which we could not introduce, as we had not a sufficient quantity of gas to spare from our lighting apparatus. Moreover, for each of these stoves we needed a small chimney, to carry off the impure air. This mode of heating, therefore, though applicable to a hall, a staircase, or a shop, would not suit our purposes. I also thought of the temporary introduction of Arnott's stoves; but they would be unsuitable, as we needed chimneys, long chimneys, for them, as they would have been of a temporary kind, and therefore must go out of the windows. On this account, the uncertainty of its answering in our case, the disfigurement of the rooms almost permanently, led me to see it needful to give up this plan also. But what was to be done? Gladly would I have paid one hundred pounds if thereby the difficulty could have been overcome, and the children not be exposed to suffer for many days from being in cold rooms. At last I determined on falling entirely into the hands of God, who is very merciful and of tender compassion, and I decided on having, at all events, the brick-chamber opened, to see the extent of the damage, and to see whether the boiler might be repaired, so as to carry us through the winter. The day was fixed when the workmen were to come, and all the necessary arrangements were made. The fire, of course, had to be let out while the repairs were going on. But now see. After the day was fixed for the repairs, a bleak north wind set in. It began to blow either on Thursday or Friday before the Wednesday afternoon when the fire was to be let out. Now came the first really cold weather which we had in the beginning of last winter, during the first days of December. What was to be done? The repairs could not be put off. I now asked the Lord for two things, viz., that he would be pleased to change the north wind into a south wind, and that he would give to the workmen " a mind to work ;" for I remembered how much Nehemiah accomplished in fifty-two days, whilst building the walls of Jerusalem, because " the people had a mind to work." Well, the memorable day came. The evening before, the bleak north wind blew still; but on the Wednesday the south wind blew; exactly as I had prayed. The weather was so mild that no fire was needed. The brickwork is removed, the leak is found out very soon, the boiler-makers begin to repair in good earnest. About half-past eight in the evening, when I was going to leave the new Orphan House for my home, I was informed at the lodge that the acting principal of the firm whence the boiler-makers came was arrived, to see how the work was going on, and whether he could in any way speed the matter. I went immediately into the cellar, therefore, to see him with the men, to seek to expedite the business. In speaking to the principal of this, he said in their hearing, " the men will work late this evening, and come very early again to-morrow." "We would rather, sir," said the leader, "work all night." Then remembered I the second part of my prayer, that God would give the men "a mind to work." Thus it was: by the morning the repair of the boiler was accomplished, the leak was stopped, though with great difficulty, and within about thirty hours the brickwork was up again and the fire in the boiler; and all the time the south wind blew so mildly that there was not the least need of a fire.

Here, then, is one of our difficulties which was overcome by prayer and faith.

For nearly three months all went on well; but at the end of February another leak appeared, which was worse than the previous one. But over this we were helped through prayer, so that without any real inconvenience the repairs were accomplished within about thirty hours. From that time the Lord has not tried us any further in this way. While I am writing this it is fine warm weather, and I have ordered in both houses the fires to be discontinued in the heating apparatuses, and, the Lord willing, a new boiler will, of course, be substituted.

Feb. 2, 1858. "From Newton" one pound. To-day I took the first active steps towards the building of the third house, when immediately afterwards I was informed by letter that a lady in London, an entire stranger to me, had ordered her bankers to send me three hundred pounds for the support of the orphans. I was also further informed in the evening that in two weeks eight hundred pounds shall be paid to me for the work of the Lord. The three hundred pounds were sent the next day, and the eight hundred pounds a fortnight after. See how, with enlargement of the work, the Lord keeps pace with the expenses, helping when help is really needed, often also giving beforehand.

During the year 1857–8, twenty-four schools were supported or assisted out of the funds of the Institution, three thousand nine hundred and sixty-three Bibles and portions of Scripture were circulated, and three thousand five hundred and thirty-one pounds expended for the aid of eighty-two laborers in various parts of the world. From these men Mr. Muller received letters containing the delightful intelligence that their labors had been blessed of the Lord. After giving copious extracts from these letters, Mr. M. adds: —

Such extracts might be greatly multiplied, and, as I said before, a large volume might easily be written; but space forbids me giving any more. I feel it, however, due to the Christian reader to state that there is good reason to believe that many hundreds of souls have been brought to the knowledge of the Lord through the instrumentality of these brethren within the last year; and may we not hope that even that which is known is not nearly all that the Lord has been pleased to accomplish through them? How seasonably, often, the help for which I had labored in prayer has come to these dear servants of Christ, the following extracts from letters may show, though hundreds of similar letters have been received by me within the last twenty years.

May 19, 1858. "I gratefully acknowledge the Lord's goodness, in the receipt of your check for ten pounds. Being brought low, my dear wife and myself, when specially waiting on him last evening, pleaded with the Lord that he would graciously send a supply this morning; and again we have the proof of his love by your letter and its contents. Bless the Lord, O my soul! With many thanks to you, in which my dear wife unites, I am," etc.

Feb. 27, 1858. " Oh, how my heart goes out towards you for your affectionate remembrance of us in our low estate! *Not a shilling* had we in the house, nor any human prospect of any money, when your remittance of five pounds reached us."

A laborer on the Continent writes on Dec. 17, 1857: "We received yesterday your kind note inclosing eight pounds. The very day you sent your letter to the post-office, the 12th instant, was a day set apart for prayer, with fasting, to ask the Lord for means."

There were also circulated during the year 1,334,791 tracts and books. Letters received from the persons who distributed them show that they were greatly blessed in awakening and converting souls.

At the commencement of the last period there were 299 orphans in the new Orphan House on Ashley Down, Bristol. During the past year there were admitted into it, and into the new house for 400, altogether 219 orphans. The total number of orphans who have been under our care since April 11, 1836, is 871.

The opening of the new house for 400 orphans, which is not a wing of the house that has been before in existence, but an entirely distinct establishment, and larger than the former, has made it needful to distinguish between these two houses in this way, that the house which was opened on June 18, 1849, is now called the new Orphan House No. 1. and the one which was opened on Nov. 12, 1857, is called the new Orphan House No. 2. The new Orphan House No. 1 is fitted up for the accommodation of 140 orphan girls above seven years of age, 80 orphan boys above seven years, and 80 male and female orphans from their earliest days, till they are about seven or eight years of age. The infants, after having passed the age of seven or eight years, are removed into the different departments for older boys and girls. The new Orphan House No. 2 is fitted up for 200 female infant orphans, and 200 elder female orphans.

Without any one having been personally applied to for anything by me, the sum of £102,714, 9s. 6d. has been given to me for the orphans, *as the result of prayer to God*, since the commencement of the work, which sum includes the amount received for the building fund for the houses already built and the one to be built. It may also be interesting to the reader to know that the total amount which has been given for the other objects, since the commencement of the work, amounts to £38,297, 12s. 11½d.; and that which has come in by the sale of Bibles since the commencement amounts to £2,222, 4s. 3½d.; by sale of tracts, £2,294, 6s. 11½d., and by the payments of children in the day schools, from the commencement, £2,138, 11s. 4¼d.

During the past twenty-two years the Spirit of God has been again and again working among the orphans who were under our care, so that very many of them have been brought to the knowledge of the Lord; but we never had so great a work, and at the same time one so satisfactory, *within so short a time*, as during the past year. I will enter somewhat into details for the benefit of the reader. There are one hundred and forty elder girls in the new Orphan House No. 1, of whom, at the beginning of the last period, ten were considered to be believers.

On May 26, 1857, the death of an orphan, Caroline Bailey, took place. The death of this beloved girl, who had known the Lord several months before she fell asleep, seems to have been used by the Lord as a means of answering in a goodly measure our daily prayers for the conversion of the orphans. It pleased God at the beginning of the last period mightily to work among the orphans, so that all at once, within a few days, without any apparent cause, except it be the peaceful end of the beloved Caroline Bailey, more than fifty of these girls were brought to be under concern about their souls, and some with deep conviction of sin accompanying it, so that they were exceedingly distressed. And how is it now?

my readers may ask, for young persons are often apparently much concerned about the things of God, but these impressions pass away. True, dear reader, I have seen this myself, having had to do with many thousands of children and young persons within the last thirty years. Had, therefore, this work among the orphans begun within the last few days, or even weeks, I should have passed it over in silence; but more than a year has now elapsed since it commenced, and it will, therefore, give joy to the godly reader to hear that in addition to those ten who were previously believers, and of whom one has been sent to service, there are twenty-three girls respecting whom for several months there has been no doubt as to their being believers; two died in the faith within the year; and there are thirty-eight more who are awakened and under concern about their souls, but respecting whom we cannot speak as yet so decidedly. All this regards only one branch of the Orphan Establishment, the elder girls of the House No. 1. In addition to this, I am glad also to be able to state that among the other girls in the New House No. 2, and among the boys also, some are interested about the things of God; yea, our labors begin already to be blessed to the hearts of some of the new received orphans.

Continuing the narrative of the progress of the new Orphan Houses, Mr. M. writes under date of Oct. 29, 1858: —

In the last Report, I stated that I was looking out for land for the third house. Regarding this, I waited day by day upon God. But for many months it pleased him to exercise my faith and patience. When, more than once, I seemed to have obtained my desire, I again appeared further from it than ever. However, I continued to pray and to exercise faith, being fully assured that the Lord's time was not yet come, and that, when it was, he would help. And so it proved. At last, in September, 1858, I obtained eleven and a half acres of land, quite close to the new Orphan Houses No. 1 and No. 2 and only separated from them by the road. On these eleven and a half acres of land a house is built. The price for house and land was three thousand six hundred and thirty-one pounds fifteen shillings, being more money than I should have seen it right to expend on the site, had it not been that it was of the utmost importance that the third house should be quite near the other two, to facilitate the superintendence and direction of the establishment. Thus, at last, this prayer also was answered, concerning which I had been waiting upon God for so many months, and concerning which the difficulties as to sight and reason seemed so great, but respecting which my mind was continually at peace; for I was sure that, as I was doing God's work, he would, in his own time, help me in this particular also. The longer I go on in this service, the more I find that prayer and faith can overcome every difficulty.

Having now obtained land, and so much, my desire was to make the best use of it, and to build for four hundred orphans, instead of for three hundred, as I had previously purposed to do. After having had several meetings with the architects, and finding that it was possible to accommodate, with comparatively little more expense, four hundred and fifty orphans, instead of four hundred, I finally determined on that number, so as to have eventually one thousand one hundred and fifty orphans under my care, instead of one thousand, as for several years previously had been contemplated. The greatness of the number of destitute children bereaved of both parents by death, — together with the greatness of the Lord's blessing, which has during all these many years rested upon my service in this way, — and the greatness of the Lord's help in giving me assistants and helpers in the work as well as means, — and, above all, the deep realization that I have but one life to spend for God on earth, and that that one life is but a brief life; — these were the reasons which led me to this further enlargement.

To this determination of a still further enlargement *I came solely in dependence upon the living God for help*, though the increase of expense for the building fund, on account of the purchase of the land, and accommodation to be built for the additional one hundred and fifty orphans more than had been from the beginning contemplated, would not be less than from six thousand to seven thousand five hundred pounds *more* than I had originally expected the total of the premises, which were to be erected, would cost; and though, in addition to this, the yearly additional expenditure for the maintenance of these one hundred and fifty orphans, beyond the intended number of one thousand, could not be less than one thousand eight hundred pounds a year. But none of these difficulties discouraged me.

Nov. 27. It is this day a twelvemonth since we began to receive fresh children into the new Orphan House No. 2. Since then the mercies of the Lord have been very many, and his help has been very great. There have been received from Nov. 27, 1857, to Nov. 27, 1858, altogether three hundred and eight orphans. Such a year I never spent in this service, — one so full of help and blessing in every way.

Jan. 4, 1859. Received seven thousand pounds, which sum was entirely left at my disposal, as the work of God in which I am engaged might more especially require it. When I decided at the end of October, 1858, to build for four hundred and fifty orphans, instead of three hundred, I needed several thousand pounds more, and was fully assured that God would give me the required means, because in reliance upon him, and for the honor of his name, I had determined on this enlargement; and now see, esteemed reader, how the Lord honored this my faith in him!

Jan. 12. From Westerham, in eighty-eight small donations, £4, 8s. 6d. Without my knowledge these eighty-eight small donations had been contributed, and were sent to me.

May 26. During the year now closing, four thousand

one hundred and forty-nine pounds seventeen shillings fivepence were expended in aid of ninety-one brethren laboring in England, Scotland, Ireland, Belgium, France, Switzerland, Sardinia, Canada, Nova Scotia, East Indies, China, and British Guiana. Also, during the past year 1,885,401 tracts and books have been circulated.

At the commencement of the last period there were four hundred and ninety-nine orphans in the new Orphan Houses No. 1 and No. 2. On May 26, 1859, there were six hundred and seventy-two orphans in the two houses, *i. e.*, in No. 1, 299, and in No. 2, 373. The total number of orphans who have been under our care since April 11, 1836, is 1,083.

Though during the past year we have not had so great and so sudden a work of the Spirit of God going on among the orphans as during the previous year, when, within a few days, about fifty out of one department of one hundred and forty girls were suddenly brought under deep concern about their souls; yet the blessing of the Lord has not been withheld even spiritually. There are already many caring about the things of God among the four hundred and twenty-four orphans who were received within the last eighteen months, and who ask it, as a privilege, to be allowed, in the summer, to take their Bibles with them to bed, so that, should they awake in the morning before the bell is rung, they may be able to read it. Out of the thirteen girls who were sent to service, nine had been believers for some time before they left the establishment.

When I began the orphan work, one of the especial objects which I had in view was to benefit the church of Christ at large, by the accounts which I might be enabled to write in connection with this service; for I expected, from the beginning, to have many answers to prayer granted to me, and I confidently anticipated that the recording of them would be beneficial to believers, in leading them to look for answers to their own prayers, and in encouraging them to bring all their own necessities before God in prayer. I likewise firmly believed that many unconverted persons would, by means of such writings, be led to see the reality of the things of God. As I expected, so it has been. In very many instances the reading of the Reports of this Institution, or the "Narrative of the Lord's Dealings," with me, has been blessed by God to the conversion of those who knew not our Lord Jesus. In thousands of instances, likewise, believers have been benefited through them, being thereby comforted, encouraged, led more simply to the Holy Scriptures, led more fully to trust in God for everything; in a word, led, in a greater or less degree, to walk in the same path of faith in which the writer, by the help of God, is walking. The thousands of instances of blessing which have been brought before me during the past twenty-four years (for almost daily I have heard of fresh cases, and often of several in the same day), have only still further led me to earnestness in prayer, that the Lord would condescend to use these publications still more, and make them a blessing to many tens of thousands of his children, and to many tens of thousands of the unconverted. And now the reader will rejoice with me, when he reads what follows. I am the more led to relate the following, that the godly reader more than ever may be encouraged to prayer, and, also, that an *accurate* statement may be given of this fact, which has been already referred to in many public places in connection with revival-meetings, and which likewise has been several times stated in print.

In November, 1856, a young Irishman, Mr. James McQuilkin, was brought to the knowledge of the Lord. Soon after his conversion he saw my Narrative advertised. He had a great desire to read it, and procured it accordingly, about January, 1857. God blessed it greatly to his soul, especially in showing to him what could be obtained by prayer. He said to himself something like this: See what Mr. Muller obtains simply by prayer. Thus *I* may obtain blessing by prayer. He now set himself to pray that the Lord would give him a spiritual companion, one who knew the Lord. Soon after, he became acquainted with a young man who knew the Lord. These two began a prayer meeting in one of the Sunday schools in the parish of Connor. Having his prayer answered in obtaining a spiritual companion, Mr. James McQuilkin asked the Lord to lead him to become acquainted with some more of his hidden ones. Soon after, the Lord gave him two more young men, who knew the Lord previously, as far as he could judge. In autumn, 1857, Mr. James McQuilkin stated to these three young men, given him in answer to believing prayer, what blessing he had derived from my Narrative, — how it had led him to see the power of believing prayer; and he proposed that they should meet for prayer, to seek the Lord's blessing upon their various labors in the Sunday schools, prayer meetings, and preachings of the gospel. Accordingly, in autumn, 1857, these four young men met together for prayer in a small school-house near the village of Kells in the parish of Connor, every Friday evening. On January 1, 1858, the Lord gave them the first remarkable answer to prayer in the conversion of a farm servant. He was taken into the number, and thus there were five who gave themselves to prayer. Shortly after another young man, about twenty years old, was converted; there were now six. This greatly encouraged the other three who first had met with Mr. James McQuilkin. Others now were converted, who were also taken into the number; but only believers were admitted to these fellowship meetings, in which they read, prayed, and offered to each other a few thoughts from the Scriptures. These meetings, and others for the preaching of the gospel, were held in the parish of Connor, Antrim, Ireland. Up to this time all was going on most quietly, though many souls were converted. There were no physical prostrations, as afterwards. About Christmas, 1858, a young man from Ahoghill, who had come to live at Connor, and who had been converted through this little company of believers, went to see his friends at Ahoghill, and spoke to them about their own souls and the work of God at Connor. His friends desired to see some of these converts. Accordingly, Mr. James McQuilkin, with two of the first who met for prayer, went, on February 2, 1859, and held a meeting at Ahoghill in one of the Presbyterian churches. Some believed, some mocked, and others thought there was a great deal of presumption in these young converts; yet many wished to have another meeting. This was held by the same three young men, on February 16, 1859; and now the Spirit of God began to work, and to work mightily. Souls were converted, and from that time conversions multiplied rapidly. Some of these converts went to other places, and carried the spiritual fire, so to speak, with them. The blessed work of the Spirit of God spread in *many places*. On April 5, 1859, Mr. James McQuilkin went to Ballymena, held a meeting there in one of the Presbyterian churches, and on April 11 held another meeting in another of the Presbyterian churches. Several were convinced of sin, and the work of the Spirit of God went forward in Ballymena. On May 28, 1859, he went to Belfast. During the first week, there were meetings held in five different Presbyterian churches, and from that time the blessed work commenced at Belfast. In all these visits he was accompanied and helped by Mr. Jeremiah Meneely, one of the three young men who first met with him after the reading of my Narrative. From this time the work of the Holy Ghost spread further and further; for the young converts were used by the Lord to carry the truth from one place to another.*

---

* Rev Dr Sawtell, in a letter to Dr. Wayland, remarks, "So scrupulous was Mr Muller about stating the facts *correctly*, and so solicitous lest a wrong impression should be conveyed, or lest any statement of importance should be made on insufficient authority, that he sent to Ireland for Mr McQuilkin, who, at his request, came to Bristol. Mr Muller there examined personally into the facts, and only on becoming satisfied of its verity, did he insert in his annual Report for 1860 the statement in regard to the connection between his Narrative and the commencement of the Irish revival."

Such was the *beginning* of that mighty work of the Holy Spirit, which has led to the conversion of many tens of thousands, and which is still going on even in Ireland, and the blessed results of which are still felt in Scotland, England, and other countries. It is almost needless to add, that in no degree the honor is due to the instruments, but to the Holy Spirit alone; yet these facts are stated in order that it may be seen what delight God has in answering abundantly the believing prayers of his children.

Seeing, then, how greatly he has condescended to own these records regarding his willingness to listen to prayer, made to him in the name of the Lord Jesus, I am delighted, at the close of another year, in connection with this Institution, to recount a few of the very many instances in which God has been pleased to answer our prayers, and to grant blessing to rest upon the various objects of this Institution; yea, blessing greater far than during any part of the past twenty-six years, while it has been in operation.

Up to May 26, 1860, Mr. M. received for the building fund the sum of £45,113, 14s. 4½d.

In May, 1859, I had in hand for the Bible, school, tract, and missionary funds, £2,009, 11s. 2½d., a balance far greater than I ever had had before. This arose not from the fact of unwillingness to spend the means which the Lord had been pleased to intrust me with, but chiefly from the fact that some large donations had come in during the last part of the previous year; and I had not, as a steward who desires to act in the fear of God, had opportunities brought before me to spend all. But much as the balance was, all the various schools, directly or indirectly connected with

---

It is interesting to find that Mr. Müller's statement of the origin of the revival accords with the account of Prof. Gibson, of Queen's College, Belfast, in his admirable work, "THE YEAR OF GRACE," prepared at the request of Gould and Lincoln, in which he details the events of the recent wonderful work of grace in Ireland. (See Chap. III. — VIII.) — ED.

the Institution, required means; the circulation of the Holy Scriptures and tracts, which objects increase more and more, needed much, in order to enter every suitable open door; and lastly, and especially, the ninety-one preachers of the gospel in various parts of the world, on my list on May 26, 1859, required a large sum to aid them. All these various objects, therefore, needed so much, that the balance, large as it was, would have lasted but a short time, had not the living God, who has been my helper from the beginning, and to whom I have looked, and looked alone, opened, in answer to our prayers, his bountiful hands, and sent in more before the balance was expended; so that, though without any human probability of meeting even one half of the probable expenses in connection with these objects, not only have I been able to meet the whole, but also, so bountifully has God helped, that though the expenses were £1,584, 7s. 3¾d. more than during the preceding year, I had not only enough, but even a larger balance was left than at the end of the previous year.

Jan. 31, 1860. On this day I received a donation of three thousand pounds, of which I took for these objects two thousand pounds. Day by day, during this period also, I had been asking the Lord for means for these objects; and day by day I had been entreating him that he would be pleased to enable me to accomplish during this period as much as during the former one in the way of circulating the Holy Scriptures and tracts, and in aiding missionary operations, though I had no natural prospect whatever, of being able to do so. My eyes were alone directed to the living God, who year after year, for many years past, had allowed me to increase the operations of these three objects, notwithstanding the continual increase of expense in connection with the orphan work; and thus I expected, fully expected, though all appearance was against it, that during this period also, I should be again helped by God, the living God. Think, then, Christian reader, how great my spiritual refreshment, when, by this one donation in a great measure, I saw these my daily prayers being again answered. In like manner may you, in your sphere of service, in your family affairs, in your business, in your profession, in your various temporal or spiritual necessities, have your prayers answered.

Dec. 9, 1859. To-day it is twenty-four years since the orphan work commenced. What has God wrought! There have been received since then altogether 1,129 orphans, and during the last two years and two months alone 469, so greatly has the work increased of late. We have now 700 orphans under our care.

Dec. 10. The following letter was received to-day from an apprentice:—

MOST BELOVED SIR:—

With feelings of gratitude and great thankfulness to you for all the kindness I experienced whilst under your care, and for now apprenticing me to a suitable trade whereby I can earn my own living, I write you these few lines I arrived at my destined abode in safety, and was kindly received by my master and mistress. Dear sir, I thank you for the education, food, clothing, and for every comfort; but, above all, for the instruction from God's word which I received when in that happy Orphan House; for it was there I was brought to know Jesus as my Saviour; and I hope to have him as my guide through all my difficulties, temptations and trials in this world; and, having him for my guide, I hope to prosper in my trade, and thereby show my gratitude to you for all the kindness I have received. Please to accept my gratitude and thanks; and I hope you will be spared many more years to care for poor, destitute children like me I am sure I shall often look back with pleasure and regret to the time I was in that happy home;—with pleasure that I lived there, and regret that I left it. Begging you to accept my grateful thanks, and with my kind love to Mr. L—, Mr. B—, Mr. W—, and Mr. S—,

I am, dear sir,
Yours gratefully,

* * * *

The Christian reader, I doubt not, in perusing such letters, will with us thank God for condescending to give such blessing, such abundant blessing, to our labors.

Feb. 14, 1860. Two pounds ten shillings sixpence, with the following letter: —

My dear Brother in the Lord Jesus Christ: —

Will you please to accept an order for two pounds ten shillings sixpence by the same post, for the dear orphans under your care? The history of this small sum is as follows. About seven and a half years ago your Narrative was put into my hands, which the Lord very greatly blessed to my soul. Six years and eleven months ago I was enabled to cast myself, my wife and family, upon the Lord, and look to *Him alone* for the supply of our temporal necessities while laboring in his glorious cause. From that time to the present we have had no claims upon any person for a single penny: nor have we made known our wants to any, or applied to any person for help, but to our heavenly Father alone; and he has supplied our need and not suffered us to be confounded, blessed be his name! My dear wife, as well as myself, from the very first had a strong desire to help you a *little* in your blessed work of love and labor of faith; but, for a long time, owing to the continued ill-health of my wife, and the growing expenses of my family, we never seemed to have any money to spare; so all we did was to *wish, desire,* and *talk about it,* and say how happy we should be if the Lord would enable us to do so. At length, we both felt that we were acting wrong, and on the eighth of August last we solemnly decided we would give the Lord back a tenth of the money he was pleased to send us, though at that time we were very poor, I may add in deeper poverty than we had ever been before; yet, under those circumstances, we were enabled in the strength of the Lord to come to the above decision and act up to it that very morning; and the peace and joy we both felt it is in vain for me to attempt to describe. The Lord has kept us firm ever since, and instead of having less for our own use, we have had even more; so, dear sir, this sum is the fruit of six months' prayers. Pardon me for troubling you with so long an account of so trifling a sum; but I want you to bless our heavenly Father for his goodness to us his unworthy servants, and to remember us in your petitions at a throne of grace.

  I am, my dear brother,
   Yours very affectionately and respectfully,
             * * * *

During the year 1859–60 there have been received for the orphans 3,542 separate sums. Of these there were 1,494 under 5s., 560 above 5s. and not exceeding 10s., 614 above 10s. and not exceeding £1, 288 above £1 and not exceeding £2, 411 above £2 and not exceeding £5, 93 above £5 and not exceeding £10, 49 above £10 and not exceeding £20, 10 above £20 and under £50, 11 of £50, 1 of £59, 19s. 9d., 1 of £62, 17s., 1 of £89, 4s., 1 of £96, 12s., 3d., 5 of £100, 2 of £500, and 1 of £1,500. Among these donations were some from East India, Australia, Cape of Good Hope, Saxony, Holland, South America, United States, from vessels on the ocean, and from missionaries among the heathen.

During the year under consideration twenty-three schools in England were supported or aided by the funds of the Institution. In all of these the teachers are persons of piety, and instruction is given not only in secular knowledge, but in the way of salvation. Without reckoning the orphans, 13,124 souls have been brought under *habitual* instruction in the things of God in these various schools; besides the many thousands in the schools in the various parts of England, Ireland, Scotland, British Guiana, the West Indies, the East Indies, etc., which have been to a greater or less degree assisted.

The total amount of means which has been expended during the last twenty-six years in connection with the schools, which have been either entirely or in part supported by the funds of this Institution, amounts to £9,275, 0s. 8½d

The number of Bibles, Testaments, and portions of the Holy Scriptures, which have been circulated since May 26, 1859, is as follows: Bibles sold, 579. Bibles given away, 1,120. Testaments sold, 409. Testaments given away, 725. Copies of the Psalms sold, 63. Other small portions of the Holy Scriptures sold, 248

There have been circulated since March 5, 1834, through the medium of this Institution, 24,768 Bibles, 15,100 Testaments, 719 copies of the Psalms, and 1,876 other small portions of the Holy Scriptures.

The amount of the funds of the Institution spent during the past year on the circulation of the Holy Scriptures is £398, 3s. 7d. The total amount spent since March 5, 1834, is £5,681, 13s. 3½d.

During the past year has been spent of the funds of the Institution, in aid of missionary efforts at home and abroad, the sum of £5,019, 6s. 1d. By this sum one hundred and one laborers in the word and doctrine, in various parts of the world, have been to a greater or less degree assisted. It is an interesting fact that these laborers are located in England, Scotland, Ireland, Belgium, France, Switzerland, Sardinia, Canada, Nova Scotia, East India, China, and British Guiana.

The laborers aided by the Institution were peculiarly blessed during the year 1859-60. While the preaching of those laboring in *foreign* lands was very useful, the brethren preaching in Ireland and Scotland were signally favored with success, and were permitted to see in a wonderful measure the fruit of their prayers and toils. A single extract only can be given from the letter of a laborer in Scotland.

A devoted servant of Christ has been laboring in a manufacturing town in Scotland, where, by means of schools, Bible classes, visiting from house to house, and preaching the gospel among thousands of the most wretched, most debased, and most ignorant, he seeks to win souls for the Lord. In this service he has been going on year after year. In a measure his labors had been blessed up to the period of the last Report, but far more abundantly since, as the following account, given by himself to me in a letter dated Oct. 28, 1859, will show : —

"This month, through which we have passed, has brought me to a point in my history which for years I have contemplated and looked forward to with deeper and more intense desire than to any anticipated event in my whole life. More than thirty years ago there sprang up in my soul a longing and craving for the effusion of the Holy Ghost on the church and on the world, such as would extend throughout the whole of Scotland. For this I have labored, and spoken, and prayed increasingly. As I grew older, the craving for this blessing grew stronger. To see it became the ruling passion of my soul, and, as years rolled away, my hope of seeing it realized strengthened apace. On this season of expected blessing we seem at length to have entered. The religious movement is creeping steadily along the whole of the west of Scotland. It has not acquired a sudden or very powerful momentum. We are, so far as I can judge, in the initiatory stage in all the points where the work has found a settlement. A sound has gone out as from the Lord; the rumor travels on, and in its course awakens the careless, opens the ear, quickens the attention, and everywhere is making preparation for something coming. This note of preparation is calling the people together. Their ear is open to listen. In every place this hearing is bringing faith in its train; men are turning to God; intensity is given to those silent cases of conviction where for months or years there has been concern ebbing and flowing with circumstances. Not a few of these have come to light through their concern all at once ripening into deep distress. Forced out of the old ruts in which they have moved, they are forced to venture their all into the hands of Jesus, and are set at liberty. Such has been the process at work here. I am continually falling in with solitary cases, and a number of these have found peace. It would take far more time than I can spare to record their history, and how they obtained deliverance."

The total amount of the funds of the Institution which has been spent on missionary operations since March 5, 1834, is £34,495, 3s. 4d.

There has been laid out for tracts and books, from May 26, 1859, to May 26, 1860, the sum of £1,650, 11s. 4¾d.; and there have been circulated within the last year 2,562 001 tracts and books. The sum total which has been expended on this object, since Nov 19, 1840, amounts to £8,064, 12s. 6½d. The total number of all the tracts and **books which have been circulated since Nov. 19, 1840, is 11,493,174.**

During the past year there were again circulated 676,600 tracts and books more than during the year before. The great number of laborers for God who have been raised up for service within the last two years in various parts of the world, and the mighty working of the Spirit of God, which has created in multitudes a desire gladly to receive tracts and books, account for this. Nor is there in these two particulars a decrease, but a continual increase. So great has been the call for tracts that of late we have sent out repeatedly 100,000 in one week, for gratuitous circulation, and sometimes even more than this. When the mighty working of the Spirit of God commenced in Ireland, I sought from the beginning to send very large supplies of tracts to Belfast and elsewhere, in order that thus the holy flame might be fanned, as it were, and that in the very outset the simplicity of the gospel might be set before the young converts. About two millions of the tracts and books circulated during the past year were given away *gratuitously*. Hundreds of believers have been engaged in spreading them abroad, not merely in many parts of England, Scotland, and Ireland, but in various other parts of the world.

At the commencement of the last period there were 672 orphans in the new Orphan Houses No. 1 and No. 2. During the past year were admitted into the two houses 70 orphans. On May 26, 1860, there were just 700 orphans under our care, our full number in the two houses, *i. e.*, in No. 1, 300, in No. 2, 400. The total number of orphans who have been under our care since April 11, 1836, is 1,153.

Without any one having been personally applied to for anything by me, the sum of £133,528, 14s. has been given to me for the orphans, *as the result of prayer to God*, since the commencement of the work, which sum includes the amount received for the building fund for the houses already built and the one to be built. It may also be interesting to the reader to know that the total amount which has been given for the other objects since the commencement of the work amounts to £51,777, 14s. 11d.; and that which has come in by the sale of Bibles, since the commencement, amounts to £2,530, 4s. 5½d.; by sale of tracts, £3,546, 19s 1¼d ; and by the payments of the children in the day schools, from the commencement £2,304, 18s. 9. Besides this, also, a great variety and number of articles of clothing, furniture, provisions. etc , have been given *for the use* of the orphans.

Day after day, and year after year, by the help of God, we labor in prayer for the spiritual benefit of the orphans under our care. These our supplications, which have been for twenty-four years brought before the Lord concerning them, have been abundantly answered in former years in the conversion of hundreds from among them. We have also had repeated seasons in which, within a short time, or even all at once, *many* of the orphans were converted. Such a season we had about three years since, when within a few days about sixty were brought to believe in the Lord Jesus; and such seasons we have had again twice during the past year. The first was in July, 1859, when the Spirit of God wrought so mightily in one school of 120 girls, as that very many, yea, more than one half, were brought under deep concern about the salvation of their souls. This work, moreover, was not a mere momentary excitement; but, after more than eleven months have elapsed, there are 31 concerning whom there is *full* confidence as to their conversion, and 32 concerning whom there is likewise a goodly measure of confidence, though not to the same amount as regarding the 31. There are therefore 63 out of the 120 orphans in that one school who are considered to have been converted in July, 1859. This blessed and mighty work of the Holy Spirit cannot be traced to any particular cause. It was, however, a most precious answer to prayer. As such we look upon it, and are encouraged by it to further waiting upon God. The second season of the mighty working of the Holy Spirit among the orphans, during the past year, was at the end of January and the beginning of February, 1860. The particulars of it are of the deepest interest. A very profitable pamphlet might be written on the subject. I have prayed again and again for guidance how to act, and have at last come to the decision *not* to relate the details, lest the dear children, who would recognize themselves in the description, should be injured; for my experience of laboring twenty-six years among children, and of having **had** to deal with so *many very young believers*, has led me to the **full** conviction *that it is injurious to make them prominent*.

If God makes them prominent by using them as evidently he is using children in these days, we have only to admire and to praise; but this is very different from ourselves making them prominent. I must therefore content myself by stating that this great work of the Spirit of God, in January and February, 1860, began among the younger class of the children under our care, little girls of about six, seven, eight, and nine years old; then extended to the older girls, and then to the boys; so that within about ten days above 200 of the orphans were stirred up to be anxious about their souls, and in *many* instances found peace *immediately*, through faith in our Lord Jesus. They at once requested to be allowed to hold prayer meetings among themselves, and have had these meetings ever since. Many of them also manifested a concern about the salvation of their companions and relations, and spoke or wrote to them about the way to be saved. Should the believing reader desire to know how it has been with these children since the end of January and the beginning of February, our reply is, we have, in most cases, cause for thankfulness. The present state of the 700 orphans, spiritually, is, that there are 118 under our care, regarding whose conversion we have full confidence; 89 regarding whom we have also confidence, though not to that full degree as concerning the 118; and 53 whom we consider in a hopeful state. To these 260 are to be added the 14 who were sent out as believers, and the three who died in the faith during the past year. It is to be remembered that very many of the children in the Orphan Houses are quite young, as we have received them from four months old and upward. During no year have we had greater cause for thanksgiving on account of the spiritual blessing among the children than during the last; AND YET WE LOOK FOR FURTHER AND GREATER BLESSING STILL.

CHAPTER XXV.

1860 — 1868.

GREAT PROSPERITY — FEWER TRIALS — INFLUENCE — THIRD ORPHAN HOUSE PRAYING FOR HELPERS, AND FOR OTHER NEEDS — REGULAR CONTRIBUTORS — REVIVALS — FOURTH ORPHAN HOUSE.

FROM this time Mr. Muller continued to prosper, and he met with no severe trials of his faith. His needs were greater than ever before, for each addition to the number of orphans involved a larger expenditure, and the widening operations in all departments of the work required a corresponding increase of receipts. But he was never brought, as in previous years, into great straits. The expenses of single days, and often, even, of successive weeks, were larger than the receipts; but the treasury was never empty. A surplus of funds accumulated in the banks, more than adequate for every emergency. The Lord rewarded the faith of his servant, which had been proved, like Abraham's, in the hours of sore trial.

He continued to receive testimonies from Christians in various parts of the world, that his example had stimulated them to a more confident trust in God's promises, and to a more systematic benevolence.

The following letter came from Scotland, in proof that a faithful steward has more talents given to his care: —

DEAR SIR: —
One of your Reports came to my hand about three years since. I have embraced the plan, which your Reports recommend, to give to

the Lord as he prospers us. I consider it now my duty to confess, that I have found it a real blessing, both temporally and spiritually. I am but a hard-working man, yet I feel it now a pleasure and a luxury to keep account of how the Lord prospers my endeavors; and ever since I commenced that plan, everything has gone on well with me. My earnings have every year been steadily increasing. I may say that I have given about seventeen per cent. for the last two years; and, though there was not any appearance of prosperity that man could see, yet all that I have given away for the last year came back with interest and compound interest.

Mr. Muller believed that all Christians should be educated in habits of cheerful giving to the Lord, but not by urgent entreaty. He says: —

To ask unbelievers for means is *not* God's way; to *press* even believers to give, is *not* God's way; but the *duty* to contribute, and the *privilege* of being allowed to contribute to the work of God, should be pointed out to believers, and this should be followed up with earnest prayer, believing prayer, and it will result in the desired end

On March 12, 1862, the third Orphan House was finished and opened, with accommodations for 450 inmates. It was begun in July, 1859, and was nearly three years in building. On the day of its completion he writes: —

It was in November, 1850, that my mind became exercised about enlarging the orphan work from 300 orphans to 1,000, and subsequently to 1,150; and it was in June, 1851, that this my purpose became known, having kept it secret for more than seven months, whilst day by day praying about it. From the end of November, 1850, to this day, March 12, 1862, not one single day has been allowed to pass, without this contemplated enlargement being brought before God in prayer, and generally more

THE THIRD ORPHAN HOUSE, ASHLEY DOWN.

than once a day. But only now, this day, the New Orphan House No. 3 was so far advanced, as that it could be opened. Observe then, first, esteemed reader, how long it may be, before a full answer to our prayers, even to thousands and tens of thousands of prayers, is granted; yea, though those prayers may be believing prayers, earnest prayers, and offered up in the name of the Lord Jesus, and though we may only for the sake of the honor of our Lord desire the answer; for I did, by the grace of God, without the least doubt and wavering, look for more than eleven years for the full answer; I earnestly importuned the Lord; I alone looked for the answer on the ground of the worthiness of the Lord Jesus, judging myself entirely unworthy of an answer; and I only sought in this matter the glory of God.

Though the expense of building the three Orphan Houses had reached nearly £42,000 sterling, yet the fund was not exhausted, for more than £11,000 remained to the credit of the building fund; and more than £9,000 to the credit of the fund for current expenses.

Many persons had become so deeply interested in the orphan work, that they contributed regularly to its support. Their gifts were often small, but the aggregate value was large. The report of 1863 alludes to some of these donors: —

A Christian, in business in Lincolnshire, has sent me week by week 10s. for some time past; and two donors have given for several years past £60 each, annually. A waiter at one of the hotels in Manchester has sent me for the greater part of the year 5s. every week; and a donor at Nottingham has also sent very many little donations as "From Needy." A Christian, in business at Manchester, dedicates a little for the orphans for every order he receives, and for every payment which is made, and sends the amount, when it has been collected for a while. Another Christian brother, in business in London, sends weekly little contributions as God prospers him. A Christian baker gives one penny to the orphans for each sack of flour which he uses; and a Christian flour-dealer one penny for each sack of flour which he sells. I have already mentioned that a widow gives one penny for each pair of shoes she sells; and a certain bonnet-maker one penny for each bonnet she makes. We have, also, gratuitously supplied, through the kindness of a firm, all the salt which is used at the three Orphan Houses. There are two servants of Christ, laboring in the gospel in dependence upon the Lord for their temporal supplies, one of whom sends the tenth part of all the Lord gives to him, for the benefit of the orphans, and the other the fifth part. The latter has done so for a number of years, and these amounts have been again considerable during the past year. One donor, with an income of about £400 a year only, has now for nine years past given between £100 and £200 of this income, year by year.

Before the third house was completed, such was the pressure for larger accommodations to receive the increasing number of applicants, and such his confident faith in God that all urgent wants would be supplied, that he formed the purpose of building two more houses, with capacity for 850 orphans, making the whole number 2,000. Among other reasons he enumerates for this great enlargement of the work, is the sense of personal responsibility to improve his special talents, for the glory of God, and the good of men. He says: —

In connection with the foregoing reasons stands also the fact, that the Lord has been pleased to give me gift for this work. I do not take credit to myself for this. There is not the least honor due to me on account of it. The germ was first implanted by the Lord, and he caused it to grow and to increase. The gift which he had been pleased to impart, for such service, was used, at first, while the work was small; for I began with 30 orphans. Afterwards were added 36 more, and then after a year again 30 more, and finally, after the lapse of several years, 30 more. Thus, for above thirteen years, the number of orphans under my care never exceeded 126; but then it grew to 300 with the opening of the New Orphan House No. 1, and with the opening of No. 2, to 700; and now, with God's blessing, it will shortly be 1,150. Thus, with the enlargement of the work, the gift, which the Lord had been pleased to give to me, was further and further developed, as the whole work grew up under my sole and immediate direction.

Now, while there is not the least honor due to me for all this, as God called me for the work, fitted me for it, has sustained me in it, and caused my experience to grow with the work; yet, on the other hand, I feel responsibility laid on me, still further, to the utmost of my power, to make use of this gift and experience, and therefore to enlarge the work, as here proposed.

It was easier to fill the house with orphans, than to obtain the necessary teachers and helpers. Many who had applied for places had, in the mean time, found other positions, or proved unsuitable. But Mr. Müller carried the matter to the Lord in prayer, and was not disappointed:—

Instead of praying *once* a day with my dear wife about this matter, as we had been doing day by day for years, we met daily *three* times, to bring this before God. I also brought the matter before the whole staff of my helpers in the work, requesting their prayers. Thus I have now continued for about four months longer in prayer, day by day calling upon God three times on account of this need, and the result has been, that one helper after the other has been given, without the help coming *too* late, or the work getting into confusion; or the reception of the children being hindered; and I am fully assured that the few who are yet needed will also be found, when they are *really* required.

Mr. Müller gave the broadest application to the command of the New Testament, " In all things by prayer and supplication, with thanksgiving, let your requests be made known unto God." He not only looked to God for the daily supply of money to meet the wants of the orphans, and for teachers and assistants to care for them; but he felt the need of divine help in all the details of his work. He was often perplexed by difficulties in finding good places for the boys, when the time came for them to leave the Orphan House, and found relief in prayer: —

In the early part of the summer, 1862, it was found that we had several boys ready to be apprenticed; but there were no applications made by masters for apprentices. As all our boys are invariably sent out as in-door apprentices, this was no small difficulty; for we not only look for Christian masters, but consider their business, and examine into their position, to see whether they are suitable; but, if all other difficulties were out of the way, the master must also be willing to receive the apprentice into his own family. Under these circumstances, we again gave ourselves to prayer, as we had done for more than twenty years before, concerning this thing, instead of advertising, which, in all probability, would only bring before us masters who desire an apprentice for the sake of the premium. We remembered how good the Lord had been to us, in having helped us hundreds of times before, in this very matter. Some weeks passed, but the difficulty remained. We continued, however, in prayer, and then one application was made, and then another; and since the time when we first began to pray about this matter, last summer, we have been able to send out altogether eighteen boys; and the difficulty was thus again entirely overcome by prayer, as every one of the boys, whom it was desirable to send out, has been sent out.

When sickness came into the houses, he implored the Lord for deliverance, and the prayers were not in vain: —

During the past year it pleased the Lord to exercise our faith greatly with reference to scarlet fever and the hooping-cough. In September, 1865, the scarlet fever broke out at the New Orphan House No. 2, in which house there are 200 infant girls and 200 elder girls. It appeared among the infants. The cases increased more and more. But we betook ourselves to God in prayer. Day by day we called upon him regarding this trial, and generally two or three times a day. At last, when the infirmary rooms were filled, and also some other rooms that could be spared for the occasion, to keep the sick children from the rest; and when now we had no other rooms to spare, at least not without great inconvenience; it pleased the Lord to answer our prayers, and in mercy to stay the disease. There were in all **36** children ill of the scarlet fever at No. 2, but not one died of the disease. The same malady broke out also at No. 3. But the Lord dealt there very gently with us; only 3 children were ill of the fever, and all recovered. At the end of the year 1865 the hooping-cough appeared among the 450 girls of the New Orphan House No. 3. This disease was very general in Bristol, and many children died in consequence. Parents and others, who have an affectionate heart, and who feel for the suffering of children, can easily suppose how our hearts were affected, when we heard these dear children laboring under this trying malady. But, while we thought it right to take all the necessary precautions with regard to the spread of the disease, and to use the needed remedies, yet our chief and universal remedy, prayer and faith, was again resorted to. We trusted in God, and betook ourselves to him, and we were not confounded. When it is considered that we have 1,150 orphans in the three houses, and that the hooping-cough was so general in Bristol and the neighborhood, and in many instances so fatal, the hand of God, in answer to constant daily prayer for several months, regarding this disease, is marked enough, in that we had only in all the three houses seventeen cases of hooping-cough, and that only one child died in consequence of the hooping-cough, this dear little girl having constitutionally very weak lungs, and a tendency to consumption, which followed the hooping-cough.

Similar help was given in the prevalence of small-pox in 1872: —

When the trial had come to its height, and many children were laid down in this disease, we proposed that as many of the whole staff of teachers, matrons, etc., as could leave their post, should, in addition to secret prayer, and our regular meeting for prayer, meet day by day for prayer regarding this heavy affliction, in order that we might humble ourselves under the mighty hand of God, and seek his merciful deliverance. From the day we did so, there has been a marked and most decided difference. The fresh cases have been few comparatively, and the deaths have been very rare. The few children who are now ill, are all convalescent, with the exception of one.

The receipts were very unequal. The expense of a single day would often exhaust the receipts of the entire week.

There was still need of prayer and faith. In the report of 1864, Mr. Müller alludes to this:—

Let no one take it as a matter of course that means must come in, because the work is large, and well known, and Reports are issued. For donations might be received, and even many, yet the income might be entirely inadequate to the outgoings. Take, for instance, the very last day before the one on which I am writing this, *i. e.*, May 20, 1864. The income of the whole day, in twelve sums, was £6, 14s. 9d., but the outgoings were £53, 8s. 5d. Take the day before that, May 19, 1864. The income was £32, 2s. 3d., in again exactly 12 different sums; but the outgoings were £213, 9s. Take this very day on which I am writing, May 21, 1864. The income for the orphans has been £2, 3s. 7d.; but I have already paid out £25, 4s., yet there is a bill of £46, 18s. 5d. more before me to be paid, and I know not what other heavy demands may further be made upon me this day. Now we did receive on the 19th £6, 14s. 9d. in twelve donations, on the 20th £32, 2s. 3d. in twelve donations, and to-day £2, 3s. 7d. in three donations. There were therefore many **donations** received during these three days, yet how entirely inadequate to meet the demands; for the total income was only £41, 0s. 7d. during the three days, and the outgoings £292, 1s. 5d.

Mr. Müller was cheered in his work by numerous letters from those who had been under his care, and felt that they owed their success in life to the training they had received in the Orphan Houses. Extracts from their letters are given in his annual Reports, and they overflow with gratitude to God and to Mr. Müller. They uniformly remember the Orphan House, and send gladly little sums to help forward the good work. We give a few extracts:—

Feb. 1, 1866. — From one of the orphans, formerly under our care, a believer, and now in service £4 for missions, with the following letter: "Dear Mr. Muller: you will be surprised to hear from me again so soon, but I will give you my reason in the history of the enclosed sum, which I am thankful to be able to offer for the missions. I had saved a nice sum from my earnings, until I was moved in reading your Narrative to send you a portion of it. The inclination was again renewed, and I put a certain small portion by, intending it for a last resource, in case of sickness, or death, that I might not prove a burden to any one; thinking it presumptuous to leave myself entirely without, as I had *no one*, humanly speaking, to look to for the least help. But, dear sir, I have received such benefits, such manifestations of God's care and goodness towards me, I was constrained to return him the little in my power, to help forward the glorious work of spreading the gospel, that others thereby may be brought to enjoy the same unspeakable blessings, through the knowledge of that gospel; and I felt I was doing a very ungrateful, neglectful act by keeping this money lying, when there is much to be done."

Feb. 15. — Received 5s. from two orphans, now in service, with the following letter: "Beloved and respected Sir: will you please to accept the enclosed trifle towards the Building Fund, as we should esteem it a great pleasure to contribute one stone towards the erection of another Orphan House, that other dear orphans, who are left as we were, may be blessed with a similar happy home to that which we enjoyed so long. We often think and talk of the happy days spent under your fatherly care, and trust that you will long be spared to be the orphan's friend. Please to accept our heart-felt thanks for all the kindness and care you have bestowed upon us."

Sept. 27, 1867. — The following letter, with 5s., was received from an orphan who more than ten years since was sent out to service, after she had been about ten years un-

THE FOURTH ORPHAN HOUSE, ASHLEY DOWN.

der our care: "Dear Sir: may I be permitted to ask your acceptance of this small donation as a token of gratitude for the great kindness I received whilst under your fatherly care; and may you, dear sir, long be spared to be a father to the fatherless, and a friend to the orphan. Often do I look back to the period of my childhood spent in the Orphan House, and feel grateful that I was one of the number permitted to find shelter in so good a home. You will, I have no doubt, dear sir, be pleased to know that I am still in the same situation as when I last wrote to you, where I have been now nearly nine years, and am still very comfortable. Dear sir, I wish you many happy returns of your birthday, and hope you will long be spared with health and strength to see many more, and to carry on the noble work you have undertaken."

July 3, 1871. — "I have been taught by your life, dear sir, that there is something truly noble and grand for a man to live for; there is nought more noble than the cause for which you have spent and are still spending your valuable life, and for which cause I hope to spend mine, namely, the cause of Christ. Will you please accept the most grateful thanks of an orphan, for having placed me with a kind master and mistress, with whom I have learnt the trade of decorating, painter, paper-hanger, etc.

In March, 1866, the plans for the two new houses were ready, and in April tenders were received from contractors to build them. Mr. Müller supposed that the building fund accumulated, £34,002, 2s., was of ample amount to meet all expenses. But the prices of building material and wages had so increased since the previous houses were built, that it appeared from the estimates of contractors that £7,000 more would be needed.

Now, what was to be done under these circumstances?

My decision was made instantly. My heart longed to build two more houses to the honor of the Lord for the benefit of poor children, bereaved of both parents by death; I had brought before the Lord many thousands of prayers during the past five years; there were many hundreds of orphans waiting for admission, and their number daily increasing (for during the past year alone, as stated before, 611 were applied for to be admitted); but I could not contract debt; I would not sign contracts, which I had not money in hand to meet. Should it be said: "But your work is so manifestly the Lord's work, it is surely according to his mind, that destitute children, who have lost by death both parents, should be cared for, so that you need not be afraid to build, though you have not yet all the money in hand, for God will surely help you: my reply is this. Just because it is the Lord's work, and manifestly his, therefore I can wait, patiently wait his time. When his time is come, he will give to the last shilling all I need; but if I commence before his time, which I should do were I to begin that for which I have not the means, it would be like saying: "God has not money enough to pay for his own work;" and, instead of acting in faith, I should act presumptuously. I therefore did this. As I had ample means to meet the contract for No. 4 (for separate tenders were given in for the two houses), I accepted it, and a written agreement was made between the contractor and myself, that on Jan. 1, 1867, or at any time previously, I may accept his tender for No. 5 also, but I shall not be bound to do so. If it shall, therefore, please the Lord, by the 1st of Jan., 1867, to give me about £7,000 more than I have now in hand, the contract for No. 5 will be signed; but I cannot go in debt.

It is gratifying to know that the amount needed was received in time to make the tender binding. Jan. 1, 1867, he writes: —

On the 26th of May, 1866, I needed about £7,000 more than I had in hand, to be able to accept the contract for No. 5 without going in debt; but by the 31st of Dec., 1866, the Lord had so graciously helped, as that a little more than £7,000 had come in by donations and interest, so that a day before the 1st of January, 1867, I was able to accept and sign the contract for No. 5, the contracts for both houses being £41,147. I had now the desire of my heart given to me, regarding this point also, and had the precious recompense from the Lord, in having received all the money from him for this object without going in debt. Thousands of times I had asked the Lord for the means needed for building these two houses, and now I had, to the full, received the answer.

It appeared also in the end to be providential that the sum needed for both houses was not in hand, when the contract for house No. 4 was signed. Mr. Müller writes, at a later date: —

It is necessary here to state, that, if even all the money had been in hand on May 3, 1866, to contract at once for both houses, yet only one house could have been gone on with; for the houses are so large, that no contractor in Bristol has sufficient scaffolding to begin the two houses at once, but there must necessarily intervene between the commencement of the one and the other eight or nine months. This difficulty could only have been overcome, had there been sufficient money in hand, by having two different contractors, which was for many reasons very undesirable, or by employing one of the great London contractors; but if the latter had been done, the two houses would have cost about £7,000 more than they now will cost.

The year 1866 was memorable for two powerful revivals at the Orphan Houses. There had been, in previous years, especially in 1859 and 1860, seasons of marked religious interest, in which a number of the orphans gave evidence of a genuine change of heart. But each of these revivals of 1866 was more powerful than any which had gone before, and the latter gave a signal display of divine power. The first began at the opening of the year, and, without any apparent cause, more than a hundred girls were suddenly in earnest about their souls, and, months after, gave evidence that a new life had begun in them.

The other revival began in the conversion, on her deathbed, of one of the girls. The account, by Mr. Muller, is full of interest: —

When now this dear girl was convinced of sin, and made so unspeakably happy through faith in the Lord Jesus, she manifested the deepest concern about the salvation of her young friends and companions in the new Orphan House No. 3, and sent several messages to them from her dying bed, entreating them to seek the Lord. On Sunday, May 27, 1866, she found peace in the Lord, and on Tuesday morning, May 29th, she fell peacefully asleep in Jesus. Her thoughtlessness and carelessness regarding the things of God had been well known among the orphans, and her conversion and her messages were now used by the Lord as the instrument of the most extensive and glorious work of the Spirit of God that we ever have had among the children, during the whole time that the orphan work has been in existence. I write after the lapse of five weeks, reckoning from the death of Emma Bunn, and about *350 orphans* in the new Orphan House No. 3 alone, *have since then been led to seek the Lord, and the greater part of them have found peace for their souls, through faith in the Lord Jesus.* These dear children, formerly almost all careless and indifferent, and most of them much like what

Emma Bunn had been, have their prayer-meetings among themselves, as often as they can, and, in other ways, give joy to our hearts.

Another revival, with even more wonderful results than those of 1866, was enjoyed in 1872. The small-pox was prevailing at that time in the Orphan Houses, and there were a number of deaths, not only among the children, but also among the teachers and helpers. God was pleased to mingle mercies with affliction, and a profound religious interest manifested itself in all the houses. Its good fruits were delightful. Mr. Muller says: —

I have just received the statements of all the matrons and teachers in the five houses, who report to me, that, after careful observation, they have good reason to believe that *729 of the orphans under our care are believers in the Lord Jesus.* This number of believing orphans is by far greater than ever we had, for which we adore and praise the Lord.

It is worthy of note, as indicating the sovereignty of God, in the *special* gifts of the Holy Spirit, that these revivals of 1859, 1860, 1866, and 1872, have been the only ones of *remarkable power*, in the history of the Orphan Houses. One might suppose that so large a company of children, under the best religious influences, and directed by a man so mighty in prayer as Mr. Müller, would be visited every year with revival influences. But while prayer was answered daily in providential mercies, and food and clothing were never wanting, the spiritual gifts were more rarely bestowed.

In November, 1868, the fourth house was opened, with

accommodations for 450 orphans. The labor involved in making preparation to receive this large number of new inmates was so great that the opening of the fifth house was postponed for more than a year. The correspondence alone was immense, involving the writing of several thousand letters, for Mr. Muller was very particular in learning the history of all the families from which the orphans were taken. Of the other work required, he says: —

It is difficult for those who are not acquainted with the practical working of such an Institution to enter into the great amount of labor connected therewith; but were they to see all the many thousands of articles of house-linen, and all the many thousands of articles of clothing required for only one such Orphan House for one hundred and fifty children, they would easily perceive **how it comes that I have not yet been able to open No. 5.**

CHAPTER XXVI.

1868 — 1872.

DONATIONS — FIFTH ORPHAN HOUSE — HABITS OF BENEVOLENCE — DEATH OF MRS. MÜLLER — MR. WRIGHT AN ASSOCIATE — PLACES FOR THE ORPHANS — OBJECTS OF THE INSTITUTION — ORPHANS LEAVING THE INSTITUTION — SPECIMEN OF ARTICLES DONATED — NOTE FROM MR. MÜLLER RESPECTING BOOKS AND ACCOUNTS — ANNUAL REPORT FOR 1872.

SOME interesting facts in the Reports of 1868 and 1872 are worthy of record: —

March 30. — Received also from a laborer in the gospel, who preaches without any salary, and trusts in the Lord for his temporal necessities, 12s., with this statement: "Dear Mr. Müller: I desire to enclose 12s. for your work for the Lord, and trust he will continue to supply all your need. He loveth a cheerful giver; for he is the *most* cheerful giver, who gave us his dear Son, and with him freely gives us all things. The Lord led me five years since, to begin with a tenth to give to him of all he sent me for my use; and, by his grace, he has helped me to go from a tenth to a seventh, then to a fifth, now to a half of all he gives me. As the work increases, and helpers come forward to the work, so he has enabled me to share with them."

April 6. — From California £4, with the following letter: "Dear Sir: on reading your Narrative I found that, after many years of profession, I was only producing leaves; for, according to your remark, I was living up to my means, forgetting the command, 'Deny thyself and take up thy cross and follow me.' By the help of God I was enabled to examine myself, and made an effort to deny a luxury. After trial I found that I was better without than with it. The produce is twenty dollars, which I transmit to your care for the use of the children in your Institution, and will feel thankful if the merciful Father accepts this gift from an aged sinner, bordering on eighty."

June 3.—Received to-day £51, 5s., with the following letter: "My dear Sir: I enclose my check, value £51, 5s., to be applied, £20 for missions, £20 for the dear children under your care, and the balance for yourself £11, 5s. I send this in acknowledgment of God's mercies. having had great losses in business, and feeling truly thankful that I am in a position to bear them, and still to carry on my business as usual, with the prayer that God may keep me humble at the foot of the cross of Christ."

Jan. 1, 1872.—"My dear Sir: through the Lord's goodness I am enabled to send you herewith £125; £5 for your own expenses, and £120 in aid of the work under your care. It is now ten years since I first sent you anything, and about the same time since I began to give systematically to God's work, through reading of your Narrative. Like many others I can say, that God has made up to me all that I have given and far more. I trust you are in good health, and feeling assured that all is going well with you, I am, yours faithfully, * * * *."—This Christian gentleman has sent me during the last ten years more than £5,000 for the work of the Lord; he has sent as God has been pleased to prosper him; and his testimony is, "that God has made up to him all that he has given, and far more."

Jan. 29.—Received £2,000 with the following letter: "Dear Sir: I send you £2,000, the produce of the sale of some property, which has given me much trouble of mind, and the proceeds of which have been devoted to the Lord's service. It is become evident that *he* saw it not good for me to hold so much, and therefore allowed its possession to be rather a curse than a blessing. That it may prove a blessing by your appropriation of it, under his guidance, is the prayer of, yours truly, * * * *." This letter is full of instruction. 1. The Christian gentleman who sent this money is anything but covetous; for he had for about twenty years sent me much for the Lord's work, and for many years about £200 annually; yet he considered that he held *too much*. So other disciples of the Lord Jesus may hold *too much*. 2. The writer states further, that, because the Lord saw it not good for him to hold so much, he allowed its possession to be rather a curse than a blessing. Shall not all of us seek to be profited by the experience of this Christian gentleman? Are not all of us, naturally, to a greater or less degree, fond of possessions, and therefore aiming rather after a curse than a blessing? 3. Possessions, small or great, are just in so far of value as they are used for the Lord.

In the Report for 1869 is recorded a striking instance of the increase which follows liberal giving:—

This poor cripple began with a very small proportion. She gave one penny per week; but God blessed her planting a piece of waste land with potatoes, so, after this, that she found she possessed in potatoes, etc., 1858, £10. She gave now $\frac{1}{2}$d. per day, viz., $3\frac{1}{2}$d. per week, instead of one penny per week, and at the end of 1859 she had in potatoes, etc., £15. In 1860 she gave double as much as the year before, and had at the end of the year £20. In 1861 she gave 2d. daily, or 1s. 2d. per week, and her property was, by the end of 1861, increased to £30. During the year 1862 she gave 3d. per day, and found herself possessed, at the close of the year, of £45. In 1863 she gave 4d. per day, and had at the end of the year £63. During the year 1864, this poor cripple was able to give away 6d. per day, and yet had at the close of the year more than at the beginning; for she possessed now in pigs, potatoes, etc., £75. In 1865 she increased her contributions to 8d. per day, and had at the end of the year £86. In 1866 she gave after the rate of 10d. per day, and her property amounted, at the close of the year, to £93. During 1867 she gave 1s. per day, and this poor cripple possessed now, in pigs, etc., property to the amount of £150 at the end of the year of 1867.

The fifth house was opened Jan. 6, 1870, having accommodations, like the third and fourth, for 450 orphans, and, with the others, for 2,050 in all. But it was not at once filled, though the number of applicants exceeded the ample provisions made. The prevalence of measles and scarlet fever made it undesirable to receive many new-comers, and the death of Mrs. Muller, in February, who for thirty-four years had been his most efficient helper in the orphan work, almost paralyzed progress. The grief of the orphans was great at the loss of their benefactress, and those who had gone out from the Institution in previous years requested the privilege of contributing something for a monument over her grave. The privilege was granted, and the gifts flowed in so freely that a sum fourfold larger than was needed soon accumulated.

In Nov., 1871, Mr. James Wright married the only daughter of Mr. Muller, and was designated as the successor on whom the responsibility of the Orphan Houses would rest, in case of Mr. Müller's death. For thirteen years Mr. Wright had been one of the most valuable helpers in the Institution, and Mr. Müller and his wife had made it a matter of constant prayer, that he might be fitted of God for the leadership of the work. In Feb., 1870, Mr. Muller, after the death of his wife, proposed to Mr. Wright to become his associate with the view of succeeding him at death; but Mr. Wright was not ready to assume so grave a responsibility. Soon after his own wife died, his feelings

THE FIFTH ORPHAN HOUSE, ASHLEY DOWN.

changed, and he felt it would not be right to shrink from a plain duty. This step was a great relief to Mr. Müller. He says: —

By the Lord's kindness I am able to work as heretofore, I may say with little hindrance through illness; yet, as I am sixty-six years of age, I cannot conceal from myself, that it is of great importance for the work, that I should obtain a measure of relief. This relief, however, can be really only given to me by one who stands in a similar position to the work, and who, when I am away, or when I may feel it desirable to have real rest, could do all I ordinarily do in directing. On this account I have, therefore, not only appointed Mr. Wright as my successor, in the event of my death, but have, also, associated him at present with me in the direction of the Institution, which year by year increases in extent.

The large increase of expenditure involved in the opening of the fourth and fifth houses brought no anxiety to Mr. Muller. He knew that the Lord, who had helped him hitherto, would support him under the heavier burdens. Nor was he disappointed. He writes in 1870: —

"Though the current expenses of the Institution were far greater during the past year than during any of the previous thirty-five years, yet we abounded more than ever."

He rejoiced, also, in the assurance that the end for which he commenced the experiment was reached. The success of the Orphan Houses during so many years, in which no debts were ever incurred, nor were the orphans in want even for a single day, was a standing proof of the power of prayer. Who, in the face of such facts, could deny or doubt that God answers the prayers of his people, who trust only in his help? Mr. Muller says: —

The greatest of all the spiritual blessings, however, resulting from this work, I judge to be this, that the Reports which have been issued in connection therewith, have not only been instrumental in the conversion of many sinners, by leading them to see the reality of the things of God, but have, also, in the cases of many thousands of Christian persons, as their letters have testified to me, during the past thirty years, been a great spiritual help to them, in comforting them, leading them more fully to cast their burdens upon the Lord, increasing their faith, showing to them practically and experimentally that the Living God is still the Living God, and in other respects benefiting their souls. This point was the great and chief end of the establishment of the orphan work, that thus God might be glorified. This end has been answered beyond the largest expectations which I had in the year 1835.

It is one of the aims never lost sight of by Mr. Müller, to train the orphans under his care for the practical work of life. He is not content with giving them a pleasant home, and a good education. He longs to make them useful members of society, and skilful workers in the world. His success has been most gratifying, for the training of his institution is one of the best recommendations for any boy or girl. There is a large demand for the orphans, who are sent out every year to service or to trades. The girls are generally sent to service, and the boys to different trades. On this point Mr. Müller says: —

We uniformly prefer fitting the girls for service, instead of apprenticing them to a business, as being, generally, far better for their bodies and souls. Only in a few instances have female orphans been apprenticed to businesses, when their health would not allow them to go to service. If the girls give us satisfaction, while under our care, so that we can recommend them to a situation, they are fitted out at the expense of the establishment. The girls, generally, remain under our care till they are about 17 years old. They very rarely leave sooner; and, as we receive children from their earliest days, we have often had girls 13, 14, yea, above 17 years under our care. They are instructed in reading, writing, arithmetic, English grammar, geography, English history, a little of universal history, all kinds of useful needlework and household work. They make their clothes and keep them in repair; they work in the kitchens, sculleries, wash-houses and laundries; and, in a word, we aim after this, that if any of them do not do well temporally or spiritually, and do not turn out useful members of society, it shall at least not be *our* fault. The boys are, generally, apprenticed when they are between fourteen and fifteen years old. But *in each case* we consider the welfare of the *individual* orphan, without having any fixed rule respecting these matters. The boys have a free choice of the trade they like to learn; but, having once chosen, and being apprenticed, we do not allow them to alter. The boys, as well as the girls, have an outfit provided for them; and any other expenses, that may be connected with their apprenticeship, are also met by the funds of the orphan establishment. It may be interesting to the reader to know the kind of trades to which we generally apprentice the boys, and I therefore say, that, during the *last* twenty-one years, all the boys who were apprenticed were bound to carpenters, or carpenters and joiners, basket makers, shoe makers, tailors and drapers, plumbers, painters and glaziers, linendrapers, printers, bakers, grocers, hair-dressers, ironmongers, tinplate workers, confectioners, hosiers, builders, millers, gasfitters, smiths, outfitters, provision dealers, sail makers, upholsterers, wholesale grocers, chemists, seed merchants, umbrella makers, or electro plate manufacturers. The boys have the same kind of mental cultivation as the girls, and they learn to knit and mend their stockings. They also make their beds, clean their shoes, scrub their rooms, go errands, and work in the garden ground round the orphan establishment, in the way of digging, planting, weeding, etc.

Mr. Müller is a man of methodical habits, and has a perfect system in the distribution of the orphans in the different houses, in the daily management of the work, and in the time for admitting visitors, and conducting them through the establishment. He gives a brief statement of the order followed in classifying the orphans, and in admitting visitors: —

The new Orphan House No. 1 is fitted up for the accommodation of 140 orphan girls above eight years of age, 80 orphan boys above eight years, and 80 female orphans from their earliest days till they are about eight years of age. The infants, after having passed the age of eight years, are removed into the department for older girls. The new Orphan House No. 2 is fitted up for 200 infant female orphans, and for 200 older female orphans. The new Orphan House No. 3 is fitted up for 450 older female orphans. The new Orphan House No. 4 is fitted up for 210 boys of eight years old and upwards, 208 infant boys under eight years of age, and 32 older girls, to do the household work, 450 in all. The new Orphan House No 5 is fitted up for 210 infant female orphans, and for 240 older female orphans.

The new Orphan House No. 1 is open to visitors every Wednesday afternoon; the new Orphan House No. 2, every Tuesday afternoon; the new Orphan House No. 3, every

Thursday afternoon; the new Orphan House No. 4, every Friday afternoon; and the new Orphan House No. 5, every Saturday afternoon; but the arrangements of the establishments make it needful that they should be shown at those times only. No exceptions can be made. The first party of visitors will be shown through the houses at half-past two o'clock, God permitting; the second at there o'clock; and, should there be need for it, the third and last party at half-past three o'clock. As it takes at least one hour and a half to see the whole of each establishment, it is requested that the visitors will be pleased to make their arrangements accordingly before they come, as it would be inconvenient should one or the other leave before the whole party has seen the house.

In the report for 1872, Mr. Muller, in addition to a particular review of the year, gives a summary of the work accomplished since the foundation of the Scriptural Knowledge Institution. It indicates the wonderful growth of the work, and the fulness of the divine blessing granted to his labors.

THE OBJECTS OF THE INSTITUTION ARE: —

1. To *assist* day schools, Sunday schools, and adult schools, in which instruction is given upon *Scriptural principles*, and, as far as the Lord may give the means, supply us with suitable teachers, and in other respects to make our path plain, to *establish* schools of this kind.

There are altogether sixty-five schools, entirely supported by the funds of the Institution (40 day schools, 14 Sunday schools, 11 adult schools); and that during the past year twenty-one schools were assisted, viz., 8 day schools and 13 Sunday schools. From what has been stated it will likewise be seen, that in the sixty-five schools, entirely supported by the funds of the Institution, there were on May 26, 1872, altogether 4,747 scholars. The total number that frequented the schools of the Institution, entirely supported by its funds, from the beginning, amounts to twenty-seven thousand four hundred and eighty-eight, viz., there were 16,455 in all the day schools, 6,275 in all the Sunday schools, and 4,758 in all the adult schools.

2. The *second* object of this Institution is, to *circulate the Holy Scriptures.*

The number of Bibles, New Testaments, and Portions of the Holy Scriptures, which have been circulated from May 26, 1871, to May 26, 1872, is as follows:—

    4,493 Bibles have been sold.

    6,728 Bibles have been given away.

   37,635 New Testaments have been sold.

   16,596 New Testaments have been given away.

    6,826 Copies of the Psalms have been sold.

    4,083 Copies of the Psalms have been given away.

    9,414 Other small portions of the Holy Scriptures have been sold.

25,671 Ditto, given away.

There have been circulated since March 5, 1834, through the medium of this Institution, 75,392 Bibles, 139,218 New Testaments, 13,605 copies of the Psalms, and 132,134 other small portions of the Holy Scriptures.

3. The *third* object of the Institution is, to *aid missionary efforts.*

During the past year was expended of the funds of the Institution, for this object, the sum of £11,640, 9s. $4\frac{1}{2}$d. By this sum one hundred and eighty-seven laborers in the Word and doctrine, in various parts of the world, were, to a greater or less degree, assisted.

The total amount of the funds of the Institution, which have been spent on missionary operations since March 5, 1834, is £116,337, 16s. $5\frac{1}{2}$d.

4. The *fourth* object of the Institution is, *the circulation*

of such publications as may be calculated, with the blessing of God, to benefit both believers and unbelievers. As it respects *tracts for unbelievers*, we especially aim after the diffusion of such as contain the truths of the gospel clearly and simply expressed; and as it respects *publications for believers*, we desire to circulate such as may be instrumental in directing their minds to those truths which, in these last days, are more especially needed, or which have been particularly lost sight of, and may lead believers to return to the written Word of God.

There has been laid out for this object, from May 26, 1871, to May 26, 1872, the sum of £1,118, 11s. 7d.; and there have been circulated within the last year more than three million six hundred and eighty-four thousand (exactly 3,684,842) tracts and books. The sum total which has been expended on this object, since Nov. 19, 1840, amounts to £20,956, 10s., 4¼d.

The total number of all the tracts and books, which have been circulated since Nov. 19, 1840, is above forty-two millions and a half (exactly 42,578,554.)

5. The *fifth* object of the Institution is, to *board, clothe, and Scripturally educate destitute children* who have lost BOTH parents by death.

At the commencement of the last period there were 1845 orphans in the new Orphan Houses No. 1, No. 2, No. 3, No. 4, and No. 5. During the past year 260 orphans were admitted into the five houses now in operation; so that the total number on May 26, 1872, would have been 2,105, had there been no changes. The total number of orphans who have been under our care since April 11, 1836, is 3,835.

Without any one having been personally applied to for anything by me, the sum of £370,535, 1s. 0d. has been given to me for the orphans, *as the result of prayer to God*, since the commencement of the work, which sum includes the amount received for the building fund for the five houses. It may also be interesting to the reader to know that the total amount, which has been given for the other objects, since the commencement of the work, amounts to £154,253, 2s. 3¾d.; and that which has come in by the sale of Bibles, since the commencement, amounts to £5,354, 18s. 10d.; by the sale of tracts, £10,440, 15s. 11¾d.; and by the payment of the children in the day schools, from the commencement, £3,987, 0s. 7½d. Besides this, also, a great variety and number of articles of clothing, furniture, provisions, etc., have been given *for the use* of the orphans.

Mr. Müller is constantly receiving not only contributions in money, but a great variety of useful articles, which are regularly sent to a shop provided for their sale. The following list as a specimen of such articles, given anonymously during the first six months of the year, will not be without interest to the reader, as showing by what an endless diversity of means resources are furnished for the work in which Mr. M. is engaged: —

June. A bead bag, a bouquet-holder, 6 gilt brooches, a gilt bracelet, a waist-buckle, and an agate heart. — 5 pairs of knitted travelling shoes, a compass and thermometer, a court-plaster case, a guinea piece, 2 half-franc pieces, a copper coin, 4 rings, a brooch, a gold pencil-case, a pair of earrings, top of a seal, and a gold waist-buckle. — A silver watch-guard, a small brooch, a breastpin, and a ring. — 12 pairs of garters. — A sofa tidy. — A small stereoscopic box. — 6 frocks, 6 shirts, 4 pocket-handkerchiefs, 2 pairs of socks, 2 nightcaps, 12 kettle-holders, 2 pair of wristlets, 4 thimbles, 2 brooches, steel slides, a bracelet, and waist-buckle. — A bead mat, 2 bags, a penwiper, 3 book-marks, and a scent bag. — A pencil, 2 pairs of spectacles, a smelling-bottle, a pocket-book, some gloves, stockings, combs, and various articles of clothing, etc., together with a half-sovereign

July. An old silver watch, an old metal watch, and an old shilling. — 2 coats, 1 jacket, 1 waistcoat, 1 pair of trousers, and 1 pair of gaiters. — 5 dresses, a body, and two shillings. — 9 pen-wipers, 4

babies' shirts, 9 mats, 1 pair of baby's boots, 2 nightcaps, 6 pinafores, 2 pairs of watch-pockets, 1 ribbon mat, 1 pin-cushion, 2 needle-books, and 3 book-markers. — 2 dolls, 2 dolls' hats, a pair of bracelets, a pincushion, a needle-book, a shaving-cloth, a sampler, 2 pairs of cuffs, a kettle-holder, a penwiper, a pair of baby's shoes, a book-mark, a bag, a watch-guard, a pinafore, and a pamphlet. — 2 buckles, a smelling-bottle, some mock pearls, 3 hair bracelets, a hair ring, and a wig.

August. Some fancy envelopes. — A ring, 2 shirt-studs, and a watch-hook. — A pattern for a collar. — A ring from Stroud. — 12 new bonnets. — A brooch, a bracelet, a book-marker, some cuffs, a pattern for work, and some trimming. — A frame for ladies' work. — "From the friend at Devizes," 2 skirts of dresses, a jacket, and a shawl. — Some pencil lead for polishing. — Some knitting and sewing cotton. — 2 old wedding rings. — 3 balls. — 8 book-marks, 4 postage-stamp cases, and 6 pin-cushions.

September. A parcel containing some worsted, some brass thimbles, bodkins, and needles. — 4 black ostrich feathers, 1 white ditto, 4 colored drawings. — 3 pairs of socks, 6 pairs of stockings, and 2 waistcoats. — A pair of patent renovators (or flesh gloves). — A small work-bag of silk and straw — A guinea piece, a lace habit shirt, a pair of lace sleeves, and a French cambric handkerchief. — 3 collars, 1 pocket handkerchief, and 1 pair of sleeves. — 2 flannel petticoats, a table-cover, a silver wine-strainer, a silver marrow-spoon, 1 sugar spoon, a punch ladle, 6 chemises, and 6 pinafores. — A small hamper of books. — 1 alpaca coat, 1 check waistcoat, 1 pair of trousers, 3 pairs of shoes, 1 travelling cap, 1 pair of spectacles in case, 2 pair of boots, 5 muffetees, 1 pair of gaiters, 1 pair of boots, 8 copper pens, 1 pair of slippers, 1 black leather bag, 1 pair of new boots, 1 coat, 1 waistcoat, 5 pairs of gloves, 1 pair of braces, a necktie, a dressing box, 2 brushes, 3 razors, a stiletto, a pair of spectacles, and 2 pieces of teeth set in gold. — 12 book-covers, 7 small ditto, 1 small box, 4 ditto in one. — A large box of toys. — A collar. — A large tea-chest, containing 160 articles of ladies' dress, etc. — A dress, three bodies, 3 berthas, a waistband, a pair of cuffs, a feather, an ornament for the hair, some artificial flowers, some whalebone, and some pieces of ribbon. — A cloth mantle, a velvet jacket, and a muslin ditto.

October. 3 pairs of crotchet ladies' slippers, and 1 pair of child's ditto. — A pair of gilt bracelets, a collar, a pair of cuffs, and a pair of worked sleeves. — 2 paper mats, a bead ditto, a plaister case, 3 needle-books, 5 small cushions, 4 pin-cushions, 2 pen-wipers, a book-mark,

2 little baskets, a little bag, a doll, a pair of candlestick ornaments, and 6 napkin rings. — The parcel also contained 5s. from "Hephzibah." — An urn-stand, a bag, and a mat. — A collar. — 6 pence purses. — 3 dolls' bonnets. — "A Canadian lady's purse." — 9 pairs of boots, 3 pairs of shoes, and a single boot, all new.

November. A box containing 5 bonnets, 2 muslin jackets, 1 silk ditto, 1 silk body, 3 muslin dresses, 1 silk ditto, 1 barege skirt, 18 pairs of fine stockings, 17 pairs of coarse ditto, 3 pairs of boots, 3 stockings, 10 chemises, 3 pairs of drawers, 5 night-dresses, some pieces of ribbon, and a few artificial flowers. — 6 pairs of night-socks. — A riding habit, a box, a silk body, some velvet trimming, some satin ditto, 2 waistbands, some fringe, some satin ribbon, a feather, a scarf, a veil, and a pair of woollen sleeves. — 3 silver coins. — A silver tablespoon, some satin trimming, and a frill. — 4 dresses, a skirt, a jacket, 3 children's skirts, and 2 frocks. — A small gold pencil-case, a gold breastpin, and a pair of small gold earrings. — A collar. — 3 antimacassars, and a baby's cap. — 2 silver coins, and a pair of silver shirt-studs. — 7 boys' shirts. — A jacket and a feather. — A jacket, a pair of drawers, 2 chemises, 2 nightcaps, 5 skirts, and 1 body. — 4 pairs of new boots, and 2 pairs of new shoes. — A crumb-scraper.

Mr. Muller, as a faithful steward, renders an annual account of all sums received, and how disbursed by him (see opposite page), to which is appended an "Auditor's Report." Mr. M. says: —

The audited accounts, together with the books containing the income and expenses, may be inspected by the donors. I particularly state this, because I do not publish a list of the donors, nor do I mention their *names* otherwise, *in order that there may not be held out the least temptation of giving for the sake of worldly applause;* but, at the same time, as I do this work in the light, it can bear the light, and therefore any donor can satisfy himself, if he please, that his donation is accounted for.

To avoid mistakes, delays, and other difficulties, I would request that all letters for me should be directed to my house, No. 21, Paul Street, KINGSDOWN, BRISTOL.

GEORGE MÜLLER.

THE INCOME AND EXPENSES OF THE INSTITUTION, FOR 1871-72.

...ome of the first four Objects, from May 26, 1871, to May 28, 1872.		£	s.	d.	The Expenses connected with the first four Objects, from May 26, 1871, to May 26, 1872.	£	s.	d.	The Income for the Orphans, from May 26, 1871, to May 26, 1872.	£	s.	d.	The Expenses for the Orphans, from May 26, 1871, to May 26, 1872.	£	s.	d.
...nce in hand on ...6, 1871		2,417	4	4¾	For the Home Schools	2,284	8	1¼	By Balance in hand on May 26, 1871	14,726	2	5¾	The current Expenses in connexion with the five Orphan houses	23,163	2	3¼
...ations		14,002	8	7¾	For Bibles	1,942	13	10	By Donations in Money	18,964	2	3¾	For the Apprentices	577	1	3¼
...e of Articles for the purpose		45	0	0	For Missionary Purposes	11,640	9	4¼	By Sale of Articles given for the purpose	762	0	10¼	For 24,000 copies of the Thirty-second Report, and 5,250 copies of the Supplement	315	16	0
...of Tracts, &c.		509	5	1	For Tracts	1,118	11	7¼	By sale of Reports	171	17	2¼				
...of Bibles		548	2	0¼	For Postage	39	13	7¼	By Cash paid on behalf of Orphans	238	5	9	For Postage and Carriage of Boxes and Parcels	110	11	6¼
...ol Receipts		359	7	6	For Stationery	10	17	0¼					For Stationery	22	3	7
					Balance in hand on May 26, 1872	844	14	0½					Balance in hand on May 26, 1872	10,673	13	11
		£17,881	7	7		£17,881	7	7		£34,862	8	7¼		£34,865	8	7¼

...ncome from the Building Fund, from May 26, 1871, to May 26, 1872.	£	s.	d.	Expenses in connection with the Building Fund.	£	s.	d.
...unt received up to May 26, 1871	105,255	14	2¼	Expended up to May 26, 1871	100,033	10	9
...ations in Money	18	7	0	Expended since May 26, 1871, on the Five Orphan Houses	1,001	17	9
...of the Fields	90	1	0	Balance in Hand on May 26th, 1872	5,276	14	5¾
...rest	948	0	2				
	£106,312	2	11¾		£106,312	2	11¾

..., July 5, 1872.   We have carefully examined these Accounts, and find them correct.   H. S. TIREMAN.
H. M. BECHER.   SAMUEL BUTLER.

CHAPTER XXVII.

A VISIT TO THE ORPHAN HOUSES — ATTENDING CHURCH — INTERNAL ARRANGEMENTS — FOOD — EDUCATION — HEALTH.

IN a brief history of the Orphan Houses, prepared by Mr. W. Elfe Taylor, of England, is a chapter devoted to an account of a personal visit, with a full sketch of the internal arrangements, and of the appearance and occupation of the orphans. We give the larger part of it, as full of interest for American readers : -

It is a striking sight to watch the orphans passing through the streets of Bristol, on their way to attend divine worship. Every Sunday morning they may be seen marching, two and two, up and down the hilly thoroughfares of that ancient city, on their way to Bethesda Chapel, where Mr. Muller ministers, there to hear the words of eternal life expounded. Each Orphan House contributes its troop of two or three hundred children — the boys and girls being marshalled in separate bands, and accompanied by their different masters, matrons, and teachers. True indeed is the saying so often in substance heard expressed : "That silent stream of children is the most powerful sermon ever preached in the city of Bristol."

It was on a fine autumnal afternoon in October that we paid a long-promised visit to this remarkable Institution. As we briskly walked up the hill which separates what is called Ashley Down from the city, the woods in the distance were already clothed in the various hues of autumn, affording to the thoughtful mind a striking instance of that law by which the beneficent Creator makes even ruin and desolation minister to the pleasure and happiness of his creatures. Altogether the walk is one of the prettiest out of Bristol, the road being studded with neat, elegant villas on each side, and though so near a city resounding with the din of business, the neighborhood of Ashley Hill is as quiet and retired as if situated in the heart of the country.

At length we came within sight of the New Orphan Houses, and truly vast erections they are, of almost interminable length. On entering the grounds in which two of the houses stand, we passed the lodge, a neat little cottage on the right, and proceeded along the pathway by the side of the carriage-drive, which, together with a well-trimmed lawn, and some pretty flower-beds, separates No. 1 House from No. 2. There are large pieces of ground surrounding each of the houses, devoted to the cultivation of vegetables. The perfect order and neatness characterizing everything outside the establishment gave us a good intimation of what we might expect within; nor were we disappointed.

On ringing at the entrance, we were admitted by a respectable female into a stone hall, and thence up a staircase into the waiting-room, already occupied by several visitors seated in groups and chatting together in subdued tones. Books and pamphlets were spread out on a table, near which sat a well-dressed young person sewing. She was placed there to receive the money from any visitors who wished to buy Mr. Muller's Reports, or the Narrative of his life; but none were asked to purchase.

The Orphan House No. 1, which contains usually 140 girls above seven years of age, 80 boys of the same age, and 80 infants of either sex, was that we first visited; but in describing it we shall follow that order which seems best fitted to give a clear understanding of the establishment, and not that in which the different parts are — to save time — shown to visitors.

There are three school-rooms, — boys', girls', and infants', — all large, airy, cheerful-looking apartments. The girls', which is shown first of the three, is very spacious and lofty, situated on the ground-floor, and well fitted up with the best modern maps and other helps for learning. As our party, numbering some sixty or seventy, entered, we beheld about one hundred and twenty girls, sitting at work at low desks; all clothed alike in blue print frocks and neat pinafores, and with their hair cut short behind, but arranged with the greatest neatness. On a signal from the principal teacher, who was stationed on a small platform, with a desk in front, the girls all stood up and placed their hands behind them. At another signal one of the orphans struck up a cheerful song, which the rest at once joined in, and all marched out in single file, with as much precision in their steps as any of our modern volunteer corps would exhibit. The effect of this sight was really very striking; and he who can witness unmoved these helpless orphans winding their way between the desks, to the music of the touching songs which they sang, one after another, must indeed be made of very impenetrable materials. As they passed round the ends of the desks in front of the visitors, who lined the walls on either side, I looked carefully at the features of each child, and, although in some cases I saw evident traces of disease, inherited, doubtless, from the parents whom they had lost,* still there was a general appearance of health and of cheerfulness in their happy faces.

Then we were taken to the girls' "cloak and shoe room," where we found a vast number of serviceable plaid cloaks hanging up around the room, for winter wear. Each girl, too, has three pairs of shoes for use, — a mark of sound economy on Mr. Müller's part, as every *paterfamilias* well knows.

The boys' school-room does not materially differ from that of the girls. There were, at our entrance, about 80

---

*From the statistics in Mr. Muller's possession, it is said that upwards of two-thirds of the parents have died of consumption.

boys seated at desks, dressed all alike in blue cloth jackets and corduroy trousers. Their appearance was certainly that of vigorous health. They looked sturdy, good-tempered fellows. At the word of command they all rose from their seats, and marched one after another between the desks to the air of some spirited song, just as the girls had before. Two separate rooms are appropriated as work-rooms also, — one for the boys, and one for the girls; the former are taught, a few at a time, to knit and mend their own stockings, and the girls to make their own garments, under the superintendence of a teacher who does the cutting out for them. Then come the play-rooms, one for boys and another for girls. These are large, lofty rooms, with a few low forms, and nothing else in the shape of furniture. These are, of course, only intended for use in bad weather, at least in the case of the boys. For there is a capital court for playing in for each class of orphans, and swings and other apparatus for exercise and play. The girls' play-room was provided with large cupboards, divided into small pigeon-holes, one for each child, well stored with dolls, dolls' houses, and a variety of other toys, the gifts, sometimes of relatives (who are allowed to visit the orphans once a month), sometimes of ladies, who present them to the teachers to be used as rewards.

The infant department in the Orphan House never fails to arrest the attention of visitors. Would that we could adequately bring before the reader the "infant school," with its two hundred little ones, or nearly so — many not more than three years of age. A prettier sight we have rarely witnessed than that of these destitute children, all marshalled in perfect order at a word of command, and marching round the room to the sound of their own merry voices. Then they proceeded in very soldier-like style to the gallery, and, when seated, sang two or three very pretty songs. One was: —

> " The little watch goes *tick, tick, tick,*
> So many times a minute;
> And as it goes so *quick, quick, quick,*
> What can the watch have in it?"

The words in italics were sung with particular emphasis and spirit.

Another was: —

> " Oh, we're all sawing — saw, saw, sawing —
> Oh, we're all sawing, at our pretty Infant School!
> The saw goes up and down, with a *push, push, push,*
> And through the log it cuts, with a *whish, whish, whish.*"

At the word "*push*" the little creatures suited the action to the word, and so with the corresponding word in the other lines of the song.

We must say a few words about the "infant nursery." Some infants, it should be remembered, are taken in so young that they are literally *babies*, and these are nursed in a small comfortable room by a motherly-looking head nurse, assisted by two or three of the elder girls. It was a touching sight to watch these helpless infants toddling about with pretty horses or dolls in their hands, and some in the arms of their nurses. Around the room, too, we noticed several little basket beds in which these tiny babies might be placed, when overcome with sleep, with all the fondness of a mother's love.

Many visitors seem to regard as one of the prettiest sights in the whole establishment the "infants' wardrobe." It was a room about twenty feet long, and ranged on each side of the room stood painted deal presses, divided into small pigeon-holes, in each of which were laid by, neatly folded up, small duplicates of all the various articles of clothing worn by the infants. The one side was set apart for the girls' wardrobes, each little pile of clothing being crowned by a pretty little straw bonnet, and each garment being most carefully and neatly rolled up and pinned together. On the opposite side stood the same number of presses for the boys' clothes, and on the top of each tiny wardrobe that occupied the pigeon-holes there was placed a little blue cloth cap. It is a fact, that scarcely any part of the house affects strangers so much as this infants' wardrobe; and it is a common thing to see tears in the eyes of one and another of the visitors, as they gaze on the exquisite order and nicety which prevail on every side, and think of the tender love which had so wonderfully cared for the smallest wants of these helpless little ones.

Next to the infants' wardrobe room comes the infants' dormitory. At the end of the dormitory is a passage on each side of which are situated the private rooms of the matrons and teachers. These were most comfortably furnished, and quite in keeping with the station of those who occupy such positions in the Orphan Houses. Each individual has a separate apartment.

The infants' dormitory, to which we have referred, is a spacious room, with abundance of air and light — filled with little tiny bedsteads. These are all of iron, painted of a light yellow color, and many fitted round with railings to preserve the younger babes from falling out. The beds are ranged in three rows from one end of the room to the other. There is no other article of furniture in the room of any description. Four larger beds — two at each end of the room — are occupied by the elder girls who take charge of the forty little orphans who nightly sleep in this cheerful room. Forty other infant orphans occupy the corresponding room to this, which we were afterwards shown.

There is a third bed-room for girls, in which 140 female orphans sleep — two girls occupying one bed. The same marvellous cleanliness of floors, and spotless purity of quilts and bed-clothes, with which our party was so impressed in the infants' dormitory, strikes us here. One good woman, in the height of her amazement, exclaimed, looking at the well-scrubbed boards, "Why, you might eat your dinner off them!" Another visitor, of the opposite sex, whose face was an index to the benevolence which filled his heart, observed, as he gazed at the beds, with the bedclothes folded down with the utmost nicety and precision: "Ah, they would never have slept in such beds if their parents had lived!" Great indeed was the admiration which this comfortable apartment elicited from our party. But it is impossible to describe the effect with pen and ink; it must be seen to be understood. At the end of the room there is a small window, opening into a bedroom occupied by one of the teachers, who is thus enabled to overlook the movements of the children. We afterwards saw the dormitories for boys, which it is unnecessary to describe, as they correspond exactly with the one just mentioned, except that only forty children sleep in each. Besides these, there is a smaller dormitory with eight beds in it for the elder girls, usually called "house-girls," as they are engaged in house-work, and are on the point of being sent out to service. Each of these has the privilege of a good strong box to hold her clothes in. These girls daily assist the servants in the general work of the house.

After we had seen the infants' wardrobes, we were invited to inspect two other wardrobe rooms. The first we came to was the boys'. The arrangement of this room exactly agreed with that containing the infants' clothes. Each boy has a square compartment, in which to keep his clothes, with his number marked, in one of the large deal presses that line the room. Six boys, we were told, are draughted out to take charge of the wardrobes, and see that everything is kept in proper order. When their term of service is expired, their place is supplied by six others, until each boy in the house, of a fit age, has taken his turn. The boys have each three suits of clothes. The girls' wardrobe room corresponded with that for the boys, except that it is much larger. There were the same lofty painted deal presses, subdivided into innumerable little pigeon-holes.

The girls have five changes of dress. Three blue print frocks for ordinary wear in the house, a lilac pattern dress for Sundays during the summer months, and a brown merino dress for winter wear. The girls make and mend all their own clothes. Six girls in rotation take charge of all the female wardrobes of the house; just as in the case of the boys.

The dining-room where all the orphans take their meals is a spacious apartment filled with long narrow tables and forms, all as white almost as the paper on which the reader's eye is now fixed. While we were inspecting this room, we noticed some of the elder girls employed in spreading the snow-white table-cloths for the evening meal. Others at the same time entered the room with trays loaded with bread-and-butter. Soon afterwards, some hundreds of cups filled with milk-and-water were placed upon the tables; but the orphans were not called to tea until after the visitors had left.

It may be interesting here to add a few particulars respecting the other meals of the children, which we obtained from our conductor. The food of the orphans at breakfast is always oatmeal porridge; they use milk with it. No doubt this wholesome food is one cause of the healthy, ruddy appearance of the orphans generally; for notwithstanding a strong prejudice against it in this country, a more wholesome, nutritious article of diet certainly does not exist. The dinner provided for the children varies almost every day. Monday there is boiled beef; Tuesday, soup, with a good proportion of meat in it; Wednesday, rice-milk with treacle; Thursday they have boiled leg of mutton; the following day they have soup again, and on Saturday bacon; on Sundays they always dine on rice with treacle, in order that as few as possible may be kept from attending public worship. The orphans breakfast at eight o'clock, dine at one, and take tea at six.

The kitchen of the establishment should by no means be overlooked. Here we saw the cooking apparatus, one of the most improved description, in which one small fire performed a variety of offices even at distant parts of the room. We were particularly struck with three huge upright copper cylinders which we found were used to boil the porridge in. A long pipe connects them with the fireplace; they consist of two vessels, the one inside the other. The steam is admitted through the pipe into the space between the outer and inner vessels; and a short time is sufficient to make the porridge boil. The cooking apparatus altogether is probably the most complete and efficient anywhere known.

We went into the store-rooms also. One was full of shoes, caps, haberdashery, etc. Another contained a large abundance of sheeting, blankets, calicoes, and such-like articles. A third was crowded with provisions of various descriptions, Scotch oatmeal in barrels, good wheaten flour in sacks, large quantities of meat, bread, sugar, etc., etc. We saw the bake-house too, and the washhouse. In the latter was an American washing machine, where wooden balls do the work of human knuckles. There was also a singular machine for wringing the clothes, called a Centrifugal Drying Machine.

Another apartment is called the "shoes and cloak room." Every child in the house has three pairs of shoes. The girls all wear cloaks of a green plaid in winter, and shawls in summer. Then there are the "washing-places." They are furnished with baths; and all around the walls were hung bags containing the brush and comb belonging to each child, and the number of the said child painted over each. The greatest care seemed to be taken to insure thorough cleanliness in the children, and to guard against the spread of infectious complaints, should they at any time exist.

It may be added that the children all rise about six o'clock in the morning. They retire to rest, the elder children about eight or nine, the younger an hour earlier. The teachers conduct religious worship every day, at half-past eight in the morning, and just before tea in the afternoon. They have two holidays in the year, at Whitsuntide and Christmas. But the orphans never leave the house on these occasions, except, as stated before, in company with their teachers. The beautiful manner in which the girls decorate their rooms at these holidays with their own work — festoons of artificial flowers, etc. — is one of many significant indications of the healthful, free, and cheerful spirit pervading the entire establishment.

We add a few remarks on the subject of the education of the children, and the effects of the system of training adopted by Mr. Muller on the health and bearing of the orphans.

As regards the education of the children, the girls are instructed in reading, writing, arithmetic, English grammar, geography, English history, a little of general history, and in all kinds of useful needlework and household work. They make their clothes, and keep them in repair; and Mr. Müller well observes in one of his Reports, "If any of them do not do well, temporally or spiritually, and do not turn out useful members of society, it shall, at least, not be *our* fault." The boys go through the same course of instruction as the girls, and they learn to knit and mend their own stockings. They also make their beds, clean their shoes, scrub their rooms, and work a little in the garden ground around the orphan establishment, in the way of digging, planting, weeding, etc.

There are some points connected with the education of these orphan children especially important to notice. For instance, there is evidently a more earnest desire to educate and discipline the mind, and draw out the kindly affections, than to cram the head with a large variety of knowledge, which may be, to say the least, of very questionable utility to children in their sphere of life. And in proof of the success which has attended this system of education, the general admiration expressed by visitors may be referred to. We would particularly mention a recent visit of some distinguished statesmen and members of Parliament,— Lord Stanley, Sir John Pakington, Lord Robert Cecil, Sir W. Miles, and others. It would be difficult adequately to convey the admiration and surprise which these illustrious persons expressed at the general character of the Institution, and the principles on which it was conducted. But what they especially noticed, whilst in the class-room, was the precision and accuracy with which the children were able to write from dictation. One of these noblemen observed, indeed, that the writing from dictation of some of the children exceeded those which he had lately inspected at one of our large National Institutions.

As regards the religious teaching imparted to these destitute children, it may be well to state, that the most diligent efforts are made to render them familiar with their Bible. The great doctrines of religion, in which all evangelical Christians agree, are carefully taught them, without, so far as we can learn, the slightest sectarian bias.

Another point of exceeding importance in any account of this noble Institution is, *the happy effects of judicious care in regard to diet, ventilation, cleanliness,* and also *the encouragement of cheerfulness and invigorating exercise.*

We are informed by those who are intimately acquainted with the Orphan Houses, that these results are strikingly observable in the appearance of the children who have been longest in the Institution, as compared with those who have recently entered. It is even asserted by competent judges, that any intelligent person conversant with such matters would find no difficulty in pointing out, with considerable precision, those orphans who have been recently received. But the most significant fact that can be mentioned in illustration of the foregoing statement, is the following. During a period of five years, the average rate of mortality has been rather under *one* per cent.! When this is considered in connection with the circumstance that all the children, having lost both parents, may be presumed to inherit from them diseased and weakly constitutions. too much importance can hardly be attached to it. It may be added, that in many cases where the children on entering the Institution have exhibited symptoms of scrofula, these have gradually disappeared under the effects of the combined influences stated above.

The Christian philanthropy of Mr. Müller carries with it, therefore, a double blessing. It provides a comfortable home for helpless orphans, and trains them to become intelligent and useful citizens; securing for them a happy childhood and a useful life. It teaches also that hereditary diseases may be checked or eradicated by wise care; and religion adds to length of life no less than to the happiness of community

CHAPTER XXVIII.

A REVIEW OF FIVE YEARS' WORK — CONTINENTAL TRAVELS, AND VISIT IN AMERICA.

1872–1877.

IT has long been the fervent prayer of Mr. Müller that his last days might be made his best days. The records of the last five years show how graciously God has answered his servant's prayer. In the preservation of his physical strength, in the ever increasing field of his influence, and in the manifest favor of Heaven which attends his work, we see a fulfilment of the promise, " them that honor me I will honor."

Reviewing his work for the year ending May 26, 1873, Mr. Muller notices the special exemption from sickness enjoyed at the Orphan houses and the presence of God's spirit there; the increase of schools and of the circulation of tracts. One day he wrote, " The income the past five days has been so small that it would not cover one-fifth of the expenses, but I am expecting again larger, much larger sums." The very next day over $4,000 were received. The reader will remember, in this connection, that no debt is allowed to accrue, and that latterly there always has been a surplus from day to day.

The gifts this year, as always, come from the rich and the poor, the aged and the young. One sends a penny each on 681 apple trees sold; two children $8, saved in a year by giving up sugar; $58 from a commercial traveller, a self imposed tax on each chest of tea sold, and $15 from an aged man who made bee hives. Thank offerings for the birth of children, restoration from sickness and other blessings, are continually recorded. One is happy in his deliverance from the curse of tobacco, another has saved money to use for the poor by riding in third class cars. A company of soldiers, " water drinkers," send their gift. A man sends enough to support an orphan a year, saved by giving up his pipe and bottle, about $65. Letters from 187 missionaries contain items of deep interest. All of these laborers are connected with no society and have no regular salary, but are in a position of simple dependence on God for temporal supplies. Those in China, Spain and Italy speak of persecution, but glory in the grace that has made them conquerors.

The balance on hand May 26, 1873, is $26,000. A year later, May 26, 1874, we read " My soul doth magnify the Lord for his kindness in connection with this Institution! I have just finished writing the history of the last eighteen years, completing the history of the forty years of its existence. The Lord, as in former years, has met its heavy demands. All the requirements He has graciously supplied, we owe nothing. When it is considered that above forty thousand pounds are required to keep up the work, and that we have to look to our Heavenly Father to supply it, without being able to reckon upon any certain income, the reader will see that the very fact of the existence of the Institution is to be reckoned among the special mercies of the past year." Eight more day schools and five more Sunday schools are added, and the number of orphans cared for is set down as 4,408, from the beginning. Twenty-five octavo pages are filled with acknowledgments of gifts from all parts of the world, in money, in cast-off jewels—the folly of wearing which the owners had been brought to see —and in articles of merchandise useful in the Orphan houses. A christian butcher sends a penny on each sheep received; a house builder a pound for every house erected; yeomen send first fruits of harvest, and property holders send hundreds of pounds which represent the cost of insurance which they save by trusting ships and houses to

God's care. Not every believer can see the propriety of this. Some regard the neglect to insure a criminal indifference. Let not him that eateth condemn him that eateth not.

The list of donations is an emphatic argument in favor of systematic benevolence and illustrates, from the experience of the donors, the pecuniary prosperity which follows the habit of generosity in giving regularly, as God gives to us. To dispose of articles of expensive table ware, brooches, ear rings and other trinkets, a room is used in the Tract warehouse for their sale. "We never had bazaars, nor intend to have any, but sell the articles in an ordinary way." New articles are also made by friends and sold here for the benefit of the orphans. The amount spent for the year in circulating tracts and books is recorded as $5,650, and the number circulated 3,775,771. In the five orphan houses there were 1,992 children May 26, 1874.

For the year ending May, 1875, Mr. Müller reports 269 orphans admitted; 23 deaths; 3 expelled on account of the corrupting influence they exerted; 56 boys sent out as apprentices, and 147 girls as servants; 1,995 remaining. He again testifies to the praiseworthy labors of the helpers, teachers, nurses and care-takers, and records a balance of $42,030 on hand. Twenty-six pages of fine type give extracts from the letters of 179 missionaries, which abound in facts of marvellous interest.

The report of 1876 states that the Institution still enjoys the uninterrupted smile and help of God, and that it not only is kept out of debt, but that the surplus steadily enlarges. The 178 missionaries report revivals and spiritual increase; the tract and book department circulates the truth in a dozen languages and 9,822 scholars are taught in the 110 schools. These latter are in both christian and heathen lands. This wonderful success Mr. Muller attributes to his humble endeavor to "do the Lord's work in the Lord's way," looking alone to Him for guidance and aid.

EVANGELISTIC WORK.

"During the past year, from May 26, 1875, to May 26, 1876, I have been absent from Bristol by far the greater part of the time. For about forty-three years my ministry in the Word was almost entirely confined to Bristol and Clifton, as I was very rarely preaching in other places. Of late years, however, it has been more or less in my heart to seek, not only by my publications, but also by the living voice to benefit my fellow-believers, especially the younger among them, through my experience during the past fifty years in which I have known the Lord, and through the measure of knowledge I have of the truth. This desire I was able to begin to carry out in March, 1875, when I left home with my dear wife on a preaching tour; for my dear son-in-law, Mr. James Wright, who has for three years assisted me in the direction of the Institution, could now be left in charge with the whole work, reporting to me day by day about it, and whom I might assist with my judgment in difficult cases. On this first tour I preached at Brighton, at Lewes, in London, Sunderland and Newcastle, and was abundantly confirmed that God would have me further thus to be engaged through the great blessing which the Lord condescended to give during the fourteen and a half weeks. I saw it His will for me to leave Bristol again after I had been there as long as various matters required my presence, and especially also to give some time for rest to my dear son-in-law and to my dear daughter. After this we set out again, and I preached further in London, at Kilmarnock, at Saltcoats, at Dundee, in Perth, in Glasgow and the neighborhood, in Dublin, at Leamington, Warwick, Coventry, Kenilworth, Rugby, at the Victoria Hall in Liverpool and in other halls in Liverpool, at Kendal, Annan, Arbroath, Montrose, Edinburgh, Aberdeen, Ballater, Crathie, Braemar, Inverness, Wick, Reading, etc. As during my first tour the Lord was pleased to bless my labors everywhere among the believers and, in not a few instances, also to the unconverted, so it was this second time also, only still more abundantly, and I became more and more convinced that it is the will of the Lord that I should, as much as possible, and as far as this Institution permits me to be absent from Bristol, spend the evening of my life travelling from place to place, to seek to strengthen the disciples and further to instruct young believers by the measure of knowledge and experience I have. In this my service I have been in England, Scotland and Ireland, most cordially received by many hundreds of ministers both in and out of the Establishment; and so abundant have been, everywhere, the openings that, if I had had five or ten times the time and strength I had, all could have been employed in entering the open doors which the Lord set before me, though I have preached hundreds of times. This preaching tour had no connection whatever with the Institution."

He then, as now, declined to narrate his Bristol work, lest he be suspected of being out on a collecting tour, whereas his sole errand was to help young converts, thousands of whom, in the United Kingdom, had been awakened in connection with the labors of Mr. Moody and others.

With the exception of Manchester and Birmingham, Mr. Müller visited every place in which the American Evangelist had been. From these two places urgent solicitations were received, but the call to the Continent seemed to be more imperative. Notwithstanding the physical strain attending these protracted labors of 1875–6, Mr. Muller says, "I state to the praise of the Lord that, with scarcely a day's exception, I have been in very good health during the whole year, and, though I have been privileged to labor more abundantly than ever in the ministry of the Word and also in other ways, I am now as well able to labor, physically and mentally, as fifty years ago, though I have nearly completed my seventy-first year. The Lord has, during the past year, again caused abundant spiritual blessing to rest upon the various departments of the Institution. I record to the praise of the Lord, that during the past year, while needing more means than ever, we also received more than ever during one year. Thus the Lord showed that He needed not my being in Bristol to supply the work with means, but was willing to listen to my prayers and those of my dear fellow-laborers in Bristol, while I was absent. Thus, also, according to my judgment, the Lord, among other points, in this particular likewise, set His seal of approbation on my absence from Bristol and on my being engaged as I have been."

LAST REPORT, MAY 26, 1877.

"The faithfulness and the kindness of the Lord are great! We have found it thus, in connection with this Institution, more than forty-three years; and we expect that thus it will be in future also. God has proved to us His faithfulness year after year, during this long period; and His kindness to us has been beyond all expectation! Our desire was to honor Him when, on March 5, 1834, we began this Institution; and He has ever since shown how ready He is to honor those who honor Him. Year after year He has been pleased to enlarge this Institution, supply its necessities, and cause abundant spiritual blessing to rest upon its operations. For all this we adore and praise Him! All the very extensive buildings connected with the Orphan Institution and the very many schools, at home and abroad, have been mercifully preserved, during the past year also, from fire and other calamities. The Lord has been pleased to let abundant spiritual blessings rest upon the various departments of the Institution.

If the income of forty-one thousand five hundred pounds, during the past year is added to the income during the previous years, it will be seen, that we have received altogether, simply in answer to prayer and the exercise of faith, without applying to anyone for anything, seven hundred and fifty thousand pounds sterling (nearly four million dollars). Should any of the readers, who are not acquainted with the former reports, ask what has been accomplished through these seven hundred and fifty thousand pounds, we reply: Sixty thousand children or grown up persons have been taught in the various schools, *entirely* supported by the funds of the Institution, besides the tens of thousands who have been benefited in the schools which were *assisted* by its funds; above nine thousand eight hundred now frequent the schools; above one hundred and thirteen thousand Bibles, above two hundred and ninety-five thousand Testaments, and one hundred and ninety-eight thousand smaller portions of the Holy Scriptures, in various languages, have been circulated since the formation of the Institution; and above sixty millions of tracts and books, likewise in several different languages, have been circulated. There have been likewise, from the earliest days of this Institution, Missionaries assisted by its funds, and of late years more than one hundred and seventy in number. On this object alone one hundred and sixty-three thousand pounds have been expended from the beginning. Also 5,199 orphans have been under our care, and five large houses, at an expense of one hundred and fifteen thousand pounds, have been erected and fitted up for the accommodation of 2,050 orphans. As to the spiritual results, I will here say nothing; indeed, eternity alone can unfold them; yet, even in so far as God has been pleased to allow us to see already the results, we have reaped abundantly, and do so more and more every year."

The Income of the first four Objects, from May 26, 1876, to May 26, 1877.

	£	s.	d.
By Balance in hand on May 26, 1876..	356	19	4¼
By Donations.....	13,176	11	3¼
By Sale of Articles, given for the purpose............	161	13	6
By Sale of Tracts, etc.............	660	4	2½
By Sale of Bibles..	717	17	8
By School Receipts...........	1,429	9	10¼
	£16,502	15	10¼

The Expenses connected with the first four Objects, from May 26, 1876, to May 26, 1877.

	£	s.	d.
For the Home Schools..........	6,653	7	9½
For Bibles.........	1,374	4	10½
For Missionary purposes........	7,173	12	10
For Tracts........	1,136	14	2
For postage.......	83	4	2
For Stationery....	9	12	10
Balance in hand on May 26, 1877..	71	19	1¼
	£16,502	15	10¼

The Income for the Orphans, from May 26, 1876, to May 26, 1877.

	£	s.	d.
By Balance in hand on May 26, 1876..	10,520	13	10¾
By Donations in Money..........	23,687	2	0½
By Sale of Articles, given for the purpose............	435	17	6
By sale of Reports	125	16	7
By Cash paid on account of Orphans...........	594	14	2
	£35, 274	2	2¼

The Expenses for the Orphans, from May 26, 1876, to May 26, 1877.

	£	s.	d.
The current expenses in connection with the five Orphan Houses..	23,199	18	3½
For the Apprentices.	739	19	6½
For 22,000 copies of the thirty-seventh Report, and 5,500 copies of the Supplement..........	222	8	9
For postage and carriage of boxes and parcels............	142	15	9½
For Stationery.....	32	10	1
Balance in hand on May 26, 1877......	10,936	13	5¾
	£35,274	2	2¼

The Income for the Building Fund, from May 26, 1876, to May 26, 1877.

	£	s.	d.
By Amount received up to May 26, 1876............	109,000	8	11¾
By Rent of the Fields..............................	90	1	0
By Interest.	619	0	6
	£109,709	10	5¾

Expenses in connection with the Building Fund.

	£	s.	d.
Expended up to May 26, 1876......................	105,909	2	4¼
Expended since May 26, 1876, on the Five Orphan Houses..	1,376	10	10
Balance in hand on May 26, 1877....................	2,423	17	3½
	£109,709	10	5¾

We have examined these accounts and find them correct,

H. M. BECHER,
SAMUEL BUTLER.

Bristol, July 13, 1877.

"When in the year 1835 I began the Orphan work I had, in doing so, particularly in view, through this work to prove to the world at large and to the church at large, that the Living God is now, as thousands of years since, the Living God, and that we may reckon on Him, as those did who really knew Him thousands of years ago. That end has been particularly answered by this Institution. Tens of thousands of souls have indeed been converted through the operations of the various objects of the Institution, for which I adore and magnify the Lord; but the greatest blessing, which I have reason to believe, which has resulted from it, is, that thereby hundreds of thousands of children of God, in very many parts of the world, have been encouraged, in all simplicity, to trust in God. While I am writing this, at Nimwegen, in Holland, another precious proof of this kind has just been brought under my own eyes, of which I have had, I might almost say, numberless instances: it is this: A Christian evangelist, simply through reading about the Orphan work in Bristol, had it laid on his heart to care about Orphans, and was encouraged by my example, solely in dependence on the Lord, to take them up. He began in the year 1863 with three at Nimwegen, in Holland, and he has at present 453."

Institutions have also been started in America on the same plan, which, in their infancy, are reaping their first fruits in a prosperity manifestly and peculiarly unlike that which results from other methods. As this leaven of faith continues to work, there will go on a revolution in the whole system of solicitation of funds through salaried agents, as well as by means of bazaars, lotteries, suppers and other entertainments which pauperize Christianity in the eyes of the world, and which, as too often conducted, are perilous alike to health and virtue. Although Mr. Muller, in his preaching, abstains from reference to these, he enunciates those general principles which, if applied, would uproot these evils which exist in this age of extravagance, of religious sensationalism and high pressure. *Do God's work in God's way* is his oft repeated admonition. He would not unite the church and the world, nor act according to worldly maxims of policy in advancing the interests of the church.

The duty and blessedness of systematic giving is another axiomatic truth which stands out in all his spoken or printed words. On page 24 of the report for 1877, he says:

"I commend to such of the Christian readers, who are not already in the habit of giving to the poor or the Lord's work, in proportion as the Lord is pleased to give to them, through their business or profession, through presents, through legacies, etc., to do so. That is the way of obtaining blessings to our souls, because we act according to the principle laid down in 1 Cor. xvi, 2: 'Upon the first day of the week let every one of you lay by him in store, as God has prospered him.' In this way we find that double if not ten-fold, is the blessing which we receive from God, when He prospers us in temporal things; and it is one of the ways in which we honor Him with our temporal things; whilst, if this is not done, and we keep all, or almost all, to ourselves, then the very prosperity in temporal things will be found to be injurious to the inner man. It is just this, why Christians should be in such earnestness on this point and be habitually returning to the Lord for His work or His poor as He may prosper them. Should it, however, be said, How much shall I give of that which I receive? The answer is, the Holy Scriptures of the New Testament lay down no rule. It is left to the children of God to act according to the measure of knowledge and grace they have received. The appreciation of what God has done for them in Christ should guide them. We have, however, not to lose sight of this, that, if the Israelite was commanded to give the tenth of all he received, in the Lord Jesus, who knows the power of His precious blood, shed for the remission of his sins; who has the whole revealed will of God in his hands; and who has received the Holy Ghost, and who is partaker of the heavenly calling, should certainly not do less than the Israelite. Then the Israelite, in addition to this *tenth*, had many other expenses in connection with his being a worshipper of the true and Living God, such as the not sowing the seventh year, the going three times a year to the Lord's Tabernacle or Temple, etc. [some scholars estimate that *half his income* went for religious purposes.] We should not say that because we are not Jews, and because no commandment is given, therefore we may do less than the Jews. Far be this from him who knows the power of the precious blood of Christ! My advice is this: If the reader has as yet but little knowledge and little grace let him accordingly, begin with a small per centage, yea, though it were ever so small a per centage, only let him be true to God, and put aside for Him habitually as He may be pleased to prosper him. In this way blessing for the soul will be reaped, will be abundantly reaped, and soon will the desire spring up in the heart, to increase the proportion of our returns to the Lord. This way will more and more lead the heart to such a state, to be only a steward for the Lord and to be willing to stand with all we have and are before the Lord as His stewards. The great spiritual blessing which I have received in my own soul, from acting on these principles for more than forty-seven years, leads me to write as I do. The money thus set apart for the Lord should be put aside, and out of that which is thus put aside, when calls come upon us, to give to the poor or to the Lord's work, we should then take. How different will it be to take from such a store (provided we have not yet grace to give all to the Lord if it were necessary) from what it would be, if there is the anxious reckoning, whether the gift can be afforded or not. We should not give for the sake of receiving, but only to please the Lord; yet this is God's way of acting, and according to the plain teaching of the New Testament, which states: 'Give, and it shall be given unto you; good measure, pressed down and shaken together and running over, shall men give into your bosom.' Luke vi. 38."

From the following condensed statement it may be seen, at a glance, how Mr. Muller acts out his own principles. He has no property and no income on which he may rely. Trustees hold the Bristol property and he never takes out a penny for his temporal need from what is sent to the orphans. But in answer to prayer, God has always moved others to send to his servant abundant means for his personal support, money which is so designated at the time by the donors. Now in revealing this chapter of his private history, he says with emphasis, " I seek not the praise of men, but the glory of God; the real profit of my fellow disciples, hoping that they may act on the same principles, if they have not already. *All we had* was the Lord's and we stood with our all before the Lord, for my beloved wife was of one mind with me. We lived by the day, looking to the Lord, and kept nothing for coming necessities, such as sickness, loss of friends, or of income." On his second marriage, November 30, 1871, to Miss Susan Grace Sangar, whom he had known more than twenty-five years as a consistent believer, he had "joy to know that she possessed no property, which fitted her the better to be my wife." Only $1000 remained of the property once possessed by her, and that was given to the Lord's work before their marriage. He also states that he always labored without being chargeable to any one, and "never received a single fee as a preacher of the gospel or for anything I did in connection with the pastoral position. Let none suppose that I do not naturally care about money. Left to myself I should even now become a lover of money and hold it fast, for I am naturally a calculating man. But as long as grace is in exercise, I calculate with regard to the eternity that is before me and also that, since the Lord Jesus became poor, it becomes me to give back to Him in return. Will not my dear fellow servants in the gospel consider the Lord's faithful dealings with me?"

Beginning with 1831, after relinquishing all emolument in connection with the pastorate at Teignmouth and continuing to the present time, we have the following record. Fractions are omitted.

1831	Rec'd	£151	gave away	£ 50	1838	Rec'd	£350	gave away	£160
1832	"	195	"	70	1839	"	313	"	140
1833	"	267	"	110	1840	"	242	"	80
1834	"	238	"	120	1841	"	238	"	80
1835	"	285	"	110	1842	"	329	"	130
1836	"	232	"	80	1843	"	326	"	140
1837	"	307	"	140	1844	"	267	"	100

1845	Rec'd £	433	gave away	£220	1860	Rec'd £1054	gave away	£ 800
1846	"	399	"	180	1861	" 1097	"	847
1847	"	412	"	180	1862	" 1067	"	876
1848	"	474	"	240	1863	" 1172	"	961
1849	"	413	"	190	1864	" 1230	"	1024
1850	"	402	"	180	1865	" 1365	"	1131
1851	"	465	"	220	1866	" 1602	"	1362
1852	"	445	"	190	1867	" 1847	"	1579
1853	"	638	"	368	1868	" 1838	"	1577
1854	"	697	"	440	1869	" 1800	"	1559
1855	"	726	"	466	1870	" 2067	"	1713
1856	"	781	"	500	1871	" 2171	"	1570
1857	"	836	"	566	1872	" 2240	"	1637
1858	"	1029	"	768	1873	" 2770	"	1819
1859	"	1037	"	776				

The account from which we copy closes with May 1874, but we learn from Mr. Müller that the total amount given away from his private purse to the present time, November, 1877, is, in our money, over $180,000.

He adds, " I have allowed my family the necessities and the conveniences of life. I do this still, if not even more as I am increasing in years ; but I have ever guarded against extravagance in any way, lest my stewardship be taken from me. The reader would be mistaken, if he supposed, that, as soon as the Lord has sent me means, my aim is to get rid of them as fast as possible, as if it were a crime to possess a ten pound note. This is not at all my way of acting. Whether I have much or little I desire to look on it as a steward would and not as an owner. I seek grace to give a part, or all, if He would. Often the Lord brings before me needy saints besides those sixty-eight poor believers whom I seek habitually to help ; or some unbelievers or special claims in His work." Thus two legacies amounting to $5000 received on January 1, 1874, and just before, with an unappropriated balance on hand, enabled him to spend a large amount for the Lord's work.

Mr. Muller also signalizes the duty of waiting on the Lord in humble, active faith. He believes in prayer, as perhaps no other man living believes in prayer, but he is no less a believer in WORK. Not only does he spend hours in communion with God and His blessed word, but he toils as few men can toil. Not only does he preach eight times a week with comparatively no fatigue, though seventy-two years of age; travel by day and night to meet appointments; receive uncounted callers, and attend to an overwhelming correspondence, but he has the faculty of keeping other people at work. For example, he has eight secretaries engaged in answering the 30,000 letters received every year. Thousands of his reports are sent by post, to applicants in all parts of the world. Mr. M. believes most thoroughly in the use of types, and every publication of the millions that yearly are issued at Bristol is a vehicle of information. When he preaches he wishes the most commodious church and desires that the services be widely advertised. He has sagacity, keenness, perseverance and toilfulness united with his humility and childlike trust. He prays as if God was to do all, but labors as though success rested on himself. A stranger seeing him as he sits silently, even in company, saying little, and with his eyes looking downward, as if in constant intercourse with the unseen, would perhaps take him for some religious mystic, pietist or quietist. But, though not of the world, he realizes that he is in the world, and he knows how to use it without abusing it. He utilizes every proper auxiliary in doing his work. The success he has had in selecting his instruments of service proves that he has been endowed with that wisdom which cometh down from above. Then he has in his quiet, modest way more real magnetism than many who are more eloquent men than he is. He is not attractive in speech or gesture. He has no "enticing words of man's wisdom," but he talks to the people in simple words, "which are thunder, because his life is lightning," to borrow Jerome's sententious figure. He talks familiarly in his reports. Having stated that the past forty-three years he has spent nearly a million dollars in the missionary department of his work, he says: "We have reason to believe that there are a thousand millions of souls who have never heard the Gospel preached, and that therefore at least nineteen out of every twenty, if not forty-nine out of every fifty, are not privileged as we who know the Lord Jesus have been. It is an awful consideration, that the vast majority of our fellow-men have never yet had the light of the Gospel; have never had salvation, through faith in the atoning death of the Lord Jesus, preached to them. Have we sufficiently pondered this? Has it had a practical effect upon our lives? And what effect has it had? 1. Has it led us to earnestness in prayer? Day by day should we pray, that God would abundantly bless the labors of all His servants who preach the Gospel at home and abroad. Every day that we neglect this we neglect what, as believers in the Lord Jesus, we ought to attend to. But we should also pray for those who are engaging in preaching the Gospel at home and abroad, that they may be upheld and strengthened, both as to their outward and inward man. 2. But if we are sincere in our prayer we shall do more than this."

He then shows that prayer without effort and faith without works amount to nothing. Some ought to go personally to the heathen, trusting in God for support, not to any society or human helper. In this Mr. M. speaks "not by commandment" or as being a law to others, but as Paul, 1 Cor. vii. 7, who said, "I would that all men were even as I myself, but every man hath his proper gift of God, one after this manner and another after that." A second method is to liberally aid those in the field. Mr. M. says: "How can we suppose that we love the Lord Jesus, if we do not practically show our interest in the labors of those who, often with their lives in their hands, seek to spread that Gospel, to which we owe our spiritual life, peace, joy, yea every thing with reference to eternal realities? Now what are we doing to help these Missionaries and Evangelists? How much of our time do we devote for them? How much of our money do we give for them? What self-denial in the way of dress, luxury, pleasure and sight seeing do we practice on their account? Do we all spend as much as the *twentieth* part of our income for this object? What have we been doing during the last year, for missions? Let us examine ourselves, let us be honest to our own hearts! Life will soon have come to an end. Our one brief life will soon be over. And then, in the retrospect, shall we be able to say that we did what we could?"

It is a marvel that any who know the activity and practical industry of such a life as the Bristol Evangelist leads, should ever apply the term "*cant*" to his docility of faith and say that "he professes to pray for everything and uses no means."

SUMMARY OF RESULTS.

Mr. Muller, in giving statistics, warns his readers that mere numerical magnitudes are of little account in God's sight. "We should labor on in this service, prayerfully, and believingly labor on, even though for a long time we should see little or no fruit; yea, *we should labor on as if everything depended on our labors*, whilst, in reality, we ought not to put the least confidence in our exertions, but alone in God's ability and willingness to bless, by His Holy Spirit, our efforts for the sake of the Lord Jesus. And what will be the result of laboring on patiently in such a spirit? We find the answer in the epistle to the Galatians, vi. 9: 'Let us not be weary in well doing; for in due season we shall reap, if we faint not.' Observe, in *due* season. The whole of our earthly pilgrimage is a sowing time, though we may be allowed to see now and then already in this life, fruit resulting from our sowing to a greater or less degree; but if it were not thus, or if comparatively but little fruit were now, in this life, reaped, the *due* season is coming. At the appearing of our Lord Jesus all will be made manifest; our reward of grace will be given to us for our patient service then; and in the prospect of that day we have patiently to continue in well doing. But this patient continuing in well doing calls for much prayer, for much meditation on the Word of God, and for much feeding on the work and person of our Lord Jesus, in order that thus our spiritual strength may be renewed day by day." This last sentence ought not to be forgotten in this age of outward, bustling activities, when in keeping other vineyards, one is apt to forget his own.

Mr. Müller's work is in five departments.

I. ORPHANS.—During the past year 247 orphans were admitted into these five houses, so that on May 26, 1877, we should have had altogether 2,242 orphans had there been no changes. But of these 2,242 orphans, 40 died during the past year. Of those who died, fourteen were young infants, and thirteen had been some time decided believers before they fell asleep in Jesus. Twenty-four out of the 2,242 were delivered up to their relatives who, by that time, were in better circumstances than when we received the children, and were on that account both able therefore to provide for these orphans and also felt it their duty so to do. Twenty-four orphans we were obliged to return to their relatives, because either on account of their physical or mental state they could not be sent to situations, or their deportment had been such that we could not recommend them to masters and mistresses. Thirty-nine of the boys were apprenticed, of whom nineteen were sent out as Christian lads. Three girls were sent out as pupil teachers, and one hundred and twenty-nine to situations, so that on May 26, 1877, we had only 1,983 orphans under our care. The total number of orphans who have been under our care from April, 1836, to May 26, 1877, is 5,199.

The girls who are received into the establishment are kept till they are able to go to service. Our aim is to keep them till they shall have been sufficiently qualified for a situation, and especially, also, till their constitution is sufficiently established, as far as we are able to judge. We uniformly prefer fitting the girls for service, instead of apprenticing them to businesses, as being, generally, far better for their bodies and souls. Only in a few instances have female orphans been apprenticed to a business, when their health would not allow them to go to service. If the girls give us satisfaction, while under our care, so that we can recommend them to a situation, they are fitted out at the expense of the establishment. The girls, generally, remain under our care till they are about 17 years old. They rarely leave sooner; and, as we receive children from their earliest days, we have often had girls 13, 14, yea, 17 years under our care. They are instructed in reading, writing, arithmetic, English grammar, geography, English history, a little of universal history, all kinds of useful needle-work, and household work. They make their clothes and keep them in repair; they work in the kitchens, sculleries, washhouses and laundries; and, in a word, we aim after this, that, if any of them do not do well temporally or spiritually and do not turn out useful members of society, it shall, at least, not be *our* fault. The boys are, generally, apprenticed when they are between 14 and 15 years old. The new orphan house No 1 is fitted up for the accommodation of 140 orphan girls above eight years of age, 80 orphan boys above eight years, and 80 female orphans from their earliest days, till they are about eight years of age. The infants, after having passed the age of eight years, are removed into the department for older girls. The new orphan house No. 2 is fitted up for 200 infant female orphans and for 200 older female orphans. The new orphan house No. 3 is fitted up for 450 older female orphans. The new orphan house No. 4 is fitted up for 210 boys of eight years old and upwards, 208 infant boys under eight years of age, and 32 older girls to do the household work—450 in all. The new orphan house No. 5 is fitted up for 310 infant female orphans and for 240 older female orphans.

Without any sectarian distinction whatever and without favor or partiality, the orphans are received in the order in which application is made for them. There is no interest whatever required to get a child admitted, nor is it expected that any money should be paid with the orphans. Three things only are requisite: *a*, that the children should have been lawfully begotten; *b*, that they should be bereaved of BOTH parents by death; and *c*, that they should be in needy circumstances. Respecting these three points strict investigation is made, and it is expected that each of them be proved by proper documents; but, that being done, children may be admitted from any place, provided that there is nothing peculiar in the case that would make them unsuitable inmates for such establishments as the new orphan houses. I state here again that no sectarian views prompt us, nor even in the least influence us in the reception of children. We do not belong to any sect, and we are not, therefore, influenced in the admission of children.

The income for the orphans has been kept distinct from that for the other objects, and I purpose to keep it so for the future. Donors may, therefore, contribute to one or other of the objects exclusively, or have their donations equally divided among them all, just as it may appear best to themselves. If any of the donors would wish to leave the application of their donations to my discretion, as the work of God in my hands more especially may call for it at the time, they are requested kindly to say so when sending their donations.

Without any one having been personally applied to for anything by me, the sum of £493,048 3s. 8d. has been given to me for the orphans, *as the result of prayer to God*, since the commencement of the work, which sum includes the amount received for the building fund for the five houses.

II. BOOKS AND TRACTS.—There has been laid out in

this department from May 26, 1876, to May 26, 1877, the sum of £1,136 14s. 2d.; and there have been circulated within the last year 3,466,774 tracts and books. The sum total which has been expended on this object, since Nov. 19, 1840, amounts to £27,336 3s. 0¾d., about $136,000.

The total number of all the tracts and books which has been circulated from Nov. 19, 1840, to May 26, 1877, is 60,408,215.

Nearly three millions of the tracts and books circulated during the past year, were given away *gratuitously*. Hundreds of believers have been engaged in spreading them abroad, not merely in many parts of England, Scotland and Ireland, but in various other parts of the world.

III. HOME AND FOREIGN MISSIONS.—This is a third object of the "Scriptural Knowledge Institution." During the past year was expended of the funds of the Institution for this object, the sum of £7,173 12s. 10d. By this sum 173 laborers in the Word and doctrine, in various parts of the world, were, to a greater or less degree, assisted.

With regard to these 173 laborers in the Gospel in various parts of the world, whom we sought to assist during the past year, I repeat, that they are not the Missionaries of the Scriptural Knowledge Institution, nor do we bind ourselves to give them a stated salary, for this would lead them out of the position of simple dependence upon God for their temporal supplies; but when we hear of any man of God laboring for the Lord in the Word, whether in a more public or private way, whether at home or abroad, who is not connected with any society, nor in the way of receiving a regular salary, and who seems to us to stand in need of help, and is working in such a spirit, as that, with a good conscience, acting in the fear of God, we could help him with the means with which donors intrust us; we are glad to assist such a one.

Seventeen pages of fine type are filled with brief extracts from missionary letters.

A brother writes from Tunghwa, China:—"We had a meeting of the native preachers here a week ago. After the ordinary business was over, such as giving an account of their work at the stations where they labor, their encouragements and discouragements, etc., we had a meeting in the evening for prayer, praise and exhortation. One of the native brethren gave a very precious and stirring address from Phil. iii. 12-14. We partook of the Lord's supper afterwards, and we all enjoyed it very much. We seldom have such a treat. Thank God! we have the fountain of blessing to drink at wherever we are. You will be glad to hear that the Lord is giving us much encouragement at some of our out-stations. They are not satisfied with ordinary Buddhism, and as Christianity holds out future happiness, many are inclined to give it a favorable hearing. Pray, dear brother, that many of them may find rest to their weary souls by trusting in the blood of Jesus."

Mr. C. writes again on February 26, 1877:—"During the year 1876, we received into the church twelve very hopeful converts. Since the new year we have received other five, and we have still six or seven hopeful inquirers, whom we hope to have the joy of receiving soon. Many of those who have confessed Christ recently, have heard the gospel for years; some of them for ten years. This encourages us to go on sowing the seed, and to believe that, in due season, we shall reap if we faint not. I would like to mention one good feature in the character of most of these new converts, and that is, that they speak of Jesus to others, and they do so without any hope of getting money from me for doing so."

One of the Chinese converts, Mr. M., of Ningpo, writes, "emphatically a brawler, and such a brawler! She is the landlady of the house in which house I lived for six years, hearing and seeing daily almost, such sounds and sights, all in connection with this woman, as would vex the soul of a man less righteous than Lot. She was not only 'a brawler,' but she was 'a Jezebel.' I think I could, in an English court of justice, bring home to her the murder of one, if not two, poor little wretched daughters-in-law, that she had purchased to be wives to her sons. Many a time have I myself rescued one of these miserable little things out of her cruel hands. Mr. C. once pulled her out of a canal into which she had jumped, when in a fit of passion, and in which she would probably have perished had he not been prompt to deliver her. She has heard the gospel for years, and we feared was gospel hardened. We were impelled one day to pray openly for her by name. She heard of it and a change at once came over her, more and more deep, year by year. Finally she began a prayerful life, and after two years longer waiting was baptized, a brand plucked from the burning."

A native Chinese preacher, laboring among his countrymen in British Guiana, writes joyfully of his work and its results.

H. O. writes from New Zealand in a similar strain. Mr. G., in Australia, says, "It has pleased the Lord to bless my endeavors. For many weeks I rode nearly 100 miles a week on horseback, distributing tracts, giving Bibles where I found a house without one, and preaching Christ to all with whom I came in contact. Regular preaching was carried on in Echma and Moawa. This work was much owned of God. The Lord gave us one soul at our first service and subsequently continued to bless, so much so, that my colleague remains teaching Christ with acceptance and blessing. A church will soon be found and steps are already taken for the erection of a place of worship."

From Madrid and other Spanish towns cheering letters come. Converts stand firm, having, in the face of difficulties, resisted the conventionalities of their country, giving up work on Lord's day and so being free to join with their brethren in worship and service. "At the present time we have some eight or nine candidates for baptism and members for the church, some of whom give us especial joy. We need heavenly wisdom to discern between real and false coin, but for this we count on God, who giveth to all men liberally and upbraideth not. One of this number was turned out of her employ for confessing Christ, and her faith was tried for some little time; but God heard her prayer and others on her behalf, and a place has been opened for her in the house of some Christian."

Mr. G. L. writes from Barcelona:—"We had over a thousand children and parents up the mountain, and gave them a treat after David's fashion, when he dealt to every one of Israel, both man and woman, to every one a loaf of bread, and a good piece of flesh and a flagon of wine,' with the addition of boiled chestnuts and figs. Six omnibuses brought up the 'wee ones' from their various schools, while the elder came on foot, accompanied by teachers and parents. It was truly a 'children's agape.' The teachers told me that it was impossible to control the joy of the little ones who came in the coaches, as all along the route they would sing some of their favorite hymns. As they were returning, and ready for the start, some of them said, 'Don George, shall we sing going along?' 'Sing! why not? If you do not the very stones will cry out.' In nothing has this government shown more folly, or brought down on themselves more ridicule, than in their recent orders that our children were not to sing too loud in the schools for fear the Roman Catholics should be disturbed; *caught*, they mean, by the golden chains of Jesus' love songs. Yesterday I saw a young shepherd tending his sheep upon the opposite piece of ground to our house. He had just been using 'sling and stone' to frighten a straying sheep from danger, or which was going on forbidden ground. Our children observed, and touched perhaps with the spirit of the minstrel, who sought his king by the aid of song, struck up 'The Ninety and Nine,' in Spanish. The shepherd stopped and listened, drew near and leaned on his staff, a cigarette died out between his fingers—his sheep had strayed a long way ere he moved, which was not until the children had finished and begun another song. I have heard mothers in different parts of this land, singing a lullaby of these precious hymns. Yes, we will make the people ballads; the government may put many chains, and beat with many stripes, and thrust into inner prisons, and make the feet fast in stocks; but so long as the enemy cannot tie our tongues we shall triumph in Jesus, 'the name high over all, in heaven or earth or sky.' It will be with the gospel in Spain as it was with a poor man whose ejaculations in meetings tried a nervous sister, who, seeing the man in want of a pair of boots, said to him, 'John, if you will suppress your exclamations I will give you a new pair of boots.' John being in want accepted the offer, and for a Sunday or two kept quiet, but after a time the fire burned, and John jumped up saying, 'boots or no boots, I must praise the Lord.' Among our visitors were the children of the Gypsy school. Some of these girls and boys, can now read and write. The tenderness the other children showed them formed a fine contrast to Roman Catholics, who never mix with other children. Last week we held meetings for prayer for Sunday schools; a larger number attended than we have yet held. The large school room at Barcelona was filled to overflowing; several recited portions of the Scriptures; short addresses and pointed prayers followed. Some of our eldest scholars have formed a Young Men's Christian Association. Native agency is more and more developing itself, in schools, in preaching, in prayer meetings and in distribution of the Word and tracts. Another gem is about being translated from the hospital to shine forever in Jesus' crown. She has been now fifteen months under our care, is eighty-nine years old, one of nature's nobility; she came into the hospital a poor blind Romanist, with beads, cross and rosary; gradually the light of free salvation, through one Mediator, broke in upon her mind; and for a long time past Jesus only has occupied her soul. It is pleasant to see her maintain, with a very clear intellect, the assurance of her faith in Jesus as her Saviour; during the past month she has counted the days, constantly saying, 'end of October shall finish my days.' On the first of November she had a stroke which has left one side dead and her tongue speechless, but the eye is not dimmed; 'tis sweet to see her raise her aged hand, pointing upward, as if to say:

> 'Yonder's my house and portion fair,
> My treasure and my heart are there.'"

Mr. P., laboring in the neighborhood of Cosham, Hampshire, writes on September 23, 1876:—"I am thankful to tell you that the work of the Lord is prospering amongst us. Our chapel here and mission room in a neighboring village are filled with hearers. Souls are saved. We have received several into fellowship lately, and others are candidates. O how gracious the Lord is, to let us see some fruit!"

Mr. T., laboring at Portsmouth, writes on February 12, 1877:—"You will, I am sure, be glad to learn that since I last wrote to you the Lord has given a continual stream of blessing in Gospel testimony. Lord Radstock gave his last address in our hall last evening; great numbers had to go away for want of room, and I should think that over 250 remained to the after meetings. Not less than seven or eight left rejoicing in their new found peace. There have been many very striking cases of conversion."

From the slums of London, Mr. L. writes on April 18, 1877:—"Adoringly and gratefully I would tell of great blessings and ask you to raise a note of thanksgiving. We have had one continued stream of blessing this year; not one meeting but what we have had to rejoice over in some way. Our prayer meetings have been wondrous times, filling my soul with adoring gratitude and unspeakable joy. At some of our meetings twenty-two, twenty-four, twenty-eight, and even thirty have led in praise or prayer. You will remember that our people are the very poorest of the poor, and most of them brought up from the deepest depths; many of them not able to read. Their utterances are certainly very simple and unpolished; just their every day expressions, but oh, the manifestation of confidence, faith, love, peace and rest is very blessed. Praise God with me, my brother, for this precious fruit of much painful toil."

IV. BIBLE DEPARTMENT.—Mr. Müller reports as follows:

"We sell Bibles and Testaments to poor persons at reduced prices, or, if the cases be found suitable, give them altogether gratuitously. In cases of needy schools, carried on in the fear of God, it would be joy in the Lord to us to supply them with as many copies of the holy Scriptures as they may require. This applies especially to all Missionary efforts in forign lands, or to any Scriptural means which are used to spread the truth of God in the dark places of our land.

Our particular aim, in circulating the Holy Scriptures, is to seek out the very poorest of the poor, through visits from house to house, in order to find out the need of the Holy Scriptures, and to supply persons either entirely gratis or on the payment of a small amount. With this we especially combine the furnishing aged persons with copies in large type, a point of great moment, as the smallness of type, even where a copy of the Bible is possessed, would keep many aged persons from reading it; and, also because it is well known that Bibles, printed in large type are, up to this present day, expensive, considering the means of the poor. We have been greatly assisted in these efforts of searching out the most needy persons, destitute of the Holy Scriptures, by many servants of Christ who, in England, Scotland, Ireland, Italy, Spain, Nova Scotia, Canada, British Guiana, the East Indies, Australia, Africa, China, &c., have sought to circulate God's Holy Word.

7,155 Bibles have been sold the past year, 792 given away; 33,406 copies of portions of the Word have been sold and 3,074 given away. There are 200 styles of English Bibles kept in stock, ranging from 12 cts. to $25; also 30 kinds of Testaments and copies of the Scriptures, or portions of them, in Hebrew, Greek, Russ, Swedish, Spanish, Welsh, Danish, Dutch, French, German, Italian and Portuguese. The amount spent the past year on this department is $6,870, and since 1834 $24,000. The report adds,

During the past year we have continued, by the help of an earnest Christian brother, to introduce the Holy Scriptures into the factories and mills of Lancashire, Yorkshire, Derbyshire and Nottinghamshire. Many thousands of copies of the New Testament and many Bibles have been thus placed again in the hands of men, women, boys and girls working in these factories and mills; and this work steadily is going on. This colporteur goes from one mill to the other, and from one factory to the other, and often disposes of hundreds of copies in one place. The expense to meet this is considerable; but the greater the efforts which are being made to put aside the Word of God, or to do without it, the more it becomes the disciples of the Lord Jesus to circulate it with earnest, believing, expecting and persevering prayer.

V. SCHOOL WORK.—The object is to aid day schools, Sunday schools and adult schools if taught on Biblical principles.

1. By day schools taught upon Scriptural principles, we understand day schools in which the teachers are believers,—and in which the way of salvation is scripturally pointed out,—and in which no instruction is given which is opposed to the principles of the Gospel. During the past year seventy-five such day schools were entirely supported by the funds of the Institution. Of these seventy-five schools there are four in Bristol, one at Callington, in Cornwall, one at Kenilworth, in Warwickshire, one at Howle Hill, in Herefordshire, two at Walham Green near London, three on the Blackdown Hills, in Somersetshire,

four at Barnstaple, three in Exeter, two at Purton, in Gloucestershire, one at Cubitt town, London, one at Saul, Gloucestershire, one at Yeovil, Somersetshire, one at Bishopswood, Somersetshire, one at North End, near London, one at Chittlehamholt, Devon, one at Hopton, Suffolk, five at Cardiff, Wales, three at Kilburn, London, one at High Bickington, Devon, two at Plymton, Devon, one at Portsmouth, one at Stroud, two at Ludlow, one at East Brent, one at Brentford, one at Plympton Underwood, one at Bow, one at Shaftesbury, and one at King's Stanley. These are the home schools, besides which there are fourteen in Spain, four in India, two in Italy, and six in British Guiana. Besides these seventy-five day schools, entirely supported by the funds of the Institution, eight other day schools have been assisted, one in Dorsetshire, one in Worcestershire, four in Devon, one in Wiltshire, and one in France.

The number of the pupils in the home day schools, on May 26, 1877, was 5,396; in the Mission day schools, 1,726, in all 7,122.

The reader cannot but see that the Lord's manifest blessing rests upon the schools. I have of late years given myself especially to the enlargement of the school department, as in years before that to the increase of the orphan work, in order that children, from their early days, may be grounded in the Word of God, as the powers of darkness make every effort to put it aside.

2. Sunday schools, in which the teachers are believers and in which the Holy Scriptures alone are the foundation of instruction, are such only as the Institution supports or assists; for we consider it unscriptural that any persons, who do not profess to know the Lord themselves, should be engaged in giving religious instruction.

There are thirty-three Sunday schools connected with the Institution, which are entirely supported by its funds. In these thirty-three Sunday schools there were, on May 26,

1877, altogether 2,487 scholars. There were likewise, during the past year, thirty-four Sunday schools, to a greater or less degree, assisted by the funds of the Institution. Of the thirty-three Sunday schools, entirely supported by the funds of the Institution, ten are in Spain, seven in British Guiana, three in Gloucestershire, two in Somersetshire, three in Devonshire, one in Cornwall, two in Hampshire, three in Middlesex, one in Suffolk, and one in Warwickshire. Of the thirty-three Sunday schools, which were only in part supported, two are in Somersetshire, three in Devonshire, one in Wiltshire, eight in Middlesex, two in Lancashire, one in Warwickshire, one in Suffolk, one in Surrey, one in Shropshire, one in Worcestershire, one in Staffordshire, one in Cheshire, one in Herefordshire, one in Buckinghamshire, two in Hampshire, four in Wales, and one in Ireland.

3. In adult schools, also, all the teachers are believers. There are now six adult schools, with 166 scholars connected with the Institution, which are entirely supported by its funds. Of these there are three in Spain, one in India, one at Callington, and one at Walham Green.

From the foregoing statement it will appear that there are altogether 114 schools entirely supported by the funds of the Institution, (seventy-five day schools, thirty-three Sunday schools and six adult schools,) and that, during the past year, eight day schools and thirty-four Sunday schools were assisted. From what has been stated it will likewise be seen, that in these 114 schools, entirely supported by the funds of the Institution, there were, on May 26, 1876, altogether 9,775 scholars. The total number that frequented the schools of the Institution, entirely supported by its funds, from the beginning, amounts to 60,110, viz., there were 39,921 in all the day schools, 13,443 in all the Sunday schools, and 6,746 in all the adult schools.

The amount of means which was expended during the past year, in connection with the various schools amounts to £6,653 7s. 9½d. This does not include £1,948 11s. 11d. expended on the Mission schools alone, which is charged to the Mission fund, to which it more properly belongs. There has been expended on the home schools from the beginning of the Institution £43,802 7s. 3¼d., or about $220,000.

CONTINENTAL TRAVELS.

"During the greater part of the past year, accompanied by my dear wife, I have been absent from Bristol on a preaching tour on the Continent of Europe, and preached repeatedly in Paris. In Switzerland I preached at Berne, at Zurich and the neighborhood, at St. Gallen and various neighboring places, at Herisau and the neighborhood, at Glaris and the neighborhood, at Schaffhausen, at Winterthur and at Basle and various places in the neighborhood. In Alsace I preached at Mulhausen and Strasburg. In the Kingdom of Wurtemberg I preached at Stuttgart, Kornthal, Ludwigsburg, Reutlingen, Ober-Urbach and Heilbronni. In the Grand-Duchy of Baden I preached at Carlsruhe, Constance, Gernsbach, Heidelberg and Mannheim. In the Grand-Duchy of Hesse Darmstadt I preached in the Capital Darmstadt. In the Kingdom of Prussia I preached at Frankfort on the Maine, Bonn, Cologne, Dusseldorf, Dusselthal, Wesel, Mulheim on the Ruhr, Gladbach, Reydt, Vierseu, Créfeld, Duisburg, Essen, Elberfeld, Barmen, Cassel, Halle, Berlin, Stettin, Hanover, Bielefeld, Soest and Ruhrort. I preached also in the free town Lubeck. In the Kingdom of Holland I preached at Nimwegen, Arnheim, Utrecht, Amsterdam, Zeist, Haarlem, Leyden, the Hague and Rotterdam. Altogether I preached *three hundred and two* times *in sixty-eight places*, most of which were large towns. To every place I had been invited by letter, as through my labors and writings I have been for more than thirty years as well known on the Continent as in England.

"I have referred to this preaching tour in order that the Christian friends who read this, may follow my past labors on the Continent with their prayers, that the Lord would be pleased abundantly to bless them; for the Continent of Europe, as a whole, greatly needs such labors. I also do so because I intend, if the Lord will, after some time, to go again to the Continent to labor there further in this way, as I have yet sixty-three written invitations for various parts of Germany, Switzerland and Holland, which I have not been able to accept. Yea, even from Vienna and Petersburg I have received letters, to request me to go there.

"The abundant blessing which the Lord has been pleased to allow to rest upon these my labors everywhere, encourages me to go on with this service, and to spend the evening of my life in going from city to city, country to country, as long as the Lord gives me health and otherwise makes my way plain."

During his European tour Mr. Müller frequently met his former beneficiaries. Their joy and gratitude were touching to behold, as after long years they saw their benefactor once more. Letters from them breathe the same spirit of thankfulness. One writes:

"It is with gratitude I look back upon the years I spent in the *dear* orphan house; they were happy years. And how much there is for which I have cause to be thankful! The education I received there, and all the tender love and kindness from all around. But most of all I rejoice with thankfulness when I remember it was *there* I was taught to know Jesus as mine, and to trust in a loving Father, who never forsakes those who trust Him. Please accept the enclosed."

Not only did his orphans, and others among the lowly, flock after him, but the rich and titled, barons and princes, honored themselves by showing attentions to this venerable apostle of faith and charity. Among these was the Queen of Würtemberg, sister of the Emperor of Russia, who solicited a private interview with Mr. Muller at Stuttgart. A letter sent to the writer from Berlin, early in the spring of 1877, speaks of the intense interest and enthusiasm awakened among the people, multitudes of whom filled the largest sanctuaries wherever he went.

VISIT TO AMERICA.

Mr. Müller's "LIFE OF TRUST" has had an unprecedented circulation in America since 1860. There has been a desire to see and hear the author, naturally awakened by its perusal. Very many pastors and leading laymen have personally, at Bristol, and by letter, solicited a visit, but without avail. A united effort, however, among brethren of different evangelical bodies has prevailed with the preacher to reconsider his plans and to leave the work pressing on him, in Germany, for a year's sojourn in the United States and Canada.

Mr. Muller and his wife arrived at Quebec Sept. 1, 1877. He had an aversion to journeying by the sea, but, providentially, was spared any discomfort from sea-sickness. On Monday, Sept. 3d, he spoke twice at meetings in Quebec; on Tuesday he left for Niagara Falls by the way of Toronto; thence direct to New York, arriving at the Pierrepont House Saturday morning. Private hospitalities had been tendered but were declined, the seclusion of hotel quarters having been found to be more restful.

During these few days about forty written invitations were received from American brethren desiring the services of Mr. Müller, which were regarded by him as indicating that he had not mistaken his course in coming to these shores. A telegram at Quebec from Rev. Dr. Talmage offered Brooklyn Tabernacle for Mr. M. Sept. 9. The weather was delightful and this spacious audience room was filled with about 4,000 people. The senior professor of the Lay College, Rev. J. L. Chapman, offered a prayer of invocation, rendering earnest thanks for the long looked for presence of this beloved brother. For sixteen years Mr M. has received hundreds of written and personal solicitations to come to America, but not till last spring did he yield. A letter from representatives from five denominations persuaded him that it was God's will that he should come. During the singing of the following original hymn to the tune "Webb," Mr. Muller was deeply affected:

> Servant of Christ, we greet thee!
>   Beloved of the Lord!
> Within His courts we meet thee
>   With gratitude and praise,
> For what God's grace has taught thee
>   Through all these fruitful years,
> And for the marvels wrought thee
>   In answer to thy prayers.
>
> We bless the Hand that led thee
>   From youth to green old age.
> Which day by day hath fed thee,
>   And thy dear orphan flock;
> That Hand thy head did pillow,
>   When on the ocean's breast,
> And o'er each swelling billow,
>   In safety bore thee here.
>
> Thro' future days, still guiding,
>   Thy Master will provide:
> In restful faith abiding,
>   Thy wants are all His care.
> And may thy life, O Brother!
>   Lead us this path to choose,
> Turning from one another,
>   And trusting GOD ALONE.
>
> Smile, Father, on this meeting
>   Of these Thy children here
> O speak Thy loving greeting
>   To every heart to-day!
> And when in heaven, all glorious,
>   Thy gathered saints shall stand,
> May each of us, victorious,
>   Be welcomed there by Thee!

Rev. Prof. E. P. Thwing presided, by request of the absent pastor, and read a letter of welcome from

Dr. Talmage. Prof. Thwing spoke in substance as follows:

"This meeting and greeting, my honored brother, is a spontaneous expression of gratitude to God, and of affection for yourself. This is not the place for any eulogistic review of human deeds, but rather for thanksgiving for what His power has wrought in answer to the prayer of faith and the labor of love. We meet you, brother, with no studied phrase and garnished rhetoric, but with brief and heartfelt greetings we welcome you and your beloved companion to America, to this city of churches, and to Brooklyn Tabernacle. I give you this hand in token of the love that is felt not only by this people and community, but by all Americans who have known your long and patient toil for the orphan, your work as a minister of Christ, and above all, your 'LIFE OF TRUST.' The story of God's dealings with George Muller has been in the hands of Americans for seventeen years. It is stranger than fiction—and yet, with all its romantic interest, but the simple corroboration of the promise, 'Ask and ye shall receive.' Christians here have longed to see you. Pastors of churches and teachers of sacred learning have felt the need of a more practical conception of the cardinal truth, that God is and that He is the rewarder of those who diligently seek Him. We have desired that the members of our congregations and of our seminaries might see and hear one who has furnished the present age the most conspicuous illustration of the power and willingness of God to answer believing prayer. We want to possess 'like precious faith,' which, while it does not supersede but rather intensifies human exertion, relies utterly on God. We can possess it, for 'if *any* man do His will, *him He heareth.*'

"But I will not keep this vast assembly from the feast promised them. We invoke upon you and your dear companion the choicest of benedictions. You have disappointed scores of cities on the Continent to come to America, but we feel that you have not mistaken your way. You did not solicit an invitation. On the other hand, you declined more than one individual request, lest you might seem to 'intrude on the churches,' and only consented when concerted action convinced you that God was calling through these pastors and teachers who formally solicited your presence. And now, sir, I do but repeat the sentiment which numerous letters and messages authorize me to convey to you, when I say, thrice welcome to these shores, to our churches and colleges, our homes and our hearts. Tarry in this fair city by the sea, at least till after your seventy-second birthday, that September 27 may be indeed made memorable to you and to us, in grateful recognition of what God has done through you for 5,000 destitute orphans, and in recognition of the still grander and wider work you are doing in the world as an apostle of faith in an age of materialistic unbelief."

The sermon by Mr. Muller was on the text, "Ask and ye shall receive," and exhibited these salient points: that our petitions should be purely to advance the glory of God; should be offered in the name of Christ; with hearty faith in His power and willingness to grant them; with a willingness to wait, and without "regarding iniquity." Under the last point he said that purity of motive rather than absolute sinlessness of life was required. No one lived who sinned not. He gave but a few incidents, reserving to Monday and Tuesday evenings following a recital of his work in England. He at that time spoke to large audiences at Clinton Avenue Church, Rev. Dr. Budington, pastor, and on the following Tuesday he preached in German at the Church of the Covenant, Prof. Thwing pastor.

Sept. 8, Mr. and Mrs. Muller visited the Brooklyn Asylum and were greeted by over 300 boys and girls, besides a large number of the managers and friends. The pulpits of Brooklyn were offered to Mr. Müller most heartily and he spoke four times in Plymouth Church, at Dr. Wild's, at Central Church, Tompkins Avenue Church, Lafayette Avenue, at the Methodist, Baptist, Lutheran churches, and other places. One object of the American tour being to reach the German population of our cities, Mr. M preached repeatedly in Newark and elsewhere in his native tongue by request of German Christians.

Rev. Dr. Cuyler says in the Evangelist: "At first sight every one must be struck with his resemblance to the late Theodore Frelinghuysen. He is tall, straight as a brigadier, and has a countenance of singular benignity. His German brogue is rather agreeable. He told us the familiar story of his "life of trust," and how wonderfully God had answered his prayers. The old story was all the more interesting when it came from the lips of the devout worker himself. There were two things in his address which delighted me exceedingly. The first was, that, in founding his Orphan House he had discarded all British toadyism for great names, and, instead of appointing a Duke or a Lord, he had appointed "his Heavenly Father to be its President." This was a very characteristic step. But it occurred to me that if it was reverential and wise in Müller to make the Lord "President of the orphan institution," "it was equally wise in the Lord to entrust its practical management to so shrewd a financier and sagacious philanthropist as George Muller. The whole success of the enterprise at Bristol is due to a happy combination of divine oversight with human energy and good sense. There is no miracle in the success of Mr. Muller's efforts. He simply believes in God with the filial faith of a child. And then he lays hold of God's work with all the energy and sagacity of a sensible man, and God prospers his undertakings."

October 19, he went to Boston and began his work there in the vast Tabernacle erected for Mr. Moody. In vitations from Providence, Worcester and Newburyport: Amherst and Wellsley Colleges, and many other places in New England left little time for the continuous preaching in Boston which Brooklyn and New York had enjoyed. The winter of 1877–78 Mr. Müller intends to spend in the principal cities south and west going as far as San Francisco, and returning to England in June. That an abundant blessing may crown his work for Christ is the united prayer of all believers.

vitat
A